THE WORLD HIS FIELD

THE GLOBAL LEGACY OF LOUIS L. KING

Robert L. Niklaus

CHRISTIAN PUBLICATIONS, INC.
CAMP HILL, PENNSYLVANIA

✠ CHRISTIAN PUBLICATIONS, INC.
3825 Hartzdale Drive, Camp Hill, PA 17011
www.christianpublications.com

Faithful, biblical publishing since 1883

The World His Field
ISBN: 0-87509-816-9
LOC Control Number: 2004102517
© 2004 by Robert L. Niklaus
All rights reserved
Printed in the United States of America

04   05   06   07   08   5   4   3   2   1

Unless otherwise indicated,
Scripture taken from the HOLY BIBLE:
NEW INTERNATIONAL VERSION ®.
Copyright © 1973, 1978, 1984 by the
International Bible Society. Used by
permission of Zondervan Bible Publishers.

*Note: Italicized words in Scripture quotations
are the emphasis of the author.*

In Appreciation

Esther Martz King
more than any other person
helped her husband
please God

CONTENTS

Preface: A Towering Leader on Loan vii
Author's Note xi

Chapter One: Forcing the Issue (1955) 1
Time Markers • Handicaps and Opposition • Benign Neglect Stateside • Bangkok Breakout • "As Iron Sharpens Iron" • Straight Talk on Finances • Other Lively Issues • Ripple Effect

Chapter Two: Making of the Man (1915-1935) 23
Time Markers • Caper Turned Conversion • Formative Factors: Home and Family • Formative Factors: Church and Pastor • Mentor Treasure • Strength from Sickness • Enter the Alliance • A Mantle Conferred?

Chapter Three: Proving the Promises (1935-1938) 41
Time Markers • Spartan School • Issues of Finance and Health • Miraculous Healing • Financial Bonanza • Proctor Problems • Role Models • First Love • Hooked in a Hut • New Life • A Hike for Life • Ring in the Rain • India Beckons

Chapter Four: Pastoral Toughening (1938-1946) 65
Time Markers • Bleak Invitation: North Tonawanda • Semi-Vows • Basics Camp • Wedding Glitch • Faith and Finances • Learning Curve • Balance in Ministry • The Work of an Evangelist • Interrupted Journey • Animated Suspension: Westmont • Right Praying • Two-Way Growth • Reluctant Move • Continuous Revival: Lincoln • India at Last, Almost

Chapter Five: The Proving Grounds (1947-1953) 95
Time Markers • Holding Pattern • Ship Bound for India • Junior Missionaries • Language Ordeal • Disillusionment • Ma-Bop Factor • Rookie Resolve • Pioneering in Palanpur • Broadband Ministry • One Tour Too Many • Winding Up, Not Down

Chapter Six: Call of the Church (1954-1956) 127
Time Markers • "Ready to Go, Ready to Stay" • Meager Provisions • Policies and Procedures • "The Present Unsettled Condition" • A Matter

of Discipline • *First and Second Kings* • *Issues of High Finance* • *Pre- and Post-Bangkok Conference* • *Baliem Valley Crisis* • *"Dog in the Manger"* • *Record-Breaking 102* • *New Era Dawning*

Chapter Seven: Wheels in a Wheel (1956-1962)......161

Time Markers • *Getting Acquainted Globally* • *Perils of the Path* • *Secret Sources* • *Trend Toward Apostasy* • *Attempts at Seduction* • *Second Asia Conference: Urban Spark* • *Strategic Shift to the Cities* • *Mass Movements* • *One Chief's Faith* • *Jaffray School of Missions* • *The People Factor* • *Reality Reminder*

Chapter Eight: The World His Field (1963-1968) 201

Time Markers • *Double-Duty Mom* • *Widening Circles* • *Collision in Gabon* • *A Better Way* • *Meeting of Equals* • *Congo Crisis* • *Another Side* • *Indigenous Vindication* • *Banmethuot Massacre* • *The Bottom Line*

Chapter Nine: Full Stride Worldwide (1969-1978)...239

Time Markers • *Focused Style* • *Marching on the Airwaves* • *God Encounters* • *Ripley-Style Response* • *Evangelical Ecumenism* • *The Wheaton Declaration* • *Green Lake Conference* • *1975: Pivotal Year* • *New Base* • *New Coalition* • *Stretch Marks* • *Strong Finish*

Chapter Ten: "Stay on Course!" (1978-1987) 281

Time Markers • *Keeping in Touch* • *Tough at the Top* • *Centennial Goals* • *Doubling Progress* • *Hope Amid the Rubble* • *Drawing the Line* • *Showing the Way* • *Laying the Tracks* • *Easter 100 Churches* • *Mission Accomplished*

Epilogue: "The Church; and the Church; and the Church"
   (1987-present)..321
Bibliography..325
Index..331

PREFACE
A Towering Leader on Loan

Dr. Donald McGavran, probably the leading missiologist of the last half-century and founding dean of the School of World Mission at Fuller Theological Seminary, paid The Christian and Missionary Alliance (C&MA) its greatest compliment. He declared it the leading missionary society of the past century.

Alliance culture has made its people slow to embrace such commendation, believing that too much self-congratulation is deadly and may even constitute a mortal sin. There is absolutely no question, however, that much of the success in C&MA missions is due, humanly speaking, to Dr. Louis L. King. As missionary, Mission board leader and then president of the denomination for more than forty years, his influence remains unmistakable and enduring.

No person in ministry has influenced me more. My wife Ruth and I served under Dr. King as missionaries to the Philippines, and again when he was president and I was his successor as vice president for Overseas Ministries. Despite a difference of eighteen years in age, seven inches in height and in the amount of topside hair—not to speak of opposite personalities—we connected from the moment of our assignment overseas.

It was his single-handed intervention that sent me to Ph.D. studies and then (lovingly yet militarily) to teaching in Canada. He asked me to lead the overseas work of the Alliance and later encouraged me to "let the call of the Church be the call of the Lord" when I was nominated to follow him as C&MA president.

His greatest personal contribution to me, as to many others, was that he believed in me more than I believed in myself. His confidence encouraged me to have faith that God could use me. What better gift than this?

This book is about Louis King's monumental direction that eventually included over a thousand missionaries, many more church workers in North America and a worldwide community of believers numbering in the millions.

How did this come about? The answer was clearly his unshakable theological conviction that every church in the world is capable of three irreplaceable achievements: the ability to govern itself, the ability to support itself and the ability to multiply itself. This it can do free of crippling, if well-meaning, dependence on the North American Church for money, people and strategy.

The World His Field chronicles how Louis King took the indigenous church policy—halfheartedly implemented before his time—and made it the cornerstone of his leadership. The Alliance under King and his capable staff had a vicelike grip on the belief that the New Testament Church is an indigenous church. Systematically, North American support for overseas pastors and churches was withdrawn and national churches were organized and dislodged from missionary governance.

This freedom was not an end in itself. As national churches gained confidence in supporting and governing themselves, slowly but surely some began to achieve the ultimate goal of all true missionary work: Receiving churches became sending churches. They supported workers to unreached people groups within their own borders and in other countries. To facilitate the sending of workers abroad, King provided initial funds to help in such critical needs as travel tickets and schooling for children of the new missionaries.

Progress toward this goal did not come easily or cheaply, as is well documented in this book by Dr. King's friend and gifted assistant, Robert Niklaus. Niklaus is without question the denomination's most able missionary writer. Drawing on his background as a former missionary to Congo-Kinshasa, as director of communications at the C&MA National Office and as author of several Alliance histories, Bob provides an important record of Alliance history in its era of greatest achievement and growth. And, in the writing, he has avoided the tendency to canonize a great leader despite his high esteem for the man.

I believe most Alliance people know very little about Alliance principles and strategies overseas that have made us successful under God. Stories about individual missionaries and indigenous church leaders are abundant and pleasant to hear, but little is known about the tracks on which the missionary work has moved forward.

It is high time for a new generation to read the record. And it helps to "tell the story behind the story" of a towering leader on loan by the Almighty to show us the way. Read this book, so well written, and be biblically proud of a great person and a wonderful page of Church history.

You may be persuaded that Dr. McGavran's tribute was not overstated.

David L. Rambo
President (1987-1996)
The Christian and Missionary Alliance/USA

AUTHOR'S NOTE

Award-winning historian William Manchester wrote in his introduction of *The Last Lion*, "There can be no enlightening life that does not include an account of the man's times. This need for context is even greater when the central figure is a towering statesman."[1]

This story is more than the biography of a mortal but giant-sized man in the evangelical world missions movement. It is contextualized in an era of The Christian and Missionary Alliance (C&MA, the Alliance) that ignited a remarkable global growth that continues to this day.

The underlying universal principles and personal convictions that made this sweeping advance possible are the focus of this book. When writing, I always wore a prickly hair shirt branded with the words, "So what?" Any episode or fact, no matter how entertaining, was discarded if it did not contribute to the legacy of intangibles forming the foundation of accomplishments that justifiably have won widespread commendation for the C&MA in Canada and the United States.

Pinned to the wall of my mind have been photos of Alliance leaders, lay workers and supporters—all who need to understand this foundation while plotting the future of their ministry. This is not an unreasonable hope. When David Howard spoke to archivists, scholars and mission agency administrators in a consultation at Wheaton College, he said, "It is vitally important that the leadership of any mission should understand fully their heritage." His experience in writing the history of the World Evangelical Fellowship, which he led for years, enabled him "to give leadership based on a firm foundation of who we were and where we had come from."

Louis King appreciated this reality as much as anyone. In Daryl Cartmel's doctoral dissertation on the Alliance, he commented,

[King] pointed to the Jews and their sustained ability to maintain a common tradition and a uniqueness among other peoples. His suggestion then is that the reason for this persistent identity has been the strength coming from a remembered heritage. The application of this is that unless the C&MA retains a clear vision of its founder's intents and its track record, it will succumb to the forces of attrition which he sees as having eroded the testimony of so many of our churches.[2]

In a position paper on the topic, King wrote, "In such a situation we need to look backward, to explore our foundation; inward, to discover our motives; forward, to settle our positive purpose. The powerful force of memory will be an aid to keep us true to our purpose for being, and certain concerning our destiny. As with Israel so with us; let a consideration of certain aspects of our past do its destined work."[3]

The reader will note in this book a profusion of direct quotes by King. This was intentional. More than anyone, he knew the events of his day and what he thought about them, so it was best to record them in his own words. He was marvelous and unstinting in his cooperation, unsparing of himself and others in his recollections. His keen memory, despite failing health and advanced years, was exceptional. In recording more than 600 pages of interview transcripts, I encountered little of the malady that afflicts many people in retirement: "The older I get, the better I was." People may question some of his comments, but this book is about his life and his work and how he viewed it all.

A word needs to be said about the "Time Markers" introducing each chapter. I believe the Alliance is not an accident of history, but a movement born in the theological, political, economic and cultural dynamics of the era. It is destined to play a God-given role on the world scene. Pick any hot spot in the international panorama today and most likely you will find the Alliance is either there now or has been in the past. The random sampling of events and trends in the international and national arenas, in the communities of world religions and in the North American C&MA are meant simply to put the Alliance in the context of the times.

Just as achievements by the Alliance were not the result of one man, neither was the writing of this book solely my work. Jewel Hall, King's former secretary, and Esther, his wife, were totally indispensable as my intermediaries with him in bringing this project to completion. So was my wife, Jan, who for years put up with lost weekends and holidays for the sake of the book, and who supported me in my writing through a months-long period of spiritual and physical ordeal unlike anything I had experienced previously.

I could count on David Rambo for a long succession of encouraging phone calls and perceptive comments. David Moore was unstinting in his meticulous review of the text—and candid comments offered in sensitivity and respect. Anne Moore, with her experience as a third-generation missionary and her heritage of grandparents who were associates of A.B. Simpson, provided suggestions that led to richer veins of thought that I had overlooked. After spending many hours in gathering and researching historical photos, she worked technical magic with Photoshop software to enhance the value of those chosen for the book.

Arnold Cook and Melvin Sylvester gave invaluable Canadian perspectives to the record. Dr. Joseph Wenninger, director of the archives at the National Office, and his assistant, Patty McGarvey, could not have been more cooperative. Daryl Cartmel's unpublished doctoral dissertation, completed posthumously by his wife Beatrice and graciously made available by her, proved extremely helpful.

Each of the King sons—Paul, David, Stephen and J. Mark—added family touches with humor and honesty. Although I am fearful of leaving out some people who cooperated in the project, here are the names of other reviewers who scrutinized the draft text: Elsie Barney, Donald Bubna, Gerald Carner, John Corby, James Davey, John and Helen Ellenberger, David Kennedy, Marion Kerr, Bernard King, T. Grady Mangham, Paul Morris, Arni Shareski, Fred Smith, Thomas Stebbins, Harry Taylor and David Volstad.

This biography could have gone the way of many wannabe manuscripts were it not for key people at Christian Publications, Inc. The project, begun with encouragement by Dr. K. Neill Foster, former publisher and president, came to completion through the editorial work of Douglas B. Wicks, publisher; David E. Fessenden, former senior editor; and Gretchen Nesbit, assistant editor. To each one I express gratitude for helping bring to the international Christian community the exploits and timeless insights of a remarkable man of God.

Ken Burns, producer of the award-winning TV series *The Civil War* and other documentaries on America's past, commented on what he believed to be the significance of his work: "We cannot possibly know where we are going unless we know where we have been." I have done all within my ability to show where we have come from, as well as how and why. I trust this record will help those who decide where the C&MA goes from here to "stay on course."

—Robert L. Niklaus

Notes

1. William Manchester, *The Last Lion: Winston Spencer Churchill, 1932-1940* (Boston: Little, Brown and Company, 1988), p. xvii.
2. Daryl Westwood Cartmel, "Partnership in Mission" (doctoral dissertation, School of World Mission, Fuller Theological Seminary, 1980), p. 63.
3. Louis L. King, "Remembrance: One Motive for Missions" (position paper for the Foreign Department, 1974), p. 1.

ONE
Forcing the Issue

Time Markers 1890 1900 1910 1920 1930 1940 1950 **1955** 1960 1970 1980 1990 2000 2010

A Nigerian volunteer serving with the British army in India wrote to a friend at the end of the Second World War: "We all overseas soldiers are coming back home with new ideas. We have been told what we fought for. That is 'freedom.' Well, we want freedom, nothing but freedom."

Plenty of his fellow soldiers from the British and French colonies in Africa had a similar experience. When their white officers urged them with pep talks about the fight to safeguard freedom, the irony was not lost on them, and the silent question coursed through their thoughts: "Whose freedom?" Their conclusion was the same—and it was far different from what their European officers had in mind.

With the war emergency over, England, France and Belgium assumed their colonial rule over Africa would stay the way it was: they the "white fathers" and the Africans their "children." At first the British ignored a young Ghanaian, Kwame Nkrumah, who confronted them with, "We demand the right to misrule ourselves." The French treated with contempt Sekou Toure, a fiery young union leader who spouted Marxist slogans in Guinea. Belgium considered Patrice Lumumba a rabble-rouser.

The winds of freedom that began stirring after the war rose to a roar across the continent in the 1950s. In one decade the last vestiges of "the white man's burden" of colonial rule in Africa were obliterated forever.

The same winds swept through Asia. The French marched back into Indochina to reclaim their role as colonial masters. The Dutch were determined to reassert their rule over Indonesia. Prime Minister Winston Churchill, so magnificent in his fight against Nazi tyranny, failed to understand the same sentiments by India toward England. "I will not preside over the dismemberment of the British Empire," he vowed.

But Japanese conquests brought enormous changes to all of Southeast Asia. White colonial rule was destroyed. Nationalist movements rose against

The World His Field

Japan and did not fade away after victory. They had seen their colonial masters mauled in battle, humiliated in defeat. Their foreign occupiers were not invincible, they concluded. And in 1945 the battle was joined.

For the British, it took two bloody and brutal years of conflict in India before the realization dawned that they could not hold on to a subcontinent and population so massive it dwarfed their nation many times over. India became a sovereign nation in 1947.

For the Dutch, the sprawling 17,000-island colony of Indonesia was just too much to hold together. Emerging from years of Nazi occupation, they did not have the stomach to wage a protracted war against nationalists who viewed them as oppressors. After years of struggle, Indonesia became a republic in 1950.

For the French, the denouement came in 1954. At a fortress in northern Vietnam called Dien Bien Phu, French troops were pounded during a fifty-five-day siege by Ho Chi Minh's forces. France not only lost the battle and 4,000 men, it lost the war and all of Indochina.

As a countervailing trend to the collapse of colonial territories, new alliances were forming. In 1954 eight nations in Asia formed the Southeast Asia Treaty Organization (SEATO) in Manila. SEATO opened its central command center in Bangkok the following year. The mutual defense group's purpose was to contain communist aggression in that part of the world.

In 1955 representatives from twenty-nine nations met in Bandung, Indonesia, to form a "nonaligned bloc" of countries opposed to imperialism by greedy governments both East and West. Although lacking in economic and military might, these developing nations put the world on notice that they would no longer tolerate the subjugation of their peoples and territories by foreign powers.

★ ★ ★

These powerful dynamics in the world, both dividing and uniting, had profound implications for the Alliance during the 1950s. Over 700 missionaries were serving in 22 foreign countries, supported by giving to the General Fund that for 1955 was a record $2,887,000. The number of believers in overseas churches surpassed the 90,000 mark. Baptisms in 1955 were a record 10,659 worldwide.

Bangkok, Thailand, in 1955 was something other than its exalted name, "Great City of Angels."

Forcing the Issue

Founded in 1782, Bangkok was originally like a loose-jointed, floating dock on polluted waterways. Temples and royal palaces rested on low-lying ground while most ordinary dwellings swayed on thick bamboo rafts lining rivers and canals serving as both water supply and sewage disposal.

By the 1950s the capital of Thailand had expanded into a sweltering urban sauna crammed with people and buildings. Buddhist shrines fronted most properties. Back alleys reeked of garbage. Canals, not streets, still carried much of the traffic. Cars were outnumbered by three-wheel bikes that served as taxis. The city appeared more reminiscent of the past than looking to the future. The economic explosion that would turn it into a heady metropolis was still years away. The "Great City of Angels" it was not.

Steamy, seedy Bangkok seemed hardly the place to convene a conference destined to send shock waves around the world. Yet the gathering would impact C&MA missions and reverberate throughout other evangelical missions circles as well.

Louis L. King, area secretary for Alliance missions in Asia, determined to do just that. He invited C&MA Mission chairmen and church leaders in Asia to attend a conference in Bangkok in October of 1955. The agenda would focus on understanding and applying principles of indigenous church policy commonly referred to as self-support, self-governance and self-propagation. The Bangkok conference would add a fourth: self-expression.

Handicaps and Opposition

In today's arena of missions, approving a strategy to establish strong indigenous churches would be a no-brainer. In a world consisting almost totally of sovereign states, the obvious logic is that national churches ought also to be free.

But in the mid-1950s, when colonies and subjugated countries were moving toward freedom, many Alliance missionaries—and even some national church leaders—opposed the policy of independent national churches as dangerous and unwise. They voiced apprehension about the risks of having a conference in Bangkok devoted to indigenous church strategy. And the conference convener, the new area secretary Louis King, was himself part of the risk.

The World His Field

King had spent only one term of missionary service in Gujarat, India, before being promoted to regional responsibility. It was hardly enough experience, it seemed, to qualify him to lead a potentially explosive convocation that would impact hundreds of missionaries with many more years of honorable service than he had mustered. He had arrived in India overage (thirty-one years old) by Mission policy, with more children than Mission policy allowed (three instead of two) and having had no formal studies in linguistics or missiology.

Furthermore, during his six years in India, King had earned the reputation of a rebel—not something to endear him to colleagues entrenched against change. Though he gave generously to the local church, he had refused to pay a required contribution into the central church treasury as did most of his peers. He had refused to hold an office in the church as was customary. He had refused to limit his ministry to the narrow confines of the Mission and national Church, enjoying congenial relations with other missions, including World Council of Churches (WCC) denominations like the Methodists and Presbyterians.

And, perhaps the most serious disqualifier to fellow missionaries who spent agonizing years mastering the local language of their posts, King never adequately learned the vernacular. He used Indian interpreters for all his teaching and preaching.

This short, balding, slightly built man with rimless glasses and starched white collar did not exude a commanding presence, and his credentials as a missionary were slim at best. Yet he was going up against the likes of William Newbern, a near-legendary missionary to China and Hong Kong. Newbern vowed to attend the Bangkok Conference and give a speech that would "blow the whole thing away."

King was well aware of Newbern's position. "He felt the progress of the gospel had been at such a cost and it had been with the lives of missionaries," he explained. "To get ahead, Newbern believed missionaries had to use money, and they had to help this way. The poverty of the national peoples ruled out their doing it alone. If we stopped helping, we would stop the progress of the gospel. It would be just a backward step instead of a forward one. He believed it would be heartless on our part to do so."

Another Alliance icon, Robert Roseberry, dubbed "the Bishop of West Africa" by his colleagues, was equally opposed. He cabled the conference that he was adamantly against the meeting and the concept of an indigenous church.

Both Roseberry and Newbern were totally faithful to their ministry of sharing the gospel despite hardships; they were deeply committed to seeing Asians and Africans become stalwart Christians. Yet they saw no conflict between trusting God for their work but not trusting Him to raise up viable indigenous churches led by the people they were mentoring.

Their attitude reflected the thinking of many of their colleagues who looked upon the indigenous people as children. Even by the late 1950s when strong winds of change were blowing across colonial Africa, many "natives" had never been invited into a missionary's house. If they had cause to visit the mission station, they stood on the lawn or porch and stated their business through the window to the white man or woman inside. In Asia, some missionaries professed great love for the people—but had no problem with entering the post office, marching to the head of the line and expecting prompt service.

Robert M. Chrisman, chairman of the Thai field, was to host the Bangkok Conference, yet he too had struggled with the philosophy of nurturing the national Church to become a free and equal partner in ministry. After Jewel Hall, his Mission office secretary, arrived in Thailand in November of 1950 and looked around the country, she asked him, "Where's the national Church?" That question, repeated by about fifty other new missionaries who arrived in Thailand after the war, unsettled Chrisman.

The national Church had in fact just been organized in 1951 after twenty-five years of missionary work. But it was far from self-supporting. Half of the Mission's budget was used to support national workers.

Chrisman believed "self-support is a good policy, but it doesn't always work. Our churches are in the rural areas and the people are so poor. We told our Thai pastors and evangelists that if they would leave everything to serve Christ, we would take care of them. Do we go back on that agreement and say, 'From now on, you're on your own'?"

Chrisman struggled long and deeply over the issue. Hall remembers, "He took from 8 to 9 o'clock each morning, Monday through Saturday, with his office door shut to read the Word and pray for guidance."

His defense of Mission subsidy came under attack from two directions. The first, of course, was the newly appointed area secretary for

Asia. King's negative experience with foreign funding of indigenous church work in India prompted him, upon taking office, to begin promoting the importance of self-support for the Asian churches.

The second was the example set by newborn believers among the lepers in Khonkaen. The dreaded disease made them hated and feared outcasts in Thai society. They were not even welcome in Buddhist temples. Advances in medical science, however, made it possible to put the disease in remission, if not bring healing.

Armed with this drug in 1951, missionaries William Kerr and Betty Johns, RN, conducted a series of clinics among the lepers of Khonkaen. The work was so successful, burgeoning to thousands of patients, that the government was shamed into taking responsibility for the operation.

More importantly, many people afflicted with leprosy were won to Christ through the compassion of the missionaries. Two of the first things they did were to erect their own chapels—mere roofs of palm branches, but churches nonetheless—and support their own church workers.

This deeply impressed the Thai Mission chairman. If outcast and totally impoverished leprous people could organize their congregations on a self-supporting basis, why not the much richer Thai Christians?

Finally convinced that the policy was right, Chrisman initiated a program in early 1955 that eventually would eliminate Mission grants to the Church over a period of four years. He did so with a heavy heart but a clear mind. By the time the Bangkok Conference convened later the same year, the move toward self-support had been firmly established.

The Thai field had another objection to the proposed conference. It opposed mixing Asians and missionaries together in the same facility. Although the Thai people had a rich and refined heritage dating back thousands of years, they were not welcomed into missionary homes or the Bangkok guesthouse. Missionaries were afraid they would not know how to act because of cultural differences, such as for example, urinating on the bathroom floor—a worry that turned out to be justified during the conference.

Benign Neglect Stateside

The most serious obstacle to indigenous church policy, however, did not arise overseas. It lay closer to home—at "260," as the C&MA national office on Forty-fourth Street in New York City was commonly called.

Forcing the Issue

Agreement on the principles of free and viable overseas churches had been around for a long time. Harry M. Shuman, C&MA president, convened a special conference in 1926 to scrutinize objectives of the Alliance. A.C. Snead, foreign secretary, participated in the conference. At the heart of the report was a call urging that "strong, virile, indigenous church[es]" be established as soon as possible. It read, in part:

> There are many tribes and tongues who have never yet heard; and in all our discussion and decisions this thought is in the background. In considering the budget of various fields, the purpose included the increasing of the efficiency of the work and the building of a strong, virile, indigenous church.[1]

The conference viewed self-support as a key component in forging strong national churches and failure to pursue this goal as an obstacle to world evangelization:

> In other words our failure in self-support constitutes our greatest hindrance to worldwide pioneer advance. We feel solemnly convinced that our power as a Missionary Society in its pioneer program will be mightily enhanced if we see to it that our present indigenous churches take over responsibility for their work, thus releasing money and men for new enterprises.[2]

The report was approved by the Board of Managers in 1927 and referred to the Foreign Department (now the Division of International Ministries). Some attempts were made to implement its findings, but the strategy was not vigorously pursued; neither was it widely known nor embraced.

Meanwhile, the practice of making overseas workers dependent on the Mission continued. King later noted, "During the first four decades ... national pastors, evangelists and Bible women—even students in the Bible schools—were supported almost entirely from North American funds."[3]

The 1926 document emerged again in 1951 when another Board committee was convened to study the issue. It concluded that the earlier report contained all that needed to be said on the issue and recommended its implementation to the Board. It was again approved, sent to the office of the foreign secretary in 1952—and again lost from view.

At the 1955 annual policy-making General Council in Philadelphia, the Council committee on missionary work heard about the report but knew little of its contents or where it could be found. King, just returning from an overseas trip and going directly to Philadelphia, was met by the question, "Where's that report?" He was unable to answer the question but knew someone who would locate the document if it were still around. He called Edna Figg, his secretary and longtime worker at "260," and told her to find the report and hand-deliver it to him at Council.

The committee compared the 1926 and 1951 calls for strong indigenous and self-supporting churches with available statistics about the overseas work. It learned that the number of "native workers" had increased from 1,294 in 1930 to 1,985 in 1950. Twenty percent of these workers were on the Mission payroll in 1930, and that percentage remained the same two decades later. However, the number of workers supported by both the Mission and the Church had doubled, while those paid by the Church had decreased by twenty percent.

The conclusion was compelling and alarming. Instead of moving toward healthy, viable indigenous churches, the trend was in the other direction. Statistics seemed to indicate that instead of advancing toward the official goal of establishing overseas churches, many soldiers in the worldwide C&MA army of missionaries were following a different order: "About face. To the rear, march."

The 1955 General Council in Philadelphia concluded that the indigenous church policy was not being implemented in some fields and not consistently practiced in any field. The delegates responded, "Enough, already!" They mandated that the section of the 1954 manual "regarding the indigenous church be put into effect by every Field Conference, Chairman and individual missionary; and that every effort be made to cause such legislation to operate successfully."[4]

The Board of Managers report on which the Council committee based its findings was more strongly worded, taking a firm position concerning missionaries who were dragging their feet in establishing strong indigenous churches:

> That when policies are finally adopted as law in the Society, every conference and individual involved shall put the policy into effect and shall make every effort to cause it to operate successfully, and
>
> That, if after study and consideration, any individual feels he cannot be loyal to the policy, he shall either be transferred to an area where the policy does not apply or he shall be permitted to retire from the work, and

That in the event any individual does not feel willing to retire but still feels he must oppose the policy, the Foreign Department shall request the individual to find service elsewhere.[5]

No clear answer emerges as to why the indigenous church policy sputtered and stalled between 1926 and 1955. Dr. Snead, foreign secretary during the whole time span, participated in discussions on the topic in 1926, 1951 and 1955. Initially he supported the strategy and initiated the development of an autonomous Church in Congo after 1926. But the mandate made little headway among the other mission fields.

It may have been that the Foreign Department was understaffed or, in later years, that the foreign secretary was too frail physically to tackle the complex issue. On different occasions, Snead would interrupt a discussion with King and ask him to return later. Then, after resting and praying, he would recall King to resume their meeting.

But a basic difference in principle about the indigenous church cannot be discounted. After the 1955 Council in Philadelphia issued an ultimatum against further stalling on the self-supporting church policy, Snead reluctantly conveyed the decision to all the overseas fields.

King recalled, "Snead's general attitude was, 'I believe in the indigenous church policy. I think it is the right policy, but I don't want to deny the gospel to anybody. If I have money to pay for an evangelist or a catechist, I don't see why I shouldn't be able to do that for the advance of the gospel.' He couldn't see that it did not really advance the gospel."

Bernard S. King, C&MA treasurer at the time and no relation to Louis, noticed the difference in the two men's attitudes on the policy: "Dr. Snead, although one of the great, early authorities on the indigenous church, nonetheless treated it with benign neglect. But Louis King was ready and determined to force the issue."

Within two years Snead would retire from office after thirty-seven years as foreign secretary.

Bangkok Breakout

Although the 1955 Council drew the line on further delay in applying indigenous church strategy, it imposed no deadlines. Delegates left the responsibility of setting timetables with the Foreign Department. King agreed. "My view," he said, "was that the churches themselves had to make the decision. It could not be imposed from outside."

Eager to follow up on the mandate by Council, he offered to organize the first regional meeting to see that the policy was implemented overseas as quickly as possible. But there was one further obstacle to overcome: funding. No money had been allocated in the departmental budget to finance such a gathering in 1955.

Bernard King showed up at the area secretary's door with an unexpected solution: "My mother has died and we are settling the estate. I will give several thousand dollars from the estate so you can go ahead with the conference."

"I don't know if Bernard ever realized it," King said, "but were it not for this contribution, we would hardly have gotten airborne."

And airborne the participants came, and by ship, and overland. Seventeen national church leaders converged on Bangkok in October from 10 mission fields in which the Alliance had been instrumental in establishing 1,500 church groups with 52,000 members. Their passports varied in colors and languages, indicating the explosive energy of a missionary movement that had taken the world to heart: India, Cambodia, Hong Kong-China, Indonesia, Japan, Laos, Philippines, Thailand, Vietnam and the Tribes of Vietnam.

Delegates ranged across the whole spectrum of age, culture, education and experience. From Maharashtra, India, came the urbane Raghuel P. Chavan, representing a church with a history dating back to 1887 but still clinging to Mission subsidy. Z. Dawan, uncomfortable in his hot, ill-fitting Western suit, represented a self-supporting church among the head-hunting Dayak people of Kalimantan, Indonesia. Saly Khounthapanya spoke for a fledgling church in Laos, still in the process of formation and seeking all the help it could get, while Le-van-Thai shared experiences of the Vietnamese Church, which had already been self-supporting for years.

By October 26, 1955, opening day of the conference, all thirty delegates were present in Bangkok—with a few minor miracles along the way. Dawan told how his only hope of reaching the coast of West Kalimantan in time to catch a plane to Bangkok depended upon a downpour within a matter of hours to raise the interior river to a level that would take his boat to the coast. He spent most of the night in prayer. Early the next morning rain began to fall and the river rose, much to the astonishment and awe of the boatmen.

Forcing the Issue

The delegation from India had almost given up hope of attending the conference because of visa complications. Through a series of unusual developments, their visas became available at the last possible moment—just before the plane took off.

Not everyone came to the conference with eager anticipation. According to Jewel Hall, called down from her work in Korat to be the conference secretary, several Mission chairmen arrived early to discuss some sticky issues, finances being one. "We're going to have problems when the nationals get together and compare what they're being paid by the mission," said one chairman. "What will happen if word gets out that Laotian workers get more than missionaries in Thailand?"

They could have saved their breath. The church delegates would not be interested in how to get more money from the Mission but less—even to the point of zero subsidy.

All the delegates stayed in the Mission guesthouse, a Thai-style wood building with verandas and high ceilings, faded paint and a rather shabby overall appearance. They slept on canvas cots in dormitory-style rooms and ate together. King had been firm on this, overriding objections by the Thai Mission committee. "I insisted we were going to have this sharing arrangement. In my travels I had known some missionaries that would not allow nationals to move from the porch into their home. They never had them sit at their table to eat with them. I wanted an example that would change this."

After some initial awkwardness, the delegates settled into a comfortable arrangement—as much as anyone could be comfortable in oppressively hot Bangkok, coming to the end of the monsoon downpours and staying in a house without air conditioning. Meals served cafeteria-style, however, were another matter. Paul L. Morris, chairman of the Gujarat Mission in India, remembers emphatically, "The menu was a mixture between Eastern and Western cuisine, and it didn't work!"

The camaraderie that built during the week proved to be one of the best features of the conference. Asians and missionaries mixed with each other, visiting around the tables, greeting people they had never met, showing interest in what was happening in other countries. This cementing element went on continuously day and night.

The mingling of participants had another effect: Newbern was disarmed. The chip on his shoulder disappeared as he observed how the

The World His Field

Asians performed. They scrutinized reports in light of the Bible, dealt honestly with each other and interacted confidently with missionaries. His speech to "blow the whole thing away" stayed in his pocket.

Secretary Hall had another problem. "There were twenty-nine men and one woman—and one bathroom. I made sure I was first up at 3 a.m. to bathe before anyone else stirred." She then typed up a report that carried the gist of the previous day's meeting. When King came down to breakfast, he found the report alongside his plate. He realized Hall, in an unfortunate comparison, "was like a demon for work," an impression that would soon drastically alter her missionary career.

"As Iron Sharpens Iron"

The day-long meetings were held at the American Bible Society center three blocks away from the mission guesthouse. The conference room was plain, large and cool, enabling the delegates to huddle in different areas. Only sixteen of the Asians had a working knowledge of English, so the other thirteen clustered around interpreters who gave running translations of the proceedings in seven languages. The area secretary insisted at this and all future such conferences that each delegate understand the discussions in the language of his preference.

Morris said the way King organized the conference "was a stroke of genius." The national churches doing the job right, primarily in the Philippines and Vietnam, were on exhibit and reporting what they were doing.

He said, "Le-van-Thai from Vietnam, and Florentino de Jesus from the Philippines, reported beautifully on how the indigenous church was functioning in their country where the missionary was a missionary, the Church was the Church, and they didn't cross; they worked side by side.

"The two men took the lead at the conference, boldly stating their position, backing it up with experience and doing it calmly, not critically. They were real gentlemen. The churches in some countries, like India, that were just plodding along on bases that were not scriptural, could see how it is really done the right way. The missionaries didn't have to say it. Asians did, and their message was well received. It was much like Proverbs 27:17: 'As iron sharpens iron,/ so one man sharpens another.' "

R.P. Chavan, president of the Maharashtra Synod, was also deeply impressed with the structure of the conference. "As Dr. King always emphasized, this and all the other conferences held for the development of the national churches were not legislative conferences; there were no rules or regulations, no votes and no compulsion. You were to hear the spiritual messages and reports . . . and each one could take what was good and needed to his own church as the Holy Spirit would lead."

King opened the conference with the keynote address. Instead of preparing a word-for-word text in advance, as he usually did, his message came together while he was en route. "I had no notes. I had not prepared, but I knew precisely what I wanted to say and how I wanted to say it. I had been mulling over these things ever since the conference had been determined."

Instead of laying down the law, he opened the Bible and spoke about Christ, the Head of the Church. Previous years of experience in the pastorate and as a missionary to India had infused him with a deep conviction in the power of God's Word to work God's will. Passionately and relentlessly, in a strong voice that belied his short stature, he challenged the conferees with what the Scriptures said about the Church. He compelled them to respond not to him but to the Lord.

"In the Bible Jesus Christ is called the Head of the Church, and just as our head controls our body, so Jesus the Head of the Church is to control it. He is to be its supreme Ruler. All authority is to stem from Him. He is the Head of all things in the body. The mission is not to be the head; no missionary is to usurp this right. Jesus Christ alone, without any rivals, is to be the Head of the body."

He told the delegates that the Lord "has certain ways of exercising His authority. . . . Jesus Christ rules His Church first through the rule of love in the heart; secondly, through clear instructions in the Bible; and thirdly by applying the principle of the cross to all duties."[6]

King stated his conviction that "all that needs to be known about the Church is in the Book." An example of this was the church in Corinth, which faced many problems familiar to the delegates in their own countries—issues like factional strife, immorality in the Christian community, lawsuits between believers, marriage and divorce, Pentecostalism, life in a heathen society and money.

On the last issue, money, he pulled no punches because it would be one of the foremost topics of discussion. Referring to a report from Thailand, he said, "When one of the brethren asked the Thai delegate,

'How is it that Christians did not tithe?' his answer was, 'Why tithe when the mission pays the bills?' " King's comment: "The mission was standing between the Thai Christians and their obedience to Christ the Head of the Church in the matter of tithing."[7]

King concluded his message by saying, "The sum of it is—Jesus is the Head, the mission is not. We don't want to take the crown from His head. No one should look to us. No thing or no one ought ever to rob Christ of His rightful authority in the Church. We sincerely desire to establish the New Testament type of Church."[8]

Straight Talk on Finances

The Vietnamese representative, Le-van-Thai, said that the purpose of the conference was to strengthen self-support in the churches and "that he personally wished to reaffirm the very important thought that every church should be self-supporting and *strongly* self-supporting." Some delegates may have disagreed with him, but the issue went right to the heart of a truly indigenous church.

Missionaries quite often believed that when they supplied the money they had a responsibility to oversee how it was to be used. Dr. Snead challenged this thinking in his report to the 1956 General Council in Omaha: "Oftentimes it has been felt, in fact has been made Mission policy, that so long as the Mission provides any funds for the support of the church and its activities, the Mission must control the church to that extent.

"We believe that the church in every mission field should be self-supporting as well as self-governing and self-propagating, but to require that self-government can only be realized in direct proportion to self-support is not a proven policy."[9]

The topic of money generated some of the most interesting exchanges of the conference. Thai pastor Chom Phoopharot closely questioned the participants about the level or non-level of self-support in each country. The disparity was quickly apparent: some churches totally free of subsidy, some completely dependent, others somewhere in between.

He then commented, "If self-support is the ideal—and we are agreed it is the ideal—then why are we not practicing self-support in an equal manner throughout all the fields? If we think mission subsidy is the ideal, then why are we not practicing mission subsidy on all fields? If we know what the ideal is, why don't we practice the ideal all over?"[10]

King thanked the Thai pastor for bringing up a topic that might not otherwise have surfaced. He recounted that since 1926 it had been the desire of the Alliance "that we adhere to the principle that every church shall be self-supporting from the beginning."

Then why was it not happening on all fields? King was hard put to explain the disparity. "Because of certain circumstances, some fields 'temporarily' compromised in implementing the policy. In some instances," he admitted, "the temporary methods have lasted for years. That is the reason for this conference, to let you know about the areas that have obeyed and how glorious their results have been."

Dawan's report on the work in West Kalimantan illustrated this principle. His report especially sparked lively interest because it was clear that this church located among one of the most primitive people groups of Indonesia was strongly self-supporting.

Bins were placed outside each church on Sunday morning. Believers tithed one-tenth of their goods: one egg in ten, one chicken in ten, one container of rice for every ten from the harvest. On Monday the offerings were put in dugouts and taken to the trading center. Money from the sale of goods supported the pastor.

Hiralal Raysingh of the Gujarat Synod in India, asked, "We have heard that each church carries out its own responsibility. Suppose there are ten or twelve churches in an area and one church is weak. Would the other churches help that church?"

Dawan replied that they used to have a central treasury that paid all the pastors. But the district conference "decided they would no longer guarantee the wages of the pastors of weak churches because it was obvious that then they were just going to stay weak."

Raysingh persisted: "In the Gujarat Synod we have sixteen churches and among those sixteen there are fourteen church buildings. One small church desires to build its own church, yet it does not have the strength to do so. This one small church requested permission of the Synod to solicit funds from other churches. Permission was granted. The church is doing this now."

Dawan told of a church, most of its members Chinese, that asked funds of others for building a church. "The Dyak churches have never asked for funds in that way. Today, the Chinese church has a roof, that is all; the Dyak churches are all completed."

The exchange between Raysingh and Dawan captivated the group. The former was a polished leader of one of the oldest and most advanced C&MA churches in Asia. Yet he was learning from the latter, a short, unlettered pastor with aboriginal features in a rumpled suit leading a church among a jungle people one generation removed from headhunting. Stating that in Gujarat a central pastors' fund helped small churches, Raysingh admitted that the work the Dyaks were doing, with each church supporting itself, "is most praiseworthy."

Other exchanges were more pointed. Y No, representing the Tribes field of Vietnam, said that although the Church felt itself like a babe or weak child still unable to walk or care for itself, and thus would enjoy further nurturing by its mother, the Mission, they were ready to try to support themselves. "We are not going to ask the Mission to give us money any more, but if after a while the Mission should conclude we still need help, we would be glad."

Then, with perhaps a shade of sarcasm, he continued, "We want to do the right thing; and because the missionaries know the right thing—because they have been told by New York—we won't tell them what to do; we shall do what we are told to do. Perhaps you are not happy to hear what I have had to say, but I thank you for listening anyway."[11]

E.F. Gulbranson, field chairman in the Phillipines, wondered politely if Y No's referring to his church as a baby "wasn't slightly incorrect because it is God who is our heavenly Father and not the Mission, and God does not bring one child into the world differently from another, but all His children are able to walk from the beginning as it has been proven."[12] He urged that the churches look to their real Father and not to their "father-in-law."

Ouch Chan, the Cambodian delegate, agreed that God was the Father of those children, but he bluntly reminded the group that God was not the one who gave the money to help take care of the children—the Mission did. "I don't know who is right or who is wrong, but if in the beginning the Mission had done the job properly, it wouldn't be so difficult for us now."[13]

Some of the Asian delegates wanted to hear what Dr. King had to say on the subject, but de Jesus of the Philippines intervened. "I am sure that it is better to hear from the nationals rather than the missionaries, especially Mr. King. I have been with the missionaries for about thirty years and with the Mission as an official worker for almost twenty-five years; thus I can say that the program of self-support, self-propagation and self-government did not take place overnight.

"There were many heated discussions and feelings, but under the goodness of the Lord and the instructions and advice from our parent society, we were able to go forward and now have no regrets.... So, the Mission is really showing love to us, although at times it might sound as if they are cruel to let us go. Personally I would not be what I am right now if I had not been willing to be pushed to make the most of myself."[14]

The report of the Findings Committee at the end of the conference summed up the issue of self-support with this laconic observation: "From the experience of the national churches in Southeast Asia it is apparent that mission subsidies have hampered rather than aided the growth of the Church."

The Indian delegate Chavan listened intently to all the discussion, especially Dawan's account about the self-support basis of his church. As he compared the West Kalimantan situation to his church in India, he became greatly distressed. "If they can do it," he thought, "why can't we?"

He went back to his room and bed, physically sick from the stress of conviction. He addressed the conference the next day and confessed how upset he was by what he had heard. Chavan made up his mind what he would do when he returned to India.

Other Lively Issues

Not all the issues were Mission-Church relations, nor were they all critical of the Mission's performance. Delegates were equally vigorous in their scrutiny of each other's work. One discussion involved how well the gospel progressed in Europe and America while the Orient had been slow even to hear the gospel as well as accept it in large numbers. A participant asked, "How do you account for that?"

One of the Philippine delegation jumped to his feet. The response came in a rush of words: "We Orientals are so selfish, we want everything for ourselves and lavish it on ourselves, to get what we can for free and use it but not pay anything ourselves. God knew that this was our disposition and that the gospel would not prosper in our hands so He sent it to the West, to Europe and America, where they would obey it and give like they ought to."

A major issue of the Bangkok gathering closely linked to self-support was self-governance. J.A. Dulaca, president of the C&MA Church in the Philippines, chaired the meeting that discussed the topic. He related that after World War II, when the congregations were challenged to organize as a national Church, "it seems that in the early days we were always trying to get some guidance from the Mission, but our missionaries said we were to solve our own problems."

After Dulaca became president of the Church, he went to a missionary with a certain problem. "What is *your* opinion?" the missionary countered. "I hesitated to give it," he admitted, "because I thought what I had decided would be wrong. But he encouraged me and so I spoke my opinion. He in turn said, 'That is my thought, too.' "[15]

One Filipino delegate, de Jesus, added that even when the missionaries offer suggestions, "that does not mean that because it comes from them it is God's program. When we seek the mind of the Lord we make a step that is in the right direction." The discussion gave substance to King's assertion in his opening remarks to the national church leaders: You have Christ who is the Head of the Church; you have the Bible that tells you all you need to know about the Church; you have the Holy Spirit who can show you the right way to go.

The question of a Church constitution flowed into the discussion. Le-van-Thai reported that to date the Vietnamese Church had worked through three such documents and had concluded that the shortest and clearest constitution was the best policy. Dulaca concurred, commenting that the constitution of the Filipino Church was very simple and enduring because it had been drawn up by a few nationals who had no knowledge of law but who depended upon the Holy Spirit for guidance.

He recounted humorously how a few years previous "a legalist in the church organization had tried to convince the national Church its constitution was so simple as to be ridiculous." He framed a more complex constitution that was presented to the Church conference. The delegates reviewed it and concluded they would need the help of lawyers to understand it and promptly voted it down.

Among other topics discussed, the principle of self-expression made it clear the Asian churches could not be lumped together in a one-size-fits-all mold. Congregations in some countries like Vietnam and Hong Kong placed great emphasis on decorum. But Pastor Potu of Indonesia said that churches in his country had a big problem with noise and confusion in their services. He explained that converts brought with them their former habits based on the belief that the more noise the better because this hindered the evil spirits from taking over the meeting.

He asked advice from other delegates on the question of kneeling to pray. Pastor de Jesus responded that Muslim converts had no problem with kneeling because they were accustomed to that. However, the churches did have a problem with another habit: sitting on the floor instead of on benches. Pastors had to discourage the practice in church services because before very long the converts were lying down and loudly snoring.

Even the dress code came under scrutiny. In Indonesia if preachers came to a village too clean and too well dressed, they were considered proud. In India, suits were required. In Hong Kong, speakers were expected to wear white shirts, not colored ones.

King recalled one stifling day in India when he removed his suit coat before preaching. He was rebuked by a church leader. (That incident may account for his habit for many years of wearing a suit and tie no matter how torrid the temperature—much to the discomfort of missionaries who felt they had to do likewise when appearing with him.)

Ripple Effect

The Bangkok Conference in 1955 was like the epicenter of an earthquake. Its impact rippled throughout the churches of Asia and far beyond. R.P. Chavan went home to Maharashtra, India, and confronted the missionaries over the issue of mission subsidies to the Church. "You started giving and you stop giving. That's the only way. You started the practice, so just stop it."

They worked out a schedule of decreasing funds until the Church would be on a self-supporting basis. Chavan was bitterly opposed by some of his fellow pastors because they had a rough time adjusting to self-support. Even the missionaries supported the plan reluctantly. They thought the step was too harsh, too risky. "Remember," said Morris, "some of the missionaries for fifteen, twenty—even forty—years had known nothing else but being involved in governing the Church and paying the pastors. The change was just about as hard on them as for the national Church."

The same scenario was played out across the world where Alliance missions and churches worked together. King himself was left with many disturbing memories. "There were many problems, many aching hearts," he recalled years later. "Among church people, pastors and missionaries, not a few spiritual crises occurred. Some thought and even propagated that compliance with the Council-mandated requirement was a terrible setback . . . a certain wrecking of the work that had been built up at such sacrifice of human life and costly endeavor."

Some missionaries attempted to scuttle the indigenous church policies of self-support, self-governance, self-propagation. A few had to be called home or forced "to find service elsewhere," and in bitterness spread damaging accusations against the Alliance and in particular its area secretary for Asia. A number of indigenous pastors deserted to other missions willing to pay them. Congregations were lured to well-funded denominations all too eager to gather them into their fold.

Yet in 1960, just five years after the Bangkok conference, King could say confidently, "All C&MA overseas pastors were entirely dependent upon national sources for financial support."[16]

Morever, he was already looking beyond the achievement of national churches paying their own way. "Self-support is not an end in itself," King believed. "Only after pastors and churches are in a self-support basis will they consider supporting a missions program." *That* was his ultimate goal.

National churches were truly indigenous, no longer dependent on foreign financing that made them suspect among their own people. Overseas church leaders were free to develop the work in ways consistent with their culture, no longer accountable to guardians of foreign subsidies. Missionaries discovered new and fulfilling relationships, no longer suffering in the role of paymasters with deep pockets, badgered by disgruntled employees.

In short, Alliance missions and churches worldwide were poised to embark together on an era of unparalleled growth when they would be partners together in a global missionary effort. The seismic shifts were precipitated by one man who stood firm in his beliefs about free and viable overseas churches. While many new and younger missionaries agreed with King on the indigenous policy, some of the most respected and influential veterans opposed his efforts.

Emerson once wrote, "If the single man plant himself indomitably on his instincts, and there abide, the huge world will come round to him."

Louis L. King, emerging as a missions leader of world rank, had come a long way from his boyhood days on a farm in rural New Jersey.

Notes

1. "Covering Letter," *Minutes of the Board of Managers* (New York: Foreign Department Conference of The Christian and Missionary Alliance, October 7-14, 1926).
2. "Report #2: Preamble to the Report on Self-Support," *Minutes of the Board of Managers* (New York: The Christian and Missionary Alliance, 1926), p. 128.
3. Louis L. King, "The Risks and Rewards of Self-Support," *The Alliance Witness*, October 1, 1980, p. 19.
4. "Report of the Committee on Foreign Department Report," *Minutes of the General Council 1955 and Annual Report for 1954* (New York: The Christian and Missionary Alliance, 1955), p. 267.
5. *Minutes of the Board of Managers* (New York: The Christian and Missionary Alliance, 1952), pp. 32-3.
6. Louis L. King, "Christ the Head of the Church," *Report of the Asia Conference* (New York: The Christian and Missionary Alliance, 1956), p. 17.
7. Ibid., p. 24.
8. Ibid., p. 27.
9. Alfred C. Snead, "Report of the Foreign Department," *Minutes of the General Council 1956 and Annual Report for 1955* (New York: The Christian and Missionary Alliance, 1956), p. 71.
10. King, *Report of the Asia Conference*, p. 119.
11. Ibid., p. 62.
12. Ibid.
13. Ibid.
14. Ibid., pp. 49-50.
15. Ibid., p. 51ff.
16. King, "The Risks and Rewards of Self-Support," p. 19.

TWO
Making of the Man

1915-1935
Time Markers

The year 1915, when Louis King was born, represented a muted slice of Americana. It was a time for small events to make headlines as people tried to wrap themselves in the naïve and numbing cloak of political isolationism. But rumbles and dimmed flashes on the international horizon reminded the nation that momentous issues ignored do not go away—they gather strength for the inevitable storm.

The 1917 infusion from America of fresh troops and materials on the war-weary battlefields of Europe hastened an armistice. Flushed with victory and still pumped up by the propaganda campaign, Americans looked elsewhere to channel their euphoric optimism. One result was the Interchurch World Movement (IWM) based on the assumption that the world was ready for mass conversions to Christianity. Under terms of the IWM, the mainline churches agreed to coordinate activities. Among other goals, the world's mission fields would be divided among the various denominations to eliminate competition and promote efficiency.

The IWM promised to raise $200 million as a start for the fund, and the total budget for ten years was estimated at $1 billion. The organization used advertising to promote support. One of the jingles ended with the punch line, "Christ needs big men for big business." Few donors agreed with this message, and the IWM became a colossal flop.

Conservative Christians did a bit better. In 1886, college students flocked to Dwight L. Moody's summer school at the Mount Hermon School in Northfield, Massachusetts. One group of 100 returned home vowing, "God permitting, to become foreign missionaries." They became known as the "Mount Hermon 100."

Within two years the group mushroomed into the Student Volunteer Movement for Foreign Missions with 2,200 young members. Its goal was "evangelization of the world in this generation." By 1920, 47,000 students from 800 campuses belonged to the movement; 8,100 missionaries were sent abroad. But by the end of the decade, enthusiasm ebbed, and the movement ceased being a key factor in world missions.

★ ★ ★

The C&MA in North America experienced no such drastic swings, but rather a steady, if not dramatic, growth. At the 1915 annual meeting in Nyack the overseas work could report a record number of conversions (2,728) and baptisms (968). Nearly 270 missionaries were working out of 100 stations. "The work is largely unaffected by war except for transportation and the increased cost of living," the report said. For example, the annual average support for a missionary in Congo was only $500 per person.

By the 1918 Council, founder A.B. Simpson was able to attend several sessions after a prolonged illness. But a report noted, "We have all felt this Council has marked the passing of a crisis and the dawning of a new era. The going down into the shadows, on the part of our beloved President, and his emergence in newness of life, we believe to be typical of the movement at large."

Simpson was too weak to participate in Council the following year. In late October 1919, Albert B. Simpson slipped into a coma after enjoying one of his most cherished activities: praying for missionaries.

Simpson's vision lived on. The 1925 Council recalled one of his strongest challenges: "God has called us in the Alliance, not to a thousand minor points of testimony, but to stand for certain great essentials, principles, and aims—the fullness of Jesus, the evangelization of the world, and the hastening of His coming. Surely this is sufficient to enable us to keep rank and to be of one heart to make Jesus King."

The Alliance was able to hold off the consequences of recession for several years, but by 1933, the Great Depression forced the Board of Managers to slash missionary allowances by two-thirds. Stricken by the hardship imposed on missionaries, the board challenged delegates to General Council, stating that "it had reached a point where no further reductions should be made, and that we should take a definite stand in faith and trust the Lord to provide funds necessary for the carrying out of His work."

C&MA president Harry M. Shuman admitted in 1935, "We can say without exaggeration, that the past three or four years have been the most trying in the entire history of the Society." That didn't stop the Alliance from adding Gabon to its pioneering advance overseas. Fortunately, an eleven percent increase in offerings over the previous year made possible the highest average allowance to missionaries since 1931.

By then the work done by 443 missionaries and their "native workers" had increased to 479 organized churches and numerous smaller, unorganized groups. Baptisms overseas in 1934 numbered more than 8,100, the equivalent of approximately one-quarter of the entire membership in North America.

Thailand, where the Bangkok conference would be held later, could not have been more remote from New Jersey, where Louis King was born on November 30, 1915.

It represented all the exotic mysteries of the Orient: an ancestral religion of innumerable gods and ornate temples, an incomprehensible language and an inscrutable culture, a hothouse climate and a land smothered in dense, tangled forests, an extravagant, gilded monarchy and life-cheap poverty.

Grenloch, where the King family moved shortly after his birth, nestled modestly among tidy garden farms of New Jersey, comfortable in its Protestant ethic and untroubled by big-city vices. Little could go wrong in a hamlet with only two stores, a post office and no saloons (it was the Prohibition era). The hamlet's link to the outside world was a serpentine country road that slowed encroachments of urban growth.

The L.L. King of Bangkok in 1955 was equally far removed from the untested, youthful Louis King of Grenloch in the 1920s, who was yet to undergo the making of a man. Quiet and serious, he alternated between farm chores and school, with scant time for the rough-and-tumble antics of boyhood or the first stirrings of romance. No one could have predicted that this unremarkable boy, who submitted without struggle to a stern Presbyterian upbringing, would one day challenge the status quo of a global missionary enterprise, turning it on its head.

Caper Turned Conversion

The orderly, no-nonsense environment of his upbringing ruled out any levity in matters of religion. But an uncharacteristic caper in the guise of religious quest brought Louis, age fourteen, to the most transforming experience of his entire life: spiritual conversion.

The World His Field

George Senior, a friend of the family and a respectable widower, was sweet on King's mother's twin sister, Ida Dennis. She was not similarly inclined. In fact, Aunt Ida, age forty-three, was firmly determined not to let any man complicate her settled life. No amount of encouragement or conniving by relatives could deflect her from her desire for spinsterhood—not until religion provided a convenient pretext for her suitor to try again.

Aunt Ida had gone off for a week in late August to Delanco Camp near Camden. Its camp-meeting program, in the old-fashioned Methodist tradition, was replete with rustic tabernacle, sawdust floor, mourner's bench and red-hot evangelists. But if she thought to escape the widower's attention, she was wrong.

George Senior suggested, and Louis concurred, that going to an evangelistic tent meeting at Delanco Camp would be a fine way to pass a summer evening. And should they chance upon Aunt Ida, well, what a surprise! The plot turned out far differently from what either one imagined.

Louis didn't remember much about the service, the speaker or his topic. At the altar call, however, he was overcome with a fierce compulsion that if he didn't do another thing in his whole life he had to "hit the sawdust trail" and find peace with God at the other end.

Rising from his knees, he recognized his co-conspirator at the same altar. It was the night that forever changed both of their lives. Perhaps the event softened Aunt Ida's heart, because she married George Senior ten months after the one-sided courtship had begun. They joined the C&MA church in Pitman, a few miles from Grenloch.

For Louis, the last vestiges of the caper cleansed in a rush of tears, that evening of August 27, 1930, would always be remembered as "the turning point of my life. The change was total and permanent." The making of a man after God's heart had begun.

Formative Factors: Home and Family

Louis's conversion may have been unexpected, but it was not done on impulse. Conviction had been building in him for a long time from different directions—home life, church activities and especially his pastor.

Louis was born into a religious home. He was the fourth of five children; Marie, Ralph and George were older, Mildred younger. All would grow up to be respectable church-going people. Mildred would join Louis in an awakened sense of intimacy with God. Gifted in music, she was occasionally a soloist on Percy Crawford's weekly radio program for youth.

His mother, Cordelia King, led a godly life well before he was born. He described her as an attractive woman with lovely hair and a beautiful voice. Never idle, she sang hymns while she worked around the house. He would often stop what he was doing and listen to her singing.

But Cordelia was no softie; she was an enforcer. She oversaw a smooth-running household like a vigilant skipper—always topside. She spent her evenings during the school year supervising all five children in their homework—intensive sessions around the dining room table, lit by an oil lamp. No one went to bed until the lessons were completed. And if for any reason one of the children crossed the line, he or she was sent to bed early. The worst penalty imaginable was to go straight to bed after church without the special Sunday dinner. Delicious aromas wafting upstairs from the kitchen to the banished was something akin to capital punishment.

Raymond King, husband and father of the family, began following Christ when Louis was about eight years old. He was reserved but not cold, hard-working but not aloof from family life. Of slender build, about six feet tall with dark, curly, gradually balding hair, he was pictured in Louis' boyhood memories as "a dapper dresser. When he went to church he wore a derby, the only one in our area to do so. He was a reader and a quiet gentleman, simply a good man in the best sense of the word. I can never recall his speaking loudly to us children or punishing us in any way. My mother did that."

Raymond had known only a brief childhood. Born to a middle-aged father who died when he was eleven, Raymond, an only child, had to leave school and earn a living for himself and his mother. Though tragic, this experience enabled him later to manage a small garden farm of ten acres, yet provide well for the family. He was enterprising and innovative, gradually acquiring acreage from two adjacent farms, hiring migrant workers and introducing overhead irrigation. He had the soil analyzed each year to determine what fertilizer to use. In the peak months of summer, he usually sent a truckload or two of produce every day to the Philadelphia vegetable markets.

During winter months he raised carnations wholesale in two large greenhouses. As word spread about his skill in raising flowers, he gained a steady market in surrounding towns. King relatives still own a florist shop and business in the area.

Hired help did not exempt the children from chores. While his brothers took care of the horses and cattle, Louis had to feed 60 pigs and 300 laying hens before breakfast. And when he returned home from school, more work awaited him. Little time was left for socializing or amusement.

But home life was far from dour monotony. With no skating rinks or cinemas in the small community—Louis saw only about four movies in theatres during his entire life—the children had to organize their own entertainment: parlor games, baseball on unplowed fields and swimming in two nearby lakes in the summer. The family shared a ritual of entertainment each evening when, chores done and homework pending, they gathered around a battery-run radio and listened to *Amos 'n Andy* or *Uncle Abe and David*.

Tough times strengthened family bonds. Raymond King lost heavily in the Depression years, forcing him to sell off all the farm machinery, release hired hands and depend on greater effort by the children. Cordelia did her part, serving up plain fare for the table and cutting costs with a merciless efficiency that would have won the respect of a comptroller. When the children's clothes wore out, she replaced them with handmade items from muslin feed sacks.

Economic conditions eventually brightened and so did the family fortunes. Years later, as father and son passed the bank in the family's blue Buick, Raymond asked, "Louis, do you see that cracked wall over there?" When the puzzled boy said no, his father chuckled, "Oh, I thought my account in the bank would crack the wall, it's so good."

The King parents worked together to provide a wholesome home life built on Presbyterian values. This heritage meant a serious application of biblical standards, especially the Ten Commandments. Moral issues were either black or white with no ambivalent shades of gray between. Swearing and filthy talk were not only forbidden, they were nonexistent. Louis remembered, "We couldn't even say a bad word in our family. It was just not permitted. I don't even recall *thinking* a cuss word. That's how strong the parental influence was."

Out of respect for God's Word, nothing was placed on top of the Bible. No picture of Christ hung on the wall, not even on a religious calendar, because that would violate the Second Commandment. Honoring the Sabbath dictated activities of the weekend. Clothes were cleaned and laid out on Saturday, buttons secured and shoes polished. Most of the cooking for the Sunday main meal was done on the previous day so worship would not be preempted by kitchen work. The Lord's Day meant going to church morning and evening.

Reading religious literature or taking a walk on Sunday were permissible, but not sports. The children learned the consequences of breaking that taboo. Louis recalled, "My brothers and I went to a neighboring farm on a walk one Sunday afternoon. They were not spiritual people at all. They enticed us to play ball in the backyard. While playing, my brother George fell and broke his leg."

Such was the reputation of Mrs. King that the neighbors' concern was not only for George, but also, "What will Cordelia say about this?" It was a big event in the family and Louis recalled, "None of us ever forgot that he had broken his leg on the Lord's Day."

Respect for Sunday was a powerful conviction for him. "When I was at Nyack and saw students leave the hillside to go downtown Sunday afternoon to buy ice cream," he said, "it was something very foreign to me. Even when I became a pastor, my observance of the Sabbath to keep it holy was such that I could not buy anything on that day. It grieved me a great deal to see people buy gasoline or stop at an ice cream parlor after the evening service and have a good time as a group."

Formative Factors: Church and Pastor

The Grenloch Presbyterian Church was the center of community life. Louis remembered it as "ardently Presbyterian of the early Scottish sort," referring to the stern Covenanters who sacrificed their lives rather than recant under torture and death by the English overlords.

Constructed with granite rock and topped by a bell tower, the church was built for the ages and meant to dominate the surrounding flat farmlands. It had that kind of prominence in the King household, about a mile away.

Flanked by modest stained-glass windows and furnished with hardwood pews to accommodate about 150 people, the sanctuary's rather sparse appearance was softened and dignified by pipe-organ music. Here, every Sunday morning and evening the King family was sure to be found. Attendance in the adjoining Sunday school rooms, with high ceilings covered with metal-pressed tiles, was also a given, not an option, for the family.

The sanctuary was usually well-filled, a tribute to the church's pastor. William Topping served the Grenloch community during Louis's growing-up years and had a permanent impact on him. In retrospect, might it not be that in the providence of God Pastor Topping was sent specifically to that small town for such a time in young Louis's life? His influence on Louis would reverberate in global dimensions.

In strictly pragmatic terms, Pastor Topping was too big for the small village parish. A Princeton Seminary graduate, he was a keen scholar, a dynamic preacher and a wise pastor who considered visiting the homes of his parishioners an essential part of ministry. In fact, his previous pastorate had been a much larger congregation in suburban Washington, D.C. But the pressures of ministry and the demands of an influential pulpit caused him to suffer a nervous breakdown. He sought a small church in which to continue his calling, and Grenloch welcomed him gladly.

About 6 feet in height, weighing 200 pounds and crowned with baldness, Pastor Topping was an imposing person. He was not the smiling type, but neither was he dour. He considered preaching a sacred calling, not a fun thing. "He was very dramatic in the pulpit," Louis said. "Even with all of his good scholarship and capability in exposition, sometimes he was very energetic, moving from one side of the pulpit to the other. He wore a cutaway coat and at times he was so powerful in his preaching that he would rush across the platform with his coattail sticking out—he looked like a swallow with its tail flapping."

King as a young high schooler had vivid recollections of another powerful preacher. "I heard Billy Sunday at the Pitman Camp Meeting, and he was impressive! He came on the grounds with a police escort and they marched him and 'Ma' Sunday right up to the entrance of the open-sided tabernacle.

"The two of them walked rapidly down the hard-packed dirt aisle. She, wearing a big, floppy straw hat, was given a front-row seat while he went to the platform. Just sitting on the platform Billy Sunday looked like a man trying to get out of a cage. He was so restless. His aim was to start preaching and, from the way he acted, he could hardly wait.

"He began preaching and it was very dramatic. Before long he took off his coat and flung it on a chair. A little deeper into his message, he ripped off his tie and undid the stiff collar attached to the shirt by a collar button. He threw them behind him and rolled up his sleeves, all the while getting more dramatic in his preaching.

"There was an upright piano next to the platform just a little taller than the raised floor. He stepped on the piano top and preached from there for a while. Then he got up on the pulpit, a big one with a slanting desk and two flat sides. With one foot here and one foot there he spoke with great power. He finally ended the sermon by shinnying up the center pole and preaching from there. Talk about a boy being impressed, I was!"

But it was not Billy Sunday's gymnastics, nor Pastor Topping's energetic pacing, that struck fear in Louis's heart. More than anything, it was the powerful week-by-week biblical and evangelistic preaching in his home church that got to the teenager.

The pastor bore down hard on the need to keep the Ten Commandments, but he always coupled that message with two other points: "Keeping the Ten Commandments will not entitle you to heaven," and "You must be born again."

The preaching provoked a struggle in Louis. Strict observance of the law in his family upbringing fostered a spirit of self-righteousness in him, yet good behavior gave him no peace of heart. He remembered, "The preaching was such that I was afraid many nights as I went to bed that I might die unsaved before morning. I would lie there with my hands folded over my chest like I would be in a casket.

"I knew I was not born again. There was no doubt in my mind that I was a sinner, despite all the religious rigors of living as we did in the home. The necessity of the new birth lay heavily on my mind, but still I did not yield."

Then came the caper with Aunt Ida's suitor. All the influences—home, church, camp meetings and pastor's preaching—converged at the Delanco Camp altar. The teenager's life was changed forever.

Mentor Treasure

The fruits of Louis's spiritual conversion became immediately apparent. "As soon as I got home that night, instead of reporting to my parents about the lark we were on, I told them I had found Christ as my Savior. I had a wonderful assurance that the Lord had written my name in the Lamb's Book of Life, and I had a real heart change.

"The immediate evidence of it was that I began going to midweek prayer meeting in our Presbyterian church, and that's where I became engrossed in the study of prophecy that our pastor was engaged in at the time. I was the only young person who went to prayer meeting, but diligently without fail I was there on Wednesday night. The other evidence of my new birth was that I began reading the Bible daily in a quiet time with the Lord."

The lone young man among the twenty older people on Wednesday evening quickly caught the pastor's attention. A rare friendship developed, the older a mentor and the younger a student, though neither thought to put it in those terms.

The parsonage, next door to the church, was built of sturdy granite like the church. Louis became a frequent visitor, always finding a welcome. Their conversation might begin casually, but it inevitably led to spiritual and theological matters. They made a curious duo: the erudite, sixty-something clergyman and the serious young teenager who soaked in everything passed to him.

Pastor Topping lent Louis classics like A.J. Gordon's *The Ministry of the Spirit* and *The Life and Epistles of St. Paul,* by Conybeare and Howson. He also introduced him to the denominational magazine. His wife assisted the legendary Dr. Samuel Zwemer, "apostle to the Muslims," who edited the missions section of the publication. After Louis read the periodical, the Toppings made a point of discussing important articles with him.

The elder scholar ignited in the young convert a lifelong interest in prophecy. "He had all the charts and paraphernalia on the subject of pre-millennialism," Louis noted. However, many of their discussions centered on something more contemporary: the modernist versus fundamentalist debate in the Presbyterian Church. The denominational seminary at Princeton, only forty-five miles away and Topping's alma mater, was at the center of the controversy and being torn apart.

The widely respected J. Gresham Machen had left Princeton and with some other evangelical faculty members founded Westminster Seminary in Philadelphia. Pastor Topping sided with this group. A Presbyterian rebel of another sort, Carl McIntyre, pastored a nearby church. He started his own protest group, but his abrasive tactics and militant attitude alienated the highly principled pastor of Grenloch.

Discussion in the parsonage about modernism and fundamentalism (in those days, a respectable term) expanded to include other schools like Drew Seminary and other denominations like the Methodists. On one occasion, the pastor produced a book written by a liberal professor at Drew, pointed out the pages where the author was offbeat theologically and let Louis take the book home to study it.

Conversations in Topping's manse on the liberal controversy had a profound effect on the young believer. Looking back from the perspective of his retirement years, King noted, "The discussion conditioned my mind as to theological niceties and how truth can be compromised in a way that looks all right in the beginning—'It's just a little thing'—and how it can grow into something terribly serious. I think he so influenced me that even to this day I can smell heresy afar off and take a stand at the early stage."

The pastor and his student did not always agree. Through study of the Scriptures, Louis became convinced he needed to be baptized by immersion rather than settle for sprinkling as an infant. Topping explained the Presbyterian position on baptism, but Louis did not accept it. "I told him that I really believed I should be immersed because I had been baptized before I was converted and this ought to be a testimony of the conversion experience and I wouldn't be satisfied until that occurred."

"Well, then," the pastor responded, "I'll do it for you."

"Oh no, sir," he replied. "You don't really believe in baptism by immersion so I don't think you should do it."

Louis arranged with the Pitman C&MA pastor to be included in their next baptismal service. One Sunday morning that summer the congregation had such a meeting before Sunday school at a nearby lake. He was symbolically "buried in the waters of baptism and raised in newness of life." Changing clothes, he hurried back to his home church in Grenloch for morning worship.

Louis looked back on those years of mentoring by Pastor Topping with lifelong gratitude. "To me it was invaluable. I think to pour yourself into another person is a wonderful way to influence him for good, especially if you have high ideals about expositing the Word of God, holding true to the fundamentals of the faith and in spiritual verities and experiences. It can't be beat."

It was a dimension he would later incorporate into his own ministry. "I was always a pastor looking for and praying for people who would give themselves wholeheartedly to the Lord for ministry, either as a missionary or as a preacher of the Word. I saw it succeed." In the course of his decades of work, he would play a quiet, decisive part in positioning in key roles of the Alliance more young colleagues than anyone realized.

In retrospect, Louis recognized the relationship with his pastor as a rare blessing. Mentoring has become a disappearing art of ministry. The contemporary pastorate with its multiplicity of roles and pressure of demands generally has meant forfeiting this personal involvement simply because it requires too much time with individuals. But the rhetorical question might be asked, What would have happened to Louis King and where would the C&MA be today were it not for Pastor Topping?

Strength from Sickness

Shortly after his conversion, Louis fell sick with a serious case of pneumonia that after two weeks left his heart badly damaged. Although just a new believer, he did not blame God or question his salvation. He accepted the affliction in stride, but it forced him to revise his whole lifestyle. Previously a strong young man well conditioned by farm work, he now tired quickly, struggled with weakness and had to use his strength sparingly. Even climbing a flight of stairs at home left him breathless.

Gone were the days of carefree games with his peers and doing his full share of chores on the homestead. During his high school years at Woodbury, New Jersey, he sat alone in study hall while his classmates played football or softball on the sports field. In the summer his brothers headed for a swim in the lake, but he stayed behind. His list of responsibilities at home had to be revised to spare him exhausting work.

But Louis refused to indulge in a pity party. Instead, he played the compensation card. If he could not develop the muscles of his body, he would power up his mind. He disciplined himself to listen intently in class, focusing on the teacher like a laser beam. After school he returned home to reconstruct the day's lessons in notebooks. Gradually he achieved nearly total recall.

He maintained the same discipline when he went to college, sitting through hours of lectures without lifting a pen. Then later in his room he reproduced in writing almost verbatim all that had been said. The same intense application applied to reading books and other material. After absorbing the text like a sponge, he would squeeze his memory dry, letting the information flow onto paper. Once there, it was his to keep.

The practice would give him an almost legendary ability to grasp and retain information, names and faces. Innumerable times missionaries would return home from overseas after years of absence, ready to identify themselves to King—only to be greeted by name and asked details about their families or work.

Making of the Man

His ability to focus attention with intensity and without emotion on someone would have made a federal prosecutor squirm with envy. It unnerved many of his colleagues, especially candidates who were being interviewed about their call and qualifications for ministry.

Once, a young missionary determined to turn the tables on the formidable foreign secretary. Called into King's office to receive an assignment, he sat totally motionless across the table, staring at his boss without comment or a flicker of emotion as the project was unfolded. King abruptly stopped and demanded, "Why are you staring like that? Do you understand what I am saying?" The young man nodded, relaxed and said to himself, "Gotcha!"

Enter the Alliance

Shortly after Louis's conversion, another development took place that would change the course of his life. The Grenloch Presbyterian Church ceased Sunday evening services. Where would the King family go to draw the Lord's Day to a fitting conclusion?

Aunt Ida and her husband, now members of the Pitman Alliance church, influenced the answer to that problem. Raymond King would load his family into the black Ford touring car and drive to Pitman, about six miles away.

They did so with Pastor Topping's blessing, because he was favorably disposed toward The Christian and Missionary Alliance. While pastoring the Presbyterian church near Washington, D.C., he became acquainted with an Alliance missionary couple, the Birrels, who attended his church while on furlough from China. "He thought the world of them," said Louis. "They set the standard for the Alliance for him."

Topping also knew of John Turnbull, who was starting an Alliance work in Philadelphia, and had invited him to be the Easter sunrise preacher one year. The Canadian-born minister had served as an Alliance missionary in India before entering pastoral work in the United States. His better-known brother was Walter A. Turnbull, who served as foreign secretary and treasurer of the C&MA.

Disillusioned with the theological battles of his denomination, the Grenloch pastor confided in his young friend that if he had it to do again, he would not have entered the ministry with the Presbyterian Church. Only his impending retirement and the denominational pension plan kept him from making a switch. He even recommended that Louis attend the Missionary Training Institute (later Nyack College). "You'll have enough to contend with as a Bible student, without the doctrinal conflicts in Methodist or Presbyterian schools."

Attending an Alliance church may have appeared at first to Louis to be a good decision. But under the Sunday-evening preaching of Pastor Sturgis and later Pastor J.V. Krall, two crises quickly surfaced: sanctification and the call to ministry. They would cause him a great deal of struggle until resolved.

Sanctification was presented as a life-transforming, ongoing experience in which the Holy Spirit is welcomed into the believer's life just as personally and decisively as was Christ at the moment of salvation. Through the person's total surrender to God, the Holy Spirit would empower the believer to live a holy life and be fruitful in service.

The thought of power for witnessing immediately resonated with the young newcomer at the church. "At the time I was deeply concerned that I couldn't and didn't witness as I should to my fellow students and friends. I had this very strong conviction that unless people believed in Christ, they were lost. I would have my devotions before going to school in the morning and I often asked the Lord, 'Please help me to speak to others today about their relationship to Christ.'

"But when I got to school, my ability to witness just failed. I'd have a lump in my throat, or I would talk about the weather, but never witness—and this struggle grew and grew. I had to have an experience with the Holy Spirit to give me the ability to speak to people about God."

However, coming into that relationship was not a quick and easy experience. He went to the altar many Sunday evenings to receive the Holy Spirit but nothing happened. "People would gather around me to pray. They would open the Bible and show me how to be sure I was filled with the Holy Spirit. I would go through the prayer, saying what they told me to pray. I would get up from my knees, expecting something to happen and it never did. So months later I would be back at the altar again." This battle would go on until his senior year in high school.

The problem was not God or the doctrine, but the person. Louis was struggling with giving up his own ambitions. "Underneath all of that seeking," he admitted later, "was my growing conviction that I must be a preacher, not a doctor." He learned that it is a dangerous thing to invite the Almighty into one's life to handle a problem because, as C.S. Lewis noted, "Once you call Him in, He will give you the full treatment."

For as long as he could remember, Louis had wanted to be a doctor. It was almost an obsession. It spurred him to be a good student and motivated him to direct all his studies through high school in preparation for a medical career. He added extra courses in science, history, Latin and French. Even his reading habits were dictated by this ambition—no novels or other frivolous reading for him!

Nor was his fixation a wasted dream. His mother's uncle was a wealthy man who lived in Philadelphia. Louis's middle name, Ladner, was in honor of this relative, something that pleased the elderly gentleman greatly. Before he died, he set aside money in his will for his namesake's complete medical education.

It was even suggested that if Louis attended the University of Pennsylvania, he might stay with his great-uncle's daughter, who lived quite comfortably. She owned two vehicles—one of them driven by a chauffeur—and had a maid to look after the house. What more could a modest-living farm lad ask for?

Compare that arrangement and the income of a medical doctor to the average Alliance pastor's salary and the whole struggle comes to life. "I realized by that time if I were to be a preacher, it would be with the Alliance," he admitted. "I knew they lived on a freewill offering and some of them eked out a very bare existence and all that goes with that kind of life. That was my battle."

Added to that battle was the prediction about him made by an Alliance missionary to India. James Brabazon was speaking in the missions conference at the Pitman church. Aunt Ida and her husband entertained him in their home and invited the Kings after an evening service for some refreshments so they personally could meet the missionary.

On the following day when the twin sisters again were together in Ida's home, Brabazon came into the room. He said to Mrs. King, "The Lord told me in private prayer last night that your son, Louis, is going to take my place in India." She tucked that pronouncement in her heart, pondering its meaning over the next four years. Her son, however, shrugged it off: "It didn't mean two cents to me at the time what Mr. Brabazon said."

The question of Louis's future came to a head in early May of 1934, when he was a high school senior. His parents had been pressuring him to register at the University of Pennsylvania or some other school for his premedical studies. Fully supportive of his ambition to be a doctor, they could not understand his reluctance to choose a school. He had not told them of his suspicion that God wanted him in the ministry, not the medical profession, and the struggle that caused.

One evening after his family had gone to bed, he stayed up to read his Bible. It was not a planned encounter with God, but a deep conviction settled down on him. He had to face the decision, so why not now?

He came to the final verses of Matthew 9: "Then he said to his disciples, 'The harvest is plentiful but the workers are few. Ask the Lord of the harvest, therefore, to send out workers into his harvest field.' "

What followed was one of the most vivid experiences of his entire life. "The words hit me like a ton of bricks. I sat there for a long time fighting the idea of not being a doctor and instead being a preacher, and this in obedience to Christ. Finally, about the midnight hour, I decided I would have to settle the whole issue then and there. I dropped on my knees and prayed."

The struggle was not only about the "bare existence," as he put it, of an Alliance pastor on freewill-offering support. It was more basic: the conviction of a call to ministry. Louis had to be sure that it was God speaking to him, not something worked up in his own mind.

"I wanted to be dead sure because of the certainty of failure if I were not indeed chosen by the Lord of the harvest. In . . . those days the fact of a call was a weighty matter whether you were Presbyterian, Methodist or Alliance. It had to be something you could put your finger on and say, 'I *know* I'm called.' Unless I felt that way and had a conviction that the Lord had called me, I didn't think I should start studying for the ministry."

The doubts and questions cleared away when Louis came to the realization that God indeed was speaking and he needed to obey the call. "The burden lifted immediately and I was filled with considerable ease and joy. In fact, it was almost joy unspeakable that the issue was settled. I was totally surrendered to be the Lord's witness."

He would recoil in later years from the mentality that the ministry was something to be settled on a trial basis: "It makes a big difference in a person if he is certain before he starts instead of trying it out to see if it suits him. If the conviction is strong that this is what God intends you to do, you won't deviate from it."

The question now for young Louis was how to tell his parents, who still believed he was headed for the medical profession. On the following Lord's Day (May 10, 1934), he lingered while the others set out for church. This was not unusual since the church was only a ten-minute walk from the house.

That particular Sunday was his mother's birthday, and Louis intended to give her a gift she would never expect. He wrote her a letter about his call from the Lord to the ministry and about how he would have to give up medicine. "I remember putting into the letter I would rather be a saver of souls than a saver of bodies. I signed my name with love and put the letter on her mirror where she would see it the first thing she got home." Then he too was off to the morning service.

He lingered at church until the whole family returned home and learned about his decision. He dreaded the moment he would walk in the door, wondering what they were thinking. He need not have worried. The first person he met was his father. He quietly told Louis he had read the letter and liked it.

His mother was equally supportive, but she had a question. Remembering the words of Brabazon, the missionary to India, she asked, "Are you sure you will be a pastor and not a missionary?" He confidently replied, "I am just going to be a preacher."

That Sunday was memorable to Louis for another reason. "At the time I didn't think of my surrendering to the call of God as a coming of the Holy Spirit to help me deal with the problem of witnessing individually to people. But after church I spoke to one of my high school buddies, Herbert Madcliff, about knowing Jesus as his personal Savior. Other times on the school bus I had choked when it came time to witness, but this time was different."

His friend replied, "I've been wanting to talk to you about that for a long time." As they knelt at a back pew of the church, Louis led his first of many people to the Lord. It was a wonderful affirmation that the Holy Spirit had taken control of his life, giving him power to share the gospel. "I immediately realized that my reluctance about being a preacher had kept the Holy Spirit from enabling me to do this," he remembered. "Now that I was totally the Lord's, He had given me this freedom."

A Mantle Conferred?

The parallel series of experiences up to this point in the lives of Albert B. Simpson, founder of the C&MA, and Louis L. King was striking:

- Both were the fourth of five children in their respective homes.
- Both were born into modest, rural communities away from big-city distractions.
- Both were raised by godly parents who laid great stress on keeping the Ten Commandments—especially honoring the Lord's Day.
- Both were instructed in the *Shorter Catechism* and the staunch Presbyterian tradition of the Scottish Covenanters.
- Both were gripped by a sense of conviction for sin and a fear of impending death.
- Both were born again spiritually when in their teens.
- Both were avid students and each was blessed with almost total recall.
- Both, while still in their teens, were convinced by the call of God to the ministry—although Simpson came to the conclusion willingly while King struggled for years.
- Both were prayed for by missionaries linked to their futures—John Geddie, serving in the South Sea islands, dedicated the infant Simpson to the ministry; James Brabazon predicted King would replace him in India.
- Both would conclude that the practice of infant baptism was unscriptural and would seek baptism by immersion outside the denomination.
- Both were physically frail due to sickness in their youth; Simpson endured an emotional breakdown and King suffered a heart condition.
- Both would later experience divine healing that enabled them to pursue their calling with a vigor that left younger men gasping in their wake.

Simpson, still living when King was born, died four years later. Could it be that a mantle passed from one to the other? It could be argued that next to the founder himself, Louis L. King had a greater impact on the worldwide work of the Alliance than any other person.

THREE
Proving the Promises

1935-1938
Time Markers

When Louis King left the family farm in 1935 to prepare for the ministry, his father hoped to provide financial support. But Raymond King's optimism was premature. The Great Depression that forced the closure of thousands of small farms still held the nation's agricultural economy in its paralyzing grip. In the middle of the Depression, farmers owed more than $9.2 billion in mortgages, yet it was estimated that a farmer had to grow the equivalent of nine bushels of wheat to afford one pair of shoes.

Somehow the nation managed to lurch onward in fits and starts. Researchers at the Johns Hopkins Medical Center perfected antibiotic sulfa drugs in 1936. A year later Joe Louis knocked out James Braddock, and Amelia Earhart and her copilot disappeared over the Pacific Ocean. A radio dramatization in 1938 of H.G. Wells' *War of the Worlds* caused thousands of Americans to panic, fearing an invasion by Martians. Walt Disney issued his first full-length movie, *Snow White and the Seven Dwarfs*.

The warnings of another great war grew louder. Italy invaded Ethiopia in 1935; Germany formally denounced the disarmament clauses of the Treaty of Versailles and Hitler reintroduced universal military conscription. His goose-stepping army marched into the Sudentenland area of Czechoslovakia a year later. Germany and Japan signed an anti-Communist pact, forging the Rome-Berlin Axis.

Nazi Germany opened the concentration camp of Buchenwald to eliminate political prisoners in 1937, the same year the Soviet Communist Party began the Great Purge. Within a year, an estimated 10 million Russians had been eliminated. Japan showed no mercy to civilians overrun in its invasion of northern China.

Germany took over Austria in 1938. Nazi thugs launched *Kristallnacht* (Crystal Night) in the Fatherland, destroying the homes, businesses and synagogues of

The World His Field

Jews, and sending 30,000 to concentration camps. It was the worst pogrom in German history to date. Britain's prime minister Neville Chamberlain flew to Munich to sign a pact with Hitler that would stem the black tide and ensure "peace in our time."

★ ★ ★

The North American C&MA's problems were miniscule in comparison. In 1935 President Shuman reported a problem that would persist in the Alliance: Congregations, called "branches," were organizing more missionary conventions than the total of missionaries available to participate in them. He noted that conventions in principal cities had begun to vie in importance with "great summer gatherings."

In the decade between 1926 and 1936, the Alliance in North America registered an increase of 10,000 members, representing a 40 percent growth to 35,000 members. Overseas in 1937, 470 missionaries lived in 140 mission centers on 20 fields. Allied with over 1,900 indigenous workers, they ministered to 50,250 members in 582 churches.

Commenting on financial figures for 1938, Shuman noted that the financial depression forced drastic retrenchment upon many foreign missionary agencies. Such was not the case in the Alliance. "We believe we can truthfully say that no ground was actually lost, and that the shortage in allowances was much less severe than that experienced in our missionary ranks during the earlier years of our history . . . for the past three years and seven months it has been possible through His goodness to send out full allowances to the missionaries."

Financial woes for the nation, in contrast, persisted to the end of the decade and beyond. Ironically, one historian noted, the Great Depression was not ended by brilliant economic strategies of government advisors, but by the demands of war. The country's labor force was fully employed and its industries in full operation by 1943.

On a hill overlooking the Hudson River and the village of Nyack, New York, stretches a long, eye-catching building with the charm of another era. Victorian in style but with a modern facelift, Simpson Hall rears above the treetops as if to demand respect today, yet at the same time hinting at a fascinating yesterday.

It was known as the Institute Building in Louis King's student days, and it still ranks as dean of structures on the Nyack College campus. Its beginning can be traced back to 1897 when it was the newest addition of a school founded fifteen years earlier in midtown New York City.

This building where Louis would spend three eventful years of learning was the nerve center of the school known in his day as the Missionary Training Institute. The steep, undulating hillside campus, punctuated with rock outcroppings and shaded by tall trees, had a personality of its own. Given the school's regimented schedule, students often jokingly changed the name "Missionary" to "Military."

Indeed, founder A.B. Simpson envisioned his institute as the "West Point of missions." The description had more to do with the school's tight-ranked program than its proximity to the famed service academy a few miles upriver. Yet there was a crucial difference between the two institutions: The sole purpose of Simpson's school was to equip men and women to make peace, not war, by reconciling people to God the world over.

Spartan School

The young freshman from Grenloch would find much to enjoy on campus, but it was not necessarily a fun place. Simpson intended the school to be narrowly focused on providing the essentials of ministry to "God's irregulars," i.e., laypeople with neither time nor resources—nor, perhaps, inclination—for lengthy seminary studies. But they were impassioned to take "the whole Bible to the whole world."

Although he was himself a seminary graduate, "Simpson was blunt in his distaste for the theoretical education that led nowhere," notes "The School that Vision Built," a centennial history of Nyack College. He wrote,

> We have no fault to find with the principles of the trained ministry. The only criticism is about the kind of training. How often it is merely intellectual, scholastic, traditional, and many of us have found by sad experience that God has to put us to school again to unlearn much of what man had crammed into our brains, and then sit at the feet of Jesus and learn of Him.[1]

Louis and his freshman peers in the class of 1938 would find the schedule at Nyack, as the school was commonly called, conducive to spiritual development. The first bell of the day jangled through the five-story, multipurpose Institute Building at 6:00 a.m. to rouse them; another rang thirty minutes later, calling its residents to personal prayer before the third bell summoned them to breakfast. Classes began with prayer. Mid-morning chapel attendance was required. Students were encouraged to attend daily prayers at noon in the chapel. They were expected to join one of several missionary prayer groups on Friday afternoons. Testimony meetings followed supper in the dining rooms three evenings a week.

A "quiet time" at the end of the day was considered the best way to wrap it up. At 10:30 p.m. the main light switch was pulled, darkening the building except for halls and bathrooms. The "early to bed and early to rise" practice was to help students to their knees in prayer early the following morning when the whole routine began again.

The biggest campus event of the week was the Friday night missionary meeting. It was considered a high honor to be asked to participate. The meeting featured the best music the school had to offer and carefully chosen speakers who were articulate missionaries or renowned mission leaders of the evangelical movement. The missions committee that prepared the programs was also entrusted with the spiritual tone on campus and was considered more influential than the student council.

School regulations exerted an almost puritanical control over relations between the sexes. By design, the Institute Building chapel was located midway between the north and south dormitory wings.

> This chapel stands between the two sections of the building and separates them by an impassible barrier. The ladies occupy the one section, and the gentlemen the other, and there is thus no possibility of that free interchange which would be so undesirable in an Institute of this kind, except on specified occasions and under proper oversight.[2]

Every noontime, a sign posted in the lobby of the building drew an invisible but inviolable line that governed the social activities of the students. One day it read, "Men exercise north, women exercise south." The following day another sign reversed directions: the men on the road south, leading to Tappan; the women on the road north, leading to downtown Nyack.

It would appear that the divisions of north and south on the "Hillside" were like the cultures of East and West, "and never the twain shall meet." But as Louis would demonstrate, not even arbitrary points of the compass could keep determined couples apart.

The regulation would continue until 1941 when the new school president, Thomas Moseley, made short work of it. "The new social rules have been much appreciated," he noted in his first annual report. "The north and south road rule, which caused so much heartache in times past, has gone forever."

Issues of Finance and Health

It must have been quiet in the blue Buick on that August day in 1935 when the King parents and their son headed north to Nyack. Their thoughts lingered on concerns for the future. Would farm income, not yet fully recovered from the Depression, enable Raymond to pay his son's way through school? That was unquestionably his intention, but was it realistic? Louis had already spent a year working on the farm after high school graduation to help the family financial situation. Was it too soon to release him?

There was no hope that the generous bequest set aside by Cordelia's uncle would be available. It had been designated with the understanding that Louis would prepare for a medical career, not the ministry.

And what about their son's heart-weakened condition? He had managed his handicap fairly well during high school, even turning it to advantage by concentrating on his studies and disciplining his mind. But college life with its accelerated schedule and peer pressure would be something else. Could Louis keep up?

His parents' concern intensified when they saw his dormitory. Wilson Hall, a rather dilapidated structure, was downhill from the Institute Building's dining rooms and Pardington Hall's classrooms. A series of stairs up a steep incline connected the dormitory with the central campus. There was no way Louis could manage that climb. Even the few stairs at home left him perspiring and breathless.

The Kings immediately went to the registration office and explained why the dorm arrangement was unacceptable. The registrar reassigned Louis to a first-floor room in the Institute Building. Again, the handicap worked to his advantage, for the room was across the hall from the apartment of E.R. Dunbar, dean of men.

The World His Field

"Daddy" Dunbar quickly sized up the new freshman. Something more than their similarities in height and build, rimless glasses and conservative suits with starched collars awakened the dean's interest. Young King's serious demeanor boded well for his college experience.

That first impression was soon confirmed. Unable to participate in the men's extracurricular activities that often took precedence over the academic pursuits of other students, Louis honed his ability to concentrate on learning. He followed class lectures without uncapping his pen, then went to his room to take notes on all he had heard. Instead of spending hours on the basketball court, he went to the library and checked out collateral reading, especially in history.

Far from being frustrated by his curtailed campus life, Louis loved it: "It was like an unending Alliance camp meeting." He formed enduring friendships with classmates, many of whom, he recalled, "would one day run the Alliance." Paul Henry, Louis's lifelong friend, pursued a successful pastoral ministry before becoming superintendent of the Western Pennsylvania District, one of the largest and most staunchly Alliance regions of the nation. Elmer Fitch followed the same course, culminating his work as the leader of the Midwest District. Milton Baker eventually headed the overseas missionary work of the Conservative Baptist denomination at the same time King held a similar office in the C&MA.

The emphasis on fellowship in his freshmen year was deliberate. Although women constituted a majority in the student body, Louis seemed not to notice them. He took part in late-night "gab fests" in the dorm, but when discussion turned to coeds, he fell silent. His interests lay elsewhere for the foreseeable future—but that would change sooner than he imagined.

Miraculous Healing

The ministry of Berachah Home, a retreat center for spiritual renewal and physical healing, was also a transplant from New York City. It was housed downhill from the Institute Building in a handsome Tuscan-style villa acquired in the purchase of the Nyack property in 1897. Simpson had opened the first "healing" center in mid-Manhattan as an integral part of his core message, the Fourfold Gospel that exalted Christ the Healer as well as Savior, Sanctifier and Coming King.

He never popularized his healing ministry lest it label him a miracle worker and draw attention away from Christ. But Simpson fervently believed that Christ's redemptive work included the body as well as the soul, since both were ravaged by sin and needed redemption.

> "The Lord Jesus has purchased and provided for His believing children physical strength, life and healing as freely as the spiritual blessings of the Gospel," he taught. "We do not need the intervention of any man or woman as our priest, for He is our Great High Priest, able to be touched with the feelings of our infirmities, and it is still as true as ever. 'As many as touched him were made perfectly whole.' "[3]

One of the early guests in Simpson's Manhattan-based retreat centers was a prominent New York businessman, E.G. Selchow, whose company owned among its products the popular game Scrabble. Selchow's life, however, was anything but fun and games. His physician warned him to get out of the business or he would die within a year or two. He checked in at Simpson's Home for Faith and Physical Healing and experienced a miraculous healing. In gratitude he financed the first Berachah Home in 1884.

The retreat center in Nyack may not have played a conscious role in Louis's thinking, but it represented on the Nyack campus a visible affirmation of the Alliance position on divine healing. Given his own physical liability, he realized divine healing was an issue he could not sidestep or ignore. In late November of 1935, the young student knelt alone in his room and without fuss or fanfare claimed Christ as his Healer.

The test of his faith came soon after. He and Dunbar had established an exercise routine of walking along the road in front of the Institute Building. The dean of men probably did so to keep a close watch on his young charge lest he overdo it. About a quarter-mile down the road, the level stretch abruptly started a steep, winding climb. At that point the two would walk back to the campus.

But in the week after Louis trusted God for healing, he told his mentor that he wanted to continue to the top of the hill. Dunbar objected with concern, but Louis insisted. They walked to Inspiration Point at the crest of the hill and then turned back. Louis experienced none of the familiar difficulties of a weak heart. Not then, not ever—not even years later, when he maintained a travel-heavy schedule. He was indeed healed.

The World His Field

His experience was similar to Simpson's miraculous recovery from broken health. Convinced that the Bible taught divine healing, the Alliance founder claimed the promise and committed himself to use "the blessing to the glory of God and for the good of others." His biographer, A.E. Thompson, wrote that the following weekend Simpson was invited to hike up Mt. Kearsage, a 3,000-foot mountain. Up to that time, even a slight elevation was hard on his heart, but he knew that refusing the invitation would be an act of unbelief.

The C&MA centennial history, *All for Jesus*, picks up the story as told by historian Thompson:

> The first steps of the hike threatened to be his last. Then Simpson sensed another Presence, a source of strength if he claimed it, and he did. "When I reached the mountain top," he testified, "I seemed to be at the gate of heaven, and the world of weakness and fear was lying at my feet."[4]

Financial Bonanza

Louis went home for Christmas vacation several weeks after being healed. He was eager to share the good news with everyone. But the joy he expressed made even more difficult the bad news his father had to tell him.

"I'm awfully sorry," Raymond said, "but the situation due to the Depression—I still haven't reached the financial goals necessary for us. Would you leave school and come back to help with work on the farm, at least for the next semester, until we can get over this problem?"

Louis was stunned. So recently restored miraculously to health and loving every minute at school, he wanted with all his heart to get back on the bus to Nyack in January. But what could he do? Willingly but with great heaviness, he agreed to suspend his studies. After Christmas he packed his suitcase to go back for the remaining classes and exams of the first semester, then drop out of school for however long it took to help the family recover financially.

The final lunch before he boarded the Greyhound bus was subdued and difficult. Unable to keep silent, his mother burst out, "Louis, I can't believe that you are going to have to leave Nyack! I know we don't have the money to support you for another semester, but somehow I don't think it's possible the Lord will let you down."

As if on cue, the telephone rang in the living room. "Louis, it's for you," Cordelia said with a puzzled look. It was her cousin, the one responsible for executing Louis Ladner's will. "We've decided you should get the money from my father's will," the cousin said. "There will be no need to answer how you use it for your schooling. Where should it be sent so you can draw on it at will?"

Louis recited the school address as if in a dream. To reassure him, she said, "The money will be there in a day or two. You just go on your way." He remembered to hang up the phone, but rushing back to his parents he forgot about the door between the living and dining rooms. It smacked him in the face, breaking his glasses.

The bus ride that afternoon back to Nyack was as joyful as the one homeward before Christmas, each in a different circumstance but both for the same reason: God's faithfulness.

Proctor Problems

Now supported with funds that would see him through school and his first year in the pastorate, Louis addressed one aspect of campus life he considered time-consuming and having no academic value. To keep operating costs down, Nyack had a regulation requiring each student to contribute several hours of work each week on campus. Some were assigned to clean halls or bathrooms, some to kitchen or laundry detail, others to building and grounds maintenance.

Convinced he could use his days to better advantage than pushing a broom, Louis requested Dunbar to release him from the work crew. The dean refused in his deep rumbling voice: "That's the rule and there are no exceptions."

The disappointed freshman may have wished he had kept silent. His work assignment was changed from floor sweeper to proctor, the equivalent of today's resident assistant. For the next two and one-half years he would be responsible for maintaining law and order on one of the dormitory floors of the Institute Building.

Louis was in for "some interesting times," as he laconically put it. You would think that young men destined for the pastorate or mission field would be exemplary students in a Bible institute. Wrong.

He remembered three fellows in particular as "difficult chaps." Kimber and Jacob Bellig came from Pennsylvania with an attitude. "I don't think Jake was a Christian at the time," Louis said. Fred Jackson was even worse. Converted only a few weeks before applying to Nyack, he was accepted only because the registrar broke all the rules of admission. Jackson reciprocated by breaking every rule on campus once he was there. "I won't go into detail, " King commented, "but he was a rascal."

The new third-floor proctor quickly encountered a disciplinary challenge. The Bellig boys, Jackson and some others had a habit of sneaking off to New York City and beating the dorm curfew by climbing in a first-floor window after midnight. "Boys will be boys" didn't wash with Louis. "Sin is sin, and righteousness is righteousness," he insisted. "There's no smoothing one over into the other."

He reported the misconduct to the dean but wasn't happy with the response: "You're the proctor, so that's your problem. Deal with it." Cringing from the prospect of punishing his peers, Louis begged to be released from his post. Dunbar held fast: "We want you to keep your job and find a solution."

"So," King later said ruefully, "I got into the business of discipline early on." He approached the confrontation in a businesslike manner. He first identified and verified the charges against the Belligs and their coconspirators. Then he faced them with the charges in a calm and deliberate manner that demolished their cockiness and excuses. His final step was to mete out punishment; they were "campused," restricted to their rooms except for classes and meals. He left the door open for restoration of social privileges if they mended their ways.

As an administrator, King would later refine this procedure when he was forced to discipline wayward associates. Whether close colleague, dear friend or mere acquaintance made no difference. "Sin is sin, and there's no smoothing it over," he insisted, but always with the ultimate purpose of restoring the wounded worker to ministry. It would be one of the most heartbreaking aspects of his responsibilities. Some people enmeshed in the process would be put off by his calm demeanor—unless they saw the anguish filling his eyes.

In the case of his devious fellow students with a yen for the Big City, the pain paid off. "The matter was settled in a day or two," he said. "It probably saved them for the future." Both Bellig brothers would have successful pastorates: Kimber served churches in Western Pennsylvania; Jacob led the innovative, mega-sized Neighborhood Church in Castro Valley, California, for many years.

Fred Jackson, missionary pilot in Indonesia, would become one of the first Alliance martyrs in World War II. For about a year he flew a mission-owned amphibious plane for the Alliance, ferrying personnel and supplies to remote parts of Borneo (now Kalimantan). When the Japanese invaded the island, he could have flown to safety and rejoined his wife in America, but he felt his place was with his colleagues who could not escape.

Jackson volunteered to help the Dutch forces. He airlifted their sick and wounded to medical help on the coast, carried their dispatches and reported enemy movements. When Borneo fell, he was thrown into the Long Berang internment camp with about 120 other Americans and Europeans. In the summer of 1942, Japanese soldiers murdered Jackson and the other adult male prisoners; later they finished off the women and children.

All this was hidden from Jackson in the spring of 1936 when he "got back on track" under the watchful eye of proctor King. But even had he known what the future would hold, he probably would not have changed course.

Some of the activities that occurred on Louis's watch were more humorous. Schoolmate William Miess recalled a skunk incident. The animal had fallen into a ground-floor window well directly under the fourth-floor bathroom window. While Miess "painted" the skunk with a flashlight beam, Jackson bombed it with a metal lamp stand. But even from four floors up, the missile failed to kill the skunk. Another classmate tried to finish it off with a hard-thrown chair rung—only it crashed through a window on the floor below, just in time to allow the skunk aroma to filter through the whole building.

King's formal application for ministry failed to mention one of his leadership events gone awry. Fourth-floor residents debated what to do with a chipmunk trapped in a food box. They decided that higher authorities needed to be consulted. With Louis leading the delegation and the frightened chipmunk in a hat box, they knocked on the dean's door.

"Mr. Dunbar," announced the young proctor in a heavy voice, "we have a bad boy here." But when the chipmunk was dumped on the floor, it scurried into the dean's bedroom with the gang in hot pursuit, pawing through the clothes closet and shoving the bed from the wall in a vain attempt to recapture the culprit.

The Dunbars, who were entertaining guests that evening, were not amused.

Role Models

Given that the ultimate goal of education is to prepare a student for life, Nyack served King well. Course content would recede in significance as he took the tools of study and embarked on a lifelong pursuit of learning that yielded greater knowledge. This does not mean the school skimped on the quality of its education. Several years prior to Louis's arrival at Nyack, the C&MA General Council in 1932 had debated the future course of the school. The result was an expanded curriculum that retained an intense, demanding focus on academic preparation for ministry.

Harry M. Shuman, president, noted in his annual report to Council the following year,

> In the recent decisions of the Board and of the Council to maintain The Missionary Training Institute distinctively as a Bible training school, we believe that there was a permanent policy which was wise, and at the same time consistent with the purpose of the Founder. A first-rate Bible training school is greatly to be preferred to a second- or third-rate theological seminary or college.[5]

In addition, the example of Louis's instructors loomed larger over time than their lectures. The values they embodied as role models became an indistinguishable part of him. The ties between Dunbar and Louis, for example, survived the chipmunk affair and grew into a lifelong friendship. Whenever the younger man visited the campus after graduation, he had a standing invitation to stay at the Dunbars' residence. This was no "out of sight, out of mind" relationship.

V. Raymond Edman was unquestionably the most influential faculty member in Louis's life. He taught at Nyack during Louis's freshman year before moving to Wheaton College, where he became president. That year indelibly fixed him in the young man's mind as a role model of excellence.

Louis never forgot arising at 5:30 a.m. and seeing the light already burning in Edman's study over in his campus residence. The professor's intellectual discipline showed in his powerful lectures and preaching, always without notes.

King wrote in retrospect, "Dr. Edman lived a disciplined life. This led to a lifelong practice of going to bed early in order to rise early. If he were out in the evening at a function for the college, he would leave for home as soon as politeness permitted.

"He never rose later than 5:00 a.m. and more often at 3:30 or 4:00 a.m. for reading the Bible and prayer. He set aside at least an hour to an hour and a half for the Lord each day."[6] Louis adopted a similar schedule for his own daily life.

Edman's interest in the impressionable freshman extended beyond the classroom. On Tuesday evenings the faculty met for prayer in the chapel of the Institute Building. Edman passed Louis's room on his way to and from the meeting. He frequently stopped afterward and lingered long enough to add more than a mere greeting. Sometimes they discussed the history of missions and fundamentals of preaching, the two courses Louis took with Edman. Other times the professor questioned Louis about his collateral reading.

They never lost contact with each other. Edman's wife attended Louis's wedding and Louis invited the Edmans to his home in Wheaton during their honeymoon. When the Kings were serving in India, Edman sent books he thought Louis should read. When he lay very ill and other visitors were turned away, he welcomed Louis and spoke of the momentary prospects of heaven. Edman collapsed on the college chapel platform just after concluding a message, "In the Presence of the King." His next moment was literally in the Lord's presence. This left yet another unforgettable lesson with his former student.

Other professors were in their prime during Louis's years at Nyack. Tall, lanky Harold M. Freleigh taught Old Testament Survey from Genesis to Malachi, using a methodology of timeless value. It would help Louis later as a missionary in India when preaching on three different topics a day. Fannie L. Hess, a heavyset, slow-moving woman, drilled her students in the location of Old Testament towns and kings of Israel until the class could recite them forward and backward. "She probably knew more about Bible geography, Bible history, and all connected therewith than most of us can imagine," said John Cable.

That was high praise, coming from the head of the school. Cable himself exerted a profound influence on Louis. A scholarly gentleman with a quiet charisma, he was the "mainspring" of the semi-vows King later would formulate as he entered the pastorate.

The World His Field

Cable used every moment of class time to instruct his students—even in the opening prayer. "When class began, he would open his attendance book and place his fountain pen right in front," King recalled. "Then he would ask a student to lead in prayer. At its conclusion he would comment on the content of the prayer. Did the student mix 'thee and thou' with 'you and yours'? Did it begin with an appropriate expression of praise? Were promises of the Bible used to strengthen praise? Some students thought this was a terrible thing for Dr. Cable to do, but to me it was perfectly fitting for ministerial students to be schooled in public prayers."

One incident involving Cable made a great impact on Louis. He recalled, "In our senior year we had a social event scheduled for Saturday night. The program committee submitted the plan to the school director. He went over it carefully, asked a few questions, and approved it.

"One section was simply called an orchestral presentation. However, it was a sham put on by several of us who had no musical talent whatever. For instance, I had a violin with broken strings. The conductor, dressed in formal attire, led the orchestra with wild, swinging gestures but not a sound came from the instruments until the finale, when everyone played one horrible, discordant sound. It brought down the house. Dr. Cable was not amused.

"Another part of the program was called a poem. It was a take-off on some student coming from Western Pennsylvania over the hills to Nyack in a jalopy. It was another hilarious joke and we were all in stitches.

"By this time," King continued, "Dr. Cable was livid with anger and it was obvious. He stood and declared that the program was over. 'This is not to be,' he said sternly. 'Bring on the refreshments.' Everyone was shocked into silence. The party ended a fiasco.

"On Monday night when we gathered in a circle for testimonies and prayer after the meal, Dr. Cable came to the dining room, a most unusual appearance for him. When we finished, he stood and with great contrition apologized for his outburst the previous Saturday evening, saying it was a terrible thing to do. He felt the orchestra and poetry skits had been misnamed to deceive him and that angered him, but it was no excuse to lose his temper. Would we please accept his apology and forgive him?"

That act of humility deeply moved all the students. Louis was especially impressed that Cable dealt with it quickly and decisively instead of letting resentment build among the students, a practice he would later make his own when an administrator.

As part of his homiletics studies, Louis made a special effort to hear prominent preachers in action. One speaker in particular made an unforgettable impact on him: G. Campbell Morgan. The famed British preacher, visiting his son's church in Philadelphia, was preaching a series of messages to commemorate his sixty years of ministry.

Louis remembered him as "tall, loose-jointed, and gaunt-faced. During the service he studied each row of people clean back to the recesses of the long sanctuary. When he spoke, it was with every fiber of his being. Obviously dominated by his message, he gripped me with his overpowering rhetoric, skillful examples, and startling quotations. For about an hour, he built a solid, sustained, carefully reasoned exposition—he was truly a Bible preacher. No wonder he was an irresistible attraction to crowds of people."

Morgan, Edman, Topping, even Billy Sunday, all had an accumulative effect on the young man destined for the ministry. It showed in his own preaching. The otherwise quiet, deliberate man, always speaking without notes, would often be so possessed by the message that his voice would rise to a shout and occasionally both feet left the floor as he hammered home his main points.

First Love

So far, so good. Louis was profiting from all that the Missionary Training Institute had to offer in preparing him for the ministry. Only one dimension was lacking. Nyack was humorously nicknamed "Simpson's Match Box" because of students who found their life partners at school. That too would become a contribution of the school to Louis's life.

One of the traditions of upperclassmen was "looking over the new crop" on the hillside at the beginning of each fall semester, i.e., identifying attractive new coeds worthy of personal attention. Louis was not much interested in that tradition, but in September of 1936 he could not help noticing a young transfer student from Chicago.

Unfamiliar thoughts and feelings began stirring in the young man, who until then had had no yen for dating. He used words like "beautiful auburn, curly hair . . . attractive to look at . . . singular appearance." He would insist later that she winked at him in Greek class, but she stoutly

The World His Field

denied it—and was probably right. Love sometimes does strange things to men's eyesight. In a word, Louis was fairly smitten.

Who was this remarkable young woman who could unsettle the seemingly imperturbable upperclassman? Esther Lillian Martz was born in 1917 into a Chicago family quite similar to the Kings in Grenloch. She called herself the "caboose," being preceded by two brothers and a sister.

The Martz home provided a Christian environment carefully overseen by devout Methodist parents, William and Myrle. Her father was an exceptional man. Although his education had progressed no further than the fifth grade, he was a self-taught structural engineer who enjoyed constant employment and taught in a technical college. "Even during the Depression years," she recalled, "he was never more than a day or two without a job."

While working for the Rock Island Railroad, Martz designed a freestanding cantilevered signal system for trains that replaced the more costly frame structures. He did not register the design (which is now widely used) and received nothing from the company for his invention.

Martz was in such demand he finally felt compelled to move his family to a forty-acre farm on a lake near Allegan, Michigan, to shield them from the constant pressures of his work. He commuted by rail and ferry from Chicago to spend weekends on the farm. Not understanding the nature of his work, Esther once asked, "Why don't you finish your job, Papa, so you can stay with us?"

The Martz family faithfully attended a Methodist church and the parents were born-again Christians. But Esther remembered, "It was not until Mama and Papa heard R.R. Brown, an Alliance preacher, that they had assurance of salvation. Until then, as good Methodists, they didn't know whether they were saved or not, and felt like they needed to keep being born again and again."

Hooked in a Hut

Myrle's friend, Viola Hines, introduced the family to the Alliance through its magazine, *Alliance Weekly* (now *Alliance Life*). Wanting to return some borrowed copies, Myrle asked her daughters to accompany her to Mrs. Hines' Sunday school class. "OK," Esther agreed reluctantly, "but let's not stay for the church service."

Actually, the Alliance group was not a regular congregation. It was a "branch" that held services on Sunday afternoon so people could attend morning worship in their own churches. This was in keeping with Simpson's vision that the Alliance would not be a denomination but a movement that would muster missions-minded people from all quarters to support missions without having to leave their churches.

Neither did the building look anything like a church. It was a Quonset hut with no frills. Sunday school classes before the worship service "broke every rule in the Christian Education manual," Esther said. "Small groups were scattered all over the auditorium and adjacent rooms. It was a cacophony of voices. If you didn't like what you were hearing in your class, you could turn your ear to the teacher in another group nearby."

The Alliance branch had the potential of a total turnoff for the thirteen-year-old Esther. To make matters worse, she was accosted by a very short, humpbacked old woman she described as "homely as a mud fence on a rainy day."

"Are you one of the Martz girls?" she asked abruptly. "We've been praying for you for a long time."

Why the teenager didn't bolt for the door was a mystery of God's grace. Instead, she moved to Hines's class for young women and encountered another shocker. "I never in my life heard anything like it. The first thing that impressed me was the Bible she was holding—the gold was worn off the pages, and she knew what to do with the book. For the first time in my life I heard that the death of Christ had something to do with me."

After class someone announced that a trombone soloist from nearby Wheaton College would play in the next service. Esther nudged her mother. "Let's stay."

The preacher captivated the young girl. "Is that man going to be here tonight?" she asked.

"I think so," Myrle answered. "He's the pastor."

"Then this is where I want to be," Esther decided. Between the Sunday school teacher and the preacher, she was hooked.

The pastor's name was A.W. Tozer, a preacher and writer who would later be acclaimed throughout the worldwide evangelical community as a modern-day prophet.

The World His Field

The whole Martz family began attending the Gospel Tabernacle on Sunday afternoons following the morning service in their Methodist church. But Esther's enthusiasm for Tozer's preaching did not sit well with the church people. "I made myself obnoxious," she admitted, "because when I told the other young people what Tozer preached, the parents got upset."

Church officials especially were angered when they learned the Martz children were telling the church's children that they were sinners and needed to be saved. "You've got to get those people out of here," they ordered the pastor. When Esther heard the news, she cheered, "Hurray! Hurray! We don't have to go back there!"

Myrle and two of her sons tried to remain in the Methodist church in order to continue their work in the Sunday school, but eventually they too were told to leave. Similar experiences occurred many times in other churches and other cities as cold, formal churches forced some of their best members to leave and form their own branches or congregations. It became one of the major reasons why the Alliance movement itself became a de facto denomination until the mid 1970s when it made official what its people had already accepted.

New Life

By the spring of 1931, however, Tozer's messages began to trouble Esther. It was OK to call other kids sinners, but what about her? She stiffened her resolve not to respond. When summer came, she was glad to leave the city and get back to the farm. "I didn't count on the fact the Lord was in Michigan as well as Chicago." She heard the same truths in a Baptist church the family attended.

One night in August she went to bed with the words turning over and over in her mind: "The Lord is coming and you are not ready." Unable to bear it, she knelt by the bed and surrendered to Christ.

"I'll never forget going over to the window and looking up at the stars. It was a clear night and the dark country sky was full of gorgeous stars. I remember saying, 'The One who made them is my Father.' " With that assurance of salvation, she jumped into bed and promptly fell asleep.

The Gospel Tabernacle became the sun around which both her social and spiritual life orbited. Thursday was often the only night of the week when she was not at church. Tozer was remembered as the preacher who hung around church after the evening service and teased the Martz children while their dad helped count the offering.

His legendary wit—at times scathing in the pulpit—was gentle and playful with the girls. One evening Tozer asked sister Margaret, "Do you ever get stiff in the joints?" When she nodded uncertainly, he went on, "Well, you better stay away from such places."

Esther gravitated toward the Women's Missionary Prayer Band. Each woman had a special continent or country of interest and reported news to the group. Ever watchful, Hines invited Esther to be a prayer partner when the group split into pairs to pray. The teenager received a college-level survey of information about Indochina, Viola's special interest—at least until knees aching from prolonged praying distracted her.

Esther became convinced her future was missionary work in Africa, especially after she met Helen Sherwood, whose married name later was Martin. A member of Tozer's church and home on furlough from West Africa, Helen was just the right person at the right time. Esther admitted "dogging her steps and worshiping the ground she walked on."

She asked Helen's advice on what school to attend in preparation for ministry overseas. Her response: "If you want solid biblical study, go to Moody [Bible Institute]. If you want spiritual life and missions, go to Nyack."

A Hike for Life

After graduating from a two-year junior college in Chicago, Esther took the train east to enroll at Nyack. It is fortunate that she was highly motivated, because her first experience at Nyack was less than inspiring.

Two older students met her at Pennsylvania Station in New York City and took her to the old Institute Building that housed both men and women at the time. "We got there about 10 o'clock at night," she recounted. "When I walked into the room, it was a dismal sight: The iron beds had nothing but thin straw mattresses; the cracked linoleum covered only part of the floor; a 25-watt bulb hung by a single black wire from the ceiling; the window had no curtains. 'Oh no!' I thought."

After her escorts left, Esther turned off the feeble light and knelt by the window. It was a beautiful night. The flashing beacon of a lighthouse on the far shore shimmered across the broad, black expanse of the Hudson River, called the Tappan Zee by early Dutch settlers. Lights in historic Tarrytown, home of George Washington Irving and the Sleepy Hollow legend, seemed to blink coded messages to the canopy of glittering stars overhead.

"Lord, this is where You want me, and I am so thankful," she prayed gamely, and she went to bed.

The young lady from Chicago adapted quickly to the hillside routine that fall of 1936 and enjoyed her studies. She anticipated an uncomplicated future: two years of school and then off to Africa as a single missionary. "But if I were to marry," Esther admitted praying before going to Nyack, "please, Lord, don't let me marry someone who will conk out along the way." In November a student whom she had not yet met was waiting by her mailbox in the post office. He had other plans for her life.

The encounter happened shortly before Thanksgiving, a very special time at Nyack. Students did not go home for the holiday, so the school went to extra lengths to soften the pain. The north-south regulations were suspended for the day, permitting students to be together. One special feature was a feast at noon, spread grandly in the traditional manner with all the trimmings. An afternoon hike around the mountain was organized for couples and singles.

Louis had determined to ask Esther, the fetching transfer student, to join him on the hike. It was an incredibly difficult step for him because he had never before dated a girl—or even asked. Simply put, he was nearly paralyzed with fear. When she stopped at her mailbox, he walked over and blurted out, "Are you engaged?"

Seeing her shocked expression at his faux pas, he stuttered, "I mean, do you have someone to hike around the mountain with you?"

For Esther, as well, it would be the first date in her life. This was partly because she was better in athletic sports than most fellows and that put them off. And it didn't bother her greatly that she was overlooked. She had other things on her mind during her growing-up years.

She accepted his blundered invitation and, flushed with elation, hurried back to her room to announce the news. Her roommate thought it was wonderful, but a girl down the hall had a different reaction. She had been bested by Louis in an argument and thought he was a very difficult person.

Esther also asked Miess, one of Louis's friends, about him. He answered, "Did he ever give you one of those looks? When we get out of line, all he has to do is look at us and we head for the hole."

The Thanksgiving Day hike was memorable—and strange. Louis enjoyed every minute of it but had little to say. Esther recalled, "It was a two and one-half hour walk around the mountain and he said no more than two or three sentences. We'd talk to other people as they passed us, but didn't talk to each other. It was crazy, absolutely crazy. I went to my room afterward and said, 'That's it. I'll never hear from him again.'"

But she did—that very day. Louis called and asked to spend the evening with her. It was a light supper because of the noon feast, followed by a testimony meeting in the chapel. Louis's testimony added one more humorous twist to their first date.

Esther remembered, "Louis stood to give his testimony about the heart condition he had when he came to school the previous year. But now, he said, the Lord had healed him from that problem—and the whole room exploded in laughter. There I was, sitting next to him after our first date. I was wearing a really red dress and I turned the same color. He didn't even know what they were laughing about."

Ring in the Rain

From then on, Esther began to observe Louis at every opportunity. She liked what she saw. "He was not one to fool around like other fellows who were at school for the fun of it. He knew why he was there and was all business."

Apparently Dunbar also liked what he saw because he took the unusual step of giving his fourth-floor proctor a special dispensation several days after Thanksgiving. School regulations permitted couples ninety minutes in the sitting rooms at both ends of the Institute Building on weekends if they signed up in advance. The dean of men gave Louis a birthday card with a handwritten note: "You are hereby given permission to weekly parlor dates with Miss Martz."

The parlor dates followed the unusual pattern set by the Thanksgiving Day hike. To overcome his shyness, Louis studied sources like the *New York Times* to make sure he had enough to talk about when they were together. While couples in the other half of the parlor were "very romantic," Esther said with a laugh, they discussed world events or points of theology. Yet both were also comfortable with silence and often sat quietly, simply relishing the time together.

Other opportunities presented themselves as well. Couples were permitted to walk to classes together—provided they proceeded "at a normal pace," the regulations stipulated. It was also tolerated when couples met "accidentally" in the post office area. The mailbox would become something of a symbol in their relationship, not only because of the brief contacts but also the notes they wrote to each other. "At first we communicated better by letter than we did by conversation," Esther joked. After they were married and Louis was traveling overseas, he would write a letter every day to his wife and she to him.

Louis had other ways of communicating his feelings. Because of his father's greenhouse business, no other coed on the hillside was as faithfully showered with fresh carnations as was Esther.

The courting progressed well under the amused scrutiny of their classmates. A joke began to circulate on campus: "How are the King and Queen Esther doing today?" During an interview with the Home Department about ministry in the Alliance, Dunbar asked if Louis was engaged to Miss Martz. Ever the private person, Louis deadpanned, "No." The next day he proposed.

On a rainy spring night after a parlor date, as they stood in front of Harmony Hall, where Esther was staying, he formalized their engagement with a ring. He had already written to William Martz for permission to marry his daughter. Esther recalled that the letter was "horribly short," about two sentences long.

And ever the stickler for going by the book, Louis also wrote to A.C. Snead, the foreign secretary, asking for permission to make the engagement public. When Snead agreed, King responded formally, "Having received your sanction of an engagement between Miss Esther Martz and myself, I am writing to inform you of its being made public."

As if such a matter could be kept secret on campus. That very evening students gathered around Esther in the Institute Building as she showed off her ring. When Louis saw they were crowding her, he pushed his way through and stood directly in front of her, glowering at the group. "He was protecting me," she explained, very pleased.

India Beckons

Throughout his three years at the Missionary Training Institute, Louis's attention focused on the pastorate. He had not deviated from that goal since high school. But he was present in a chapel service in his senior year at Nyack when the leader read a telegram that would drastically alter his future. Alliance missionary James Brabazon had died suddenly while serving the Lord in India.

A wave of memories swept over Louis: his mother, visiting her sister in Pitman; Brabazon, speaker at the church's missionary conference, telling Cordelia that God revealed to him that her son would replace him in India; he, Louis, dismissing the notion out of hand. Now, four years later, India beckoned.

After chapel, he skipped classes and went directly to his room without a word. The Bible, meditation and prayer would be his agenda for the rest of the day. By evening he reached several conclusions. He would apply for missionary service but not mention India. He was not prepared to let one man's opinion constitute his call. If God wanted Louis in India, He would get him there on His own.

This young man, who arrived at Nyack as an untested teenager with a weak heart, was coming of age. He had been healed; he had completed his courses; he had proven himself in leadership; he had found the ideal mate and lifelong friends; and he had won approval as a candidate in what some knowledgeable observers called the foremost missionary movement of the century.

But the Alliance first required its overseas candidates to spend several years in home service. Why send someone abroad if he or she were unable to succeed in the relatively sheltered and familiar environment of the homeland?

Louis L. King, man in the making, was about to embark on another phase of preparation fully as life-forming as his days on the hillside.

Notes

1. Robert L. Niklaus, "The School that Vision Built," *Missionarian 1982* (Nyack, NY: Nyack College, 1982), p. 9.
2. Ibid., p. 13.
3. Robert L. Niklaus, John S. Sawin and Samuel J. Stoesz, *All for Jesus: God at Work in The Christian and Missionary Alliance Over One Hundred Years* (Camp Hill, PA: Christian Publications, Inc. 1986), p. 55.

4. Ibid., p. 41.
5. Harry M. Shuman, "Report of the President," *The C&MA: The Thirty-Sixth Annual Report* [for the year 1932] (New York: The Christian and Missionary Alliance, 1933), p. 8.
6. Louis L. King, "In the Presence of the King," *The Alliance Witness,* April 15, 1987, p. 25.

FOUR
Pastoral Toughening

1938-1946
Time Markers

In 1939 the world accelerated down the slippery slope toward a bloodbath beyond the imagination of decent people. Britain began universal military conscription and joined France in a pledge to protect Poland if it were invaded. When Hitler's legions swarmed across the border on a trumped-up charge of Polish aggression, Britain and France declared war. The Second World War began.

The Alliance overseas experienced only "minor disruptions" despite the European conflict. Discarding one aspect of a free-spirited movement, the North American headquarters developed the first annual budget.

What had the Alliance done up to that point? Shuman explained, "It has been the custom to operate on the basis of the Council Budget which is framed in accordance with the needs of the several departments of the work without special reference to anticipated income. Each month all fixed bills were paid; and if shortages occurred, they were deducted from allowances."

No wonder the missionaries—and headquarters staff—were put on pro rata support repeatedly in the early decades of the movement! The formula is still familiar to some Alliance pastors in small, struggling churches: Pay the bills first, and if there's money left over, pay the preacher.

The "Day of Infamy," December 7, 1941, dragged the US into the war against the Axis powers—Germany, Italy and Japan. The conflict closed Alliance fields in the Far East: China, French Indochina, Thailand, Philippines, Netherlands, East Indies (now Indonesia). Of the missionary force, thirty-five men, forty-two women and forty-four children were interned.

Looking ahead, the Alliance authorized a special reserve to accumulate funds for use after the war when missionaries would again serve overseas, especially in Asia. Displaced missionaries and new recruits were routed to Africa and South America. A plan was drawn up to send 250 new missionaries within 5 years.

The C&MA missionary effort held steady during those war years. Of the 476 licensed missionaries, 252 were in active service overseas. Giving to the General Fund reached an all-time peak of $1,332,000 in 1944.

★ ★ ★

General Council of the C&MA in 1946 reviewed the costs of war. Ten adult missionaries and one child died in captivity. Destruction of Mission properties amounted to many thousands of dollars. Overseas churches suffered heavily.

That same Council approved the sending of forty-two new missionaries. The list of active overseas workers rose to 522. The special reserves collected to finance the resumption of work in closed areas amounted to $714,860.

This unrelenting commitment to world evangelization was building on a foundation laid years earlier. Shuman, for example, had reported to the 1927 General Council that the district superintendents "were entirely unanimous" in declaring that "the prime objective of all our service at home is the taking of the Gospel to the perishing millions in the regions beyond. As expressed by one of our brethren, 'No Christian work that comes to the vanishing point before it reaches the threshold of the heathen world is worthy of our time or attention.'"

Overall giving to the General Fund rose to a record $1.5 million, a tribute to the sacrificial leadership of pastors across North America, especially considering the modest size of the Alliance community: 14 districts with 928 branches and churches; 1,070 licensed workers; and 50,011 baptized members.

They were ready to get on with world evangelization, but already roadblocks were appearing. In 1946 Winston Churchill gave his famous speech at a college in Missouri, warning, "An iron curtain has descended across the continent." War returned to Vietnam; the French bombarded Haiphong and Hanoi, killing 6,000 people in an effort to force the surrender of Ho Chi Minh's forces.

The cloistered days of Nyack's academic year were coming to an end in the spring of 1938. Classrooms in Pardington Hall soon would empty; dormitory halls of the Administration Building would fall silent; jangling bells in both places would stop ringing out the daily schedule. The invisible chasm of the "Great Divide" between north campus and south campus would soon close, no longer keeping apart men and women.

For the class of '38, graduation held other challenges. Instructors who for three years had dominated students' thoughts would no longer invite, entice, stimulate, cajole, force or shame them into the larger world of ideas and realities. Chapel services that too often had substituted for neglected personal devotions would no longer provide a crutch of inspiration. Friendships that in many cases had superseded family ties would now themselves be subjected to separation, replaced by loneliness and uncertainty.

"Am I ready for this?" was the question uppermost in the thoughts of many seniors. One by one, they mentally began peeling away from their close-knit circles as the future beckoned. Most of Louis King's friends decided they were not yet ready for ministry so they applied to other colleges and seminaries.

Not Louis. "I came to the decision not to go further in schooling. Money was not a problem. There was enough to pay for another year. I concluded that I had learned enough at Nyack about how to study the Bible, what books to read and how to get ahead as a minister of the gospel."

Thus began a lifelong discipline of study as structured as the school bells that signaled the succession of classes on the hillside. In addition, he enrolled in that informal graduate school of experience, where he would learn from men of the highest quality—and they from him—across a broad spectrum of confessional and professional backgrounds.

So while his peers sent off applications to Wheaton College, Asbury Seminary or New York University, Louis applied for pastoral ministry in the Northeastern District of the C&MA. He wrote to the superintendent well in advance but for weeks received no reply. That silence continued right up to graduation day. A half hour before he joined the other seniors to begin the solemn procession to the final ceremony, Louis checked his mailbox one more time. There was a letter from the district office with some welcome news.

The newly formed Alliance church in North Tonawanda, New York, was looking for a pastor. The superintendent had scheduled Louis to candidate the following Sunday, just five days later. Would he go?

The World His Field

Louis quickly responded and in a few days took the train across New York to the next great epoch in his life. Inexperienced and eager, just out of school and anxious to get started, he would have agreed to anything for nothing. And that's just about what happened.

Bleak Invitation: North Tonawanda

The Alliance church in this factory town near Buffalo was just three years old, growing out of a series of tent meetings conducted by a woman evangelist. The congregation of nineteen members, most of whom were mill and factory workers, met in a remodeled old brick and cement-block theater on a busy corner. It was in the middle of a Polish-tradition, blue-collar community, dominated by a large Catholic church three blocks away.

Some of the new Alliance people had converted from that church, generating bad feelings in the strongly Catholic neighborhood. The simmering anger occasionally erupted, especially when another person defected to the Protestants; windows in the small church had been smashed and worshipers' car tires slashed.

The pastoral candidate, fresh out of Nyack, arrived in North Tonawanda with only two sermons written and memorized—just enough for the Sunday services on May 15, 1938. He forgot part of the morning sermon, so the service was shorter than usual. The evening meeting went better and longer.

The governing board interviewed him after the service. They did not embellish the situation: There was no parsonage, so he was on his own; the church could not afford benefits—indeed, probably had not even thought about them.

His salary would be only the loose change in the offering plate (which, over the next nine months, averaged $3.51 per week). Even with these drawbacks, the candidate was not discouraged. The thought of negotiating a salary package was foreign to him.

While the board further considered the matter, Louis sat quietly in the dimly lit auditorium, studying the worn theater seats and the faded curtains that flanked the stage in heavy, long folds. The men returned with their decision: "We are extending an invitation to you to be pastor of our church. Will you accept?"

The instant response: "Yes."

When asked later why he agreed to such a bleak offer, he said, "I wanted to preach!" But there was more to his decision than the itch to be in the pulpit. "In my daily devotions I was so committed to the Lord and His guidance that I had no hesitation and no fear that I was missing the mark."

That settled conviction applied to his experiences and decisions would become over the years a hallmark of his life. One of his cherished quotes was from an old book, *A Guide to True Peace*:

> We should give up our whole existence unto God, from the strong and positive conviction, that while we are faithfully endeavoring to follow him, the occurrence of every moment is agreeable to his immediate will and permission, and just such as our state requires. This conviction will make us resigned to all things; and accept from all that happens, not as from the creature, but as from himself.[1]

He began immersing himself in hours of personal study and prayer early each morning. Then he went about the day's business, confident that the Lord would direct his decisions and control all the events that would come to him—no hesitation, no questioning, no looking back. Few leaders would probably risk following that creed, but decades of exceptional service would verify that it worked for King.

Semi-Vows

On the long train ride back to Philadelphia and home the next morning, Louis had plenty of time to reflect on the future course of his ministry. Sensing the need to lay some ground rules, he interrupted his train trip at Tarrytown and crossed the Hudson River to Nyack. He rented a dorm room at his alma mater and secluded himself for as many days as he felt he needed to settle on principles that would be the framework for his life as a minister of the gospel.

He cautiously labeled his resolutions "semi-vows, because if I broke any one of them, I would not have sinned," he explained. In this respect, he differed from A.B. Simpson, founder of the Alliance. As a new believer at age 18, Simpson drew up a 900-word "Solemn Covenant" and vowed to honor it throughout his lifetime.

Originally listing eleven semi-vows, Louis settled on nine and scrupulously followed them during nine years in the pastorate and six years in India. Several continued to influence his schedule even during his decades of administration. In response to a request by an Australian pastor years later, he listed them:

1. Arise, shave, dress and be working at my desk before the first man in my congregation left his house for work.
2. Insofar as possible, begin preparations for going to bed at 10:30 p.m.
3. Study a minimum of five hours a day, but strive for eight.
4. Study every word of the New Testament in the original language.
5. Write in full two sermons a week—one expositional, one evangelistic.
6. Preach without notes.
7. Visit every member or family of the church once a month while the church is small enough to do so. Stay no longer than twenty minutes. Never leave without prayer and the reading of Scripture. [Eventually he would memorize whole passages to share when visiting parishioners.] When in a larger pastorate, devise a system for shepherding the flock adequately.
8. Give a weekly lecture like a seminary Bible course; prepare and preserve notes that could become a commentary.
9. Read textbooks that are used in college classrooms in order to stay abreast with current thought and development.

Later he added another semi-vow based on Job 31:1: "I made a covenant with my eyes/ not to look lustfully at a girl." His reason for this additional principle? "Preachers, I found, were having trouble morally and I didn't want to be one of them."

In an article much later in life, he linked this additional semi-vow to something he had read in Alexander Whyte's writings: "The eye is the shortest road to the heart, and like all other short roads it is cram-full of ... traffic. For one assault that is made through my ear there are a thousand assaults made through my eye."[2]

Basics Camp

The North Tonawanda Alliance church would be the first and smallest of King's three pastorates over the next nine years, but in many respects it would be his most important. It would be the training camp for basics that largely would determine the future content of his service.

Looking back over those early years, he said, "In embryonic form, everything I needed to learn happened in that church in one way or another. Situations would be dealt with by principles I never had to alter.

And fortunately, the experiences came in small enough amounts I was able in my beginning stages to handle. Anything catastrophic would have thrown me."

These basics were deeply embedded in the young pastor's disciplined study of the Scriptures. As with any aspiring servant of God, discipline was the key; without it, Louis's personal life and ministry would have gone nowhere.

Discipline was not a newcomer to Louis's life. The boyhood years on the farm—rising early to do chores before school and then after—played a formative role that would mark him for life. Likewise, the crippling heart condition that had forced him as a teenager to narrow his attention to mental development now fitted him to spend hours in study and sermon preparation.

A church family, the Tylers, took in the new pastor and treated him like a son, giving him free room and board. Without having to worry about such things as grocery shopping or housekeeping during his first months in North Tonawanda, Louis was able to get into the disciplined practice of his semi-vows and devote himself to study and visitation.

The freedom from household chores especially enabled him to get a very early start to his day. Indelible in his memory was the lighted window in the Nyack faculty residence where Dr. Edman was at work before his students at Nyack were even up. King's heart was also stirred by the story he read about a student at Oxford, Joseph Alleine, not yet twenty-one, but who described himself as "infinitely and insatiably greedy for the conversion of souls."

King wrote, "Daily he was up at or before four o'clock, and on Sundays, sooner. He would be much troubled if he heard any workers at their trades before he was at his duties as God's minister to lost people."[3]

Wedding Glitch

Esther visited North Tonawanda after graduating midyear at Nyack in January 1939. After the couple worked out details of the April 14 wedding, she resumed the train trip to Chicago to prepare for the great event.

The wedding weekend was an eye-opener for Esther's fiancé. Louis, with his bent toward formality and decorum, was surprised by Tozer's relaxed attitude toward the double-ring ceremony for Esther and her sister Margaret. As officiating pastor, he told the two brides-to-be, "There are

The World His Field

no tracks to run on for this one since there are two of you. So do it any way you want. Nobody is going to say anything."

Louis's puzzlement must have intensified during the rehearsal the following day when the moment came to exchange rings. Tozer leaned forward and, with a twinkle in his eye, whispered, "Now, Louis, if the ring won't go over her knuckle, don't put her finger in your mouth and push it with your teeth."

The groom thought he was joking. But shortly before the ceremony was to begin, the pastor and the groom's men were called out of the church side room, delaying the wedding and leaving the groom alone to wonder what was going on. Eventually they returned without explanation. What happened was one of the worst nightmares for such an event: The best man, William Moreland, had lost the bride's wedding ring.

The ceremony proceeded so smoothly Esther failed to notice that her ring indeed did not fit. Immediately after the wedding, the best man and an usher disappeared. Only later, after a long wait for Moreland to return and the reception had started, did Esther notice the ring she wore belonged to her sister-in-law.

With perfect timing the best man reappeared at that moment, soaking wet, with the ring clutched firmly in his hand. Moreland explained that after the service he scoured in vain the sidewalk and gutter in front of the church for the missing ring, all in a heavy downpour. He found it back at the house, where it had slipped out of his vest pocket into his suitcase.

As perhaps a harbinger of lean times to come, the newly married couple had to use money from their wedding gifts to pay their way from Chicago back to New York.

Faith and Finances

If North Tonawanda was basics camp for Louis, it was also a training ground for Esther, especially in finances. Realizing their pastor would need more income as a married man, the congregation's loose offering increased from $3.51 per week to $3.59. "I was worth eight cents," Esther quipped.

The new couple's living quarters, however, doubled. Louis exchanged his single room with the Tylers for two rooms with the Behrnses, an older couple. The husband had become a believer shortly after King arrived at the church. Louis and Esther had a standing invitation to share all meals with their hosts except when they were invited out, which was frequently. Esther would go downstairs early to help Mrs. Behrns in the kitchen and clean up. She said, "I run out of adjectives to describe how generous and caring they were."

Married life was still more expensive, however, and living on less than four dollars a week was a serious challenge. But Esther did not complain, believing the congregation could not afford more. The grim days of the Great Depression lingered on like a chronic illness in the factory town. "I had received enough teaching in the Scriptures that the Lord would provide," she said. "We lived on Philippians 4:19: 'My God will meet all your needs according to his glorious riches in Christ Jesus.' "

Holding to that promise, she said, "kept us hopeful, not apprehensive. We accepted the finances as part of our spiritual training. We learned everything we needed as a basis for future ministry. We learned to trust the Lord for a dollar so when later we had to trust the Lord for millions for the work, the experience was there. God would supply our needs because 'the cattle on a thousand hills' (Psalm 50:10) are His."

Louis had already applied that principle of faith to the finances of the church before they were married. When he came to North Tonawanda, the congregation owed over $150 in heating bills, and obligations for the church's previous location were still unpaid. People were giving a mere pittance to missions—and even less to the pastor's support.

"Money was hard to come by, and I determined these needs should not be laid on the people," Louis conceded. "Rather, I should pray through the matter and not drive the people away by insisting on money, money, money. Eventually all the bills were paid and giving to missions rose to $1,000. All of this was in answer to prayer without any announcement from the pulpit or advertising of the needs."

The Kings honored the same principles of trust and prayer to their family finances when they moved to an apartment of their own. They determined not to disclose their needs to their parents, friends or church family, but rather to God alone. Every Saturday evening they sat at the kitchen table, gathered all the bills and anticipated expenses for the following week and laid them before the Lord in prayer. During their ministry in North Tonawanda and beyond, they paid every bill on time. "The Lord never defaulted," he said.

That is not to say funds always came easily. On one occasion they were confronted with a bill for $30 due the following week. It was a large sum for them, and nothing extra had come in the offering beyond the usual $3.59. They checked the mailbox every day for perhaps other help, but nothing came. On the night before the bill was due, they went to bed without any money to pay it.

Around 5 o'clock the next morning the doorbell rang. When Louis opened the door, no one was there but on the floor lay a blank envelope. It contained exactly the amount needed. They had no idea where the money came from.

Several weeks later they were invited to supper at the home of the postmistress of North Tonawanda. "I asked you to come because something happened three weeks ago that is altogether the first time I have had such an experience," she explained. "I was awakened at a very early hour, an uncommon thing for me. I had the strongest impression that I should give you thirty dollars and I could not go back to sleep. So I got up, put the money in an envelope and left it under your door. Then I rang the bell and left."

She continued, "I am a Baptist and not used to this sort of thing. Why did I do it? Was it of the Lord?" Louis assured her that indeed it was and explained why.

An even greater need arose when the Kings' first son, Paul Lloyd, was born. Very early on a Sunday morning in March 1940, Esther knew it was time to go to the hospital—quickly. The Pontiac coupe Louis had purchased with some remaining funds from his uncle's bequest was in the garage because he was unable to pay the license renewal fee. In fact, the only money he had was fifty cents. When he called a taxi, even that pocket change was spent. They barely got there in time: The baby was born at 4:12 a.m. Leaving Esther and the baby at the hospital, Louis had to walk back home and later to church for the morning service.

During the next week, the young pastor crisscrossed the streets. Tears streamed down his face as he wrestled with the horrors of unpaid hospital costs and doctor's fees. In ten days his wife and baby were ready to go home but Louis still had no funds to pay the bill so they could be released. "I might have had to stay and wash the dishes," Esther joked.

But that was unnecessary. Mr. Behrns, their host and friend, accompanied the pastor to the hospital and paid the bill in full. The doctor, although a Catholic, charged nothing for his treatment of Esther over the months.

The years at North Tonawanda taught the pastoral couple to appreciate their church family. "Everyone was going through a lot, so they looked out for each other," Esther remembered. "Most of them knew what we were going through even though we didn't make a big deal of it." The small congregation had paid a stiff price to start the church, and if the pastor and his wife were ready to struggle along with them, the people would take care of them somehow.

One woman kept an eye on little Paul's clothes. When he outgrew one outfit, she bought him a new one. Another woman made sure he had shoes that fit. Someone else supplied diapers, "the cotton kind you don't throw away," the young mother noted.

Other families in the church followed suit so that the Kings were seldom home for supper. Two ex-Catholic couples, both of Polish descent, often invited them for a meal. They knew the pastor's financial status because one was the church treasurer and the other the financial secretary. But they honored the Kings' request to keep such matters confidential and did what they could to help.

As the congregation grew, eventually more than doubling in size, pastoral support gradually improved. Esther said that her husband's favorite hymn those years was "God Will Take Care of You," and He certainly did.

Learning Curve

Louis's work at the church introduced him to many valuable experiences, such as how to deal with problem parishioners. Perhaps the most unexpected and hurtful episode was with his first host. The man had generously opened his home when Louis first arrived and treated him like a son. But he had another side to his personality. Louis described him as a hard-nosed, self-righteous gentleman who thought he was boss of the congregation.

Without warning in a governing board meeting, his former benefactor pulled out a sheet of paper and listed eleven things the young pastor was not doing right, according to him. Louis was stunned, not knowing how to reply. He didn't need to. Other board members spoke up in support of him and put their disgruntled colleague in his place. He continued to serve on the board. And because the pastor did not have to defend himself or rebuke his elder, Louis's relationship with the old gentleman continued unbroken.

"That experience taught me that if I were doing a good work, I would not need to be defensive. The Lord would work it out. But if my efforts did not measure up, they were not worth defending anyway."

The pastor's learning curve with the congregation sometimes found him on the receiving end of lessons from unexpected sources. As a result of his healing experience at Nyack, Louis had become convinced he should trust the Lord for all ailments and not resort to medicine. But the time came when he suffered from a high fever and hacking cough that no amount of prayer changed. The problem became apparent to the congregation.

Two women parishioners came to see how he was doing—a switch for the pastor who was used to doing the visiting. Instead of lecturing him, one of the women brought along a bottle of cough syrup and urged him to take some. By this time, Louis was receptive to anything that would help. Almost immediately he felt better.

"The experience leveled me off on the matter of health and healing," he concluded. "I realized I shouldn't be so dogmatic. The Lord healed me once but that didn't mean that I should thereafter refuse medicine." Later in India that lesson learned would save his life.

Balance in Ministry

Louis struggled with another issue that would shape his ministry: the need for balance. Remarkable diligence in study was becoming a strength and also a weakness.

His heavy speaking schedule demanded many hours of preparation. Tuesday evenings he pursued a book-by-book Bible study, often word-by-word. Thursday evenings he devoted to subjects that would encourage people attending the prayer service. He delivered two Sunday sermons that he had written out in full and memorized. And he treated his Sunday school lesson with equal seriousness.

His study habits claimed up to eight hours a day. He pored over the Scriptures, believing that problems in the congregation were dealt with best through the progressive study of the Word, not through "preaching at" the people. He had tremendous respect for the Bible's ability to address every personal need, every situation in the church. He eventually would work through First Corinthians eleven times and cover twenty-seven books of the Old and New Testaments in systematic expository preaching over the decades.

"The messages were not very deep at first," he admitted, "and not because the congregation was uneducated. I was too young, just out of Nyack, and couldn't be very deep." But word got around town that the Alliance preacher was a gifted Bible teacher. Tuesday evening lectures attracted people from other churches and attendance eventually grew larger than that of Sunday morning.

But diligent to a fault in his hours of study and message preparation, Louis's prayer life suffered neglect. "I practically lived in the study of God's Word from early morning to night—even when I was doing other things like visitation. It became a problem of spending so much time in study I did not give much attention to prayer. Esther and I had family devotions, but my private prayer life languished.

"I found that in kneeling to pray alone, in three to five minutes I was done. I began to be bothered by my inability to stay on my knees without my thoughts wandering to the day's schedule and other matters."

Then Tracy Miller came to town. At the time he was pastoring the large Pittsburgh Alliance church, and it was in the middle of a revival. So many people were coming to church the services had to be moved to Carnegie Hall. Despite his deep involvement in the revival, Miller agreed to conduct a two-week series of meetings in North Tonawanda. The Kings were delighted to give up their bedroom so he could stay with them.

Rising early the next day for his study schedule, Louis noticed that light was already coming from under the door to the bedroom. "I could hear him mumbling and knew he was praying. He came out for breakfast with us at 7 o'clock and then, instead of asking for the newspaper, he went back to his room and was mumbling until 10 o'clock or later. I knew he was a man of prayer and that's why his church was enjoying such blessing."

When Miller went for a walk on Thursday, Louis helped clean the bedroom. He noticed a notebook on the bed, a pillow on the floor with

The World His Field

knee indents, and elbow impressions on the bedspread. Curiosity overtook him. "I took the liberty of looking at the notebook," he recounted. "One page listed prayer requests for January, the facing page, line by line, noted corresponding answers to prayer and the date. The next double page had requests and answers for February, and so it went for as far as the year to date. I was amazed at the array of requests for church needs, students away at school, Alliance matters."

When Miller returned from his walk, Louis admitted he had read his notebook and then confessed his problem of spending adequate time in prayer.

"Tracy, how do you do it? How do you stay on your knees?"

"It's a matter of habit, sheer habit," Miller answered. "You have to develop a way to keep your thoughts from wandering and letting other things come to mind. You must determine to keep them out and not get up from your knees.

"If you should go to sleep when praying, when you awake, don't get up. Just keep on getting back to your prayer requests. And you must have something before you to go from one matter to another, and the promises of God to present as an argument to Him."

That conversation between a seasoned pastor and a rookie preacher was one of the most life-changing lessons for Louis in the graduate school of experience.

The Work of an Evangelist

The imbalance between prayer and study was not the only aspect of pastoral ministry that troubled Louis. His pulpit ministry in teaching and preaching to build up the church was blessed with results. But his evangelistic outreach from the pulpit was getting nowhere even though the Sunday evening service drew a larger audience than the morning worship as people from the town came to hear him.

Faithfully every Sunday evening he preached a salvation message. And just as predictably, no one in the congregation budged during the altar call. Many Sunday nights he wept himself to sleep, grieved over his inability to reach people he knew were spiritually lost without Christ.

King was of kindred spirit with John Bunyan, who wrote in his autobiography, "In my preaching, I have actually been in real pain, travailing to bring forth children to God, and I have never been satisfied unless there has been some fruit. If not, it made no difference who complimented me. But if it were fruitful, I did not care who might condemn me."[4]

Despite the barren altar week after week, Louis persisted because he was convinced it was the right thing to do, based on Paul's admonition to another young pastor, Timothy: "Do the work of an evangelist, discharge all the duties of your ministry" (2 Timothy 4:5). A second piece of apostolic advice to Timothy also came to mind: "Do not neglect your gift, which was given you through a prophetic message when the body of elders laid their hands on you" (1 Timothy 4:14).

Louis concluded that Timothy received a special gift for ministry when the elders prayed over him. "So when I was ordained, I pled with the Lord to give me the gift of evangelism in the pulpit. As Mr. Stoddard and Mr. Isch laid hands on me when I was ordained at district conference, they didn't know that I was crying out to high heaven for the gift of evangelism. I believed I could ask for, and the Lord would give me, this gift for my ministry."

He felt little different when the prayer was finished and the conference ended. But the following Sunday night, when he again preached in his church, people were converted. From then on, though his evangelistic preaching contained none of the flair or flamboyance usually associated with evangelists, people responded to his messages calling for repentance and surrender to Christ.

Louis's experience as an evangelistic pastor had one totally unexpected result: friendship with A.W. Tozer. He had already come to the renowned pastor's attention by marrying one of the church's young people (Tozer jokingly chided Louis for stealing one of his girls from a future in Africa). That interest grew stronger one summer at the district's Delta Lake Bible Conference. The preacher from Chicago was guest speaker and the fledgling pastor from North Tonawanda was in charge of the dining room.

Finding each other's company enjoyable, they hiked through the surrounding woods together. Their conversation moved casually from one topic to another. Tozer, a keen naturalist, would break from a spiritual or theological discussion to comment on the vegetation or a startled bird as they strolled along. King, although raised on a farm, was amazed at how much more his older companion knew than he did.

All the while, the older pastor was sizing up his young friend, age twenty-three. Finally, one day he asked Louis to preach in his church. The invitation was an honor not to be refused, but the young pastor did. Not once or twice, but five times. He felt himself too inexperienced to fill such a prestigious pulpit. This resistance probably tickled Tozer because he knew many preachers who itched for the opportunity.

Louis finally relented and agreed to preach on a Sunday when he and Esther would be visiting her family. Tozer then gave him some advice. Either then or on another occasion, he counseled Louis to have both "fire and ice" in his messages—the fire of passion and the ice of deliberate preparation.

Louis was surprised by another bit of advice. "He insisted that I not preach any new sermon," he recalled. "He said it was not his own practice to use a new sermon when he was preaching away from his church. He insisted I preach a message I already knew, one that God had used to the profit of His people."

King followed Tozer's advice on the Sunday night he was guest speaker in the Southside Chicago Alliance church. Six people responded to the salvation appeal. "After that, I had it made with him," King said with a grin. "He really mentored me for fair after that."

Louis would speak many times in Tozer's church and the invitation was always accompanied by the same injunction. Years later when the two were traveling back to New York from a pastor's conference, Tozer said, "Louis, you are going to be in my pulpit in a couple of weeks. Now remember my requirement that you preach nothing new, only some of your good old sermons."

That was his parting word before continuing on to Toronto. Shortly afterward, he died.

Interrupted Journey

Events were moving along smoothly and in order toward the Kings' ultimate destination of missionary work in India. Louis had been ordained. He had more than met the requirement of successful home service for two years. He had applied for foreign service, indicating a preference for India but open for ministry elsewhere overseas should the Lord so direct. True to Brabazon's prediction, the Board of Managers appointed Louis and Esther King to the Maharashtra field in India.

In his response to Dr. Snead, dated May 28, 1941, Louis wrote, "We are praying that nothing will hinder our sailing at the earliest possible date." He was chomping at the bit, unaware of the interruptions that would repeatedly put off his plans for five long years.

The official appointment freed them to meet one more condition before sailing. Appointees were required to raise their first year's support, passage funds and $200 per person for duty charges and other expenses at their destination. By late September these obligations were met, passports secured and tickets purchased on a President's Line steamship. Louis resigned from the pastorate in North Tonawanda. They also said their farewells at a Friday evening missionary meeting at Nyack while the couple spent time at the International Headquarters in New York City to receive final instructions.

Everything was in readiness for their departure—except that it did not happen. Lowering war clouds scudding across Asia were upsetting the plans of many people. Militaristic Japan had already occupied Manchuria and Korea, invaded China and displayed a belligerent attitude toward the United States and the European colonial powers entrenched in Asia. Negotiations were going nowhere.

The King family was visiting Esther's sister in Wilmington, Delaware, one final time in November when a telegram arrived from the State Department. Astonished that the government could track him down, Louis read the message. Without detail, the telegram informed the Kings they could sail as scheduled, but they would have to leave Paul, age sixteen months, behind.

Louis hurried to New York that same day to find an explanation. After reading the telegram, Dr. Snead said, "Will you step out of the room? I'll call the State Department and talk to them."

Fifteen minutes later Louis was called back in. Dr. Snead explained, "Our government is involved in difficult negotiations with Japan and matters are not being resolved properly. The State Department is apprehensive about the future.

"If something should develop while you are on the ocean, we don't want anything to happen to children. We don't mind adults traveling on the high seas but not the children. So yes, the telegram is accurate. Your son cannot go with you."

Louis returned to Wilmington heavy in heart—perhaps like Abraham when God told him to sacrifice his only son. And what would he tell his wife? The decision confronting Louis and Esther was not as drastic in one sense as the one that faced Abraham, but it would mean separation by an ocean from their little boy for seven years. In those days, transoceanic travel was uncommon and expensive. Paul would grow up in someone else's home.

Time was short, the sailing date near and the pressure intense. With little time to ponder and pray about what to do, the Kings initially came to the excruciating decision to leave their child behind if Esther's parents would agree to care for him. Esther's mother said they would keep Paul, but jokingly said she would not promise to give him back in six or seven years.

After further soul-searching, Louis and Esther reversed their decision. He wrote to Snead to say they did not feel free to go without their son. They would wait for a more opportune time.

Another telegram traced them to the Martz home. This time the parents too were forbidden to leave the country. The order was blunt and final. There would be no travel until differences with Japan were cleared up. The goal toward which the Kings had been planning and progressing for years disappeared behind the darkening horizon in the East.

The Kings learned later that the ship on which they had bookings sailed into Pearl Harbor in the middle of the Japanese attack on December 7, 1941. The India field chairman, Raymond Smith, was on board. It seemed to him the planes were trying to sink the ship in order to block the harbor channel so no ship could escape.

Surprisingly, and uncharacteristically for one so resolute, Louis admitted to a sense of relief in the turn of events—a feeling which had nothing to do with the sacrifices averted.

"I knew that India was one of the toughest fields. I knew from being in the India prayer band at Nyack for three years that results often were not there," he recalled. "By then I had come to the conclusion that unless I saw revival under my ministry, the experience in India would be most difficult. Since I hadn't seen such a mighty movement of the Spirit, the question of whether I could cope with the situation in India did nag me. So there was some sense of relief."

Animated Suspension: Westmont

Louis may not have known where to turn next, but God did. There would be no free fall or downtime. When Esther's brother Clifford, in

Allegan, Michigan, learned that the King family was stranded in Chicago, he contacted Louis. The pastor of his church was sidelined with a throat condition and, under doctor's orders, he could not preach for a month. Would Louis supply the pulpit and stay with his in-laws?

For the next four Sundays Louis preached in the Bible Church in Allegan. On the way to the morning service on December 7, he heard the news over the car radio that the Japanese had attacked Pearl Harbor. "I knew then why the State Department had stopped our going," he recalled. "It was also immediately clear we would have to settle into a pastorate again until the war ended."

Returning to Chicago in mid-December, Louis found a letter from R.R. Brown, district superintendent. The church in Westmont, Illinois, only twenty miles from Chicago, was without a pastor. He asked King to preach the following Sunday. That one Sunday stretched into four. The church governing board then approached him. "We know your situation and we are without a pastor. You have proven yourself these several weeks so you do not need to candidate. We want you to be our pastor."

Without missing a single week after plans for India fell through, the King family was back in the ministry.

The Westmont Alliance church had an average Sunday attendance of 198, about 4 times the congregation size in North Tonawanda. King succeeded pastor Clifton Rash, who had accepted the chaplaincy of a leprosarium in Louisiana. He left a congregation that had prospered under his ministry. Services were held in the remodeled lobby of an old hotel, perhaps for the new pastor a step up from the renovated theater back in New York. The beautiful brick parsonage near the church was a definite improvement.

For the next several years, while World War II raged across the globe, the Westmont congregation flourished and the Kings were delighted with the congregation. Louis admitted, "A minister rarely has as good a time as I did at Westmont."

One new aspect of the Westmont church was a large group of young people he described as "gung-ho for the Lord." During one summer vacation Bible school, he took the high school youth and drilled them in Second Coming doctrine much as his Presbyterian pastor in Grenloch had done during his teen years.

The World His Field

The Kings made their own contribution to the growth of the congregation size in February 1943. Esther was pregnant with their second child and once again, early on a Sunday morning, she went into labor. But this time, an experienced father of one child, Louis was more sanguine. With a parting comment at the hospital, "Have a good time!" he returned to the church for the day's services. David Jonathan was born shortly after he left.

The ministry in Westmont differed in many respects from Louis's first pastorate, but his disciplined application to a schedule did not. His activities, however, began to expand beyond the limits of the church. He served on a home missions association whose purpose was to reopen churches that had been abandoned during the Dust Bowl era of the 1930s. He mentored several pastors struggling to restart churches in neglected communities.

Still listed as a missionary appointee, Louis was asked to be the Bible teacher for two Mission conference tours. Wheaton College was on the itinerary because at the time the Alliance was the only Mission organization privileged to conduct a missionary conference on campus. Edman, president of the college and a former Alliance missionary, no doubt favored the arrangement started by the college's first president, Charles Blanchard, who was on the C&MA Board of Managers during the days of Simpson.

Right Praying

The years at Westmont made possible more frequent visits with Tozer and some continued contact with John Cable, who had retired from the Missionary Training Institute. Both took part in his installation as pastor of the suburban Chicago church. Tozer commented during the service, "I don't know Louis King very well, but I can tell you he has beautiful feet because, 'How beautiful are the feet of those who bring good news!' " (Romans 10:15).

Over the years the two pastors strengthened their bonds of friendship. Tozer recommended books he thought King should read. During discussions he shared with the younger man his thoughts about the ministry. Often they prayed together.

On one occasion when Louis was in Chicago, he stopped to visit his mentor and friend. Tozer, who didn't drive or own a car, asked Louis to take him to the store. "I need to do some shopping, so let's pray before we go."

He dropped to his knees and, although they were only going shopping, Louis recounted, "he poured out his heart to the Lord to give direction so he wouldn't be frivolous in what he bought. It was mostly a worship prayer and a revelation to me."

Another prayer time had an even greater impact on the young pastor. "Tozer called to tell me that a guest speaker at his church would be staying over a day or two. He asked if I would join the two of them and Harry Post, a missionary home from Indonesia, for a day of prayer.

"We started the day in a room at the Southside Alliance Church. Before the noon hour, the guest speaker prayed an oratorical-type of prayer, rising to a great crescendo of shouts and outcries. In the midst of it, he told the Lord that Mahatma Gandhi was trying to get rid of the British in India, and had started a campaign of civil disobedience. He went on to explain to God that if Gandhi won and the British had to go, it would be a disaster for the missionaries and a tragedy for the advance of the gospel.

"Then, with a great shout, he said, 'Oh Lord, if You have to do it, kill that brown-skinned man in the three-cornered diaper and take him to heaven!' "

When the morning-prayer session was over, Louis drove the men to a restaurant for lunch. When the car pulled to the curb, Tozer whispered, "Let them out and wait for me."

They lagged behind until out of earshot of the others. "Did you hear how he prayed?" he asked.

"Yes."

"That wasn't prayer. That was for our benefit. Gandhi is not a Christian, and look at the language he used—'three-cornered diaper' and all that. Don't you pray like that! When you pray, you are in the presence of God and on holy ground. You had better watch your language."

Another defining moment happened and was recalled by Louis with mingled tenderness and awe. While the men were in prayer, the door slowly opened and in walked Cable, one of his favorite professors at Nyack, but a stern one to be admired from a distance. This day, however, revealed a different side of the venerable gentleman.

"May I say a word or two?" he asked.

The World His Field

Tozer answered, "Carry on."

This was his first time to go out after a month in the hospital, Cable explained. He had undergone colon surgery, but it was too late. He was not expected to live and did not know from one minute to the next when he would be in eternity.

"During that time in the hospital I frequently thought on what it was going to be like with Jesus and what heaven would be like," he mused. "I thought of my little son, the only one we ever had. He was the joy of our lives. My wife and I doted on him. One night we tucked him in and said good night. In the morning he was dead. The light went out of our home. A pall settled in. We were never able to have other children.

"I've thought a lot about my little son in the past month. What would he be like now? How old would he be? Would he be seven years old as he was when he died? Or would he be thirty-three years old as was Jesus when He died on the cross? Will we know each other?"

As Cable went on to reminisce, an other-world stillness settled down on the group. His visit helped restore some of the sacredness of the morning-long prayer time that had been dissipated by the histrionics of the guest speaker's prayer.

Two-Way Growth

Louis's years at Westmont reaped growth in two directions: Some more of the young pastor's sharp edges of zeal were tempered, and the congregation prospered.

One problem he had to deal with was his rigid observance of the Lord's Day, a mark of his strict Presbyterian upbringing. For years he would buy nothing on Sunday, not even gas for the car. At Nyack he looked with displeasure on fellow students who aspired to be spiritual, yet went out shopping and eating in restaurants as if it were like any other day of the week. He was grieved by the practice in North Tonawanda of church members who went from Sunday morning worship to a restaurant for the noon meal or to an ice cream parlor for dessert after the evening service.

At Westmont he realized he had grown rigid and legalistic—*he* was the one with a problem about observance of the Lord's Day. "I realized I had to get over it," he admitted. "In my study of the Bible I came to realize that this, though I would never admit it publicly, was a kind of 'works' mentality on my part to gain some additional merit with the Lord."

Consequently, he and Esther decided to go out for dessert after some evening services in Westmont. It was not something he particularly enjoyed or wanted to do, but was rather a deliberate attempt "to get over the ingrained attitude of legalism." Though it felt like backsliding spiritually, after several weeks at the ice cream store on Sunday evenings, the banana split triumphed over the attitude.

The Westmont congregation increased in size under Louis's pastoral leadership. The keystone of growth was his continued intense study of the Scriptures, which was reflected in his messages. A strong pulpit was the core dynamic of growth. Sunday morning services included fully developed and memorized sermons. Sunday evening messages focused on salvation, and people continued to seek the Lord. Midweek services featured systematic Bible studies.

Though his careful preparation of each sermon continued unabated, one part of his routine changed. Esther recalled, "He would tell me on Saturday nights what he was going to preach about. One night I said, 'You can't preach that because you have people with different persuasions in the congregation!'

"He was preaching in the book of John and coming down pretty hard on one side or the other of the Calvinistic point of view. He was really going to town on it. So I warned him, 'You are going to alienate a lot of people if you go at it that way.' "

Louis took her advice and dropped that part out of his carefully written sermon. She said, "He listened to me and nobody knew the difference, I guess. But that was about the time he stopped sharing his sermons with me."

The lecture series begun in North Tonawanda on Tuesday moved to Friday and from the church to private homes. As previously, the lessons drew a wider audience than just church members. A professor from Wheaton had been leading the group in preparation for their Sunday school lessons, but the college insisted he concentrate his energy on commitments to the school. Louis was invited to continue the Friday evening studies.

By 1944 attendance at the church had grown until the renovated hotel lobby was filled to capacity. The governing board had plans drawn for a new facility, started a building fund and purchased land in the same block as the hotel.

The anticipated building project did not mark an end to the Kings' commitment to India. It was rather a recognition that in 1944 fulfillment of that dream was still a long way off. The Foreign Department had approached them two years earlier about the possibility of going to a South American field, but the Kings declined. Their hearts were set on India.

Cecil Thomas, who had followed R.R. Brown as district superintendent, was noting their progress in ministry with great interest. He wrote to Dr. Snead in January 1945, "[The Kings] would make good missionaries, but what about their ages now? He will be thirty years old in November. He is doing a good work. If he is not able to sail soon, I shall no doubt move him to a better charge." He repeated this to Louis.

Reluctant Move

In a matter of days, Thomas followed up with a phone call to Louis: "The Havelock Alliance Church in Lincoln, Nebraska, is without a pastor. I'd like you to go candidate."

King's quick response: "I'm not interested."

The Westmont church was growing, building plans were in the works and the pastor likened his ministry to "days of heaven on earth." Why should he move?

Thomas countered with the argument that the Lincoln pastorate was bigger, more important, and would give a larger opportunity for service.

"No, I can't go," King insisted. "This is my place for now."

"Will you at least go out and fill the pulpit this Sunday? It's too late for me to ask someone else." Louis agreed—on condition that Thomas made clear to the congregation he was not a candidate.

The Sunday in Lincoln was marked with people responding to the messages morning and evening. As the guest speaker was counseling with people in the evening, a member of the governing board interrupted, directing him to another room. The men asked if he would be free to accept if they called him to be pastor.

Louis told them in clear terms he was not candidating and he would not accept a call. Ignoring this response, the men proceeded to ask what dollar amount he would need for a salary—an insensitive and distasteful question at that point.

King lost his cool. *"I am not a candidate!"* he responded indignantly. When the board persisted in continuing the discussion, Louis rose to his feet and said, "Gentlemen, it's time for me to catch the train back to Chicago. Will someone please take me?" And he walked out.

Settling down in the train compartment for the long night ride, Louis was troubled as he reviewed the board's actions. As he mulled over his response to the board, ashamed of the spirit in which he spoke, sleep eluded him.

Arriving back home next morning, he immediately called the district superintendent and explained what happened. Again he insisted he would stay put in Westmont. After hanging up, he had a lingering doubt whether Thomas had bothered to tell the church board, as he had requested, that he would not be a candidate.

Despite his assertions, Louis could not get past an overpowering sense of shame. He explained to his puzzled wife, "I did not appreciate the way things went after an unusual day of blessing. Yet there was no excuse for my attitude toward those men."

Meanwhile, the Westmont church's plans hit an unexpected snag. With the war still going full force, the building project had to be submitted to the local War Production Board that controlled the use of all construction materials. About three weeks after Louis returned from Lincoln, the Westmont church received word that its building plans were rejected. Nazi Germany was on the ropes, but Japan gave every indication of fighting to the last man. There would be no construction supplies available until the war was over.

Then King got a late-night phone call from the church in Nebraska. The secretary of the governing board quickly conceded that the men understood he was not a candidate—but would he come anyway to be their pastor?

The two events combined to give Louis a sense of release from Westmont. He accepted the invitation from the persistent church committee and the family was on the move.

Continuous Revival: Lincoln

The Havelock Church in suburban Lincoln (now relocated and called Rosemont Alliance Church) was as different from the Westmont congregation as that group was from the one in North Tonawanda. For one thing,

The World His Field

Louis's new pastorate was considerably larger than either of his two previous ones. The pastor's Sunday school class alone numbered fifty adults. The youth group had about 150 teenagers and college students.

The personality of the congregation, with its high percentage of people in skilled professions, was different as well. The Sunday school superintendent had been in charge of the city's public school system before retiring. One of the city's leading physicians taught a large adult class. Theodore Epp, speaker on the "Back to the Bible" radio broadcast, was a member. A bank cashier led the choir. Several public schoolteachers actively participated in church ministries. Young families were numerous and prolific: One Sunday morning the pastor dedicated thirteen babies, eleven in another service.

Though well-established and prosperous, the church was not without its problems. At the first meeting of the governing board with the new pastor, the men expressed a serious concern for the young people. Many were nonbelievers. Small cliques in the group were drifting into a worldly lifestyle. The board asked him to devote a number of messages directed to young people about spiritual issues.

"I can't do that," Louis answered. His was not a bully pulpit. "If you begin to aim sermons at sections of the congregation because you think they are not up to standard, you will not win them. It will only be through regular preaching of the Word as it comes up in my series of expository sermons that I will speak to the problem."

He suggested an alternative plan of action: Pray. Discussion went on until nearly midnight. The board concluded the best way to deal with the spiritual needs of the young people was not to comment publicly, but instead to quietly meet for prayer.

Without announcement, the church doors would be opened every morning from 7 to 8 o'clock. The governing board and other men would be welcome to come for however long they could pray before going on to work. The women's prayer groups, meeting in homes scattered across the city on different nights of the week, were enlisted in the prayer campaign.

The board also decided that Monday nights would be prayer and visitation times. Sunday school teachers were invited to participate with the elders, governing board members and Alliance Women volunteers. After a simple meal prepared by the women, visitation cards were distributed with information on people who were absent the previous Sunday and the names of new people visiting the church. The cards came back later in the evening with information collected from the visits. Week after week, eighteen or more people took part in the Monday evening program.

For five weeks no change was apparent in the congregation. Then unexpectedly on a Sunday evening, thirty-five people—mostly youth—responded to the message. Eleven of that group went to St. Paul Bible Institute (now Crown College) in the fall to prepare for pastoral or overseas work.

King's effectiveness in speaking to young people was not limited to his own church. One invitation he never forgot came from the State of Nebraska Holiness Association. He and another speaker were to share the pulpit in a summer convention under a pitched tent.

"A few weeks before the conference," he recalled in an amused tone, "I received a letter from the president of the association. He had received accusations that I was a Calvinist and did not believe in the 'second blessing.' I replied that certainly I did believe in a crisis experience by the Holy Spirit subsequent to conversion for life and service. He need have no fear. I suggested expositional messages from First Corinthians and he agreed."

Because people would be driving in each day for the conference, meetings were scheduled for afternoons and evenings. Louis was to alternate with another speaker. He arrived early enough on Monday to hear his preaching partner speak in the afternoon. His message was on radical eradication, i.e., once saved never to sin again. "I did not agree with him," King said, "but I would not speak about it from the pulpit. My duty was to preach Christ, not to argue."

King brought a straight salvation message that evening and people responded to the altar call. Attendance swelled each day until the tent was crowded out. And people, especially youth, responded to each invitation by King.

"On the final Sunday night," he recalled, "I preached with unusual anointing and afterward returned to the boarding house where I and the other speaker were staying. A small committee of the association came later to pay me for the week. They thanked me, saying that never had attendance been so large and with such blessing. Previously, the young people had caused them great concern because of their rebellious attitude and unconverted condition. They had to be dragged to the conference. But many of them were soundly converted that week."

The best was yet to come. In a lowered voice, the chairman said, 'We are giving you a double stipend—but please do not tell the brother across the hall."

Louis took a new approach to the midweek service in Lincoln. Realizing that the wartime shortage of gas strained the ability of people to drive to church three or four times a week, he adopted a "have car, will come" strategy for weeknight meetings. On Tuesdays and Thursdays, he drove to different parts of the city for home gatherings with church people in those vicinities. Midweek services on Wednesday continued at the church for those near enough to come.

Monday through Friday evenings the pastor was involved in one kind of meeting or another. In addition, the congregation assumed responsibility for opening a new church, Green Chapel, in a small, abandoned church building in Lincoln. The pastor added that preaching engagement to his Sunday school class and two services each Lord's Day. Completing a seven-day week of ministry, Louis and Esther devoted Saturday evenings to prayer for the following day's services.

The combined efforts of the lay leaders and pastoral couple brought about a quiet movement of revival that reached every segment of the congregation. In a matter of weeks after the Kings' arrival, the governing board realized their pastor needed help. Louis found a well-qualified young graduate from Trinity Evangelical Seminary in Illinois. As assistant pastor, John Gabrielson took over responsibilities for the music, Christian education and visitation programs.

The sustained spirit of revival had a personal implication for Louis. It was one of the aspects of ministry he felt was needed in his pastoral experience before he could embark on a missionary career in India with its faction-riddled churches and vast populations totally unresponsive to the gospel.

India at Last, Almost

The Havelock Alliance Church was well on the way to explosive growth in a nation by now exuberant in its victory over the Axis powers. The future held great promise for the church. It was carried along on the current of revival in a city brimming with possibilities waiting to be seized for the glory of God.

Then, just eighteen months into his ministry in Lincoln, Louis received a phone call early one Sunday morning that abruptly redefined the future of both pastor and congregation. Howard Van Dyck, assistant to Snead, called to say the Foreign Department had decided it was time to send the King family to India.

Amazed and confused, Louis responded, "But I'm thirty years old, have two children, and a third on the way. These conditions are contrary to the rules!"

"We know that," Van Dyck countered, "but we are putting aside those rules. You were appointed in 1941 when all the requirements were met, so we made our decision on that basis. Will you go?"

Without further hesitation, Louis answered, "Yes, we will go." He hung up and told Esther, confident of her agreement.

That Sunday morning the elders filed into his study as usual for prayer before the service, totally unprepared for what was to follow. "Gentlemen, I am announcing my resignation this morning," Louis said. "The Foreign Department wants us in New York within three weeks to board ship for India."

The announcement struck the congregation like an earthquake. But, shaken and grieved, they supported their pastor's decision and wished the family Godspeed. "They were quality people," King concluded.

But he was mistaken in thinking plans would move forward swiftly and smoothly. With no discernible good purpose or benefit, the long-postponed dream of service in India would be further delayed.

Events would sorely test Louis's commitment to his often-repeated creed, "We should give up our whole existence unto God from the strong and positive conviction that while we are faithfully endeavoring to follow Him, the occurrence of every moment is agreeable to His immediate will."

Notes

1. Howard H. Brinton, *A Guide to True Peace: The Excellency of Inward and Spiritual Prayer* (New York and London: Harper and Brothers, in association with Pendle Hill, 1839 edition), p. 73.
2. Louis L. King, "Caring for the Church," *The Alliance Witness*, June 22, 1983, p. 5.
3. Ibid.
4. John Bunyan, *Grace Abounding to the Chief of Sinners* (New York: Penguin, 1987), n.p.

FIVE
The Proving Grounds

Time Markers
1947-1953

The King family arrived on the Indian subcontinent at a time of political turmoil. The Constituent Assembly of India prepared the way for independence as a democracy in 1947 by outlawing untouchability and affirming equal rights for all, regardless of race, religion, caste or sex. Pakistan did not follow suit. Both became independent nations on August 15, ending nearly 350 years of British colonial rule over the vast area. The resulting mass movement of Hindus heading south to India and Muslims going north to Pakistan was one of the largest and bloodiest migrations in history.

In August 1948 the World Council of Churches (WCC) organized in Amsterdam with 197 Protestant and Orthodox member denominations in 44 countries. A Gallup poll indicated that ninety-four percent of Americans believed in God; sixty-eight percent believed in life after death. *Christian Herald* magazine reported that church membership stood at 77,386,000. The US Catholic catechism stated, "Outside the Church there is no salvation."

The North American C&MA registered gains in the early postwar years. By 1948 it had already exceeded the goal of 1,000 organized churches and branches. Members and adherents had passed the 50,000 mark. And in May 1949 the goal of 250 new missionaries in 5 years was reached. A young pastor, A.W. Tozer, published *The Pursuit of God*. It achieved wide recognition and robust sales and made him the obvious choice as new editor of *The Alliance Witness*.

Perhaps in part because of the Cold War and conflict in China, Korea and Palestine, the religious upsurge that began in the previous decade continued in the 1950s. Of all the belligerent World War II nations, only the United States experienced religious renewal. Whereas forty-three percent of the population had attended church in 1940, the total increased to fifty-five percent by 1950 and would continue rising to sixty-nine percent at the end of the decade.

The World His Field

Church membership skyrocketed. The Southern Baptists gained 300,000 new members between 1945 and 1950. The Catholics baptized 1 million infants a year. The depth of spiritual renewal was debatable: A Gallup poll in 1951 indicated that nearly half of all Americans could not name one of the four Gospels.

Politicians, however, recognized the power of religion in politics. Congress approved the addition of "under God" to the Pledge of Allegiance; it adopted the phrase "In God We Trust" for national currency.

The National Council of Churches (NCC) came into being on January 1, 1951. It absorbed the former Federal Council of Churches and eleven additional denominations.

A thirty-one-year-old evangelist rode the crest of the religious wave. Billy Graham had begun a three-week series of meetings under a big circus tent in Los Angeles. Attendance was impressive, but it really took off when newspaper magnate William Randolph Hearst put out a two-word staff memo: "Puff Graham." The meetings stretched to eight weeks and Graham was catapulted to national prominence. His book, *Peace with God*, would become a bestseller.

★ ★ ★

H.M. Shuman, retiring after 28 years as C&MA president, noted in his 1953 annual report that during his administration mission fields increased from 18 to 22; missionaries from 490 to 720; organized churches from 1,177 to 2,410; and church members from 17,026 to 89,828.

During the same period, income to the General Fund grew from almost $677,000 to $2,511,300. The Foreign Department scrapped the policy that missionary candidates were required to provide their first year's support and outgoing transportation expenses.

By 1953 Louis would be able to sum up six years of missionary experience in India by saying, "The main thing I learned was what we should do and not do."

But in mid-1946 he was wondering if he would ever get there. The disheartening events that followed his resignation from the pastorate in North Tonawanda were repeated after he left the Havelock Church in Lincoln in anticipation of a quick departure for India. Again it was a case of "hurry up and wait."

The three weeks between farewell from Lincoln and the booked passage on a ship for India were filled with frenetic preparations, especially for Esther. Trying to outfit three children with summer clothes for six years was a daunting challenge. What would Paul, then age six, look like as a teenager? And how much would David, age three, and Stephen, not yet born, grow in that many years?

She might as well have taken her time in shopping. Plans were abruptly and completely changed. When Louis stopped for a final conversation with Snead, he immediately learned something was wrong.

"We're awfully sorry," the foreign secretary said. "The ceiling has fallen through. As you know, the war has just ended and many people are scrambling to get back to their businesses overseas. We thought we had a secure passage for your family on a ship, but apparently it has been sold to someone else right out from under us."

Louis was so stunned he could not speak. It was "the biggest devastation I had ever experienced," he admitted.

Snead continued, "We want you to settle down somewhere and wait for us to get another booking. We don't know when that will be—it could happen again like this. We will put you on allowance right away and give you rental money for a place to stay."

Holding Pattern

So the uprooted King family repeated the familiar trek back to Chicago and to the Martz family's summerhouse on a farm in Allegan, Michigan. Louis said he was for a month or two "the most silent man you could imagine."

But if he was at a loss for words and what to do, others were not. Cecil Thomas, superintendent of the Western District, suggested he should forget India and go teach at the St. Paul Bible Institute.

Tozer was furious. He had already warned Louis he belonged in the pastorate, not overseas. He believed strongly that if the Kings went to India, they would step out of God's will. Now he demanded the Foreign Department explain why they yanked a good pastor from a productive ministry and left him sitting on a farm. He and others made such a fuss that Snead felt compelled to write a report to convince the Board of Managers that his department had acted properly.

Through it all, Louis sat in bewildered silence.

Esther was more sanguine about the turn of events. "It never occurred to me to object," she said. "Why should I? After all, I didn't have the wisdom to make decisions about what we should do. The Lord knew what was right. Why should I interfere with my puny thoughts?"

District superintendent Thomas decided that since Louis was on allowance and had nothing to do, he would take advantage of a mostly cost-free opportunity. "We've a lot of little churches in Nebraska, Colorado, Iowa and Illinois. They would be fortunate to have a Bible teacher and evangelist. Since you're on allowance, there will be no expense. We'll set up an itinerary."

For the next several months, Louis traveled thousands of miles, ministering to small Midwestern congregations that couldn't afford special speakers. The arrangement did have two unexpected advantages. He got acquainted with many churches he might otherwise never have visited, and they were introduced to a young missionary candidate who would need their prayers.

In October, during the enforced delay, the Kings' third son, Stephen Raymond, was born in Chicago. This addition to the family further complicated their departure for India.

By early 1947 Louis's impatience began to boil over. In a letter to Snead the edginess showed through. After enumerating several instances of promises left dangling, he wrote, "I do not desire to be insubordinate or over-demanding, but do you not think it is high time booking for us to India be expedited? We left our pastorate nearly eight months ago. It seems to us that something ought to be done and that right quickly!"

The foreign secretary's reply contained a certain stiffness. In defending the travel office's efforts to secure passage for the King family, he intimated that the delay was partly of Louis's own doing. "I know you would criticize us far more if we sent you on what is little better than third-class accommodations on the *Marine Adder*, where your wife and all the children would have to be in a cabin with thirty to fifty others, hot, crowded and uncomfortable."

If that implication were not clear enough, he ended the letter with some chiding of his own: "Remember, we were ready for you to sail in the fall of 1945 but the home requirements [Lincoln pastorate] held you, and then in 1946 your family matters [Stephen's birth] held you. Now let us trust the Lord that you will get out soon."

Whether this exchange of correspondence had an effect is unclear. But within a month the King family had tickets in hand—aboard the *Marine Adder*, one of the mass-produced Liberty ships used as freighters and troop carriers in the war.

Louis had one final hurdle to conquer, probably more formidable than an ocean-going vessel: Tozer's continued strenuous objections. Convinced Louis was missing God's will, he refused to announce to Esther's home congregation that the Kings would be leaving for missionary work in India. He arranged no farewell service. Neither did he request prayer for them.

When the King family was ready to take the night train at Union Station in Chicago for San Francisco, the pastor and a few church members showed up. "You would have thought they were going to a funeral," Louis remarked. "Near time for the train to depart, the little company walked with us to our Pullman car. As I mounted the steps and waved good-bye, Dr. Tozer's last words to me were, 'I don't think you should go. The Lord is going to stop you before you board the boat.' "

Louis's mentor remained steadfast in his opposition through the next six years. When the Kings returned to Chicago on furlough in 1953, Louis received a phone call. "I want you to preach on Sunday," Tozer said, "but don't give a missionary message. Just one of your good Bible sermons."

Introducing the speaker to his Southside Alliance congregation the following Sunday, he made no reference to the Kings' work overseas. He simply said, "We all know Louie King. He'll bring the morning message."

Despite the sparse introduction, Louis sensed great liberty in his preaching, "as if I were in seventh heaven." But Tozer, not yet finished with him, said, "Louis, I want to see you after tonight's service."

When the church emptied in the evening and the two men were alone, Tozer returned to his familiar refrain. "I don't want you to go back to India. You should stay in the States and preach, *and preach*."

Louis responded, "No, I'm going back," and walked out. Subsequent events would confirm Tozer's conviction. Only his timing was wrong.

Did unwavering opposition by his respected mentor hurt Louis? "It was done in a way that was never offensive or disturbing to me," he insisted. "I had no sense that he was wrong in what he did, but neither did I question that what I did was right."

Ship Bound for India

When the Kings boarded the *Marine Adder* in early March 1947, they met 140 missionaries also headed for India. Esther and the two youngest sons were directed to a stateroom with two other women. Louis and Paul went belowdecks to the steerage area with about thirty men and boys.

The large contingent of missionaries later proved a definite advantage to Louis. He became acquainted with people across a broad spectrum of denominations and mission groups. These contacts would be very helpful in his broadband ministry. Could this have been the reason for his delayed departure?

One passenger in particular stood out: Bakht Singh, an Indian evangelist of national stature. Raised in the intensely proud and fanatical Sikh religion, Bakht Singh had pored over the holy books of Hinduism and Sikhism. However, the first Bible he received was not given equal respect. He tore out the pages and kept the leather cover.

While crossing the Atlantic on a British ship during the Depression years, he attended an Anglican service in the ship's lounge on Sunday. He went out of curiosity but was greatly convicted by what he heard. He sought out Christians in Canada and became a fervent believer. Upon returning to India, he often ministered to C&MA gatherings with great effectiveness.

King's reputation as a speaker must have preceded him on the ship because he was invited to preach in the first service at sea. His preaching skill, however, was not supported by sea legs. He quickly fell seasick and for four days was confined to his bunk, unable to eat or drink.

Early Sunday morning Bakht Singh came to visit him. "Ah, you are so sick! I will go back to my room and pray."

Almost immediately the malaise left Louis. He showered, shaved and, without breakfast, preached in the "divine service" without a hitch. He must have done well because later in India he would be invited to speak in areas and to groups not open to other Alliance missionaries. He and Bakht Singh became fast friends, a relationship that also would open interdenominational doors.

Louis's truce with the rolling decks was apparently short-lived. Young Paul remembered that his dad was seasick for most of the five and one-half weeks at sea. Strangely, in all his later travels by plane, he was never airsick.

Junior Missionaries

Whether officially designated or not, career missionaries serving with The Christian and Missionary Alliance in those days were divided into two categories: junior and senior. Rookie missionaries were relegated to a subordinate role until they completed rigorous language studies, usually two years in length. At the same time they struggled with culture shock and drastic climate changes.

Their junior status frequently subjected them to decisions by senior missionaries regarding their location and ministry activity. This was an especially difficult adjustment to newcomers accustomed to a great deal of autonomy as pastoral leaders in stateside churches where they often served with distinction.

Louis and Esther encountered this reality when they stepped off the ship in Bombay harbor on April 14, 1947. They had been appointed to ministry in Maharashtra, the larger and more prominent of the Alliance's two areas in India. But the field chairman met them at the dock and said their assignment had been changed to Ahmedabad, Gujarat, over 300 miles away on the western coast of India.

No one on the field connected this decision with the fact that the Brabazons had lived in Gujarat. Nor did they know of the deceased missionary's prediction when Louis was still a teenager in New Jersey that he would take the veteran missionary's place in India.

One of the newcomers' first shocks was the torrid, humidity-drenched weather. They arrived in Ahmedabad at the beginning of the hottest season of the year when the temperature soared to 114 degrees in sopping-wet humidity. Fortunately, in a few days they would follow hundreds of missionary colleagues from all over India to the cooler hills for six weeks of respite from the shimmering lowlands.

But that very first night in the city Esther came down with a fever. Little Stephen also had a bad night. Although feverish herself, Esther fanned him until he dropped off to sleep. But when she stopped and tried to rest, he awoke crying. This continued throughout the night, leaving her exhausted and miserable.

A missionary colleague, Anna Haagen, realized what was happening and took charge of Stephen. The following night Esther slept under a mosquito net on the veranda while a rain shower cooled the air. It was the only time during her six years in India that she would be ill.

Landour, perched at 8,000 feet in the Himalayan foothills, was an institution probably unlike any other in the world. Between four and five hundred missionaries of all affiliations converged on its cooler climate during the oppressively hot months of April through June. Many missions maintained bungalows for their personnel, including the Alliance, which owned a vacation house called Fairview. In addition to well-organized religious services at Kellogg Church, the retreat center offered tennis, badminton and other recreational activities. Twice each year a ministry-related conference was conducted.

Although Landour was famous for its relaxing and congenial environment, it was also a hill of heartbreak. Woodstock, the inter-mission school for 400 students, shared the location. MKs (missionary children) in grades one to twelve lived there ten months of the year while their parents, hundreds or even thousands of miles away, answered the call to ministry. Aching hearts and loneliness spanned the distance between children and parents no matter how near or far the separation.

Paul, age seven, found out what that meant as he watched his mom and dad leave the center after six weeks. It would be a long six months before they would be reunited at Christmas. "At our parting," he recalled, "my father was tender and my mother's tears just wouldn't stop. I cried day and night for a whole week after they left. And for the rest of the school year I couldn't even look across the valley in the direction of the road they had taken down the mountain without getting choked up."

Two years later David would stay behind with Paul when the family's vacation at Landour ended. It was a particularly hard separation for Esther. She wept while sewing name tags on David's clothing. Louis watched silently and finally conceded, "He is very small, isn't he?" David was entering the first grade.

"I recall the last morning of my parents' vacation at Fairview," David said. "I left for school that morning as usual, but with the knowledge that I would be moving into the dorm at the end of that day and would not see Mom and Dad until we left for the plains at the end of the school year.

The Proving Grounds

"It was raining that day. Mom could not hold back her tears as she said good-bye. That caused my tears to flow as well as we walked down the hill to school. Paul did his best to comfort me; by the time we arrived at school, the rain had stopped and so had my tears."

The separation from their parents did not get easier. Paul remembered that when it was time to go back to Landour, David, being the younger, would often cry. Paul would tell him, "Stop your crying! You're going to make me cry too." And, of course, that made his younger brother cry all the more.

In the years to follow, when Louis was an administrator, he had to enforce the regulations sending MKs away to school. Louis and Esther understood the pain of separated families because they had experienced it themselves.

Language Ordeal

The rookie missionaries began language study right after arriving at Landour. This was—and is—in keeping with Alliance policy that the pressing priority for new missionaries was to learn the vernacular of their ministry area. Missionaries are essentially communicators; if they do not know the mother tongue of their hearers—the language of the heart—how can they carry out their mission? Other responsibilities assigned to them must not interfere with this primary task. A language teacher or coach, usually a missionary, and a local language consultant were assigned to each newcomer.

For the next two years, five hours a day, six days a week, the Kings studied Gujarati. For Louis it was admittedly an ordeal. "The language did not come easily to me. I was now thirty-one and had been a pastor for nine years with a reasonably successful ministry. I was used to that, not trying to learn how to speak all over again in a difficult language.

"To begin with, there are forty-seven letters in the alphabet, every one pronounced differently. I spoke with a very strong accent. Even worse, the daily grind of study was far different from preaching, seeing people converted and watching the work grow."

Esther fared differently. Unlike Louis, who was reticent and studious, she was outgoing and congenial, mixing easily with people. Paul Morris, a friend and fellow Alliance worker, said she learned the language as well as any first-term missionary. Her introduction to Gujarati, however, was not encouraging. On that first, hot night in Ahmedabad, trying to quiet her sick little boy while she felt no better, she heard women talking in the backyard. Horrified, she thought, *I've got to learn that lingo?*

Louis's problems with Gujarati were common for foreigners starting language studies in their thirties or older. Morris observed, "It's not simply a case of hearing it right. You've got to be able to make mistakes and laugh at yourself. That becomes more difficult the older you are."

King's inability to master the language did not render him useless. His work would be primarily in large-city populations where so many languages were spoken that people had to resort to English to communicate even with each other. This was particularly true in Ahmedabad, population 750,000, known as the "Manchester of India." It was one of the five greatest cotton textile cities of the world, drawing people from all over India. When Louis preached in English, some hearers got the message before the majority heard it translated into Gujarati.

During those ministry-sparse years of language study, he conducted a Bible study on Friday evenings. English-educated young men of Simpson Church, the city's main Alliance church, requested the meetings. On comfortably familiar ground, Louis led about twenty-five men in a book-by-book study of the Scriptures, beginning with First Corinthians. He was encouraged by their growth as they studied in context some major problems of their own church related to factional strife, money matters and lawsuits.

On some occasions he also was invited to preach to an international congregation that met Sunday nights in the large Irish Presbyterian church. Morris described the senior pastor, John H. Davey, as "probably the most successful missionary in India." He was related to James E. Davey, an Alliance pastor in the States whose son, James A., would be a prominent C&MA leader.

One invitation was especially memorable to Louis. The ministerium of Ahmedabad invited him to participate in a series of union evangelistic services during Holy Week in April of 1949. All five churches—one Presbyterian, two Alliance, one Methodist and one Church of England—supported the meetings.

The Presbyterian church, at a V-shaped crossroads like Times Square in New York City, was chosen for the meetings because of its strategic location in the city's center. A large school ground surrounded by a brick wall behind the church could accommodate thousands of people.

Before the Holy Week series began, Louis advised the ministerium that he intended to invite people to receive Christ at the conclusion of each service. The men demurred, saying it had never been done and would not be well received. King insisted, believing that the churches faced many problems because their people had not experienced the new birth by the Holy Spirit.

The objections of his fellow ministers were proven wrong, thanks in part to some Alliance missionary colleagues. Myra Wing, Ruth Blews and Louella Burley came to King's house each day and joined in prayer for the series. Louis also prepared some of his Bible study group to serve as counselors alongside the missionaries.

Louis spoke the first four nights. Attendance grew from 2,000 to as many as 4,000, many of them nominal Christians. At the end of King's first message, fifty-seven men and thirty-eight women came forward to receive Christ. Night after night people responded to the invitation.

Disillusionment

Disillusionment occurs frequently among first-term missionaries. They arrive in a foreign country on a high wave of idealism and eagerness to minister among a people for whom they profess a great love—before meeting even one. Still warming their hearts are the farewell expressions from admiring congregations.

Then follows a crashing, crushing encounter with reality. The people to whom they are called do not automatically love them in return—in fact, they couldn't care less. And the Christian community might also be rife with defects, reflecting carnal nature and the humanness of the missionaries who organized the work.

The true measure of these first-termers is not how far they plunge in disillusionment, but the level to which they rebound and get on with their calling.

An additional challenge also faced the Kings: India's political transition from British colony to sovereign nation. The passage to independence in 1947, the same year the young missionary family arrived, was paved with horrific violence, mass population shifts and convulsive political changes.

The future of Christianity in India was darkened with uncertainty. One of the leading independence leaders, Pandit Nehru, said, "Its spread was coextensive with the spread of British power and British officers; Christianity thus became the political symbol of British domination." Newcomers were subjected to suspicion and even hostility before they uttered a word or did anything.

A few months before India's independence, Alliance missionary Lauren R. Carner wrote,

> The masses of this thickly populated land have fallen prey to uncontrollable passions fanned to a flame by the recriminatory utterances of communal leaders, the wild propaganda of cheap journalism and the sinister influence of Communistic infiltration. The result has been a harvest of strikes, labor unrest, petty mutinies and communal riots all over India. If threats made in advance are any criteria of what may be expected, then what has already taken place is only a precursor of the bloody days which may be in store for this benighted country.[1]

And what of the Church? Carner continued,

> The transition period is likely to be one of physical danger to missionaries because civil strife is likely to continue, especially as the Mohammedans have refused cooperation in the Interim Government. Pandit Nehru, the new Prime Minister, is practically an atheist and friendly toward godless Russia. He has said, "The average missionary is usually ignorant of India's past history and culture and does not take the slightest trouble to find out what it was or is. He is more interested in pointing out the sins and failings of the heathen."[2]

This situation greeted the Kings when, after exerting decades of determined and devoted effort to serve the Lord in India, they finally arrived. Disillusionment was inevitable, especially for Louis. Despite all he had read and heard about the country and the national Church, he was not prepared for what he met.

Ahmedabad's main congregation, Simpson Church, numbered 800 members, and the second one, Bethel Church, counted 300 members. Many adherents were middle class and educated, a few wealthy, and a goodly number were professional people. Aging pastors in the whole region, the youngest in his fifties, projected weak leadership, providing no incentive for young men to consider the ministry.

"The churches were anything but spiritual," Louis lamented. "They were used to all kinds of fights—I mean actual fights with fists and clubs. In one annual meeting of the main church, the fighting was so bad the police had to stop it. The church was closed for several months by the authorities.

"The annual election was the churches' biggest event of the year. The people put up candidates for office, usually in two parties, one for 'democrats,' and the other 'republicans.' They fought tooth and nail to get on the governing board of the church, even buying votes."

The problem was partly systemic, partly cultural. Field chairman Kyle D. Garrison, a very godly man, had drawn up a constitution for the Indian C&MA in 1931. It provided for local churches to be organized into four church councils in each of the two Alliance regions. These eight councils elected representatives to the Maharashtra and Gujarat Synods that met annually. They also sent delegates every three years to the General Assembly.

While a good start toward church autonomy, this structure had some serious flaws. Ordained missionaries, i.e., men, were automatically members of the church and thus eligible for election to church council positions and higher posts. As a result, missionaries could, and often did, exert their influence as office holders to direct the national Church in the direction they thought it should go.

The 1931 constitution also stipulated that to have a voting voice, all local church members had to give an annual offering, the minimum of which could be determined by the local church. The constitution specified who could vote or hold office in the church. Excluded was anyone "who does not contribute his just proportion, according to his own promise, or the rules of the congregation."

Even twenty years later, a Mission leader defended this controversial practice. He described an item of business at one annual church council in which he participated.

" 'What shall we do with church members who fail to give?' That was one of the subjects for discussion at this gathering. Some were in favor of excommunicating them, but wiser counsel prevailed and that extreme step was not taken.

"A minimum amount must be given in church offerings before a member may take part in church business meetings. Our people have a flair for politics, and there are those who like to make speeches but do not take an equally active part in giving, so it has been found by experience that the privileges of church membership must be conditioned by the responsibilities of self-support."[3]

Another systemic source of contention arising from the 1931 constitution was the central fund that paid pastors' salaries. Garrison explained this system of support: "Some larger churches pay into this fund more than enough to support their pastors, thus helping the weaker churches, and ensuring that a man of ability may be appointed to a rural area without penalizing him for this consecration to difficult service."[4]

Garrison did not foresee that in reality this fund would generate resentment in the larger churches. Obligated to follow the dictates of the powerful synodal committee that determined where pastors served and how much they were paid, progressive city churches were not allowed to give their pastors what they deemed a fair salary. At the same time the system perpetuated inferior ministry in small churches by mediocre or unqualified pastors who did not need to worry about the quality of their work because they would be paid no matter how poorly they served.

Ma-Bop Factor

Underlying many of the problems in the national Church was an attitude of Indian believers toward the missionaries. It was called the *ma-bop* (mother-and-father) relationship.

As with many good things that turn sour when they outlive their usefulness, the *ma-bop* factor had a valid beginning. Daryl W. Cartmel, veteran missionary to India, chronicled the development of this problem.

> Prior to King's arrival in India as a missionary, the C&MA had maintained a mission in Gujarat for more than fifty years. They had sent missionaries there in 1893.
>
> "Before the decade [1890s] was complete, a devastating famine was experienced in Gujarat. Along with evangelism, teaching and other duties, the missionaries quickly added what ministries they could to the destitute people all around them. Two orphanages grew rapidly to larger proportions. Programs such as building churches, schools and missionary residences supplied needy families with work, finance and food they earned from their labors.
>
> During the famine time an educational system developed. Boarding schools were provided. Forty primary schools were established. Farmland was secured by the mission and assistance provided to

people to cultivate that land. Industrial training was offered in carpentry, tailoring, shoe-making, weaving and cooking. Students were assisted to obtain training as government-certified teachers.[5]

No one could fault those early missionaries for their compassion and good intentions. Even the most primitive of peoples would never turn their backs on starving children, much less the followers of Him who said, "When I was hungry, you fed me" (see Matthew 25:35).

As a strategy, however, an orphan-based church was a poor starter. Moving from orphanage to school to farm collective to Christian village meant believers were isolated from mainstream Indian life. One observer likened those early Mission efforts to American churches attempting to evangelize the nation by converting and supporting the homeless, or calling a great city to Christ by starting a mission in skid row.

Moreover, the resulting *ma-bop* dependency of Indian converts on resourceful, energetic missionaries developed into a defining relationship. "Missionaries and Indian Christians alike," said King, "saw the mission's role as improving the people, raising their status and securing for converts a place in the community. This developed into a pattern for all Mission activity.

"In retrospect," he noted, "the relation of giver to receiver, inevitable in the early stage of the work, extended over too many years. The missionaries' generosity and good will became stumbling blocks to the building up of the Christian community. Even after decades of work, missionaries still needed to learn not only how and when to help, but how and why to refrain from helping."

The cradle-to-grave mentality pervading the Church fostered an attitude that the Church existed to take care of its own. Vision to reach out to nonbelievers was weak at best. Cartmel, in his study of the Church, noted that between 1920 and 1947 the number of congregations remained static.

King wrote in a later report,

> No new congregations had been formed since the start of World War II. The number of ordained pastors had decreased, and some pastors had the oversight of two churches. They were not having converts from the non-Christian faiths. Additions to the church were from the Christian community, with new members equaling the loss by death and transfer. There was no church growth.[6]

Missionaries in later years recognized the stumbling blocks that grew out of the structure and practices of the Church. But making changes was not easy. As in many developing countries with deep respect for ancestors and traditions, Indian Christians looked with suspicion on efforts to change the ways of their elders.

William F. Smalley, retired corporate secretary of the C&MA, summed up the problem:

> In our Mission the national, and his parents in many cases, had been in our schools or orphanages. His very physical existence had depended on the missionary for leadership and funds. He had a church constitution which gave him autonomy, but it had been written by the missionaries. He was not sure he knew what it meant or how it should operate. He found it easy to accept the perquisites of independence without the attendant responsibility. He still wanted financial help.
>
> There were many differences of opinion and long discussions—sometimes not too pleasant. Well educated, well dressed, successful businessmen tried to get more help for themselves and their children. The newer missionaries and those trying to operate under the conditions of national development were told, "You don't love us the way the older missionaries did. They were like mothers and fathers to us."[7]

Not everyone in the nominal Christian community viewed the missionary as mother and father. In the nationwide agitation for independence spearheaded by Mahatma Gandhi beginning in the 1930s, a vocal segment of church people called for the expulsion of the "colonialist missionaries." Their protests were widely publicized in Gujarat. When the Kings arrived in India fifteen years later, relations between the Church and the Mission were still tense.

Rookie Resolve

After Louis completed language study and his ministry expanded to non-Alliance missions and churches in other areas, he would realize that the problems that troubled the C&MA were not localized. The same issues literally bedeviled the Christian community throughout the nation—political agitation, unbiblical principles in money and leadership practices, ugly disputes and factional rifts among the believers, dedicated but disheartened missionaries.

That fact, however, would provide him no encouragement in the early years of ministry in India. Deeply troubled and shaken for the first time in the pursuit of his calling, he questioned if he had made a wrong turn in coming to India. Maybe his mentor, Tozer, was right after all.

He conceded, "The sorry state of the church was such that one day I had to settle in my mind whether I should give up on India and go back to the States and be a preacher."

Louis shut himself away for a day and laid before the Lord this one question: "Am I in the right place?" Before sunset he had his answer. The conflict within was resolved. He took a stand: " 'Though He slay me, yet will I trust Him' to give me a ministry in India" [see Job 13:15].

But he also realized that if he were to make this resolve work, he needed a new set of guidelines, something like the semi-vows he drew up before entering the pastorate. The six points that emerged from his struggles became a declaration of intent not only for the immediate years in India but in many respects for decades to come.

1. Although a member of the church, I should decline any church office at any level in order to make way for the splendid Indian Christians.
2. With church members well educated, holding secular positions of importance and well taught in the Word, I should refrain from entering into the church's problems. I ought to depend upon the Holy Spirit to work in them as I believe He did in missionaries.
3. The church must look to its Head for all the answers and not to the mission or to me, a missionary.
4. My authority should be spiritual and emanate solely from preaching and teaching the Word of God in the power of the Holy Spirit; I should studiously avoid preaching from Scripture passages that applied to the church's problems unless they came in natural sequence in an expositional presentation of a New Testament book.
5. I must set a diligent example in witnessing to the lost and in establishing churches.
6. Although acting differently from my missionary colleagues, I must not permit my new way to cause contention in the missionary ranks. My views will need to be successfully implemented to be convincing.

The final point relating to Louis's concern about fellow missionaries reveals a sensitivity that does not show in his open criticism of much Mission activity at the time. He felt compassion toward colleagues trapped in policies with which they disagreed but were at a loss about how to change. He acknowledged that his own conclusions that emerged in crisp, confident statements were only arrived at over a period of heart-searching years.

His disagreement with Mission policy was not a personal attack on fellow workers. He often repeated that he had no problem with the missionaries and was unaware of any problems they might have with him. His working relationship with contemporaries like the Carners, Eichers, Dykes and Morrises became lifelong friendships.

That attitude extended to his predecessors in India. He held them in high esteem. Men like K.D. Garrison, John and Walter Turnbull and his own superior, A.C. Snead, were men of great spiritual stature. The several missionary generations of Schelanders, dating back to 1895, amazed him.

He was aware of the heritage left by A.I. Garrison, a second-generation missionary, who experienced a trial by faith when a gallstone attack was almost fatal. Days of acute pain and groaning gave way to months as his weight fell to ninety-eight pounds and his hair fell out. Yet Garrison believed God had promised him healing and persisted until it did happen. Later he "retired" to the Nepal border despite a heart condition. He discipled new believers even though some days he was so weak he could only instruct them for a few hours while bedridden.[8]

Louis King was neither a critic nor a rebel by nature, as his early farm years indicated. But he was an astute student of the Scriptures, and he believed that the principles found in the Bible required full obedience—even if they cut across personal inclinations and relationships.

Therefore, true to his concerns yet not wanting to isolate or alienate himself from others in the Mission, he shared the list of six points with his fellow workers. To their credit, they gave him liberty to follow his convictions. As events unfolded, some colleagues may have had second thoughts.

The first issue he confronted was what he considered the assessment practice of the Church. As a member of an Ahmedabad church, he was expected to pay at least a certain amount in order to take part in the business of the church council. This he refused to do, even though it meant that when the list of those who paid was read publicly, his name would be missing.

The pastor and several elders came to reason with him. "Sahib, we know that you give more than anyone else in the church," they said. "We know you do this without fail. But we can't put this on the books. You have not made the necessary contribution, and therefore you cannot vote. It is a poor example for our people if your name is not listed as having paid."

Louis went over carefully with them the reasons for his refusal. Giving to the Lord, according to Second Corinthians 9:7, taught that "Each man should give what he has decided in his heart to give, not reluctantly or under compulsion, for God loves a cheerful giver." If the Lord prospered a Christian, he reasoned, it should be proportionately, not an imposed tax of six rupees.

"But Sahib," the pastor countered, "we want you to do it. You would set a wonderful example."

"I don't want to set that kind of example," he insisted. "It's wrong."

When the Ahmedabad churches met in their annual church council, Louis and Esther were not allowed to vote because they had not paid their dues—which was just fine with them.

Louis's second revolt related to holding office in the national Church. The refusal brought him into conflict with his colleagues as well as national church leaders. As an ordained missionary, he was automatically a member of the Church and eligible to hold office if elected. Going into his first annual meeting after language study, Louis knew his name had been nominated for the synod committee. But being a foreigner and a newcomer, he thought it unlikely he would be chosen. Wrong.

When the vote results were announced, he was astonished to hear his name read. He immediately stood up and resigned. "The Lord did not send me to India to be a lord over His people, but to be a preacher and teacher of the Word," he declared. The Indian delegates let out a gasp. He heard some missionaries exclaim, "Phew!" but they held their comments until later.

That evening after supper in the Mission residence, the topic surfaced. Why, some of his colleagues questioned, did he think he was different from everyone else? They had to do it, why not he?

"If you didn't come out here to give leadership to the church, why did you come?" one colleague challenged.

"Certainly not to be chairman of a church council," he responded with a chuckle, saying good night and heading for bed. The discussion continued and one veteran missionary was heard to say, "If we send him home for being uncooperative, they'll just give him a bigger church."

The consensus among others seemed to be, "Let him do his own thing. His language skill is such that he wouldn't be much help on the committee anyway."

But years later the field chairman wrote to Snead about King's promotion to Asia-wide leadership. He could not refrain from commenting, "We can hardly see how a man who consistently refused any place in the Indian church in administrative capacity and whose only desk work was the writing of sermons in English, can suddenly shift his work and become a good area secretary."

Pioneering in Palanpur

An unexpected development set the Kings free for the type of ministry they desired and at the same time won the mission's strong endorsement.

Palanpur, a Muslim-ruled state in pre-independent India, long had been high on the Mission list for evangelism. With a population of 600,000 people and a major center for commerce, government and the railroads, it held great strategic importance. Brabazon had camped on its border, longing to enter and proclaim the gospel to its unreached masses, but his vision died unfulfilled with him. Now his prophecy for Louis was about to be realized.

One day shortly after completing their two years of language study, the Kings noticed a chauffeur-driven limousine stop in front of the house. A familiar figure emerged. Modak, the Indian official who had stayed in their home in Lincoln, had come to visit. He was now the district collector of Palanpur and wanted a Christian witness in the state that had been off-limits to missionaries. Would Pastor King visit Palanpur as his guest to investigate the possibility of ministry there?

The next Saturday Louis arrived by train in Palanpur, the state capital, and was met at the station by Modak. With flags fluttering on the limousine fenders and escorted by motorcycle outriders, he was whisked off to the official palace. The following morning he preached to the official's staff in his living room. Most of the civil servants were at least nominal

Christians recruited from other areas of India. "It was a ready-made congregation," Louis noted.

The Kings moved quickly to Palanpur with the full blessing of the Mission. Benjamin Bala, a bright young graduate of the Union Biblical Seminary in Yeotmal, later joined them. They started regular weekly services in a large, rented house. After they were reassigned to Ahmedabad, other missionaries continued the work.

"It all led," said Paul Morris, "to the planting of a unique and fruitful church that from its organization in early 1963 chose and supported its own pastor. The congregation also bought land, built and paid for a lovely church and parsonage—all without drawing on mission funds."

Louis received an additional responsibility of teaching two days a week at the Bible school in Mehmedabad, over eighty miles away. Taking a slow night train to Ahmedabad and an even slower local one, he got to the school the next morning in time for a full day of classes. After teaching the following day he returned to Palanpur the same way.

He was also appointed to mentor young Benjamin Bala, a responsibility he took seriously. In the Sunday services Louis preached in English for the out-of-state people. Bala did the same for the Gujaratis, but first he had to submit his messages in writing for the missionary's critique. It didn't happen often, yet one Saturday the message he submitted was rejected for "insufficient biblical basis" and had to be rewritten for the following day.

Esther's work in Palanpur differed significantly from her husband's. Accompanied by a Bible woman, she mingled freely with the people and focused on evangelizing women and children.

Bible women fulfilled a key role in evangelism. In most cases they graduated from the same Bible school as the men. Almost all were middle-aged widows who had distinguished themselves in zeal, integrity and ability. The five Bible women in Esther's time were employees of the Mission and were expected to attend the same refresher courses as the men during the monsoon season. Esther's associate was Ednaben.

Early in the morning, the two women set out to do evangelism, often not knowing where or how to do it. The opportunity might be a street corner, a communal well where women did laundry or outside a school where children in crisp, neat clothes waited for classes to start. Esther's white face and well-spoken Gujarati were an unusual attraction.

The World His Field

Ednaben held the listeners' attention with her storytelling. The two favorite narratives that they repeated many times were the "The Prodigal Son" and "The Farmer with Bulging Barns and Impoverished Soul."

The pair usually met with respectful curiosity. Only once could Esther recall a hostile experience. She and Ednaben had gone into a courtyard and were speaking to women washing dishes early one morning. A man appeared and shouted, "What are all you women doing just sitting there? Get back to work. And you two strangers, get out of here!"

Returning home near noon and after having lunch, the two women often climbed to the flat roof of the residence in the oppressive afternoon heat. Under the shade of a huge tree that sheltered them from the sun, they drank tea, discussed their work and prayed about the morning's contacts.

Esther's other role was that of mother, not only for little Stephen at home, but also for the two boys away at Woodstock. She kept in regular correspondence with Paul and David at least once a week during the school year. A nanny looked after Stephen while Esther and Ednaben followed the Spirit's leading on the streets of Palanpur to share the gospel.

Louis usually delegated family letter writing to his wife, but Paul remembered one time receiving a letter from his dad. During Paul's second year at Woodstock, a special speaker gave a series of messages on Christian living. Paul again prayed to receive Christ and wrote to his parents about his decision.

"I told them I wasn't sure I had been saved in Lincoln, but now I was," Paul recalled writing. "That prompted one of the rare letters from my father. He wrote that if I had truly received Christ when I was five, then I was already saved and didn't have to do it again. This time was more properly a rededication of my life to Christ."

He added with some amusement, "Years later, when we had conversations about Calvinism and Arminianism, my father refused to take a dogmatic position about eternal security. However, that one episode when I was eight years old seems to reveal that he at least leaned in the direction of his Presbyterian roots."

David's conversion actually did take place in India. He was nine years old when R.R. Brown, pastor of the Omaha Gospel Tabernacle (now

Christ Community Church), came to Ahmedabad for a series of evangelistic meetings. Seated in the back of the large Simpson Memorial Church, he remembers, "I realized for the first time that I couldn't get to heaven on my parents' credentials. Under great conviction, I went forward for counseling and gave my heart to God."

The scarcity of communication between father and sons did not turn them sour on missions—far from it. During his preteen years in India, Paul viewed missionary service as the "apex of vocations. I don't recall my parents ever saying or even hinting that they hoped I would become a missionary, but the shining example of their lives made a profound impact."

David's call to service was very personal. "I recall a village outside the walls of our house in Palanpur," he recounted. "The headman of the village passed away. The sound of the professional mourners could be heard for three days inside our house. That continual wailing—of no hope to ever see that person again—compelled me to commit my life to the Lord for missionary service.

"At that time, I firmly believed I would return to India, telling the good news of salvation to just such people as I had heard mourning those three days. I wanted only to serve under the C&MA. There was no other thought in my mind."

Paul would minister in Taiwan. Because India later closed to missionaries, David served in China/Hong Kong. Their younger brothers, Stephen and Mark, would become active laymen in US churches.

Broadband Ministry

The King boys had reason to be proud of their parents. Louis and Esther pioneered in a totally unreached area in Palanpur, a remarkable breakthrough.

When they were reassigned to Ahmedabad in January 1952, Esther continued her street-level evangelism with two Bible women. That meant hitting the streets early each morning in search of opportunities to share the gospel. Four mornings each week they conducted children's Bible classes. In one class she reported fourteen of the sixty-five students putting their faith in Christ. On Sundays the trio of women taught classes of teenage girls at the Simpson Memorial Church.

One incident burned itself into her memory. A Hindu man came forward to talk about Christ and offer some money. His contribution was politely declined, and he left. A few minutes later as he headed for work, he was struck by a bus and killed instantly.

Following his return to Ahmedabad, Louis began a ministry that expanded across mission lines and spread to other parts of the nation. The city ministerium again asked Louis to speak, this time to conduct public Bible lectures. Since the textile mills worked around the clock, he decided to teach in three shifts. The audiences were made up of the city's pastors, missionaries, evangelists, Bible women and a good number of high school and college young people, along with working-class laymen.

Each Thursday morning at 7 o'clock Louis taught a group in the Alliance Bethel Church; he returned at 5 o'clock in the afternoon for another meeting. Both groups averaged about fifty people. In the evening he spoke to approximately 200 people in the large downtown Irish Presbyterian church.

He lectured from a different book of the Bible in each of the meetings so those who attended all the sessions would receive three separate lessons. Assuming the speaker had been well-stocked with material from seminary studies, one minister asked which school he had attended. Louis replied it was not a seminary but a training institute in Nyack, New York, with some great teachers like H.M. Freleigh, F.L. Hess and John H. Cable.

King's impact on the Methodist church in Ahmedabad indicated the effectiveness of his preaching. The congregation was plagued with fights and lawsuits similar to Church problems throughout India, including the Alliance. In one series of lectures on First Corinthians, Louis dealt with the problem of Christians suing each other in law courts. One faction in the Methodist dispute obeyed the Scriptures and withdrew its complaint on the morning the case was to begin. Opposition by the second group collapsed, opening the way for reconciliation, an event that became the talk of the town.

With his fractured and heavily accented Gujarati, how was King able to be such an effective speaker? Enter R.B. Desai, a Methodist minister won to Christ by K.D. Garrison. He lived in Ahmedabad and had oversight of district churches. He became Louis's interpreter. People said they were almost like twins—same height, same build, same receding hairline.

"What a man of God!" King exclaimed. "We were inseparable. You couldn't tell when I stopped speaking and he began. It was the smoothest operation possible. I went over the material with him before speaking so he often knew what I was going to say before I opened my mouth."

Word of his preaching gifts reached the historic Mar Thoma Church in South India. The Mar Thoma Church traces its beginnings back 2,000 years to missionary work by Thomas, "the doubting disciple," in Jesus' original group of twelve. Twice he was invited to Travancore for meetings that lasted for weeks with up to 5,000 people attending.

One Tour Too Many

In the summer of 1952 Louis was invited to speak in three back-to-back gatherings that exacted a heavy toll on his health. The tour began in March with an Easter week of meetings in the Presbyterian church in Surat. He stayed in the same room used by David Livingstone, the famous missionary to Africa, during a visit to India.

Attendance grew as interest accelerated during the week. By the weekend the church was crowded well before the evening service began. Saturday night he spoke to about 300 teenagers. When the invitation was given, eighty young people walked to the enquiry room in spite of jeers and insults from their peers.

On Easter Sunday morning the church was crowded an hour before the service. In the afternoon, with the thermometer registering 114 degrees in the shade, 600 Christians paraded through the streets of Surat. Singing, distributing literature and holding gospel banners high, they celebrated the triumph of Christ as astonished bystanders lined the route.

Louis then traveled to the annual convention of the C&MA Maharashtra Synod near Akola. The weeklong series was held at the Katepurna campground in a mango tree orchard on the banks of the Katepurna River. The grounds had no permanent buildings so everyone stayed in tents and bamboo huts or simply camped under the trees. Meetings were held in a large tent.

The Akola region, known as one of the hottest parts of India, lived up to its reputation. Temperatures even at night did not dip below 112 degrees. Air conditioners were nonexistent. Crossing an open field to the meeting tent with missionary colleagues Bert and Artimese Eicher,

The World His Field

Louis could no longer contain himself. He burst out, "This is Purgatory!" With some amusement, R.P. Chavan, the convention moderator, remembered that King repeated the description when he entered the tent.

Chavan described Louis's speaking style as "quite challenging and excellent for the spiritual growth of the church and penetrating, uplifting the heads of people from their sinful lives to eternal heavenly life. His exposition and illustrations were so simple that even illiterate and simple people could follow the message."

Returning to Ahmedabad for the final series of meetings, Louis spoke twice on Sunday at the Bethel Alliance Church. The following morning, May 4, he drove to the church for the 7 o'clock lecture. En route he was seized by a sharp abdominal pain. He was able to complete the hour-long talk only by pressing hard against the corner of the pulpit the entire time.

Once back at the Mission house he collapsed in agony. Alarmed, Esther sent a runner with a plea for help to the English doctor in charge of the large hospital nearby. Although not one to make house calls, the doctor knew the Kings and came immediately.

He quickly diagnosed the problem. "You're having spasms of the bladder—a rare thing for Europeans. Your system is seriously depleted of minerals. Now you know what it's like when a woman gives birth to a baby. It's the same kind of contractions." As if his patient needed that encouragement!

The doctor prescribed heavy concentrations of mineral water but would not add painkillers lest complications set in unawares. So for two days Louis agonized, unable to sit or lie down without pain. After a brief respite on Wednesday the spasms returned. The only recourse was to keep him on heavy doses of mineral water and get him away from the nonstop 110-degree heat. That meant an emergency trip to the mountains, over two days away by train and bus.

The next morning, as he huddled over a tub of ice and waved a fan to circulate some cooler air to keep him from perspiring, Louis and Esther traveled to the Mission house in Landour. It took him six weeks to recover.

This was not the first physical problem Louis encountered. He had had to put language study on hold for a month because of severe anemia.

Later, in Palanpur, he had suffered an attack of malaria that reached crisis proportions. The only remedy was an injection of quinine that, if not exactly administered, would have left him paralyzed. At first the Indian doctor refused to give the injection because it was so dangerous, but when Louis grew rapidly worse, he had no choice. With the small Christian community praying fervently, the doctor succeeded.

The bladder spasms, however, were the most severe illness Louis had to endure. Given his conviction of God's control over every moment of his life, he had to believe his ordeal had some personal message. "I had nothing else to do but lie there and question what it meant," he said. "Sometimes we are sick in order for the Lord to give us an opportunity to reflect and correct something in our lives.

"So I reviewed my whole ministry. 'Lord, are You trying to speak to me? Are You putting me on the shelf for a reason?'

"Finally it came to mind that I was not declaring the whole counsel of God. I had not preached on the Second Coming since before I left the pastorate in Lincoln. There were positions and aspects I needed to work out in my studies, but all the intervening activities kept me from doing so."

Louis promised God he would correct this imbalance by preaching more on the return of Christ. For him, this was the lesson he needed to learn through the ordeal of sickness.

Although not robust in health, King's real problem was applying himself to the ministry with such intensity that his body could not keep up the pace. The lesson he learned while pastoring in North Tonawanda—God does not always heal, but sometimes permits help from medical science—probably saved his life more than once in India.

The Kings' years in the Ahmedabad Mission residence were not all spent in seriousness, service and struggles. Sometimes humor punctuated daily life.

David recalls that the gardener chose siesta time to chase monkeys out of the mango trees in the yard, whooping and yelling at them to sit still so he could hit them with a stone from his sling.

One day, unknown to David and some friends, they were playing under a big tree at the top of which was perched a bull monkey. He described what happened next: "Dad came out of the house with one of our slingshots. He let fly a stone—it must have been beginner's luck because it hit the monkey in the head. It fell like a pinball, hitting branch after branch on the way down. Dad yelled at us to get out of the way.

"The monkey died, and this did not set well with the neighbors because monkeys are considered sacred. In fact, not far from our house was a temple dedicated to the monkey god. Somehow we weathered the storm."

Like all the boys, Stephen had his own cache of memories of "Life with Father." He recalled that one day when he and David were having a tug-of-war, he fell and suffered a gash in his head. "Dad tried to console me with chocolate éclairs and hired a coolie to take me to the hospital emergency ward."

But the overanxious father got too close in watching the doctor stitch up his son's wound. A whiff of the ether fumes made him keel over, barely averting injury to his own head and damage to some hospital equipment. This was the man who, in his teens, was determined to be a doctor. Perhaps the gospel ministry's gain was not necessarily the medical profession's loss.

Winding Up, Not Down

By the Kings' sixth and final year in India, Louis participated in some major interdenominational projects. He served on the ad hoc group sponsored by seventeen evangelical groups to lay plans for the Union Biblical Seminary in Yeotmal, Berar.

He took part in the original planning committee for the Evangelical Fellowship of India (EFI). The EFI coalition of missions and national churches formally organized in 1951. A year later the group asked him to serve as associate executive secretary in tandem with Ben Wati, an outstanding Indian church leader. The plan called for Louis to extend by two years his stay in India. During that period, he would help Ben Wati get up to speed in directing EFI.

The Mission strongly favored this arrangement and sent it to New York for approval. It seemed a win-win situation for everyone. They were not prepared for the sharp dissent from the Foreign Department subcommittee: "We cannot countenance any affiliation with the Evangelical Fellowship of India. . . . It is understood [King] will return home at the regular time for his furlough."

Given his years of broadly accepted ministry, part of the time under the sponsorship of EFI, and the field committee's full agreement, the Kings had anticipated approval from New York. They had already registered their sons for another year in Woodstock. Louis had to make a hurried trip to Landour to pull the boys out of school.

While scrambling to comply with the decision and secure bookings for the return to America, Louis expressed his compliance with a discernible edge of irony in a March 30 letter to Smalley:

"A few questions have arisen in my mind after reading the strongly worded resolution.

"Does it mean that the New York board approves of our affiliation with a doubtful group affiliated with the World Council of Churches, viz. the Indian National Council of Churches, but does not approve of 'nor countenance any affiliation' with the already God-appointed EFI?

"Does it mean that an action of General Council which had clear reference to the National Association of Evangelicals and applicable to the US in its intent can be rightly applied and enforced in a foreign country?"

The Kings sailed from Bombay on April 16, 1953, to the United States via England. They would never return to India as a missionary family, but Louis's impact on the Gujarat and Maharashtra C&MA fields was just beginning.

Changes were in the offing, some due to his initiative, such as the epochal Bangkok Conference in 1955, others due to gathering political pressures in India itself. In 1954 the Mission requested direction from New York on how to make the C&MA Church of India "a completely indigenous body in full keeping with Alliance policy."

In response the Board of Managers called attention to the well-defined policy in the official manual, outlining steps already on record since 1926 and reaffirmed in 1951.

As a result, Paul Morris resigned as moderator of the general assembly of the Gujarat Synod. He was the last missionary to serve in an administrative role of the church. A Gujarati church leader admitted to him privately that the church could handle all the financial responsibilities currently carried by the Mission except for the support and housing of the missionaries themselves. The goal of a fully autonomous synod soon would be realized.

In the Maharashtra Synod, less industrialized and more rural than Gujarat, such changes would need to await the return of Chavan from the Bangkok Conference. His leadership would be decisive in bringing the whole C&MA of India into line with Alliance policy concerning the indigenous church.

These changes were still in the future as the King family boarded ship in April of 1953 for return to the States. En route to Southampton on the S.S. *Stratheden*, King had opportunity to read Donald McGavran's manuscript on people movements toward God. It was then on its way to the publisher. When King finished reading, he remarked, "When people get a hold of this book, it will change the whole concept of missions." McGavran's impact on global missions would expand when later he became the first dean of the School of World Mission and Institute of Church Growth at Fuller Seminary.

Based on his experiences and observations as a missionary in India, McGavran believed that God worked in some situations to bring whole cultural groups into the kingdom. The book, entitled *Bridges of God*, was published by the World Dominion Press and did in fact have a bombshell impact on missionary efforts.

Louis recalled his first contact with McGavran's ideas. One summer at Landour the missionary conference featured a series of lectures on group conversions. The speaker, a Canadian Presbyterian missionary, Angus McKay, had previously championed the traditional mission approach of individual conversions. He had opposed the idea of group responses to the gospel. For years he had worked at "polishing Christians" on a one-by-one basis, convinced that Indian believers could not be good Christians if they came to the Lord in groups.

But then McKay was assigned to a region of India where a people movement toward God was underway. Although highly critical at first, he began to realize that the group converts were far superior in quality as believers compared to those who came to God through traditional means. He was won over.

McKay's observations paralleled King's conclusions as he traveled across India for his speaking engagements. Those who came to Christ in family or cultural groups were far more akin to the New Testament kind of believers than individual converts who broke away from their cultural ties.

"Before that Landour conference was over," King said, "I was a convert of the group-movement concept. It was right in line with my six principles for doing missions."

When he finally met McGavran personally, the two would become close friends and colleagues. They worked together in applying group-conversion principles in several Alliance fields with great effectiveness.

King's embracing the strategy of people movements was the final lesson he learned in a long list of experiences in India. These experiences prepared him for the next level of leadership in the Alliance and involvement in the worldwide evangelical missionary movement.

"It was providential," he realized, "that my one six-year term of service was in India. It was that earliest large C&MA mission field where patterns of work were attempted. Missionaries in other countries would follow their approach to non-Christian people and their dealings with national churches."

Years later, in a Mission-Church relations study paper he went more into detail.

> I learned, therefore, as a first principle that good relations with the church are achieved and maintained when missionaries refrain from accepting administrative functions in, and forego imposing their plans upon, the church. I learned too that rapport is heightened through a missionary's diligence and success in the spiritual work of Bible teaching, evangelism and church planting.[9]

India was for Louis King the proving grounds of principles that would form the decades of service soon to open for him on a worldwide scale. And those days would come sooner than he imagined.

Notes

1. Lauren R. Carner, "India in Transition," *The Alliance Weekly*, October 12, 1946, p. 646.
2. Ibid.
3. William F. Smalley, *Alliance Missions in India: 1892-1972*, vol. 1 (Foreign Department of The Christian and Missionary Alliance, 1973), p. 539.
4. Ibid., p. 495.
5. Daryl Westwood Cartmel, "Partnership in Mission" (doctoral dissertation, School of World Mission, Fuller Theological Seminary, 1980), p. 7.
6. Louis L. King, "Mission-Church Relations Overseas—Part II: In Practice" (paper presented at Green Lake Conference, 1980), p. 2.

7. Smalley, p. 504.
8. "A.I. Garrison, A Bond Servant of Jesus Christ," *The Alliance Weekly*, May 19, 1954, p. 11.
9. King, p. 3.

SIX
Call of the Church

Time Markers
1954-1956

In March of 1954, an event in Vietnam triggered a series of events with far-reaching implications: Ho Chi Minh's troops captured the French forces at Dien Bien Phu. France's defeat spelled the end of its colonial rule in Indochina, forced the division of the country at the seventeenth parallel and started the country down the slippery slope that led eventually to Communist rule in all of Vietnam.

Despite unrest elsewhere, Americans continued to enjoy the good life and deal with some problems. General Motors assembled its 50-millionth car since beginning operations in 1916. People moved into single-family homes at a staggering rate—up thirty-three percent from the previous year. C.A. Swanson and Sons introduced frozen TV dinners.

Race relations heated up in 1955 when Rosa Parks was arrested in Birmingham for not giving up her bus seat to a white person as the law required. A city preacher, Martin Luther King, Jr., helped mobilize the African-American boycott that lasted 382 days and culminated in desegregation of the city bus lines.

The relative quiet internationally gave way to momentous events in 1956. Nikita Khrushchev denounced Stalin as a dictator who misruled the Soviet Union and committed many crimes against its people. The Communist empire began to unravel.

Presley mania caused many American teenage boys to adopt Elvis fashions: blue suede shoes, black leather jacket, double-high collar, sideburns and long, greased hair. Plastics invaded the furniture industry. The US Census Bureau reported that women outnumbered men by 1.38 million.

Billy Graham returned in 1954 from a five-month European tour on which he had conducted 300 meetings. The Revised Standard Version of the Bible reached sales of 3 million copies. The Vatican permitted priests to use English for the sacraments of baptism, marriage and extreme unction. In what was called the greatest mass conversion in history, 250,000 untouchables converted to Buddhism in India.

The religious revival in America had its critics. In his book, *Protestant, Catholic, Jew*, Will Herberg accused Christians of "flocking to church, yet forgetting Christ."

He explained, "The religion which actually prevails among Americans today has lost much of its authentic Christian (or Jewish) content. . . . Americans think, feel, and act in terms quite obviously secularist at the very same time they exhibit every sign of a widespread religious renewal." He could have pointed to Cecil B. DeMille's last film, *The Ten Commandments*. Many moviegoers described it as a religious experience.

★ ★ ★

Harry L. Turner, who assumed the C&MA presidency in 1954, commented in his first annual report the following year, "In our foreign work we have too long and too often measured our success in missionary endeavor by a statistical record of converts and baptisms. The proper criterion of success is, 'What have we done to plant an indigenous church in each [C&MA] occupied country?'"

The C&MA's Sealand plane arrived in New Guinea (now Papua) from the manufacturer in Belfast, Ireland. The 12,000-mile trip lasted 22 days and stopped in 17 countries, setting the world record for that type of aircraft. Within a week it delivered 10,000 pounds of supplies to the Wissel Lakes station. After landing missionaries in the Baleim Valley in April, it supplied them with airdrops for five months.

Turner broke with tradition in his annual report to the 1955 General Council in Philadelphia. Instead of generalities and exhortations, he proposed a series of five-year goals. The missionary staff would increase to 1,000; homeland churches would number 1,500; *The Alliance Weekly* would grow to 75,000 subscribers. Delegates at Philadelphia also took a firm position on the indigenous church policy overseas. Benign neglect of this basic strategy in missionary work had to stop.

For the first time, the C&MA's General Fund income passed the $3 million mark, a 10.1 percent increase over the previous year. But treasurer Bernard King, in his review of the fiscal year, did not let Alliance people off the hook: "Our record of past giving cannot be viewed with any mood of self-congratulation. Actually we should have needed far more than this to fully advance into the unoccupied fields."

Choosing Chicago for the year of furlough ministry was an obvious move for the King family. Esther would be near her family and home church. Louis would have opportunity to interact with his mentor, A.W. Tozer. So, after returning from India in the summer of 1953, they settled in a four-room apartment close to Esther's parents.

Louis received his missionary conference tour assignment in the fall; he would be traveling among the churches in upstate New York, down the Hudson River and out to Long Island. He worked on his messages for the eight-week tour. Esther prepared for the arrival of their fourth child. All in all, everyone settled in for a tidy, predictable year of activity before heading back to India.

It didn't work out that way. Louis's tour ended in time for him to be home when the new baby arrived. As he returned home from the hospital in the early hours of the morning, he was greeted by a chorus of three voices: "What is it?"

"It's another boy. Go back to sleep."

Persistently: "What are we going to name him?"

"We don't have a boy's name but it will have to be a Bible name," he answered.

According to the weary dad, the three boys responded, "Call him John Mark."

If there were any doubt about the appropriateness of the name, a telephone call later in the morning clinched the matter. Tozer called and, without knowing of the family's choice, suggested the newborn be called . . . John Mark. The boys had varied recollections of the event, but the newest brother grew up being called J. Mark.

"Ready to Go, Ready to Stay"

The second disruption of the family's plan for the year was much more profound, precipitating a sea change for everyone, especially Louis.

He was unaware that the Board of Managers had appointed a committee to propose reorganization of the Foreign Department. Several major factors made a compelling case for change. The overseas work had grown too large and complex—22 fields and almost 800 missionaries—for the department's small staff.

Administrative oversight of the sprawling worldwide work was based more on honor than accountability. Once out of sight of the homeland, most missionaries were pretty much on their own. Headstrong and single-minded missionaries could pursue their own agendas; inadequately prepared workers were left to follow a policy of good intentions, even if misguided. A sense of disciplined, unified strategy was often lacking.

But in the early 1950s the Alliance was poised for dramatic expansion of missionary work. Ex-GIs finished Bible school training, raring to go back overseas in the service of the Lord rather than Uncle Sam. For the most part, they were men and women trained to obey orders, especially when a clearly expressed and soundly planned order of the day was given.

The administrative weakness of the understaffed office had become increasingly apparent as the gap widened between official indigenous church policies and actual work in many areas. Snead's desire to retire from office in a few years also added pressure on the Board of Managers to reorganize the Foreign Department.

The foreign secretary was given the responsibility to set up a provisional program to expand the department's personnel. He chose D.I. Jeffrey, veteran missionary to Vietnam, and William F. Smalley, personnel secretary, to assist him on a temporary basis.

Snead's proposal for reorganizing the Foreign Department was approved by the Board of Managers in April 1953, and the hunt was on for permanent appointments. He submitted names for two area secretaries and one staff secretary to the board at its September session. At some point in the process, Tozer recommended his protégé. One board member, pastor Kenneth C. Fraser of the large Pittsburgh church, remembered his speaking up for "a godly, brilliant, young, one-term missionary to India named Louis L. King."

That was the background when the phone rang in the Chicago apartment of the Kings. The foreign secretary informed Louis that after considering several candidates for the new post of Area Secretary for India and the Far East the Board chose him "by a good majority." Would he accept the appointment? Snead needed an answer in two and one-half hours because the Board was nearing adjournment.

Call of the Church

Esther, working in the kitchen, followed the conversation with intense interest and began humming the familiar melody of a missionary hymn, "ready to go, ready to stay, ready my place to fill...."

Louis hung up the phone and laughed, partly bewildered, partly amused. What a ludicrous situation! He had no clue why the Board would choose him. "I have no management experience except running a family household. I am a Bible teacher and preacher, not an administrator! It is not in my blood," he told Esther.

But would he accept the appointment? she asked.

The emphatic answer: "No! I will turn it down."

Then Esther did something highly unusual. Almost invariably she left such weighty matters to her husband, confident in his ability to make the right decision. Not this time.

Her blunt comment brought him up short. "You keep telling people, 'The call of the church is the call of the Lord.' Why don't you follow your own advice?"

Louis admitted, "Her question hit me like a ton of bricks. Without another word I turned on my heels and, without even praying about it, I called Dr. Snead. I told him, 'I will do it, but I don't understand why they chose me. I'll just have to accept it as the call of the Lord.' "

Snead responded, "That's it!"

The principle invoked by Esther had come to King's attention when he was pastoring in Westmont. An elderly widower with a background in the Church of the Brethren, commonly known as the Dunkers, loaned him a history of the denomination. It explained that most of the pastors were untrained laymen chosen from within the congregation. A carefully reasoned principle underlay this practice: If there were no political conniving or personal seeking or family string-pulling, and if the group prayed and concluded that a particular individual should be the spiritual leader, its decision constituted a divine call.

This Dunker practice traced its origin back to the New Testament church in Antioch, "While they were worshiping the Lord and fasting, the Holy Spirit said, 'Set apart for me Barnabas and Saul for the work to which I have called them' " (Acts 13:2).

King would use that principle carefully over the years to convince men to accept leadership roles in the Alliance. On this occasion in 1953, however, he was told by his wife to practice what he preached.

Before returning to Chicago in November after his missions conference tour, he spent two days at "260," as the C&MA national office was commonly known. Snead and others briefed him on his new role, but since the position had no precedents he would have to make up most of the job description as he went along.

The responsibilities were enormous. King would oversee 510 missionaries in 11 Asian fields: Japan, Hong Kong, Vietnam (cultural and tribal), Cambodia, Laos, Thailand, Philippines, Indonesia and India (Maharashtra and Gujarat). The area comprised over half the C&MA's inclusive members and seventy-three percent of the populations that Alliance missions was committed to evangelize. Alliance work in France and Holland rounded out his world parish.

Louis would start his work on the first of January 1954. The other area secretary, George S. Constance, would begin in March because he first had to disengage as chairman of the C&MA Mission in Colombia. His work would encompass Latin America, Africa and the Near East.

King spent Thanksgiving and Christmas at home with his family. Then, before New Year's Day, he left for New York. This would be his custom for many years. The two year-end holidays would be sacrosanct, reserved for his family. But January 1 would find him somewhere on the road.

One of the first things he did when taking over the Asia desk in the Foreign Department was to invite his new secretary, Edna Figg, into his office for a remarkable conversation. "Now, Miss Figg, I don't know anything about administration. Why they elected me and why I'm here, I'll never know. I have accepted the decision as from the Lord. But I have to know how to do my work.

"You've been a field secretary in Ecuador and a secretary in this department for years. You know the system from both the field and headquarters sides. Now you will have to be my instructor. You must teach me what to do and how to carry out my duties."

Edna recalled her first impressions of her new boss: "One afternoon in the '50s, the hall door of the Foreign Department opened. A gentleman passed hurriedly by, looking neither to the right nor the left. He marched straight ahead to the office of Dr. Snead. As I caught sight of him, my reaction was—that man means no nonsense.

"As I learned to know Dr. King, I realized that he was really a very humble and amiable servant of the Lord, and also if there were to be any ulcers, it would not be he who would have them."

Edna proved a godsend. She was well organized and not easily intimidated, a thoroughly practical person given to speaking frankly. Every morning when King came to the office, she handed him a typed list of things to do for the day. She noted the letters to be written, even suggesting how to answer some of them, and then critiqued his writing. "I obeyed her very carefully," he said. "That's how I learned the ins and outs of the office."

Meager Provisions

In later years the C&MA National Office would have an efficient relocation service to help people coming on staff. But in the early 1950s, office newcomers were on their own—and assignment to "260" did not automatically mean upward mobility in financial matters, and certainly not in perks. This reality did not faze Louis and Esther, but it would have some stringent consequences during their first years in New York.

Arriving in the "Big Apple" the last week of December, Louis received permission to stay at the C&MA multistory guesthouse until housing became available in Nyack. The Eighth Avenue building wrapped around and over the street-level Christian Publications Bookstore and the Gospel Tabernacle founded by A.B. Simpson. It connected to "260" around the corner on West Forty-fourth Street by a catwalk that looked down on the stained-glass dome of the church's sanctuary.

His off-hours were spent in relative seclusion, living in a single bedroom, eating in restaurants and avoiding the time-consuming commute to midtown Manhattan. The time alone freed him for hours of prayer and meditation. But unlike the beginnings of his pastoral and missionary work, when he forged semi-vows as guidelines, he sensed no such need at the start of his new role. The set of his sails was determined, the course charted. Now he would draw on prior principles best suited for his journey into the daunting unknown.

Having no money in the bank to purchase a house, Louis and his family were dependent on rented housing owned by the Alliance. When Merrill Cottage in Nyack became available in February 1954, Esther and the four boys rejoined him. But the bungalow was to be only temporary because it was one of several properties maintained for use by missionaries on furlough in the States. Louis, after all, was no longer a missionary.

Several months later, the Kings moved to an old house in South Nyack purchased by the Finance Department and rented to the family. In addition to deducting the housing allowance from his salary, another $59 was taken out to cover the full mortgage payment of the house.

The rental fee may not seem excessive by today's standards, but Louis's total monthly salary was approximately $360. Because he was no longer considered a missionary, the customary allowance for children was disallowed. As a result, the new area secretary with oversight of a vast region and hundreds of missionaries—living in a high-cost suburb of Metropolitan New York, paying commuter fare to work and hosting meals at his own expense for missionary guests—had less income than if he were simply a missionary on furlough.

Moving into the unfurnished house on Piermont Avenue presented another challenge since everything the Kings owned fit into their suitcases. King's parents gave them a scratchy mohair sofa and some chairs, and for $30 they bought some pre-owned furniture. The boys slept on two borrowed beds. The table for eating consisted of a six-foot plywood sheet balanced precariously on chairs and a radiator. Bare floors and drafty windows added to the family's discomfort that winter.

"We were utterly ashamed to let anyone into the house because of the poverty of the place," King said. A car, of course, was out of the question at first. Esther had to depend on neighbors for a ride to the grocery store.

Difficult as the situation was, the boys did not seem to notice. "We never knew we were poor," Stephen wrote, "and Mom always had a good, hot meal for us."

There was one bright, sweet spot provided every week by Mrs. Luleich, a dedicated Christian. She and her husband operated a popular bakery in downtown Nyack. Every Saturday she sent to the King family unsold pastries and special breads that otherwise would have been thrown out. Just as manna from heaven continued until the Israelites entered the Promised Land, the supply of delectables lasted for several years, ending about the same time the Kings' income improved.

Genevieve Holton, daughter of missionary parents to China, worked at the bakery. She often delivered the goods to the Kings' door. The kindness of this attractive young bakery worker was not lost on teenaged

Paul. He later married "Genny" and they went off to Taiwan as missionaries.

The salary shock failed to rattle Louis: "It was just like North Tonawanda again. The Lord provided for our needs." Honoraria from his speaking engagements helped the family cope with what he called "abstemiously living on meager provisions."

Why would a religious organization put its leaders through such difficult times? Even as the Kings and other headquarters workers struggled with inadequate income, General Council wrestled with the issue. Many delegates and Board members lived in lower-cost areas. They could not understand why people in New York needed so much money.

Finally, after years of sharp debate, General Council set up a Committee on Salaries to review and adjust annually the income of headquarters personnel. Being a Council-mandated committee, it was answerable only to that body. The Board of Managers could accept or reject its recommendations but not change them. When it disagreed with the committee's findings, the report went back to General Council which invariably upheld the proposals.

In the late 1960s the Board of Managers decided to reduce the number of C&MA properties in Nyack, including the one on Piermont Avenue. Faced with the prospect of finding another place, Louis purchased the house. It continued to be the family home until his retirement two decades later.

While renting, Louis depended on the "company" maintenance crew in Nyack to take care of the house. But when he became its owner, he bought a handyman's "how-to" book and went to work. His first major project involved digging a deep trench around the house to waterproof the seeping foundation. Then he began painting and other repairs.

Those outside the family, however, rarely saw him in work clothes. "We had been working in the yard when Dad decided he needed something at the hardware store," Mark recalled on one occasion. "But first he went into the house, cleaned up and put on a suit." One time a friend stopped by unannounced. Louis emerged from the cellar in paint-spattered, worn-out clothes. The sight of this grungy-looking fellow, who was always "dressed to the nines" in the office, caused the visitor to burst out laughing.

Policies and Procedures

Given King's strong record of evangelistic preaching and systematic Bible teaching, it could be assumed that his first order of business as an administrator would be to promote such activities overseas.

Wrong.

"The Alliance was a spiritual movement in which it was assumed people would do the right things because they were spiritual," he noted. "But it didn't work out that way. In real life, the wheel that squeaked the loudest got the most grease. This made for some gross inequities from field to field."

The system for determining missionary allowances, for example, was what he called "a helter-skelter situation." Some fields got comfortable allowances because of the careful way numbers were kept. In other countries allowances were set low because people tracked expenses differently.

Personnel in Laos, a developing country, lived quite well on a high allowance rate, according to King. And living in a tropical climate, they dressed very casually. In Argentina, with its sophisticated society and advanced economy, men had to wear business suits. Yet the missionaries received a very small monthly allowance. In Japan, one of the world's most expensive countries in which to live, monthly support was extremely low. Mabel Francis and her sister, Mrs. Anne Dievendorf, lived like paupers—"the most sacrificial ladies you could ever imagine," he said. "When you added all the field allowances together, and sixty-five percent of the average was to be for food, the figures for the whole Japan field were very low. It was impossible to understand how they could exist."

The policy on furniture for Mission residences was another practice that varied greatly from field to field. The premise for providing basic furniture in mission-owned houses was sensible. Personnel were transferred frequently from one place to another. The cost of moving families and all their belongings was expensive and damage to furniture inevitable.

But what constituted "basic furnishings"? In some areas this meant furniture in every room, including a full dining room set and new mattresses every year if children had bed-wetting problems. In other countries the Mission provided only a table, six chairs and a food closet. "To me, this harum-scarum difference of provision for missionaries was just not right," King decided.

The use of time in some countries also troubled the area secretary greatly. "For example, in one Asian field people would leave their post to go shopping in the capital every month. When you figured the time it took to prepare for the trip, stay in the city, and return home, they spent less than three weeks a month in their work. We would never allow that in the States."

To correct this, King asked each field executive committee to do a time study of missionary work habits. This request met with resistance, even refusal, by some chairmen. He countered by requiring that all mileage and travel expenses submitted for payment be explained before they were reimbursed.

"Time banks" also became a part of field administration. Terms were established at a uniform length of forty-eight months. If a missionary wanted to leave early, the shortfall of time had to be matched by those who extended their time beyond the term duration. Such policies made an immediate difference in the work output on some fields.

Bringing a sense of order and fairness to these and other problems became a process that stretched into years. Later, as foreign secretary (now called vice president for International Ministries), King asked Smalley in his role as corporate secretary to research all the confusing and sometimes conflicting decisions generated by the Foreign Department and Board of Managers over the years. Helen Byington, Snead's secretary for thirty-seven years, did all the research. Each line item was subjected to scrutiny and then either reaffirmed or scrapped by action at the appropriate level.

The eventual result, extending into King's years as foreign secretary, was a *Policies and Procedures* manual that clearly defined a wide array of principles and practices for all Alliance overseas fields. It included such details as term limits, church building projects, health-care coverage, school and medical work, vacation time and allowances. And instead of being tucked away and forgotten in the field chairman's office, the handbook was published and placed in the hands of every missionary.

But more than just the nuts and bolts of performing tasks, the document addressed the reason why missionaries went abroad. King summarized the purpose statement: "The focus of our duty is to preach to as many as possible, win converts and have visible and multiplying assemblies of believers; these will be centers of evangelism in themselves for their territory and to regions beyond. This especially involves cities and new tribal adventures."

No longer would there be ambiguity about what was expected of overseas workers or what they could expect from the Mission. Although tedious and painstaking, the process produced a standard by which all personnel were treated equally and fairly.

Despite its obvious advantages, *Policies and Procedures* did not meet with universal jubilation, especially in Japan and Mali. Some field chairmen rejected the role of "double agent," as King unfortunately termed them. He meant that as an agent of the Mission, they were to represent accurately the field's problems and situations to the Foreign Department; as an agent of "260," they were to explain and implement faithfully directives from the homeland.

"Some of the men found this difficult," King explained, "because they themselves were independent. They were not going to operate according to strings pulled from another direction."

Resistance from several fields was such that the Foreign Department instructed King to write to each field leader. He clarified the main issue to his subordinates: The chairman is expected to carry out fully—without undermining or undercutting—the policies spelled out. Would he comply wholeheartedly? If not, he could not serve in that position. A similar letter was sent to all subsequent nominees by the fields for the job.

One unhappy chairman went so far as to bypass the normal channels and write directly to all members of the Board of Managers. He stated his objections to the Foreign Department policies—a position quite obvious by the problems he had been causing. The outcome? King said, "He was unworthy to be a field chairman and did not continue as such."

"The Present Unsettled Condition"

The first major problem on King's watch as area secretary occurred in the largest and most successful of the Asian fields. A notice in *The Alliance Weekly*, June 14, 1954, entitled "Financial Crisis in Indo-China," presented the matter in stark detail:

> The four great fields of Indo-China—Viet Nam, Cambodia, Tribes of Viet Nam and Laos—have suffered greatly during the past eight

years because of the ravages of war and political turmoil. . . . Upheaval always brings about a situation of financial instability and this has been true in Indo-China. Unrestrained inflation has practically doubled the cost of our missionary occupation. . . .

For a number of months it has been the approved policy of the Foreign and Finance Departments and the Missions in Indo-China to purchase local currency to finance our Indo-China operations on the open market in Saigon. These transactions were carried on with the knowledge and consent of the local government, but suddenly, because of the political uncertainties, this permission has been withdrawn.

The extent of this staggering blow to our Indo-China finances can only be measured by the fact that were we to keep our Indo-China Missions on the same rate of national currency under the new regulations as we did previously, it would mean $162,000 a year extra.[1]

The financial crisis required immediate and drastic steps because the Alliance did not have sufficient reserves to meet the inflated costs. After consulting with the subcommittee of the Foreign Department and empowered to make on-the-spot decisions, King flew to Saigon. He informed the assembled Indochina chairmen that their budgets would be cut in half immediately.

The obvious first step to deal with the crisis was to reduce the number of missionaries on the four fields. Men and women soon due for furlough were to leave immediately. Veterans nearing the end of their last term were given early retirement. And, in a lesser-known step, new missionaries wanting out of the troubled situation were allowed to return home without criticism or blame.

How did the still-inexperienced area secretary handle the traumatic situation? "It was a shocker," he admitted, "but everyone understood something had to be done. As for me personally, it is not my nature to have deep emotional feelings in a case like that. It has always been my nature to do what had to be done, and accept it as part of the Lord's promise in Romans 8:28: 'And we know that in all things God works for the good of those who love him.' "

Jewel Hall, Louis's secretary for twenty-two years when he was foreign secretary, observed King's ability to make the tough decisions—and not pass them off to someone else to handle. "He dealt with problems in a cool manner but I always felt he had prayed a lot before he

The World His Field

moved. And he did act swiftly. Often, after a short but careful preparation, he got there as fast as possible. He definitely was someone who shouldered responsibility in a crisis and I have to believe his being on the spot was most helpful."

Reducing the staff, however, was only part of the crisis precipitated by the meltdown of Indochina's currency. After the area secretary left, missionaries had to face the repercussions of a drastic cut in financial aid to the national churches.

For the Evangelical Church of Vietnam, *Hoi Thanh Tin Lanh,* the situation was especially difficult. The Vietnamese and Congolese national churches were the only two that had quickly implemented the indigenous church policy established in 1927. The Church's response in Vietnam was to adopt the "ladder policy"; i.e., each year the Church advanced to a higher rung of self-support, and the Mission reduced its subsidy by a corresponding percentage. By the end of five years, the Evangelical Church of Vietnam was self-supporting.

Then came conflict year after year in Vietnam. First it was World War II and occupation by Japan. When France tried to reimpose colonial rule after V-J Day, Communist forces under Ho Chi Minh led an armed rebellion. After the French were defeated and the country was divided between North and South at the seventeenth parallel, a new war soon erupted to unify the entire country under Hanoi's rule.

Following the partition, 300,000 Vietnamese fled from the north, including *Hoi Thanh Tin Lanh* believers and pastors. Eleven workers stayed behind, and most of them paid dearly for their courage. One evangelist, Tran-My-Be, was beaten and buried alive. When his wife went to beg for his body, she and a child in arms were also killed.

The phrase "present unsettled condition" summed up the turmoil as war spread to the south: Christians were attacked, churches destroyed, congregations scattered, pastors impoverished. Starvation spread as young men were drafted into the military and farmland fell fallow.

Recognition of the "present unsettled condition" moved the Mission to provide financial aid to the national Church, especially the support of pastors and workers among the highland tribes. Then the currency plummeting to half its value forced deep cuts in the Mission subsidy, causing serious repercussions. Most of the cultural Vietnamese churches, however, continued to honor the self-support policy initiated in the 1920s.

Paul Carlson reported in *The Alliance Weekly*,

> The necessary cut in our Mission subsidy to the Vietnamese nonself-supporting churches, followed by a sudden and disastrous drop in the value of the *piaster* [the Vietnamese currency], had created a situation that seemed well-nigh intolerable to our Vietnamese pastors. They insisted that an increase in their subsidy was imperative, but we, the Mission representatives, had to inform them that the budget for Viet Nam was already fixed. . . .
>
> When these facts were made known to the workers, a large section of them expressed deep dissatisfaction and voted in conference to accept no Mission subsidy whatsoever. Some were ready to take drastic action that would result in a definite split within our Society. Finally upon persuasion they decided to wait until the Joint Committee could meet. The new chairman might have a solution.[2]

The joint Mission/Church committee met for a whole day of prayer in September 1954, before hearing the report by J.D. Olsen, the field chairman recently returned from the States. The time together in prayer helped soften the blow. Olsen reported that not only would the previous subsidy cuts stand, additional sacrifices would have to be made.

"Everyone was stunned," Carlson wrote. "We sat in silence for nearly five minutes, no one knowing what to say."

Speaking for his colleagues the following day, the Vietnamese chairman said that the reduced budget would force the closing of twenty-four churches. After another caucus, he informed the missionaries that all the workers would accept the reduced budget proposal even though it was inadequate. They pledged to "stand together in faith with the missionaries, the native Church and the home constituency for the supply of their material needs."

Ha Sao, superintendent of a tribes district, pled with his workers to trust God. "If the money is short, plant rice and corn along with the Christians," he urged. "Don't even think of running back to your own villages."

The chairman of the Vietnamese missionary committee told his colleagues, "Let us be faithful in our ministry, not even seeking gain for ourselves. Let us use a pure fire for our sacrifices, and let us continue to seek the salvation of the souls of men no matter what happens to us."

King said later, "Of all the overseas churches I had to work with, the *Hoi Thanh Tin Lanh* was the most manly and biblical of all." The courageous stand of the Vietnamese churches in both the tribal and ethnic districts eventually would reap rewards beyond imagining.

In contrast, the "present unsettled condition" prompted Snead to go public with his conviction that supporting indigenous workers with North American funds was the quickest and least expensive way to reap results.

In an article published in *The Alliance Witness*, he reiterated an argument often used before and since: "If new missionaries were sent out from the United States and Canada, at least two full years of language study would be necessary before they could preach the gospel effectively. The time for missionary service in South Viet Nam may be very limited. . . . Eleven Vietnamese pastors and their families have come down from the north and are seeking service. . . .

"We are told that, in the present unsettled and impoverished conditions of South Viet Nam, support for these additional Vietnamese missionaries must come from America."[3]

Appealing to the Apostle Paul's statement, "the love of Christ constrains us" (see 2 Corinthians 5:14), Snead left little doubt how he thought that love should be expressed for Vietnam. A few months later, his position would be sharply challenged.

A Matter of Discipline

King was called back to Vietnam a year later to deal with another problem, only this involved an individual, not the whole Mission, and it required disciplinary action, not financial measures.

Gordon H. Smith had come under close scrutiny and serious questions were raised about his work. Harry Turner, the C&MA president, was ordered to Vietnam to conduct an inquiry. He was a guest of the Smiths during the investigation and then returned to New York with the conclusion, "He is a fine fellow." Disciplinary action was considered "not necessary."

The Board of Managers was dissatisfied with this verdict. Snead left a board meeting in April of 1955 to inform Louis that the decision had been taken to dismiss Smith for unbecoming conduct. And since he was one of the most widely known and supposedly successful Alliance workers in Asia, Louis was ordered to confront him personally with the charges against him. He was to remain on the field until the Smiths left the country.

The Alliance Weekly carried this terse notice of what happened:

> The Board of Managers of The Christian and Missionary Alliance regrets to inform the public that Rev. Gordon H. Smith, of the Tribes of Viet Nam Mission in Indo-China, has been dismissed as a missionary of the Society.
>
> The Area Secretary, as a representative of the Board of Managers, left New York on April 20 and personally gave Mr. Smith this information on April 27. Mr. Smith accepted this dismissal as justified and the Board of Managers prefers not to make public the reasons unless necessary.
>
> Mr. and Mrs. Smith have turned over their work in the Banmethuout area to the Field Executive Committee and left Indo-China by steamer on May 9, traveling by way of southern Asia and Europe to the United States.[4]

In a personal letter to Louis years later, Paul Carlson referred to "the kind but firm manner in which you settled the potentially dangerous misunderstanding with Gordon Smith in Banmethuout. A number of pastors told me that they needed that kind of spiritual authority in conducting the affairs of the *Hoi Thanh Tin Lanh* Church."

Even four decades later, King would not divulge the details of his encounter with the Smiths. Jewel Hall said he always kept such matters very confidential. In many instances, committee minutes contained no reference to disciplinary cases. He maintained a separate file under lock and out of sight, always hoping and praying the final entry for individuals under discipline would be "restored to service by the grace of God."

First and Second Kings

Before Louis set out to ease the financial crisis in Vietnam in 1954, he received some very practical advice from Bernard S. King, the C&MA treasurer. It reflected a growing cooperation between the two men.

They bore the same last name, were not related, yet shared similar passions for the overseas work of the Alliance. The timing of their arrival at "260" was providential, not coincidental. Together they would form a formidable team for advancing the gospel worldwide.

The two men became known informally as "First and Second Kings." They too joked about the combination. Bernard laid claim to the title "First King" because he preceded Louis at the national office. But Louis retorted that he was glad to be "Second King" because that book had more chapters.

The two leaders sometimes engaged in administrative jousting during their committee meetings. Louis knew missions and Bernard knew finances. They complemented each other's strength—though not always smoothly.

"We had precious times of discussion because Louis would fight hard for his budget," Bernard conceded tactfully, "but once the budget was established, Louis stayed with it." Louis reciprocated, saying that the treasurer was hardheaded and adamant, "all business from the word go, but excellent to work with. He had a heart for missions, doing far more than the usual treasurer."

Bernard came to his commitment to missions from a totally different direction than his colleague in the Foreign Department. A native of Minnesota, Bernard graduated from the University of Minnesota with a degree in business administration. He met Dorothy, later his wife, at the university. She was only one of 2 women among the 290 students in the College of Chemistry—and Bernard chortled, "I got one of them!"

Bernard and Dorothy settled in Lewiston, Idaho, in 1935 with the intention of becoming active in a local church while he pursued a business career. They made their life motto "Stick close to God."

Over the next three years, he sensed a totally unexpected call to ministry. They moved back to Minnesota and Bernard enrolled in St. Paul Bible Institute (now Crown College). On the student application he listed his resources as "$75 and Philippians 4:19." Three years later, he graduated with "$4,000 and Philippians 4:19." It was an indication of his future work.

Bernard felt a strong pull toward missionary service while a student. "I was one of those guys who, every time I heard a missionary, I wanted to go to the field he represented."

It was not to be. During his senior year he expressed his burden to a guest on campus, Thomas Moseley. The former missionary to China told Bernard bluntly, "Forget it. Number one, you're too old. Number two, your wife does not have Bible school training."

After pastoring the Alliance church in Lyle, Minnesota, for four years, Bernard volunteered to serve in the military as a chaplain because the war was still raging. In 1944 "the Army was so hard up for chaplains that they lowered the standards and I got in," he recalled, only half joking.

Completing basic training and chaplain school, Bernard was assigned to a combat unit of the 89th Infantry Division, which was punching its way through France and Germany. Despite downplaying his qualifications for the chaplaincy, he saw great blessing in the service. "It was revival every day," he said, "as the chapel was crowded for four or five services on Sunday, and Bible studies and other services during the week. Hundreds of young men found Christ as Savior."[5]

He grasped a strategic principle that would become a driving force in his later years as C&MA treasurer. "Everything for the front," he said. "That's what I got out of my experience in the Army. I did not want to see an increase in staff or some big setup at headquarters unless it increased the effectiveness of our work. I wanted everything possible, a maximum amount, to go to missionaries for direct impact overseas."

The opportunity to apply that principle came during General Council in 1952. By then, Bernard had returned to civilian life, pastored in Minnesota, worked as treasurer of his alma mater and served as superintendent of the Northwest District. During his five years as school treasurer, he helped solve a financial crisis. This brought him to the attention of C&MA leaders.

When his name was put in nomination for the office of treasurer, he spent the night in prayer and emerged confident he would be elected. He was, by a large margin. And further convinced that as chief financial officer of the Alliance he needed to be on the Board of Managers, he voted for himself in that election. He won by one vote. He would be the treasurer for the Alliance for twenty-five years.

Issues of High Finance

"I was awed by association with great men like H.M. Shuman, A.C. Snead, David Mason, William Christie, and other leaders of the Alliance," Bernard said of his first days in the New York office. "But I was not so overwhelmed that I couldn't see their frailties and some steps needed to correct the financial drift they had allowed to happen."

He was only the second experienced businessman to direct the C&MA's financial affairs since the founding years of the movement. David Creer, known in hard-driving New York as "Honest Dave," was a master builder credited for such landmark skyscrapers as the New York Life and the Metropolitan Insurance buildings. He served as Dr. Simpson's first treasurer, sometimes quietly paying the society's outstanding bills.

Bernard brought management principles to the C&MA's financial operation. Two stood out as major changes that benefited missions: budgetary reform and the foreign currency exchange plan.

He said, "The budget process was hopelessly mired in complexity nobody understood. It was so skewed the Board of Managers had no idea what the figures meant. For example, the budget projected for 1953 included missionary allowances, but the outlay for support of overseas workers in 1952 already exceeded the next year's budget. No one realized it so no one did anything about it. That was just one item."

Fortunately, the Alliance was surviving the confusion because it was experiencing a rising tide of giving and overall financial strength. The eight postwar years (1946-1953) saw an average annual increase of 7.9 percent. Income from all sources in 1953 totaled a record $3 million. But the system needed serious overhauling.

The new treasurer attacked the issue with an admittedly "feisty attitude and a lot of gumption." He spent many hours consulting with a reputable New York accounting firm, Lambrides and Lambrides, whose founder had become a Christian under A.B. Simpson's ministry. With the firm's backing, Bernard presented what he called "an exposé of the muddled budgetary system" to the Board of Managers. He recommended sweeping changes to bring management discipline and budgetary accuracy to the C&MA's financial system. He won strong support from the Board for his proposals.

One of the steps he instituted was a monthly meeting ten times a year with each department head. He reported on income and expenses, status of that division's performance in relation to its budget and what it could expect to accomplish in keeping with the balance.

He was able to help Louis, for example, plan for future expansion of the overseas work. Based on the Foreign Department's analysis of missionary allowances in all the different fields, he was able to project what the average cost per missionary would be and how many new recruits could be appointed for service.

Bernard's experience as a GI chaplain on the front lines gave him a personal concern for missionaries at their far-flung posts. A young missionary, for example, returned home after five years abroad and found he was refused credit cards because he had no record of financial activities. He asked the treasurer what he could do to break through this barrier. Bernard picked up the phone and called an executive in the C&MA's primary bank, the Chemical Corn and Exchange Bank. A positive credit rating was issued immediately.

One of Bernard's greatest contributions to the Alliance was his discovery of a way to improve dramatically—by tens of thousands of dollars—financial support of overseas work. It grew out of an innovative policy based on foreign currency exchange.

The 1950s was a great decade for American organizations with overseas operations. The "almighty dollar" reigned supreme in the world money markets. Foreign governments discounted their currencies to gain Yankee greenbacks. The official rate of the Japanese yen, for example, was pegged at 360 to the dollar, but was available to foreign companies in Japan at a special rate of 460 yen to the dollar. Vietnamese piasters were available in the open market for one-third the official rate.

Claire Weidman, an Alliance layman, was an officer in the National City Bank. He sent Bernard a clipping from the *Wall Street Journal* about some interesting results achieved by a foreign exchange expert. "I think it would be helpful for you to see this man," Weidman suggested.

The C&MA treasurer enrolled in a thirteen-week private seminar conducted by Franz Pick in the prestigious Athletic Club in Lower Manhattan. He sat next to chief financial officers of multinational giants like Merck Pharmaceuticals and Mobil Oil. He learned enough about the intricacies of foreign exchange to realize there were legitimate ways to leverage the value of the dollar overseas. Franz Pick became a consultant for the C&MA for a nominal annual fee.

Bernard and Louis agreed that surplus from the foreign currency exchange transactions would not be dumped into the Foreign Department operational budget. Instead, the savings would go into a special account for capital-fund projects overseas. Among them: Bible school buildings in Vietnam, a Mission headquarters property in Jakarta, the Ujung Pandang (now Makassar) Bible school in Indonesia. They also used the account to buy properties for Mission use in major cities if rental fees in seven years matched the purchase price of the property.

"The ability to maneuver financially in this way was an enormous aid for overseas work, and Bernard freely did all of this," Louis commented, "going far beyond what a treasurer was expected to do." As for Bernard, the foreign exchange venture with Louis confirmed his first impression of the new area secretary: "Here's a man I can work with." The combination of First and Second Kings would reap remarkable benefits for Alliance missions over the years.

With his pastoral background, however, Bernard also had a heart for churches in the homeland. He instituted a stewardship program—now the Alliance Development Fund—to provide funding for new churches.

Pre- and Post-Bangkok Conference

By the time Louis returned from dealing with the Smith problem in Vietnam, the 1955 General Council had already opened in Philadelphia. Esther met him at New York's international airport and they drove immediately to Pennsylvania. The next morning the chairman of the Council Committee on the Foreign Department Report asked Louis how to obtain information of previous reports and actions regarding indigenous church policy. Edna Figg, his secretary, personally delivered the documents to the committee the following day.

Council acted on the indigenous church policy as a matter of principle, but in Asia the urgency of such a course was being undermined by political events. War raged on the Korean peninsula. Although the French had been defeated in Vietnam and the country was divided into North and South, fighting continued after a brief lull. Political analysts warned of a domino effect of other nations falling to Communism. China boasted, "The East is Red." No one knew how far the Red tide would spread.

Alliance fields were literally under the gun and scrambling to meet the threat.

- *Laos*: The missionaries and national church leaders agreed on the critical need of the church to be self-governing.
- *Vietnam*: National church leaders pressed forward to prepare their congregations for hard times, both self-supporting churches and

ones partially subsidized by the Mission, especially among the tribal groups of the highlands.
- *Indonesia*: The national Church established a goal to have all local churches self-supporting by 1956.
- *Thailand*: In the aftermath of the Korean War, a sense of urgency prevailed that the Church be totally indigenous and viable. In his 1955 annual report, the chairman noted, "The mission-supported workers program was in competition with our self-supported native Church objective." The fifty Thai workers either partially or fully supported by the Mission in 1951 had been reduced to seventeen by 1955 with a comparable increase in self-supporting churches.
- *Philippines*: A Mission/Church committee jointly administered a schedule of diminishing mission subsidy. To be a voting member of the annual conference, a pastor had to be fully supported by his church.

But while current events in Asia focused attention on the indigenous church goal, the same could not be said of some other parts of the world. In a strongly worded assessment of subsidized overseas churches, the Council committee noted,

> For a number of years there has not been so much enthusiasm in favor of the developing of the indigenous church. Answers to the questionnaires about the indigenous church serve to show, not a pattern of consistency and progress, but rather a vision of confusion, a picture of inconsistency, of groping around and of uncertainty as to the goals.[6]

The committee left no room for further ambiguity about the role of Alliance missionaries vis-à-vis the overseas churches.

> The indigenous church will never be developed until we as a Society insist that it must be. It can never be developed until we send out missionaries who are willing to take the hard way and insist on the development of the church rather than the easy way of begging for money from America in order to pay more workers to do more preaching, to open more stations....
>
> Just as one of the greatest acts of parenthood is that of retreating gracefully as the child grows older, so the missionary can show best his love for the church and the Lord by stepping out of leadership and control as soon as possible. We will view without sense of loss our decreasing importance....[7]

The report continued in biting terms about "The Delusion of Paternalism":

> The easiest way to get the largest amount of quick success in our work is for the missionary to go into an area with plenty of money....
>
> The workers will do what the missionary wants. They will agree to the missionary's suggestions. They will go where the missionary sends them. They will preach what the missionary has taught them. The work will grow as rapidly as the converts are won, provided there is sufficient money coming from abroad to build more churches and support more workers and train more students. This is a short-sighted policy.[8]

Council agreed with the committee's thumbs-down verdict on overseas subsidies. It mandated implementation of the indigenous church policy.

The Foreign Department subcommittee convened after Council to follow through on this decision. Attending were: president Harry L. Turner; secretary Smalley; treasurer King; foreign secretary Snead; area secretaries King and Constance; and staff secretary Wagoner.

It was a pivotal meeting—and not pleasant. Louis described it as strident, even harsh. Bernard admitted that his impatience boiled over. "I got that way from sitting in the subcommittee meetings and my total frustration from listening to A.C. Snead talk about his vision of the Church and doing nothing about it. He was an early proponent of the indigenous church policy but later adopted a very benign attitude toward it."

Smalley as well had chafed during years of inaction by the department. He expressed in strong terms his conviction that the policy could no longer be ignored. Louis did not join in the attack on the foreign secretary's inaction, though he totally agreed the lack of implementation had gone on too long. The majority mood was clear: It was time to act.

King remembered that Snead "took it on the chin like a Christian gentleman" and realized there was no longer room to evade the issue. The subcommittee voted to send a copy of the Council report and decision to every missionary so no one could plead ignorance. It also decided to have portions of the text published in *The Alliance Weekly*, August 31, 1955, to inform the entire constituency concerning the C&MA position on development of the indigenous church.

At the same subcommittee meeting Louis volunteered to convene a conference of all the Mission and national church leaders in Asia to act on the Council mandate. (The story of that meeting appears in chapter 1.) The resulting Bangkok Conference so impressed H.E. Nelson, home secretary, that he had the entire report published and paid for from his departmental budget. "He was heart and soul an Alliance man," King said. "Mr. Nelson wanted what the Alliance was set up to be: a missionary organization."

The widening ripples of that conference reached into all the Alliance fields and beyond. Soon afterward, Raghuel P. Chavan, moderator of the Maharashtra Synod of India, attended the annual missionary gathering in Akola with other Indian delegates. "I took my Indian brethren to one side and we spent quite a bit of time discussing what to do and praying about it. We decided that we should ask the Mission to withdraw their subsidies; we would fully support our own work with no outside help."[9]

The joint group agreed on a five-year plan to reduce Mission subsidy by twenty percent a year until the Marathi churches were fully self-supporting. Chavan's next stop as moderator also of the Gujarat Synod was to carry the same message to the other churches. A strong leader among the Gujarati pastors warned the moderator he would be wasting his time because they would never accept his message. But when Chavan finished speaking to the delegates, this pastor, with tears streaming down his face, was the first to come forward and commit himself to the new direction.

Other mission groups heard how God was blessing Chavan's ministry and asked him to speak. At the national conference of the Evangelical Fellowship of India in February 1956, he spoke several times. This led to an invitation by a union meeting of seven denominations in Katepurna. When he spoke on tithing, "all 1,300 delegates rose to their feet to pledge themselves and their tithes to God," he reported.

Impact of the Bangkok Conference reached into Vietnam as well. Representatives of the Tribes work returned home committed to ending all subsidies even though their nation was reeling from the effects of war and the sharply devalued piaster. Cambodian church leaders adopted a similar step of faith.

Word went out to Alliance fields in Africa, Latin America and the Middle East that paternalism had to end. The goal of indigenous

The World His Field

churches able to stand on their own feet and attain their full stature in self-support and autonomy was the inescapable obligation of all missionary work.

Only the Middle East fields stood adamant in their determination to continue financial support of pastors and churches. The Board of Managers finally imposed a plan on the missions: a quarter reduction in subsidy funds over a four-year period. Rather than gradually reducing their overall assistance to the Arab Land churches and Jewish congregations, the missionaries used the full shrinking amount each year to support the workers they could afford. The rest were put on their own. Some pastors and congregations found other missions like the Southern Baptists and Nazarenes all too willing to pick up the tab.

Baliem Valley Crisis

The Bangkok Conference in 1955 took place midway between travels of the area secretary to several Asian countries. On his way to Thailand, King visited Laos and Vietnam, conferring with colleagues and preaching to congregations. As was his custom, he preached the same message at every stop, not deviating from his closely written text. (Bernard King quipped that you could hear every punctuation mark in his message.)

Following the conference, Louis continued his tour of the fields after Bangkok, arriving in New Guinea (later Irian Jaya and now Papua) by mid-November. His destination was the Baliem Valley.

The high, narrow plateau, guarded by jagged peaks often shrouded in heavy clouds, was surrounded by dense, verdant forest. The topography helped shield it from outside intrusion. The valley did not come to the world's attention until 1938 when the Archbold Expedition, funded by the American Museum of Natural History, penetrated its fastness. The scientific team gathered botanical and geographical specimens; it also collected considerable anthropological data about the Dani people and their cannibalistic culture still locked in the Stone Age.

Army reconnaissance flights during World War II rediscovered the isolated valley. Fascinated by its meandering river and small villages surrounded by neatly cultivated fields, the airmen romantically named it "Shangri-La." Sightseeing groups were flown over the valley until a disaster halted the fun. An army transport carrying twenty-one passengers slammed into one of the precipitous mountains flanking the Baliem.

Call of the Church

Three survivors made their way down to the valley where Dani villagers treated them kindly until they could be rescued. Then the mysterious valley lapsed back into obscurity for another ten years.

The Baliem came to the attention of Alliance missionaries when some Dani men appeared in the Wissel Lakes region. They came looking for salt in the markets of the Moni and Kapauku (now Ekari) people among whom the Mission had established churches. Spurred by the discovery of another major group without knowledge of Christ, the C&MA mobilized its resources.

Bernard King negotiated the purchase of a twin-engine amphibious plane in Ireland. An advance team prepared for entry into the valley with the thoroughness of a military operation. Supplies were carefully and sparingly selected because of the small baggage space. Veteran missionary Einar Mickelson and newcomer Lloyd Van Stone chose a young Kapauku family to accompany them. The woman and her child were important because among the highland peoples only men waged war. The appearance of Elisa and little Dorcas would signal to the Dani that the strangers were not a war party.

Equally important, the entire Alliance constituency across North America was called to special prayer in preparation for the flight to the Baliem. It would be a risky operation. Only 1,300 yards of the serpentine river could be used for landing, a stretch so narrow it allowed only thirty feet of clearance for the plane's wingspan. A floating log could spell disaster for the landing. And how would the warriors receive the intruders?

Alliance people held their collective breath and prayed as the *Gospel Messenger* took off on April 20, 1954. Not until the following day did a radio message from the Baliem report that the Dani had greeted them with intense curiosity and suspicion, but peacefully. Although the beachhead would be contested for some time, the gospel had come to stay.

When Louis arrived at the Mission base in Hollandia in 1955, the Baliem situation was still tenuous after more than a year of missionary work. No radio message had been received in five days, stirring concern that something was wrong. A quick flight to the valley by pilot Ed Ulrich confirmed their uneasiness.

Ulrich reported that on Friday, November 18, three Dani women working on the newly opened airstrip had drowned on their way home. Only one body was recovered. Attending the funeral on Saturday, the

Van Stones met hostility among the grieving relatives. One furious man cut off two of his fingers, a traditional sign of mourning, and gave them to the missionaries.

Yomeke, a friendly Dani, appeared early next day and violently shook the door of their house. He demanded that Lloyd accompany him immediately to the village chief who was very ill. From the conduct of Yomeke and his companions, Lloyd knew something bad was brewing. He told Doris that if he was not back in an hour, he was probably in serious trouble.

The chief was not sick but very angry. His first question: "Is the plane coming?" The missionary was hustled into the chief's hut and warned that some villagers wanted to kill him and his wife. Since they had come to the valley there was only trouble, the chief said. After receiving a stern lecture, Lloyd asked permission to leave.

"You're going nowhere," the chief shot back.

Just then the Mission Cessna flew overhead. For whatever reason, the tense situation changed completely. Did arrival of the plane thwart evil intentions toward the Van Stones? The chief and a group of villagers headed toward the airstrip with Lloyd. As Ulrich climbed out of the plane, a sobbing Doris met him with a frantic plea for help, thinking something had happened to her husband. As they talked, the villagers arrived with Lloyd and the tension seemed to recede.

In the discussion that followed, the chief promised to protect the missionaries from angry relatives of the dead girls. He also gave permission for the plane to return the following day with visitors. They too would be safe, he promised.

King and Ken Troutman arrived on Monday morning and spent the day visiting nearby villages without incident. The next day a boat took them upstream to another village in the valley.

"A large company of Dani met us," King wrote in his diary. "They were almost too friendly. Myron [Bromley] and Darlene Rose began giving injections. I was nearly taken apart by men who crowded close to see themselves reflected in my sunglasses. They felt me all over, pulled up my pant leg to feel my leg and stocking. A couple of fellows kept holding my hand and putting their arms around my waist.

"The crowd was thick around me, but there was no fear on my part. Lloyd, though, was evidently scared. It was just such a situation as this that turned into a terrible scene of near disaster the day another plane had crashed."

King concluded laconically, "Holding hands with me was a great practice here, but we got away safely."

Back with the Van Stones by evening, Louis participated in a Dani-style pig roast. A deep pit was dug and lined with stones. Hunks of meat were layered between white-hot stones and greens and cooked for several hours. The village chief, Yomeke, and their friends joined in the feast. Afterward Louis carefully washed his dirty hands, thinking he was done with pig fat for the day. Then Yomeke, freshly coated with grease, "came over and loved me good, pressing his body against mine."

"Dog in the Manger"

It's hard to imagine that such monumental courage and sacrifice in taking the gospel to the Baliem Valley would cause a squabble with sister missions. But it did. The fertile valley, forty-five miles long and ten miles wide, with lush terraces and well-populated villages, was an enviable target. Evangelical groups like the Australian Baptists and Unevangelized Fields Mission wanted to work in the valley. They accused the Alliance of being a "dog in the manger" by denying them entrance.

Their concern may have been the same that motivated Alliance missionaries to risk so much to take the gospel to the Dani. Here was perhaps the last tribe on earth to be evangelized—quintessential missions in its grandest form. Or perhaps it was the supposed glamour of "Shangri-La" and all the promotional value that could be reaped from evangelizing a Stone-Age people.

Could the C&MA indeed play the role of a "dog in the manger"? Unfortunately, yes.

The reason goes back to World War II when the island was part of the Dutch colonial territory that fell to the Japanese. Dutch officials, including some of high rank, were captured and thrown into concentration camps. Also imprisoned were C&MA Dutch missionaries William and Harmina Konemann. Throughout the years of internment William served as chaplain to his countrymen, hearing their confessions, conducting their religious services, counseling the discouraged and burying the dead.

After the war, broken in health, Konemann and his wife remained in Holland and played a major role in organizing a C&MA missions base known as Alliance Zendings Centrum "Parousia." He recruited workers from among the evangelical churches of Holland and maintained contact with his former parishioners in the Japanese camps. Some of the survivors were appointed to high places in the Dutch government and colonial administration. Among them were the minister of colonial affairs, the minister of education and the governor of New Guinea.

Having great respect for their former prison chaplain, and kept informed by him of Alliance work on the island, these officials were very sympathetic and supportive. The government financed the mission's medical and educational programs, paying salaries of workers and providing supplies for schools and clinics. The officials also looked to the Alliance for advice concerning other Protestant missions wanting to work on the island. Without the C&MA's nod, these groups could not move inland from the coastal region to the high mountains of the interior.

King went to Melbourne, Australia, in 1955 to meet with representatives of several missions wanting to expand in New Guinea. He explained the reason for not wanting the high valleys of the interior chopped into little mission turfs. The Alliance strategy envisioned a string of church and mission posts stretching from the Wissel Lakes to the Baliem Valley. It would link work among Moni, Kapauku (now Ekari), Uhunduni (now Damal), Dani and other people groups based on a uniform policy of establishing viable indigenous churches. To have other missions with perhaps conflicting priorities next door to Alliance centers could generate confusion and divisions among the inhabitants.

The conferees in Melbourne reached a comity arrangement. Other missions agreed to wait one year to allow the Alliance time to expand its work in the interior. If areas still remained unreached after that period of time, they would be permitted to enter.

Record-Breaking 102

The inter-mission conference in Australia was only one event that highlighted a worldwide problem for the Alliance: shortage of workers. The appointment of recruits was not keeping pace with vast new areas rapidly opening to the gospel.

There was no lack of C&MA candidates eager to serve overseas. The problem lay in a tightly controlled, closely screened, first-come-first-served procedure of screening applicants. Qualified men and women sometimes had to wait years to be appointed and posted abroad.

Smalley, in his role as personnel secretary, directed the screening process. He knew from firsthand experience "the right stuff" a missionary needed to survive and flourish in a foreign setting. He had served as a missionary in the Arab Lands, one of the harshest and most dangerous places on earth for a Christian. He went the limit in sacrifice, repeatedly placing himself at risk for the sake of the gospel. On one occasion he was jailed for thirty-five days and then expelled from the region. It was said that any candidate Smalley approved for service would make the grade.

But by 1956, the screening process was too slow and inflexible to keep up with the demand for new missionaries. "We were losing some of the best young people coming out of evangelical schools because other missions were grabbing them," Bernard King said. "Candidates were not willing to hang around three or four years before they filtered up to the top of the Alliance waiting list." The logjam had to be blown open.

Responding to a request by the Board, Smalley provided a list he had compiled of more than 200 candidates somewhere in the screening process. From this group the Board wanted 102 who could be appointed quickly for service overseas.

Arriving at a goal of 102 recruits was an evolutionary development. It began in early 1955 when the Foreign Department originally requested fifty new workers. The Board of Managers meeting in September increased the number to sixty-three as a bare minimum. In November the department concluded that even more recruits were needed. The request was raised to eighty-nine. The Board approved this revised total in its December session.

But the Foreign Department meeting in January realized that replacements as well as reinforcements were needed. Like Abraham bargaining with his angelic visitors about the number of righteous persons in Sodom and Gomorrah, the men raised the ante to 102 appointees.

The Board dispatched Louis and Bernard on a coast-to-coast sweep through Canada and the United States to interview the candidates. The two Kings enlisted the help of college faculties and district superintendents during the three-week tour. Their combined efforts presaged a new system that would involve a wider representation of interviewers in a faster, more flexible appointment process.

The World His Field

Louis and Bernard returned to New York with the names of 102 men and women whom they were confident could meet the stringent requirements for appointment. Then Bernard sharpened his pencil to see how many new workers the budget could absorb.

He knew the average cost of direct allowance per missionary amounted to $1,350 per year. He knew General Fund (now Great Commission Fund) income for 1955 had increased 6.8 percent over the previous year. He knew total income, including gifts and other income, amounted to a record $3,380,000. He compared projected income with the cost of additional overseas reinforcements.

Bernard had no way of determining at the time how churches would respond to the sending of a record group of new workers. But he did anticipate enough income growth that he informed the Board that the 1956 budget would sustain the staff increase. Supporters of Alliance missions responded to the bold decision by increasing their giving an astonishing 10.1 percent during the next year.

"It was one of the most thrilling experiences of my life," said Bernard. And Louis allowed a rare outburst of pride in Alliance people: "What other mission can collect 102 worthy candidates, appoint them and get them to the field in so soon a time!"

New Era Dawning

Snead retired from active service at the 1956 General Council in Omaha after almost thirty-seven years in the Foreign Department. He had come to New York in 1919 as assistant secretary and was later elected foreign secretary. Fittingly, he left office when overseas ministry had reached an unprecedented level of personnel and advance in 22 fields and 136 languages or dialects. The active foreign staff numbered over 780, making the C&MA the sixth largest Protestant mission in the world.[10]

He concluded his annual report to Council with a farewell note and exclamation that often punctuated his letters and reports: Hallelujah!

When Snead passed into the glorious presence of Christ in 1961, Louis paid tribute to his predecessor in office.

> His was a tall, delicate, stooping frame, in appearance meager and emaciated. He was never robust physically, but there was nothing weak about Dr. Snead otherwise.

The way in which he triumphed over insuperable difficulties was a proof of his strong faith and iron will. He never looked at the symptoms that were always present, nor did he seek the pity of any. He was always radiant in spirit, the victor and not the vanquished, and through it all he accomplished more work than many a strong man would care to face.[11]

Louis King was elected at General Council in Omaha to take the reins of the Foreign Department. The change of leadership capped a convergence of factors pointing to a new era in C&MA missions.

The same Council set goals to field 1,000 missionaries, increase the budget to $5 million and number 1,500 churches in 5 years. Waves of recruits were finalizing preparation for overseas service. Churches in North America raised their support to record levels, income that was administered by a capable treasurer at "260" with a heart for missions. Overseas churches were shaking off the confining weights of Mission subsidy and experiencing remarkable growth in strength and numbers. Missionaries were increasingly focused on their primary goal: establishing self-supporting, self-governing and self-propagating indigenous churches.

In God's providence, 1956 marked the beginning of an explosive period of Alliance missions and national Church growth worldwide. Leading the advance would be a man who neither sought nor desired the role of foreign secretary. Yet he did not shrink from the responsibility, quietly convinced that "the call of the church was the call of the Lord."

Notes

1. Bernard S. King, "Financial Crisis in Indo-China," *The Alliance Weekly*, July 14, 1954, p. 11.
2. Paul E. Carlson, "A Spiritual Answer to a Practical Question," *The Alliance Weekly*, January 20, 1954, p. 9.
3. Alfred C. Snead, "Advance Among the Tribes of Viet Nam," *The Alliance Weekly*, January 19, 1955, p. 11.
4. "Notice," *The Alliance Weekly*, June 1, 1955, p. 9.
5. Janet Kuhns, "God's Man in God's Place," *Alliance Life*, December 2001, p. 24.
6. "Report of Committee on Foreign Department Report," *Minutes of the General Council 1955 and Annual Report for 1954* (New York: The Christian and Missionary Alliance, 1955), p. 264.
7. Ibid.

8. Ibid., pp. 264-5.
9. Raghuel P. Chavan, "Indian Churches Catch a New Vision," *The Alliance Weekly*, July 18, 1956, pp. 9-10.
10. Louis L. King, "Report of the Foreign Department," *Minutes of the General Council 1957 and Annual Report for 1956* (New York: The Christian and Missionary Alliance, 1957), p. 56.
11. Louis L. King, "Dr. Alfred Cookman Snead, Man of God and Missionary Statesman," *The Alliance Witness*, April 5, 1961, p. 5.

SEVEN
Wheels in a Wheel

1956-1962
Time Markers

From 1957 to the end of the decade, the world scene was fairly quiet, but it was a calm before the storm. Fidel Castro took Cuba into the Soviet sphere, with serious results by the early 1960s. Charles DeGaulle fussed about having greater influence on NATO; when that didn't happen, he pulled France out of the mutual defense club.

The American economy suffered a sharp but short decline, then recovered in 1959. The 50-millionth Ford rolled off the assembly line. A record 68,300,000 vehicles traveled the highways, an average of one for every 2.5 Americans. Forty-seven percent of all Americans over age fourteen had cigarettes dangling from their mouths.

The decade began with the religious film, *The Robe*, and ended with *Ben Hur*. The biggest religious news of the late 1950s, however, was Billy Graham's crusade in New York City—called the most spectacular revival meetings since Billy Sunday. An estimated total of 2 million people attended the crusade and 55,000 decisions for Christ were reported.

Violence troubled the domestic American scene as efforts were made to implement the Civil Rights Law of 1960. An attempt by two black students to enroll at the University of Georgia triggered riots. A riot erupted when a black student, James Meredith, enrolled at the University of Mississippi; Kennedy sent in federal troops and ended the fifteen-hour riot, leaving two dead.

In the midst of all this turbulence and hatred, the US Supreme Court outlawed prayer in public schools.

★ ★ ★

Alliance income was hard hit by the mid-'50s recession. After a banner year of giving in 1956, the General Fund was left with a total balance of $409 in 1957. But magazine editor Tozer said circulation was doing so well that "a point can easily be foreseen when the *Witness* will pay its own way."

The World His Field

Giving to the General Fund recovered and climbed to $4 million for the first time in 1959. In his first annual report as president, Nathan Bailey spoke to 1960 General Council in Portland of his concern about the percentage of income going to missions.

He noted, "The crucial matter is that this seventy-two percent must not go any lower, notwithstanding a tendency to do so. Despite all other appeals and needs, we must hold the line. . . . To weaken at this point is to invite irretrievable disaster all along the line. The moment we do so, our donors will decrease their pledges. They will say we are becoming like the denominations around us. Once public confidence is lost, it will never be regained. Our distinctiveness, as a missionary organization, will be forever lost."

By the end of the decade, inclusive C&MA membership in North America reached 108,700, and overseas 131,800.

The Diamond Jubilee year ended in 1963. In his annual review, Bailey noted there were almost 1,200 churches in North America; over a ten-year period the net annual gain was eighteen churches. General Fund income exceeded $4 million for the first time. The first Life Investment Conference attracted 1,800 young people and Sunday school enrollment reached nearly 170,000.

For the 24 overseas fields—Taiwan being the most recent—the number of active missionaries was 876, a net increase of 216 over the 10-year period. In the same timeframe, church membership increased by 53,400, national pastors and workers by 1,280. Nearly 2,000 organized and unorganized groups were added. Another significant statistic: The number of self-supporting overseas churches grew to 2,693.

The hoped-for merger with the Missionary Church Association (MCA) failed by forty-two votes short of the majority needed for approval by the MCA membership.

The Alliance Witness, doubling in circulation over the previous twelve years, reached nearly 60,000 subscribers. But editor Tozer was not at the 1963 Council in Phoenix to give the report. He died suddenly just days before Council convened.

In 1957 Louis concluded his first annual report as foreign secretary with a statement that would characterize his leadership for more than two decades:

Wheels in a Wheel

The Alliance through the years has been called a "Movement." At its inception the Master breathed into its wheels the word, "Go." It was not, and is not now, constituted for standing still. Its equilibrium depends upon forward movement. It wobbles only when speed is slackened. It will topple over into the ecclesiastical scrap-pile if it stops; therefore it must not stop.[1]

If his analogy referred to something like a bicycle, overseas ministries was one of the wheels. From the beginning of his administration, he set in motion diverse smaller wheels within that wheel. They would propel the C&MA forward in its missionary mandate. But the road would be pockmarked with risks and costs.

Scanning the Alliance world of 1955, he could pinpoint many locations marked with the word *forward* in large letters. (Overseas statistics were two years previous.)

- The Church in Belgian Congo recorded over 2,700 baptisms.
- The Mano people group in French West Africa heard the gospel for the first time.
- The Church in Thailand reported in one year almost as many baptisms as in the previous twenty.
- The Holland-Belgium Alliance committee purchased a center in the Netherlands, opening the way for qualified Dutch volunteers eager to serve overseas.
- Alliance churches and other evangelical groups in Lima, Peru, joined in the nation's first-ever united evangelistic campaign, drawing 3,000 people nightly to a large coliseum until aroused opposition forced it to close.
- The Christian community in north-central Vietnam grew rapidly as tens of thousands heard the gospel and hundreds received Christ. Baptisms more than doubled over the previous year and another 1,500 new believers were candidates.

Yet even as King cited these "memorials of blessing," conflicts in other areas served notice that forward movement would not be a cruise in the park. Some field reports raised warning signals:

- *Gabon*: "The young church, organized only two years ago, is still very weak and unsure of itself." Its instability would precipitate a crisis threatening the future of missions in the nation.
- *Ecuador*: "This past year has brought events not seen before in the sixty years of missionary service. Not that opposition to the

preaching of the gospel is something new, but that this opposition seems to indicate official influence."
- *Syria*: "During the year our missionaries had to leave Syria and are now in Beirut." It would mark the end of missionary presence in the country.
- *Indonesia*: "Two years have passed since the Mission withdrew its financial support of the national workers. On the dark side it may be said that in general there is a feeling among the national brethren that the Mission has let them down and some pastors have quit."[2]

Getting Acquainted Globally

During that first year of his administration, King realized the need for on-site understanding of all twenty-two Alliance fields. It was one of the first inner wheels he set in motion. "I had to see South America and Africa to become further acquainted before I could make any conclusions as to improvements or what changes ought to be made. I didn't have to spend time in the Far East because I knew the area like the back of my hand," he said.

A three-month tour of South American nations in 1957 gave him some initial insights.[3] In Colombia he noted approvingly, "The Christians in every place appear to be alert and vigorous in their testimony for Jesus Christ.... No doubt this is due to their intense persecution. It really costs them to be Protestants."

But in Peru he observed that, with one exception, missionaries were pastors of the churches. "Although we probably have a grouping of the ablest missionaries in our South American fields, men of whom we can be justly proud, I am fearful the indigenous goal set forth in the *Alliance Manual* will be missed due to their great earnestness to achieve visible results quickly."

Concerning Chile he wrote, "To me, our Chilean work is the most outstanding and impressive of the five fields I visited," but he did have a tart comment on a later trip regarding the national church leadership.

He was trying to determine why statistics showed a drop in church membership. After a 1966-1967 trip to South America, he concluded, "The real problem seems to be the large numbers of static, older pastors and their removal of members from the church rolls if they didn't contribute satisfactorily or did not attend faithfully. No one seems to have thought of removing old pastors if their sermons and nonattendance to pastoral duties have created the members' lack of interest."[4]

King did visit every one of the Alliance fields early in his administration. With that accomplished, he went to the next level, visiting in each field as many mission centers and stations as possible, a practice he had begun while area secretary.

During each itinerary he absorbed information and impressions like a parched sponge. He seemed to inhale the atmosphere of cultures ranging from that of cosmopolitan Buenos Aires to the traditional cliff dwellings of Mali, West Africa.

Long car rides with missionaries and visits in their homes were often as informative as formal meetings. However, King had established a strict policy about riding with missionaries that on at least one occasion resulted in a humorous incident, according to Peter and Jerry Nanfelt, missionaries in Makassar, Indonesia.

After visiting the couple, it came time for King to go to the home of another missionary couple. When King learned that Peter's wife would take him there, he hesitated and then told William Kerr, who was present, "Tell Peter my policy about traveling."

Kerr declined, saying, "It's your policy, not mine. You tell him."

So King said, "I have a strict policy never to travel alone in a car with a missionary wife or single woman. You'll have to make some other arrangement for me."

When Jerry learned of the complication, she went up to King and said, "It's only a mile to the place and it's broad daylight. Furthermore, I have our three children waiting in the car. I just want to know what the real problem is. Because if you are worried about me, I need to tell you, Dr. King, you're not my type!"

She said he laughed all the way while in the car and was still laughing when he walked up to the next house.

King's foreign travel protocol generally grew out of experiences good and bad. At first he agreed to missionaries' requests to carry items to them provided by friends back home. But on one occasion a customs agent opened a suitcase he was bringing as a favor to a woman missionary. The distinguished missions administrator was totally chagrined when he saw it contained feminine lingerie. He did no more such favors.

Conversations with national church leaders ranked as high priorities. There was seldom time for small talk—too much to learn, too little time. Always and everywhere he posed endless questions, often without follow-up comment, and with an unblinking concentration that sometimes unnerved his hosts. Entertaining the new boss from New York was not always a fun thing. Some missionaries felt like they were under scrutiny—and often they were right.

Even meal times were not exempt from Louis's relentless search for information. When asked how he resisted gaining weight when missionaries went all out to prepare delicious meals, he replied. "I eat slowly so that when others are finishing their second helpings I am still on my first." That deliberate pace gave him the added benefit of time to keep the questions going and the answers coming.

King, however, was not totally rigid in his dietary discipline. He believed everyone was entitled to one good dessert a day. And one missionary gleefully confronted him in Vietnam: "I have discovered your weakness," she said. "It's chocolates!"

Host missionary dining rooms were not always an extension of the conference room, especially in later years as King became more comfortable in his role. Eileen Sather, missionary to Gabon, remembered a group chatting with him after supper. She wrote, "We were discussing the need for more missionaries on the field. You were indicating the number of single men being sent to Vietnam at the time.

"Elaine Battles asked, 'Why aren't you sending single men to West Africa?'

"To which you replied, 'Your field is asking for couples, not single men.'

"Elaine retorted, 'Well, you send us the single men and we'll make the couples.' " King was at a loss for words while the others burst into laughter.

On a trip to Taiwan, the dining room provided another light moment. Louis and Esther King were visiting in the home of Steve and Juniata Wible. The Chinese cook had prepared a local dish Steve described as "simulated spinach," but it was poorly prepared. After Louis chewed a mouthful for several moments he commented, "I need to make a decision about what to do with this vegetable."

Esther calmly replied, "The decision has already been made for you. Swallow it!"

Extensive travel and firsthand observation would always be a hallmark of King's administration. At the close of one year, Jewel Hall said, "Do you realize, sir, that this past year you spent just sixty-one nights in your own bed?" It was not uncommon during his years in the Foreign Department to log 100,000 miles annually.

King agreed with the comment often made that world travel is fun for everyone—except those who do it. A three-month itinerary through Europe and Africa in early 1959 listed some of the problems he routinely encountered in his travels. He reported to the Board of Managers, "Despite continually changing airplane schedules, two car accidents and two breakdowns on the road; the longest period spent in the same bed being on three different occasions of three nights each; a daily preaching schedule; attending three field conferences; traveling in West Africa approximately 3,000 miles on rough gravel roads; the usual heat; and interminable interviews with missionaries and national church leaders—no headache or physical disorder was experienced."[5]

Perils of the Path

Perhaps not every visit to a mission station was as difficult as the one he undertook to inspect the Homejo station in 1955, but it made clear the fact that he was not afraid of the tough ones. Homejo was located in the high mountainous interior of Irian Jaya.

William Cutts recalled in a letter to King, "I had a bout with scrub-typhus just before you came to Enarotoli for our field conference. Because of my being weak, you are reported to have said, 'If Bill can't come here to see me, I will go to Homejo to see him.'"

The three-day trek began with a group quietly gathered around Ken Troutman, the field chairman, King and eight bearded tribesmen half their size who were there to carry the supplies. The missionaries murmured to themselves as they sized up the area secretary in borrowed clothing, borrowed helmet and borrowed jungle boots over wool socks held up by tape. They bid him farewell with silent sympathy for the perils of the path they knew he would shortly encounter.

After a four-hour boat trip across the lake, the going got rough. "Starting overland, we slogged along in swamps, goose-stepping from one tuft of grass to the next," he wrote later. "Sometimes we slipped and sank to our hips in the mud and slime.

"Emerging from the grassy swamp we entered a water-sogged [sic] forest and forged ahead by stepping on the tangled, gnarled roots of bushes and trees. One false move might mean a muddy bath and a sprained ankle or worse."

The second day's hike was even worse as the small group crossed two mountain passes, each over 7,000 feet high. He wrote, "When a halt was called for the night, my energy was gone; one knee would hardly function and fatigue was intense. I lay on the ground in my wet clothing covered by a jacket and tarpaulin for the better part of an hour before being sufficiently revived to be able to change them."

Homejo, wedged between cloud-capped ranges, came into view on the third day. The plain, bare necessities of the station seemed like luxury to the weary trekkers. Cutts, however, recalled a detail of King's visit that showed that his boss would not surrender his privacy even in roughhewn circumstances. "We remember you as being one of our more modest guests," he wrote. "My not having proper boards for the ceiling of the first story—which was the floor of the second story—I had used split rails. And, not giving in to the desires of the nationals to know everything that could be known about the white man, you stood on top of the bed upstairs to change your clothes."

After two days of preaching, inspecting an airstrip under construction and consulting with the workers, King and his entourage returned on the long, weary route to Enarotoli. The last lap was a fitting climax of the trip. King described it:

> As we recrossed Lake Paniai ... we were plagued with a torrential rain driven by a stiff, cold wind. Leaving Mr. Troutman to handle the outboard motor, I covered myself completely with a tarpaulin. Presently my Kapauku carrier slid under too. Soon he was asleep, his naked body lying peacefully against me for the remaining three hours of the trip.[6]

Secret Sources

In addition to the firsthand knowledge of C&MA missions that he was gaining through travel, Louis had access to information about overseas work that few Alliance people knew about—and probably would not have approved of.

His contacts with leading officials of the National Council of Churches (NCC) headquartered at Riverside Drive in uptown Manhattan, had begun when he was area secretary for the Far East. The interaction increased when he became foreign secretary.

The Alliance had entered into an agreement some years earlier with other missions, ecumenical and evangelical, to establish the Associated Medical Missions Office (AMMO). It was a joint project in which diverse theological groups could join together for mutual benefit without compromising their differences. Louis was the C&MA representative on the AMMO board.

The AMMO's function was to assess the physical fitness of missionaries to cope with challenges posed by the rigors of foreign climates, especially in the tropics. When the AMMO disbanded because of a lack of missionary clients from liberal churches, the Alliance hired Dr. John D. Frame. He had a special interest in tracking down rare African diseases. While treating a missionary to Guinea, he isolated the virus that caused Lassa fever, a devastating plague in West Africa. He went beyond the call of the contract for medical exams and tried to determine as well the emotional and mental fitness of candidates. This sometimes amused his patients; other times it caused annoyance.

Louis was also a member of the board of directors of the American Leprosy Mission because of the strong C&MA commitment to ministry among leprous people in Vietnam and Thailand. As with the AMMO connection, this brought him into frequent consultation with Mission leaders of various denominations and groups.

Another point of contact with ecumenical leaders was the China Consultation. This group organized after the expulsion of foreign missionaries from the country by the Communists from 1949 to 1954. Mainline denominations that had worked in China formed a group to pool information available on religion and other aspects of life under Communism. The Alliance was invited to participate in recognition of its long-established and extensive involvement. King, as area secretary, represented the Alliance in monthly meetings at Riverside Drive.

Members funneled information from their various sources to a China expert who analyzed and compiled the material in a report to the participating groups. According to King, the information was high quality and not otherwise available. The service proved so helpful that King appointed Robert Chrisman, his successor as area secretary, to continue the liaison. William Kerr, a missionary on the Tibetan border until

China closed, followed Chrisman in the Foreign Department and on the China-watching committee.

When Louis became foreign secretary, he was asked to join a small group of highly placed evangelical leaders who maintained communications with their counterparts in the ecumenical movement. Among his colleagues were Clyde W. Taylor, executive secretary of the Evangelical Foreign Missions Association (EFMA); Arthur Glasser, head of the Overseas Missionary Fellowship; and Charles E. Ryrie, Dallas Theological Seminary professor.

It was mutually agreed that the meetings would not be publicized, nor would reports be prepared. The sole purpose of the off-the-record meetings was to get acquainted and exchange views. The C&MA officers approved of the meetings and agreed that they should be kept confidential. "Some people would cry bloody murder if they knew," King acknowledged. Yet he was so convinced of the value of such contacts for the benefit of the Alliance that he was willing to take the risk.

"From these various opportunities to rub shoulders with men of the ecumenical movement," he recalled, "I could ask questions and listen to the discussion, learning how and why they did things, and what the results were. All this gave me insights from those who had been in the business of missions much longer than I. As a result, I gained a perspective few other evangelical mission executives had the opportunity to develop."

On some occasions, WCC officials may have had second thoughts about inviting the C&MA foreign secretary to their meetings. King was asked in 1963 to be an observer and resource person for their World Conference on Faith and Order in Montreal. The agenda was to formulate the World Council's stand on social problems and moral issues.

"In the process of the discussion," he remarked, "the group concluded that Jesus Christ did not give the command to go into all the world and preach the gospel. To see them arrive at this position officially was an eye-opener to me."

However, the decision was not unanimous. King was especially impressed by a professor from a Lutheran seminary in St. Paul. He and some other conferees always went straight to the Bible to substantiate their positions.

Noting his silence in the discussion, one of the conveners said, "Dr. King, we brought you as a resource person for the evangelical community and we haven't heard a word from you. We do want you to speak up." He suggested as a starter that King talk about results of work among the cannibals in the Stone-Age culture of New Guinea, a story that had been carried in *Reader's Digest*.

King explained that since the Scriptures had not yet been published in the local vernaculars, candidates for baptism were expected to memorize with detailed accuracy key portions of the Bible. These included the Genesis account of creation, the fall of Adam and Eve, the new birth and the Lord's Prayer.

At this point, a delegate loudly interrupted. "Why in the world do you have them memorize the creation story and those other stories in Genesis? They're just myths!"

"Simply because we accept the Bible as the very Word of God," King replied. "These are essentials for being true believers and followers of Jesus Christ."

The comments stirred a lively debate between those who believed the Bible was inspired and those who did not. When the group adjourned for dinner, those who sided with King sat together to continue the discussion. "We had a lively time," King commented. The "unbelievers," as he called them, sat in another section of the dining room.

King began a long friendship with some of the men, especially Eugene Smith, head of the Methodist Board of Missions. He said, "Dr. Smith was a born-again believer and had no hesitancy in saying so. He was aboveboard in talking with some of us about the problems within the ecumenical missions."

But relationships with leaders in the long-established denominations did not blind King to the policies and strategies that smothered spiritual growth in their churches. The contacts further honed insights he had developed toward the ecumenical movement under the tutelage of his pastor in Grenloch. "I could see what eventually would happen if you turned one way ever so little. Or if you turned another way, how it resulted in blessing or loss of it."

Trend Toward Apostasy

Eventually the question was raised by NCC men in their group meetings, "Why doesn't the National Association of Evangelicals (NAE) join the World Council of Churches? We're doing identical work in many parts of the world, and we could do much more if we joined forces." (The NAE is a fraternal group of denominations and organizations that adhere to basic evangelical beliefs.)

Despite the congeniality and value of their contacts, the evangelicals had to say bluntly what divided them boiled down to one terrible issue: apostasy. The trend in World Council circles toward denial of historical Christian truths was something the NAE would have no part of.

The mere utterance of the word tossed into a group of churchmen who claimed to believe the same Bible, follow the same Lord and give themselves to the same ministry must have been like a grenade dropped in their midst. It says something of the caliber of men at Riverside Drive that the charge leveled against their organization did not end any further contact with the evangelicals. Instead, they proposed several days of discussion to explore the issue in depth, especially as it related to missions.

Their proposal, as King remembered it, was: "You claim we are apostates, so get one of your men to give us a Bible study on the subject in the Scripture. Have another one present the practical implications arising from the doctrine. On our part, we will respond to the two papers. That will be the only agenda for the meeting."

The debate took place on the campus of Malone College, a Quaker school in Canton, Ohio, in July of 1963. Dr. Charles E. Ryrie presented the evangelical perspective in a doctrinal paper entitled "The Meaning of Apostasy in the New Testament." Louis called the paper a fine in-depth study, and it drew "lots of questions back and forth. It was a very polite discussion."

Then, in a less diplomatic tone he added, "The liberals were handling Scripture, so they were trying to be very careful not to disturb us at the beginning—at least act and talk as if they were Bible believers."

Then it was King's turn to present his nineteen pages on the practical implications for overseas missions arising from Ryrie's study on apostasy. The polite atmosphere evaporated and "the sparks began to fly," he said.

There was no way, as a teenager being mentored by his Presbyterian pastor on the errors and consequences of liberalism, that he could have imagined the drama that would unfold on the campus of Malone College decades later. At that time, as foreign secretary of a major missionary movement, King would confront some of the best minds and most influential movers of the ecumenical movement in the United States. In blunt and tightly reasoned terms he took them to task over their deviation from historical biblical truths and the terrible consequences that followed.

Despite his passionate conviction for truth and aversion to error, he introduced his remarks with reluctance and humility.

> I find my assignment uncongenial and contrary to my normal attitude. I have wanted no part with those who are in a headline hurry to suspect or condemn others [a reference to Carl McIntyre]. I have sought for the temper and intelligence and justice to understand and to make this proper application to difficult matters. Many rash, ill-considered, and offensive statements have been made; but since I have been asked to prepare this paper, I shall endeavor to state the situation courteously and faithfully.[7]

King referred to Ryrie's study for the basic issue: "Apostasy is a departure from truth previously accepted and it involves the breaking of a professed relationship with God.... There is an objective, well understood and previously believed standard of truth from which the apostates depart.... The departure is willful. The very word infers it, and the actions and life of the apostates show it."

King affirmed, along with Ryrie, the conviction that apostasy would increase in scope during the church age and climax at the end, a situation he believed was now unfolding in the world. "When we place the plain scriptural accounts of the possibility, the nature and the onset of apostasy and its eschatological implications alongside certain elements in the World Council of Churches, we see a degree of likeness."

The departure from a sound theological base was the most serious charge he leveled at the religious world body and its strongest member, the National Council of Churches. Referring to the WCC's statement of faith, he noted, "Admittedly, the statement is good, but an orthodox doctrinal statement does not guarantee orthodoxy in either doctrine or life."[8]

For example, the ecumenical basis of faith makes solid reference to the Bible. But when the individual denominations and leaders attach their own meaning to the words, "according to the Scriptures" has little meaning in the final analysis.

Evangelicals hold the Old and New Testaments to be inspired, infallible, trustworthy—the supreme authority in all matters of faith, doctrine and conduct. Modernists, however, refer to the Scriptures as myths.

Neo-orthodoxy proponents say the Bible contains the Word of God and allow the reader to pick and choose what passages are inspired—much as Thomas Jefferson cut and pasted together scriptural passages he approved of to make his own version of the Bible. Orthodox churchmen elevate church traditions and declarations to equal authority with the Bible.

References in the WCC statement of faith like "gospel" and "salvation" were equally vulnerable to widely varying interpretations. Universalism, King pointed out, is the prevalent message of ninety-five percent of European clergy whose denominations belong to the WCC.

Nullifying the authority of Scripture resulted in devastating effects on the missionary work of the WCC-member bodies. He spoke of the waning of evangelical fervor: "The once firmly held conviction that those who are not born again are lost and in need of Christ's salvation is not now a strong motivation in the majority membership of the World Council."

He cited the waning of missionary passion: "For the size of their membership and financial resources, the missionary outreach of the World Council members is simply pitiful."[9] He observed also a parallel waning of godly living among rank-and-file members of the world-body churches.

King viewed these trends toward abandoning the revealed Word of God, and therefore the God of the Bible, as highly dangerous for the younger overseas churches. He concluded, "The Christian and Missionary Alliance and like-minded evangelical groups are necessarily concerned lest, by association, the same spiritual maladies which can eventuate in apostasy fasten themselves upon mission-field churches."[10]

The same held true for the sending agencies. Any organizational link with the WCC would place the much smaller NAE in a dangerous position. "The end result would be vitiated if that organization is seeking to perpetuate something that is contrary to the minority's purpose. Organizations as well as people are influenced by friendship, and evil especially seems to have more power to offset than good does."

Trends toward apostasy evident in the religious world organization left but one clear choice: "Evangelicals sincerely desire to glorify Christ by loyalty to Him and His Word; by taking the gospel to the whole world; by establishing churches of the redeemed; and by being free from that apostasy that will characterize the Babylonian church of the end time."[11]

The implications of a church in cahoots with Babylon was not lost on the ecumenical leaders and theologians: "BABYLON THE GREAT/ THE MOTHER OF PROSTITUTES/ AND OF THE ABOMINATIONS OF THE EARTH . . . drunk with the blood of the saints, the blood of those who bore testimony to Jesus" (Revelation 17:5-6).

No wonder "the sparks began to fly!"

The discussion at Malone College continued, however. The men intermingled at meal times, roomed together in the dormitories and related to each other on a first-name basis. But when the three days were over, King and his associates no longer were asked, "Why don't you join with us?"

Attempts at Seduction

In delivering his paper, King did not limit himself to theological and philosophical implications. With specific dates, names and places, he accused the ecumenical leaders of engaging in a global strategy to entice overseas churches into their one-church orbit.

He quoted EFMA's Clyde Taylor:

> The main goal of the ecumenical movement as previously expressed is to bring all Protestants and those who are called Christians into one world organization as the means by which they may express spiritual unity. At the moment this is called the unity of cooperation. However, there is no doubt that it is twofold. One is unity through organization and the other is going to be unity by union and this is being pushed at the local and national level wherever possible.[12]

Taylor also might have added "by whatever means possible," and King in his paper provided Exhibit A: Vietnam.

From 1911 to 1955, the C&MA was the only evangelical Mission working in Vietnam. The years of ministry proved fruitful: a national Church with 331 churches and approximately 53,500 believers pastored by 288 workers. *Hoi Thanh Tin Lanh* in Vietnam was self-governing, self-propagating and largely self-supporting by 1927.

Representatives of the world Church body in Geneva visited Vietnam in 1955 on a fact-finding tour. The following year a Swiss pastor with deep pockets arrived on "a mission of fellowship with the Protestant church." Over the course of seven months he visited seventy-six churches, distributing relief supplies such as rice, clothing, furniture and building materials, with the promise of more to come.

The impact on low-paid pastors and war-ravaged congregations was predictable. Some workers agitated for the *Hoi Thanh Tin Lanh* to become a member of the WCC in order to receive more benefits. But Church president Le-van-Thai and some older leaders refused, looking down the road to eventual consequences of receiving such funds. The "mission of fellowship" caused a serious but temporary rift in the Church.

The Foreign Department in New York took a dim view of the WCC's "advances" to the Vietnamese Church. King wrote a letter of protest in November 1956, to U.H. van Beyma at the World Council headquarters in Geneva. "For the World Council to deliberately and knowingly seek to purchase a church's allegiance in this way [material and financial aid] is inconceivable to us and, I trust, is not the case; but if continued can be considered by us and other evangelicals in no other light."

Then, more bluntly, "It seems to us that if the World Council of Churches desires to have a constituency in Vietnam, it should seek to raise up one of its own rather than to build upon another's foundation."

The response by Leslie E. Cooke, WCC associate general secretary, was one of injured innocence and denial. "We had all become aware of the great suffering in Vietnam," he explained. "We felt we should do something for the people of Vietnam. We wanted as much as possible to help with and through the Christian Church. We, therefore, naturally rejoice to learn that the C&MA is equally engaged in such an enterprise ... and take for granted that its purposes are as wholly non-self-regarding as we venture to believe ours to be in such a ministry."

Making clear its intentions to continue offering assistance to the Vietnamese Church, the World Council sent a second official representative to Saigon. He remained for two years, exploring ways to offer aid to the Church—and woo its leadership.

Efforts to lure the Church into the ecumenical fold became more obvious in 1958. The WCC-related East Asia Christian Council (EACC) extended numerous invitations designed to sway church leaders to the ecumenical agenda and ideology.

The EACC offered to send a delegation of Vietnamese pastors on a two-month tour of WCC-member groups in Asia, all expenses paid. It offered to assign a community-service team to Vietnam, all expenses paid. It offered to send a delegation to Japan for a literature conference; to the Philippines for a conference on industrial evangelism; to Hong Kong for a conference on Church-sponsored medical work. All expenses paid.

The EACC also offered to "share the burden" of evangelism and other activities through subsidies to local *Hoi Thanh Tin Lanh* congregations. Apparently the ecumenical leaders had not done their research. Otherwise, they would have realized that the biblically strong Vietnamese Church that practiced self-support as essential to spiritual maturity, often with great sacrifice, would not rise to the bait of foreign subsidies.

The most serious threat by the ecumenical strategists to infiltrate the Vietnamese Church was an offer to partner in theological education. The WCC would provide funds for building, equipment and supplies. It would fund the exchange of professors between the Bible institute and liberal schools. Students would be given scholarships to attend WCC-related institutions.

This initiative was an overt attempt to displace the C&MA in one of its key roles in establishing indigenous churches. Alliance policy holds that if a national church is to be truly indigenous, its workers must be spiritually and academically qualified to shoulder the responsibility of leadership. Therefore the longest-enduring commitment by the C&MA to an overseas church will be a cooperative effort in the schooling of its leaders.

Again, the Vietnamese Church leaders declined the proffered EACC help. They realized that the way to pollute a land is to poison its headwaters.

That same year of 1958, the Mission and the Evangelical Church of Vietnam embarked on a joint effort to meet the growing need for qualified workers for the Church. It would be the largest single program ever sponsored by the Mission and implemented entirely by a national Church.

The small Bible school at Tourane was stalled at its capacity level of seventy-five students. But the waiting list of applicants and of churches without trained pastors kept getting longer. The Mission took the initiative to promise a $250,000 grant to help create a larger campus. *Hoi*

Thanh Tin Lanh congregations gave generously toward the project as well. Church officials turned the first shovel on a choice site on the coastline in Central Vietnam in 1958. Design, construction and development of the campus were totally in the hands of the Vietnamese.

Three years later, the sparkling new home of the Nhatrang Bible Institute was completed. Its dedication coincided with the fiftieth anniversary of the Vietnamese C&MA.

Missionary Dale S. Heredeen, present for the occasion on July 9, 1961, described the setting.

> The campus is beautiful. It is constructed on a low hill overlooking the China Sea, and from it one has a more than 180-degree view of the ocean and offshore islands. A lush green valley and purple mountains complete the scene. Rising above the administration building, dormitories, and faculty houses is the lovely new chapel with a lighted cross that can be clearly seen in the city of Nhatrang. On the roof apex are the two words 'Good News' in neon lights. This clearly identifies the campus with the national church.[13]

King flew to Vietnam to participate in the dedication and celebration events. "When I arrived," he said, "the national church executive committee was in session. They sent word they wanted me to meet with them. I declined to do so because I should not be involved in the business of the church."

The committee sent another message, "Please come. We don't have church business to discuss."

"When I entered the meeting," King continued, "they explained how they had used the grant from the Alliance. The campus was completed debt free, but there was $50,000 left over from the grant and they wanted to return it."

King flatly refused to accept the money. "We said we would give you $250,000 and not ask for an accounting. That word stands. It's your money."

No amount of reasoning by the committee could change his decision. They later decided to put the remainder of the grant into a special account to fund extension works of the Church.

Over 100 students enrolled for the fall semester. Administration of the school was completely in the hands of the Church, headed by Rev. Ong-van-Huyen, a Vietnamese classical scholar, as dean. In addition to the 600-seat chapel, the campus contained 2 large student dormitories

Cordelia King with her children (clockwise from top left): Ralph, Marie, Louis, Mildred and George

The Grenloch (New Jersey) Presbyterian Church was Louis King's first church home.

Left: Missionary James Brabazon, with his wife Ruth, predicted Louis's service in India.

Below: King's childhood home in Grenloch, New Jersey, is still the residence of relatives.

Louis's demeanor was already serious in his teens.

Esther Martz, age 13

Esther's parents, Myrle and William Martz

What was the Institute Building during King's Nyack days is now Simpson Hall of Nyack College.

Louis King, class of 1938

Esther Martz, class of 1939

V. Raymond Edman, faculty professor for a short period at Nyack, deeply impacted Louis as mentor and model.

E.R. "Daddy" Dunbar, dean of men at Nyack, maintained a lasting interest in Louis King.

Louis King and Esther, his "queen," were the campus's surprise couple.

The Alliance church in North Tonawanda, New York, became King's first pastorate.

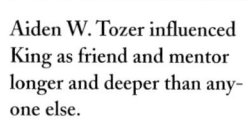

Aiden W. Tozer influenced King as friend and mentor longer and deeper than anyone else.

After their 1939 wedding, the Kings served together in the North Tonawanda pastorate.

King and Donald McGavran collaborated closely in church-planting strategy.

Philip Teng, early influenced by King, became one of Asia's outstanding church leaders.

The Wheaton Congress on the Church's Worldwide Mission, chaired by King, opened a new era of evangelical missions cooperation.

The Nhatrang Bible School in Vietnam was designed and built by the national Church.

Missions Aviation Fellowship partnered with the Alliance to provide travel to interior Irian Jaya.

Left: Bernard S. King, C&MA treasurer, worked with Louis King to secure funding for many overseas projects.

King and an official of the Three-Self Protestant Church in China.

Congo church leader Kuvuna ku Konde Mwela (far left) attended the founding meeting of the Alliance World Fellowship in 1975.

The conversion of people groups opened a new era of missions in Irian Jaya.

King worked closely with Canadian C&MA church leaders, including Melvin Sylvester, first president of the Canadian Alliance.

Jewel Hall served as King's secretary during his years of overseas leadership.

Louis and Esther King with their sons (beginning left), Mark, Stephen, David and Paul.

Following his election as C&MA president, King, joined by his wife Esther, was dedicated in prayer to his new role by Nathan Bailey, retiring president.

Retiring from office in 1987, King passed the symbolic gavel to his successor, David L. Rambo.

Above: Louis L. King, C&MA president

President King in his Nyack C&MA office

and 7 faculty residences. Classes in subjects ranging from Greek to personal evangelism were conducted in a three-story administrative/academic center.

Other buildings included a medical clinic funded by the Church and the Mennonite Central Committee, and a radio studio for the preparation of programs to be broadcast from Manila-based FEBC to all of Vietnam. The school that had begun in 1919 in a single straw house had come a long way.

After the fall of South Vietnam in 1975, the Communist regime swiftly seized the Nhatrang campus and converted it to government use. But during the fourteen years the campus was used by the Church, hundreds of young men and women received quality training for the ministry. They formed the cadre of dedicated workers who would help *Hoi Thanh Tin Lanh* to do more than simply survive under decades of official persecution. When the Church was finally recognized by the Hanoi regime in 2001, it had grown in size from 53,425 believers to an estimated 680,000 inclusive members true to the Word of God and faithful to the Lord Jesus.

The Nhatrang Bible Institute, with its short but glorious history, and the Evangelical Church of Vietnam, with its ongoing vibrant faith, are a matter of record. Credit is due in large part to mature church leaders like Le-van-Thai and Doan-van-Mieng who scrutinized the proffered aid of the World Council of Churches—and hung out the sign, "This church is not for sale."

Second Asia Conference: Urban Spark

During the same period that the World Council was offering financial incentives to the Vietnamese Church, King set in motion another of the wheels within the wheel of Alliance world missions. The Second Asia Conference convened in Saigon, January 15-22, 1958. One of its primary objectives was to reinforce the move toward self-support as an essential part of the truly indigenous church.

Since most of the delegates had attended the first Asia Conference, camaraderie was quickly renewed and deepened. The tension and uncertainty that preceded Bangkok were notably absent. Success was building on success and gathering momentum.

The format basically followed the program set for the Bangkok Conference in 1955: Asian church leaders helping each other achieve the

New Testament pattern for the Church under the Lordship of Jesus Christ as its Head. Using indigenous principles established at the Bangkok meetings as their guide, representatives from eleven missions and national churches in Asia reported on progress and problems encountered. The forty-three delegates spent long hours encouraging, advising and correcting each other.

King reported, "They probably learned more from each other and were strengthened more in indigenous methods through those conferences than through any other method used in the past." With an eye to the future, he added, "Because of their proven worth, such conferences should be held in South America and Africa in the near future."[14]

One new topic was added to the familiar themes of the Bangkok conference. Pastors from Japan, Indonesia and Vietnam presented papers on "The Missionary as a Problem to the National Church." In a gracious and loving manner, they spoke of the unwillingness of some missionaries to work closely with the Church. They encouraged all missionaries to melt and mingle with the customs of the country and the life of the Church.

The Saigon conference differed sharply from Bangkok in one respect: flourish and fanfare. Vietnamese church officials met each delegate at the airport, children presented bouquets of flowers, cameras flashed. Newspapers and radio stations publicized the meetings. The opening ceremony was filmed for news releases. The country's president sent greetings.

The closing service was even more dramatic. King described it this way:

> The setting was the big Saigon Central Church. At starting time it was crowded to capacity with about 1,000 people. There was an overflow crowd on the sidewalks in front and on the side of the large building.
>
> All the delegates were seated on the platform—the three from Japan in their kimonos; the India delegation in turbans and four yards of draperies around their waists; an Indonesian in his colorful, wrap-around skirt with shirt on the outside; the Vietnamese in their dignified high-necked black coats and neat black hats; the Filipinos with attractive embroidered shirts. What a sight to behold![15]

At the conclusion of the electrifying service, as if on cue, the audience stood and 1,000 voices roared in unison, "Hallelujah! Hallelujah! Hallelujah!"

Strategic Shift to the Cities

As he attended the Second Asia Conference, King recalled vivid memories of his first visit while he had been area secretary. He had come to Saigon five years earlier to resolve the financial crisis precipitated by the collapse of the Vietnamese piaster.

He said, "Going into Saigon for the first time was like going to Paris. The city was built beautifully, clean and neat. It had broad avenues lined with trees and French-style houses, the same you would find in a fine residential section of the French capital."

But something about Saigon was not right. "In this city of 2 to 3 million people we had only one Vietnamese church and one affiliated Chinese church. This disturbed me to no end. We had been there since 1911; this was now 1954. Granted, the Vietnamese church had about one thousand people, and the missionaries thought they were doing pretty good.

"At the time, their emphasis was to evangelize the small tribes in villages and towns in the countryside. But they were missing the 'bridges of God' concept. People who moved to the cities maintain their network of contacts back to village relatives and friends. The potential for city dwellers to evangelize the nation is enormous. To have only one church in Saigon was unacceptable. Right away, I figured something had to be done about cities, and it was in Saigon we would begin our urban emphasis."

The shift would be a major one. The C&MA historically identified itself as a pioneer mission in the tradition of the Apostle Paul: "It has always been my ambition to preach the gospel where Christ was not known, so that I would not be building on someone else's foundation" (Romans 15:20).

This often meant for the Alliance, a relative latecomer to world missions, that its workers bypassed the cities where other missions were already established. They pushed into more remote, less populated areas. That situation, however, did not apply to Vietnam, where the Alliance was the only Protestant mission.

The more King had studied over the years the potential of major city churches, the more he became convinced it was the best way to reach an entire nation. "My concept was that the city is where the money and initiative are found," he said. "In cities you get educated people who are experienced in business and finances. They are open to change; they have the ability to make decisions and carry them out. Villagers usually are not like that.

"When city people are converted and truly following the Lord and the instruction of the Bible, you have the resources necessary for church work, for theological education and other activities. You name it, you have the kind of people who get things done."

King's study of mission strategy strengthened his conviction. For example, Roland Allen in his book, *Missionary Methods: St. Paul's or Ours*, noted that God led Paul to establish churches in great cities of the Roman Empire. Before AD 47 there were no churches in Galatia, Macedonia, Achaia or Asia. But ten years later he considered his work to be done in those provinces because in each area churches were established and taking up the work of evangelism.

Allen pointed out that all the major cities chosen by Paul shared common features: Each was a center of Roman administration, Greek culture, Jewish influence and world commerce. They were crossroads of the empire. Allen called them "centers of light" from which radiated the gospel into surrounding areas and finally the entire provinces.

In contradiction of this New Testament strategy, King noted, "The concentration of evangelical missionaries, apart from a few exceptions, will be found the smallest and weakest in the largest city centers. Evangelicals tend to concentrate on going to the remote mountain or jungle people in difficult-access areas—places with 'glamour appeal.' "

Reaching the last unreached peoples and going where no others have gone with the gospel would always have a high priority for Alliance missions, he believed. "But there is a strong tendency to expend principal energies on that which appeals to the popular imagination and pass by the vast concentrated urban populations."[16]

When King saw that happening in Vietnam in 1954, he kept silent. But in 1958, during the Second Asia Conference in Saigon, the decisive moment had come to set in motion still another wheel in a wheel: urban work. It would be a bold new strategy that would profoundly impact global Alliance missions—and none too soon.

World population projections at the time, though later revised, gave a sense of urgency to King's plans and would only grow more serious. Three percent of the world lived in cities in 1800. That number rose to thirteen percent by 1900. Studies indicated that by the year 2000 the cities would claim eighty-seven percent of the world's population.[17]

The topic of urban church planting came up at the Saigon conference and was roundly discussed. It emerged again during a dinner invitation to the home of Curwin Smith, United Bible Societies agent in Saigon and a former Alliance missionary. Other dinner guests were Le-van-Thai, church president; Jack Revelle, Mission chairman; and Philip Loh, pastor of the affiliated Chinese church in Saigon.

"As we sat around the table, Mr. Thai brought up the subject of the morning: city work. I asked how the Mission could partner with the Church to launch such an effort. Ideas were bandied around and the outline of a strategy began to develop."

Based on that discussion, King returned to New York and drafted a plan for opening city churches, using Saigon as a pilot project. The executive committees of the Mission and the Church in Vietnam approved the proposal. Key points were:
1. Financial help would be given only to churches in the capitals of provinces and port cities.
2. There must be an existing group of Christians supporting their worker.
3. This group must assume at least one-third of the cost.
4. The C&MA grant (as a gift) would be one-third of the cost.
5. The C&MA would help with a long-term, noninterest loan for the other one-third of the construction cost, this loan to be paid back to the National Church for future building programs.
6. This program would apply only to the opening of new churches.
7. The C&MA would pay the rent of a meeting place for a limited amount of time.

The Vietnamese church in Saigon released several families to become the nucleus of a new congregation in the vicinity of their homes. The mother church agreed to pay the salary of the new church's pastor for six months. The Mission assigned veteran Paul Carlson to work on the project.

Lay members in witnessing bands were crucial to the campaign. Going door-to-door, they distributed literature about the planned opening of an evangelical church in their district. They invited residents to attend the opening series of evangelistic services. For eight successive weeks they blanketed the area with a series of tracts that presented the gospel, explained what the church was and offered other opportunities to know more through radio broadcasts and Bible correspondence courses.

The plan was a winner. By 1961, seven churches were started. By the time South Vietnam collapsed, Saigon had forty-three churches. Success in Vietnam encouraged the Mission and the national church in Hong Kong to develop their own urban strategy, combining elements of the Saigon plan with new ones suited for the Crown Colony. The same thing happened in Africa and Latin America. Universal principles combined with homegrown applications catapulted the C&MA into a major force in urban evangelism as well as continuing to pioneer among the most remote, primitive peoples.

And it all began with discussion around a dining table in Saigon.

Mass Movements

Even while discussions in Vietnam centered on a carefully detailed strategy for urban church planting, spontaneous people movements toward God were exploding in Irian Jaya. It would become another of the wheels within the wheel, one that could only be attributed to divine initiative, not human planning. The two approaches could not be more dissimilar, but King believed in both and supported both. The results were astonishing, a reminder that God cannot be put into a box.

As a missionary to India, King had heard about a people movement in India and was won over to the concept. Homeward bound by ship at the end of his term, he had read the manuscript of Donald McGavran's *Bridges of God*. He was "enamored" with the soundness and potential of people groups in some cultures making a collective decision to follow Christ. He believed their group act could be as valid as individual conversions in other cultures. At the time he had no way to implement the plan, but he developed a close relationship with McGavran and bided his time.

Several years passed before the opportunity suddenly presented itself in Irian Jaya. "The Uhunduni tribespeople were the first to take a definite stand against spirit appeasement, white magic and sorcery," reported Viola Post, who worked with her husband Walter in the Ilaga Valley. "On Easter Sunday morning in 1957 they burned their idolatrous charms. This was a spark that set off a mass movement toward the Lord."[18]

Missionary John Ellenberger reported how the Ilaga Uhunduni (now Damal) came to the Lord in a manner typical of the whole spiritual phenomenon. About 350 tribal people had been hearing the gospel for over a year and discussing among themselves what to do. Some put away their charms and determined to follow Jesus. A delegation came to the missionaries to announce their intention: "We and our people love Jesus and we want to put away our spirit appeasement." But they waited another month until the whole group was unified in its decision before taking the next step.

On Easter Sunday, singing "We Will Follow Jesus," over 1,000 Damal piled their fetishes, worth thousands of dollars, on a bonfire. Then they erupted in shouts and dances of joy. The same pattern was repeated again and again as whole segments of the population turned en masse to Christ.

The spiritual awakening spread to the adjoining Beoga Valley. A delegation came to the missionary, asking to follow the Lord. He advised them, however, to wait until they knew more about the Jesus way.

"Several months later," Mrs. Post wrote,

> they detained another missionary on a trip through their country, saying, "We have desired the Lord for this long time. We have one mind to follow the Lord. We won't let you go until we have burned our fetishes."
>
> They burned them the next day, dancing to express their joy. Several times the dance abruptly stopped and they reminded each other that now they had no fear of the spirits, and [rehearsed] the various things they must do in obeying the Word of God. Then joyously they would resume their dance.[19]

King reported that in 2 years over 1,000 converts were baptized. Approximately 2,000 more qualified for baptism and another 4,000 were being prepared.[20]

A similar spiritual awakening came to the Baliem Valley in 1960. King reported,

> After six years of no response, on one Sunday morning 8,000 Dani tribesmen converged on Pyramid [station]. Five thousand of them laid their devil charms and implements of war in a pile, seventy feet long and three feet high, and set it afire as they sang, "We will follow Jesus." The next day 3,000 others laid their charms and weapons on the previous day's ashes.[21]

The challenge of discipling masses of people in transit from raw, primitive paganism to new life in Christ was enormous. As missionary Gordon Larson put it, "Of course, these new converts from savage ways are weak. They lack almost everything we consider as necessary aids to spiritual growth. The language has yet to be fully reduced to writing, and the translation of the Bible will take a long time after that."[22]

When King first heard of the people movements in Irian Jaya, he knew immediately what to do. He called McGavran. "I kept in contact with him as to how to handle this, and followed his instructions very carefully," he said.

One very practical bit of advice from McGavran related to the Scriptures. He encouraged the missionaries always to refer to the Book even if it had not yet been translated into the local language. He suggested they hold the Bible in their hand as they spoke or hang it in a bag visible to the whole group. When they referred to a scriptural passage they could point to it and explain, "What I am saying is in that Book. When we get it translated, you must tie yourself to it."

The new believers, being illiterate, gathered in groups and repeated Scripture passages until everyone had learned them by heart. New Christian leaders followed the same procedure. Taught by missionaries in witness schools, they then spread out to share with village groups the Bible stories they had memorized. Since there was no indigenous hymnody, missionaries wrote new words to familiar chants. And, in a calculated and carefully reasoned step, the national Christians were encouraged to retain as much of their culture as possible, including their scanty traditional coverings instead of Western clothes.

Some of the veteran missionaries were not at all convinced of the depth or validity of group conversions. Unless individuals made personal decisions to follow Christ, they insisted, the whole aspect of personal responsibility was negated and the result would be shallow, name-only Christians.

Missionaries Donald and Alice Gibbons, first to live among the Damal, disagreed. They had read *Bridges of God* and were convinced the mass movement among the Damal was of God. They encountered considerable flack from those who thought they were encouraging something less than New Testament conversion. The Gibbonses appealed to King for guidance.

Years later they wrote to King, "We were young missionaries and some of our older colleagues questioned what was happening and others openly criticized. We've always appreciated how you investigated and then stood behind us in confirming that this was God's work, not man's. Through the years God has confirmed to everyone the work He did in the hearts of these primitive people. Of all who have followed the Lord here in Irian Jaya, none have been stronger in their faith than those who first heard the message of the gospel."

A new chapter in Church history was being enacted in Irian Jaya's mountain ranges and high valleys. The spontaneous spiritual awakening spread rapidly through the valleys from the Ilaga, to the Beoga, to the Baliem, marking its progress with large numbers of people reveling in a newfound kingdom while still at home in their familiar culture.

The annual report to Council for 1959 summed up the phenomenon in Irian Jaya:

> No government arrangement for occupation can stop the spread of the gospel; no mission boundaries can keep the building of the Church of Jesus Christ from going forward. The Dani have no idea of such boundaries; they travel freely among friends and relatives. As a result, the moving of the Spirit has now spread into other valleys occupied by other missions, and on into the Grand Valley of the Baliem.[23]

One Chief's Faith

Did the group conversions hold up over time? Michael (Buzz) and Myrna Maxey, serving as community developers with the C&MA in the area where the people movements took place in the 1950s, wrote of one man's enduring faith.

The story began in early 2001 when a military plane crashed in the mountains near Wamena where the Maxeys lived. Some villagers told Buzz of a plane circling over the valley "like a bird hit by a stone." He radioed the information to the Search and Rescue command center. The wreckage was discovered the next day by a Mission Aviation Fellowship plane. A rescue team airlifted to the site by helicopters reported no survivors, but the task remained to bring back the bodies for decent burial.

Then storm clouds blew in. Nothing more could be done until the weather cleared. Bad weather again hampered operations the next day. By the third day the situation was getting desperate for the investigators stranded at the crash site. They were drenched in freezing rain, and the altitude of 12,000 feet forced them to use a dwindling supply of bottled oxygen. Weather was becoming a crucial factor.

Maxey picked up the story:

An officer in charge of the operation asked if the tribe had any spiritual mediums or witch doctors who could move the clouds away. He offered to bring in pigs to sacrifice to the gods of the mountains as well.

Before the gospel had arrived, the people had indeed appeased the spirits with sacrifices. Now they only relied on God to move the clouds away. "Would you be willing to request God to give good weather?" he asked.

I gathered the villagers together and asked that Chief Amene pray. Amene is an old war chief who had led his tribe into battle many times. His life had been changed, and now he walks with God. Amene led in a powerful prayer requesting blue sky in the name of "my older brother Jesus and the Spirit that controls the sky."

I peeked during the prayer because the urge was so great. Next to me was the colonel with his arms outstretched and his palms turned up. Next to him was the brigadier general in charge. He too was in the Muslim posture of prayer. The soldiers had put their guns down, and the four helicopter crews stood respectfully at attention.

My heart was warmed as I listened to Chief Amene pray. He wore a tattered hat, shabby clothes and no shoes. The old warrior was weak in body and he knew little of the outside world, but he knew a lot about the Spirit, his God, who controls the skies. Amene was God's general and that day he was in charge. He possessed more power and authority than anyone else assembled on the airstrip.

As the next day dawned, we eagerly waited. What had Amene's "older brother" decided to do with the clouds that day? As the night disappeared and was replaced with daylight, we saw only blue sky clear of clouds. Helicopters flew into action, and before 8 a.m. the work was over. Nine bodies had been retrieved from the wreckage of the plane. Search-and-rescue teams and soldiers had all been rescued. Everyone was ecstatic, thrilled that the mission had been successful.

After I took everyone's picture, someone asked if we might pray again. I noticed it was one of the helicopter pilots of another faith whom I had befriended. I was honored. In my prayer I thanked God for the good weather, safety for the pilots and comfort for those who were grieving.

When I had finished, I noticed some wiping tears from their eyes. Many embraced me in sincere appreciation. With tears in his eyes, the colonel expressed his thanks, and the general put his arms around me. Having accomplished their mission, they climbed into their helicopter and were soon lifting off.

When the last aircraft was out of sight, the valley was quiet. I turned around to see my old friend Chief Amene. God's general in charge was grinning and pointing towards the sky. "The God of the skies answered. Our older brother Jesus is here," he said. I knew it. Chief Amene knew it. And the military men flying home in the choppers knew it. Then he grasped his walking stick and shuffled off into the direction of his village.[24]

God cannot be put in a box. Whether seekers come to Him one by one, or by a group decision, He can work the same miracle of enduring grace. Chief Amene knew that too.

Jaffray School of Missions

During that same eventful first term of King's service as foreign secretary, when so many small wheels were turning in the wheel of missions, he set in motion still another one. It was as distinctly different from programmed urban evangelism and spontaneous people movements as the two were from each other. Yet this new wheel would fit well with the others, adding power to the forward motion of Alliance missions. His vision was the creation of a graduate-level school to prepare overseas candidates for service in a rapidly changing world.

In one sense, the idea was not new. From 1910 to 1912, the official C&MA magazine edited by Simpson repeatedly supported the proposition that Nyack should become a multi-school campus. It would include a junior college, a liberal arts college and a three-year seminary.

In his 1911 report of the academic year, William C. Stevens, dean of the Missionary Training Institute, wrote, "Finally, brethren, 'the Nyack Missionary University!' It is already at least the cloud of the size of a man's hand on the horizon."[25]

The proposal came to General Council in 1914—and the cloud Stevens referred to suddenly evaporated. "The reason given for the council action was a shortage of money. All the limited funds during the unsettled war years were needed for overseas outreach.... However, opposition to higher education was already building. Alliance workers and lay people were well aware that the liberal movement had its source and support mainly in denominational universities."[26]

The World His Field

Princeton Seminary was just one of the schools at the very center of controversy, pushing a liberal view of theology that convulsed and divided the Presbyterian denomination. Louis was well aware of this reality, but he was nonetheless convinced of a need for advanced schooling, as were others in the Alliance. By the time he headed the overseas work, the topic was again being debated on the Council floor.

A back-page report in *The Alliance Witness* gave the rationale for such a school. It bore King's unmistakable imprint:

> Problems confronting today's missionary are particularly demanding. Permitting our young workers to plunge into the maelstroms of unfamiliar political, social and religious upheaval without proper forearming is folly.
>
> Their relation to the development and expression of the younger churches is a matter of concern too fundamental to leave for casual development. The obligation to intellectual competence and experiential apprehension in matters of Biblical authority is even more basic.[27]

G. Linwood Barney, in giving a rationale for establishment of the school for advanced studies in missions, referred to Ralph Winter in *The 25 Unbelievable Years: 1945-1969*. Winter showed how much the world was changing. He gave a chart showing that 99.5 percent of the non-Western world under foreign colonial domination prior to 1945. By 1960, when the much-debated new Alliance school opened its doors, over ninety-five percent of former colonies were already autonomous. Nine years later 99.5 percent of the non-Western world was independent.[28]

This radical reversal of political roles overseas had enormous implications for missionary work. Not only were nationals in the driver's seat politically, increasing numbers were college graduates and earning doctorates. "Standards were being raised in the new nations," King observed, "and we felt our Alliance missionaries would be considered second-class men and women if we didn't do something about it.

"Already missionaries were beginning to rub up against an ever-growing number of nationals better educated than they were. Moreover, I believed the Alliance ought to be ahead in the field of preparation. If we didn't, young people would not choose service with the C&MA."

A core group at "260" moved the discussion to an initial proposal in December 1957. William Smalley, Bernard King, George Constance and Louis King produced a one-page "Proposed Year of Special Missionary Studies." Invitation to join the planners went out to Smalley's son William (a former Alliance missionary who was at the time working with the American Bible Society) and G. Linwood Barney, chairman of the missions department of St. Paul Bible Institute. Jack Shepherd, missions department chairman at Nyack College, joined the group as well.

Later, Gilbert H. Johnson, education secretary; Harold W. Boon, Nyack College president; and his successor, Thomas P. Bailey, were indispensable in launching the Council-approved school. According to Shepherd, however, "Louis King was the prime mover in getting [the school] under way."

The new institution was called Jaffray School of Missions (JSM). Its namesake, Robert A. Jaffray, already a legendary veteran missionary to China, at age fifty-seven spearheaded the entrance of Alliance missions in Vietnam and Indonesia. He did so over the objections of "260" because at the time the Great Depression was hamstringing churches and offerings were down. He died in a Japanese prison camp shortly before World War II ended. Planners of the new school wanted it to reflect his daring, selfless commitment to the Lord's work.

A missionary interned with Jaffray in a Japanese prison camp recounted an experience that proved how appropriate it was to name the new missions school after Jaffray.

> I remember again an afternoon in 1942 when I saw an old man dreaming dreams.
>
> Sitting in a corner of a little house in which we were imprisoned in the mountains, the old man was intent in the study of a map of that great sweep of islands then known as the Netherlands East Indies. How often we'd pore over that map and mentally check off the cities and islands as they were invaded or fell . . . Singapore, Sumatra, Java and Celebes. "These, lassie," he said as I knelt by the chair, "are the areas we must enter as soon as the war is over."
>
> My thoughts were so full of the fears and anxieties, separations and tales of atrocities which had become a part of our daily life. Suddenly I realized that to him they were but passing events that never altered the program of reaching the unreached, events that never marred the dream. . . . "This is our task and I can hear the sound of a gong in the tops of the mulberry trees, and the noise of the marching feet of the mighty army of young men and women that God is preparing for the occupation of these areas!"[29]

Jaffray, as the school was called, welcomed its first class in 1960, occupying part of Nyack College's north campus. Although operating under the college's charter until it gained accreditation, JSM had its own faculty, staff and budget.

In the development stage, the school did not take its cue from other institutions of higher learning. The planners determined to break new ground that would make the school distinctly Alliance. It would be "cut from whole cloth," said one of the organizers. However, there were striking similarities between Jaffray and Simpson's original Missionary Training College organized sixty years earlier in New York City.

Both schools were homegrown; they had to embody and support priorities of the Alliance. Just as Simpson expressed dissatisfaction with seminaries of his day and the need to "unlearn much of what man had crammed into our heads," King would echo the same frustration. The C&MA standard by which all missionary activity must eventually be evaluated was its commitment to the indigenous church policy. Too often, candidates from non-Alliance schools had to "unlearn" concepts unsympathetic to this bottom-line goal before they could be useful in Alliance work.

Another basic feature the two schools shared was an emphasis on applied learning. Their one-year curricula evidenced a strong streak of pragmatism: The ultimate result of schooling was not to earn a degree but an education that prepared the student for the realities of overseas service for the Master. Neither school initially offered an academic degree, although JSM students had to possess a college degree as a prerequisite.

Entrance requirements reflected this specialized vocation. For the earlier school the only qualification required of applicants was "that they had given up all for Christ, and His work meant all to them."[30] JSM repeated the same high spiritual standard and ministry focus as well as academic requirements: "Enrollment is limited and those who apply must possess outstanding Christian character and show evidence of a missionary call."[31]

The limited-enrollment factor helped explain why there was little fanfare or promotion of JSM even though it was an historic step for the Alliance. Classes also were kept deliberately small because of the method of instruction.

In terms of educational philosophy, JSM was very different from the earlier school's formal lecture style of teaching. The new school would pioneer a method of instruction that in King's words would be a "hazard to accreditation because of the avant-garde concept of the program that Shepherd, Barney, the two Smalleys and I envisioned. By avant-garde I mean there would be a great deal of team teaching. If it were a course in missions, for example, a theology professor would be on hand as well to debate with the missions professor from a theological and biblical viewpoint."

Shepherd and Barney, the two original full-time professors, were well suited for team-teaching. Shepherd, a former missionary to China and the Philippines, was theologically oriented, very analytical and incisive, possessing "one of the finest minds in the Alliance," according to his peers. King wrote to him later, "I know of no other person who could have done what you have to launch so very well the JSM, and I don't think we'll find in any other the combination of unique qualifications that you possess."

Barney, an affable former missionary to Laos, approached his ministry from a linguist's and an anthropologist's perspective. He and his wife Elsie had been planning to work among the tribes of Vietnam. But a great turning to God among the Hmong people group in Northern Laos prompted the Foreign Department to redirect them to Laos.

With his training by Wycliffe Bible Translators, Barney reduced the unwritten Hmong language to a romanized alphabet similar to the one used in English. Although working with a tonal language, he managed to indicate the tone by final consonants. This made translation work and literature easier to print and quicker to learn.

Shepherd and Barney had already worked well together, teaching courses at St. Paul Bible Institute. Barney called their team approach "the creative nature of the interface between biblical theology and the insights of socio-cultural anthropology. At Jaffray we sought to bring these two disciplines into creative tensions in understanding, teaching and demonstrating the missionary nature of the Church."

The exchange between the teaching duo was often truly "creative tension." Each professor felt free to comment on the other's lecture, either to agree or challenge in front of the class. The students loved the exchange and often joined in, either to take sides or stake a position of their own.

On one occasion, King squared off with guest speaker David Stowe of the NCC Division of Overseas Ministries. Their topic was apostasy in the World Council of Churches. "An exciting interchange and sometimes free-for-all discussion ensued," he recalled. "Dr. Stowe admitted my presentation mirrored a fair 'image' of Protestant ecumenism as represented by the WCC."

In addition to the focus on the missionary nature of the Church and the interaction between theology and anthropology, Jaffray added a third emphasis: One must earn the right to be heard. In the brave new world of fledgling nations, Westerners could no longer assume ready acceptance based on their race or nationality. They now had to prove their worth in tangibles such as language expertise, cultural sensitivity and personal compatibility. Through a demanding curriculum and close spiritual community life, JSM students learned how to earn that right.

The Jaffray School of Missions did not have a long lifespan as institutions go. It was evolving into something more comprehensive to meet the wide-ranging needs of Alliance pastorates as well as overseas fields. JSM (1960-1974) became the Alliance School of Theology and Missions (1974-1979), reflecting that broader service to the denomination. The third phase, Alliance Theological Seminary in 1979, began an essential and permanent part of the total C&MA organization. The pivotal roles of Shepherd, JSM executive director, and Barney, dean of faculty, earned for them a place of distinction for all time in the Alliance.

The People Factor

Reviewing the big issues that crowded King's first term as foreign secretary—councils and conferences, strategies and movements, major issues debated and defended—it would be easy to overlook another dimension that was a constant throughout his public years of ministry as a high-ranking leader in the Alliance.

He was ever alert to identify people on whom he sensed the hand of God. He kept track of them, investing time to encourage and counsel them. Then, when just the right opportunity opened, he carefully but confidently expressed his conviction concerning God's leading in their lives: "The call of the church is the call of the Lord." The challenge seldom went unheeded.

He met one such promising person during an early trip to Asia. Philip Teng was a young Hong Kong pastor, tall and trim, wearing the dark-rimmed glasses favored by many Chinese at the time. Even as a young man, he was quiet and deliberate, but with a poise that spoke of inner strength.

Teng already had become well-known in Hong Kong Alliance circles. Although the son of a Presbyterian pastor, and with a theological degree from the University of Edinburgh in Scotland, he gravitated toward the C&MA. Having married an Alliance girl was one good reason why, but the quality of Alliance teaching and people also attracted him. He preached in their churches, did translation for the Alliance Press and taught at the C&MA seminary on Cheung Chau Island.

"It was obvious to me," King said after they met, "[that] he was a potential giant and I was gratified he had opted for the Alliance."

King spent almost a full day with Teng, covering a wide range of topics. On most points they were agreed, but not concerning the Alliance policy on the indigenous church. "He favored missions doing what they had always done in a traditional way," King said.

Teng questioned him on his reasons for advocating the C&MA position. "He was doing it like a student asking questions and weighing answers," King recalled. "However, by the end of the day he was quite a convert to the whole concept of the indigenous church. We even discussed how a church could be missionary on its own, and ought to be, in obedience to the Lord or else it was not an obedient church."

At the time, Teng was pastor of a small Alliance church that in itself was an amazing story. The North Point Church had invited him to preach when it formally opened. It was a rather farfetched hope, because Teng was much in demand as a speaker. Already he had preached in at least half of Hong Kong's 300 churches. It would be a concession for him to speak to a small group in a chapel hardly bigger than a modest motel room. But he agreed to come.

On the night after the service, he could not sleep. "The North Point Church came suddenly to mind," he recounted, "and I could not shake it off. It possessed me with a strange power."[32]

When the church in an equally audacious move invited Teng to be pastor, he again accepted. The congregation quickly outgrew its small chapel and several other locations, in one year accepting 100 new members.

Characteristically, the young pastor put everything he had into the work. He told how a successful dentist in the congregation offered to keep his wardrobe current with a continuous supply of quality suits. Teng accepted the offer—on condition he be permitted to use the money as he saw best. Then he put the money into the church, saying his old suits were good enough.

The burgeoning church finally moved to a major intersection of Hong Kong. Along the way, Teng added an English-language service for expatriates in the city. It also prospered rapidly. The two congregations became powerful witnesses for Christ. Heeding King's advice, Teng inaugurated missionary conventions that led to the founding of a mission-sending agency in the North Point Church. To date, the church has sent and supported dozens of missionaries in other countries.

As the North Point Church grew in prominence, Teng gained stature throughout Asia. He was invited to pastor a large church in Singapore and also to teach in a well-established union seminary. When he asked King what he should do, the response was, "Better not."

King's experience with seminaries in South America and Africa that were sponsored by several groups was not positive. "Sooner or later," he told Teng, "friction develops when one of the cooperating groups assigns to the school someone who does not preach the whole counsel of God. You ought to stick with what you are doing," he suggested. And Teng followed his advice.

Later, Teng took a sabbatical from North Point to serve as a missionary in Indonesia for one year, setting an example to the Chinese Christians in Hong Kong. He was concerned that in his absence the churches might lose momentum in their commitment to missions. Instead, they gave $117,390 (US) to support twenty-five missionaries in nine countries.[33]

Teng went on to become a towering figure not only in the Hong Kong (C&MA) Church Union and the colony's evangelical community, but also among the many expatriate Chinese Christians across the globe and in the worldwide evangelical movement. The friendship between King and Teng deepened in the decades following that decisive time in the young pastor's life.

Reality Reminder

One tragic event took place toward the end of King's second term, the kind of situation all mission leaders pray will never happen. The night of

May 30, 1962, began like any other at the C&MA leprosarium near Banmethuout, Vietnam. Nurses bedded down their patients, cooking fires of visiting relatives faded into wisps of smoke, dogs and chickens settled down for the night and lights in the staff houses blinked out one-by-one.

Not until the Viet Cong guerillas had infiltrated the station and started hammering on doors did anyone realize a raid was in progress. Because the medical people considered their work nonpolitical and it was very popular with the local population, they had thought themselves immune from the war that was destroying Vietnam. They were wrong.

Alliance missionaries Dr. Ardell Vietti and Archie Mitchell, along with Mennonite volunteer Dan Gerber, were hustled off into the jungle, but not before the guerrillas cleaned out the clinic, seizing medicines, bandages, clothing and instruments, no doubt intended to care for their wounded comrades—and probably also the reason they targeted the medical missionary for abduction. The other missionaries, including Mitchell's wife Betty, were released when the raiding party left.

Nine months passed before Grady Mangham, field director, sent a cable to New York: "Authentically reported three alive. Good health. Hallelujah!" This information came from the Viet Cong officer who had led the raid on the leprosarium and later was captured by South Vietnamese forces.

The jungle again closed its tangled curtain to cloak the fate of the three abducted workers. Not until September of 1963 did *The Alliance Witness* carry another notice that the three had been seen alive and well. "The report [from nationals whose information is considered reliable] indicates they are closely guarded but are having opportunities to witness."[34]

Mission and Church leaders in Vietnam and the C&MA in New York tried repeatedly and unsuccessfully to win the captives' release. Efforts by the State Department, the United Nations and humanitarian organizations were equally fruitless.

On one occasion, King sat across the table from a North Vietnamese officer in Saigon and pled for their return. With stony indifference the officer replied, "You are worried about three of your people. What about the thousands of my people who are missing?" Neither the Communists nor the jungle would give up their secrets about the fate of the three cap-

The World His Field

tives. As a special BBC radio feature noted in 1999, Dr. Vietti remains the last civilian woman captive unaccounted for in Vietnam.

King began his years as foreign secretary with the analogy of the Alliance like a conveyance that required forward motion to avoid toppling over in the ecclesiastical heap. In the wheel of missions he set in motion smaller ones that powered its progress. The Banmethuot tragedy was a reminder that more sacrifices and risks would lie on the road ahead. The toll exacted would make the advance costly—and more certain.

Notes

1. Louis L. King, "Report of the Foreign Department," *Minutes of the General Council 1958 and Annual Report for 1957* (New York: The Christian and Missionary Alliance, 1958), p. 62.
2. Ibid., p. 79ff.
3. Louis L. King, "Report on the South America Trip," *Report of the Foreign Department to the Board of Managers* (August 13-14, 1957), pp. 1-4.
4. Louis L. King, "South American Administrative Trip," *Report to the Foreign Department* (December 31, 1966-February 7, 1967), p. 6.
5. Louis L. King, "Report of the Trip to Holland, France, West Africa, Gabon, and Congo," *Report of the Foreign Department to the Board of Managers* (March 24-26, 1959), p. 1.
6. Louis L. King, "On the Homejo Trail," *The Alliance Weekly*, March 14, 1956, pp. 9-10.
7. Louis L. King, "The Practical Implications Arising from Dr. Charles E. Ryrie's Paper" (July 1963), p. 1.
8. Ibid., p. 2.
9. Ibid., p. 4.
10. Ibid., p. 5.
11. Ibid.
12. Ibid.
13. Dale S. Heredeen, "Buildings Built for Faith," *The Alliance Witness*, September 6, 1961, p. 10.
14. Louis L. King, "Report of the Foreign Department," *Minutes of the General Council 1959 and Annual Report for 1958* (New York: The Christian and Missionary Alliance, 1959), p. 66.
15. Louis L. King, "Second Asia Conference," *The Alliance Weekly*, May 7, 1958, p. 11.
16. Louis L. King, "Urbanization and Missions" (study paper for the Foreign Department, November 28, 1960), p. 3.
17. "Mission to an Urban World," *Church Growth Bulletin*, September 1975.
18. Mrs. Walter M. Post, "Masses Move Toward Christ in New Guinea," *The Alliance Witness*, March 11, 1959, pp. 12-3.

19. Ibid., p. 13.
20. Louis L. King, "The Gospel Outruns the Missionary," *The Alliance Witness*, February 24, 1960, p. 8.
21. Louis L. King, "Be Not Discouraged," *The Alliance Witness*, May 14, 1980, p. 6.
22. Gordon Larson, "God Moved Upon the People of a Hundred Valleys," *The Alliance Witness*, March 25, 1959, p. 13.
23. Louis L. King, "Report of the Foreign Department," *Minutes of the General Council 1960 and Annual Report for 1959* (New York: The Christian and Missionary Alliance, 1960), p. 159.
24. Michael "Buzz" Maxey, "Chief Amene," *Indonesian Insights*, April-May 2001, p. 3.
25. Robert L. Niklaus, "The School that Vision Built," *Missionarian 1982* (Nyack, NY: Nyack College, 1982), p. 17.
26. Robert L. Niklaus, John S. Sawin, Samuel J. Stoez, *All for Jesus: God at Work in The Christian and Missionary Alliance Over One Hundred Years* (Camp Hill, PA: Christian Publications, Inc., 1986), p. 128.
27. "The Jaffray School of Missions," *The Alliance Witness*, May 18, 1960, back cover.
28. G. Linwood Barney, "Jaffray School of Missions: A Vision Uncovered" (paper given at the thirtieth anniversary of the school's founding, 1990), p. 3. Quoted from Ralph D. Winter, *The 25 Unbelievable Years: 1945-1969* (South Pasadena, CA: William Carey Library, 1970), p. 12.
29. Harry M. Shuman, "Annual Report of the President," *Minutes of the General Council 1953 and Annual Report for 1952* (New York: The Christian and Missionary Alliance, 1953), p. 9.
30. Niklaus, et al., *All for Jesus*, p. 59.
31. Gilbert H. Johnson, "Report of the Education Department," *Minutes of the General Council 1961 and Annual Report for 1960* (New York: The Christian and Missionary Alliance, 1961), p. 31.
32. "North Point Alliance Church," *Foreign Field Flashes*, October 1966, p. 1.
33. "The Fields in 1977," *Appendix VI, Minutes of the General Council 1978 and Annual Report for 1977* (Nyack, NY: The Christian and Missionary Alliance, 1978), p. 133.
34. "News Flash," *The Alliance Witness*, September 18, 1963, p. 8.

EIGHT
The World His Field

1963-1968
Time Markers

In 1963 President Kennedy went to Berlin to show his support for the free citizens of the divided city. Germans will never forget his words, "Ich bin ein Berliner." It may have been his last memorable declaration. Before the year ended, he was shot in Dallas. The President's death was just one of many more deaths to come as the US sank deeper into the quagmire of Vietnam.

The year 1968 had its share of good and bad. President Johnson halted the bombing of North Vietnam and peace talks began in Paris. The dark side of 1968 included the murder of Martin Luther King, Jr., in Memphis. Race riots spread to forty cities. Robert Kennedy was shot in a Los Angeles hotel. Soviet troops marched into Czechoslovakia to put down a revolt against Communism.

The middle and later years of the decade marked the high tide and receding of the religious movement that had begun during the early war years—at least in the mainline churches. Hare Krishna and Sun Myung Moon's Unification Church attracted growing numbers. New York's Metropolitan Community Church with its following of gays and lesbians expanded into the Universal Fellowship of Community Churches. The Mormons became one of the fastest growing religious groups.

Meanwhile, evangelicals and Pentecostals gained in numbers and acceptance. Glossolalia (speaking in tongues) spread in traditional churches. Charismatic renewal cropped up on a number of campuses, including Harvard, Yale and Notre Dame.

The "Death of God" movement widened the distance between doctrinal liberals and conservatives. A *Time* magazine cover story in October 1965 blazoned the title "Christian Atheism." Pastors who had scuttled the primacy of Scriptures struggled to tell society how to behave in a world where God was deemed no longer active or relevant.

★ ★ ★

C&MA president Bailey responded to the "Death of God" issue. He told the 1968 General Council in Raleigh, "A current topic among the theologians who are always quick to consider 'some new thing' is what is now being called 'the theology of hope.' Edward B. Fiske, writing in the *New York Times*, says that eschatology, largely ignored by Christian thinkers for 1,800 years, has replaced the 'Death of God' theology as the most avant garde issue in both Protestant and Roman Catholic circles." Bailey noted that the Alliance had always held the Blessed Hope as the fourth tenet of the Fourfold Gospel.

The living God certainly had been much in evidence during the 1960s in Alliance work. The Afro-Asian Literature Conference in Hong Kong during April 1963 reported that tens of thousands of correspondence courses were in use throughout Asia; Mission presses published more than 107 million pages of literature. Each week 172 radio broadcasts overseas carried the gospel in 20 languages. Medical facilities reported treating almost 209,000 outpatients that year in their clinics and hospitals.

A preemptive strike by the military in Indonesia during 1965 averted a Communist coup and the planned massacre of government leaders and foreigners, including missionaries. The aborted coup in Indonesia and the army's brutal suppression caused Indonesians to take a new look at Christianity in 1966.

The first Alliance Youth Corps numbered ten college students sent to three overseas assignments in 1967. The murder of six missionaries in Banmethuout, Vietnam, in 1968 did not stop the North American C&MA from appointing sixty-seven new recruits. Nor did Catholic opposition in Colombia keep evangelicals from launching a national Evangelism-in-Depth effort. Some 20,000 Colombians reportedly sought Christ in the nationwide campaign.

Home secretary Pippert also appealed for more of the General Fund to make grants and loans. He insisted, "We *must* have large sums of money available for extension." He initiated the "Blueprint for Action" in December 1968 to establish 100 new churches in 3 years. It was the first coordinated program for extension efforts in the C&MA.

First he was a missionary to India. Next he became area secretary for all of Asia and the Pacific Islands. Then he moved to the Office of Foreign Secretary, still deeply involved in Asian ventures such as regional conferences, urban church planting and people movements toward God. It might be assumed he would continue to tilt toward the mission fields of that region.

Not so. The world became his field.

King's extensive travels in Latin America, Africa and Europe made clear he would follow the Spirit's working no matter where it took him. Some momentous achievements of his administration grew out of crises in Africa. He would preside over Latin American fields, historically dominated by the Roman Catholic Church, when a great shift took place in favor of the Protestants. And in every direction he would give credit to missionaries as the ones who got the job done.

Double-Duty Mom

How much would have been accomplished if his home base were weak? This is unclear. But when King was later elected president, the first thing he did was to call his wife to the platform and present her to the delegates with a moving tribute to her part in his ministry.

It was not a mere "politically correct" gesture. His world actually began at home. To his four sons, Esther was "double-duty Mom," as Stephen put it. Mark called her "a rock of stability." Louis could confidently roam the planet because she had the family well in hand.

His absence from home for months at a time was a matter of conviction, not choice. King believed that if he were obedient to the "call of the Church," God would take care of his family. As for Esther, when someone asked if at times she wished he were home, she snorted, "I wish he were home all the time."

Mark recalled, "Regrettably for me, my father's obligations took him away from home for long periods of time. Although I understood why, I missed having a father come home every night. When he did come home, he oftentimes seemed preoccupied with burdens and responsibilities. I always knew, however, that I was loved completely by both parents."

Louis and Esther made a pact at the beginning of his world-encircling ministry. They would write to each other every day. For example, Mark was six months old when his dad went on a three-month itinerary. Esther kept a daily diary of all that happened so Louis would not miss out on changes in Mark during those fast-growing first months. It was a rare and difficult day the parents did not write to each other. Esther shared with the boys most of the information she received from Louis so they always knew where he was and what he was doing.

Esther assumed her role as a single mom most of the time without breaking stride. "The Lord prepared me for boys rather than girls," she said. "I never cared two cents about fashion or all the things girls were supposed to do. I didn't like dolls either, or sitting around with a bunch of girls. I would rather be out playing baseball, even football."

She was, in a word, an unabashed tomboy. "I was," she agreed, "right from the beginning. The Lord knew what was coming so He got me ready in advance. Looking back now, though, I wonder how I ever did it. But I wasn't thrown in with four boys all at once. I just got one at a time, and took a day at a time."

Among other things, Esther taught Mark how to fish like she had when growing up. This meant he had to get up in predawn darkness to catch nightcrawlers with the help of a flashlight. Mother and son traveled to nearby Lake Welch where she rented a rowboat. She taught Mark how to row and turned the job over to him. "We didn't have fishing poles or fancy equipment," he said. "We fished like Mom did: just a string, a sinker and a hook with a worm as bait."

Stephen said that when his dad came home from work, the first thing he did after walking in the door was to kiss his wife. If the boys were home, he shook hands. Then he made a tour of the rooms to make sure everything was in order. "If anything was out of place—like letters or sewing—he would not make a fuss, just quietly open a drawer and put it out of sight," Stephen recalled.

"Invariably that weekend, we would hear Mom say, 'Louis, do you know where such-and-such is?' Many times I had seen Dad put that very object in a drawer, but he would reply, 'I don't know. Look in a drawer.' Sure enough, it was there."

In this, he was consistent with his office habit of clearing the desk at the end of the day—and dumping all the papers into a deep drawer.

Evening meals were family time. Feeding four growing boys had to be a challenge, but Stephen said his mom always prepared a hearty breakfast and a hot supper. The evening meal ended with a devotional time of reading and prayer. One of the boys was given the assignment of reading out loud a chapter of the Bible.

"When Dad was home," Mark remembered, "Sundays were extra-special days. He would arise before anyone else and set the dining room table with linen and put on classical music or choral hymns. After breakfast, usually pancakes or French toast, he would send us off to Sunday school while he cleaned up the dishes and set the table for dinner at noon."

Not that supper was a solemn event. The boys could be very irreverent. At home, Louis was not a leader of world renown. He was simply Dad, and the boys enjoyed teasing him in a way that sometimes shocked guests. "He was quick to laugh at himself and engaged in the banter," said Mark. "I think I learned how to laugh at myself from him."

Paul remembers, "In 1957, when I was a senior in high school, I started to date my future wife, Genevieve Holton, an Alliance MK from China and Vietnam. The first time I brought her home to have Sunday noon meal with us, she was outraged at how much disrespect we boys showed the foreign secretary. We were always joking around the table, and I think that in the presence of a pretty girl, the game of one-upmanship was raised a notch. In the process, my father, who was rather English in the humor department, became the butt of some jokes and the hero—or goat—in stories of family misadventures."

Table humor was not restricted to the King house. Clarence Drake, the Kings' pastor, recalled one occasion when Stephen and Mark were his guests. "I will never forget one night at dinner," he said, "when out of the blue Steve said, 'It's time for my father to cross his legs.'

"When I asked what he meant, Steve explained that at a certain moment during the evening meal, his father always shifted his seating position."

The boys' high-spirited antics did not mean "anything goes." When it came to discipline, Stephen recalled, "Mom never said, 'Wait till your father gets home,' mainly because that event could be months away. I got my share of lickings from Mom as well as Dad."

Paul agreed that there was no "time out" for the King boys: "As a child, discipline was often administered by my father, who used a belt on my bottom. It was plenty painful, but never delivered at random, out of anger or for insignificant matters. I always knew exactly what the punishment was for—usually direct disobedience—and once it was over, the matter was settled. Neither he nor my mother held it against me."

Once the boys grew older, however, all physical punishment stopped. "Throughout my teens," Paul said, "they treated me like an apprentice adult, expecting me to behave like a grown-up. If I didn't, I lost my privileges for a while. After going to college, I was considered an adult. They chose merely to be available if I wanted to talk things over. They let me come up with solutions of my own."

Being treated with fairness and respect is one of Paul's strongest memories of his father. One event stood out. On the family's way home from India, the ship stopped in the port of Aden. Paul saw some beautiful and inexpensive watches in shops lining the harbor. He begged his dad to buy him one. Louis said it would be better to wait until they got to Switzerland in ten days and he then could get a good watch.

But Paul pestered him until Louis relented—and warned he would only buy one watch. "I couldn't have been happier, putting on that watch and going back to the ship," the boy said. But sure enough, the watch stopped running before the ship cleared the harbor.

"I saw some beautiful watches in Lucerne and for about the same price we paid in Aden," he continued. "I was heartbroken but didn't dare say a word to my father. I learned a lesson about patience and greed."

While still in their young teens, the King boys were encouraged to pursue their individual interests. Paul chose the more academic activities, becoming editor of the Nyack high school newspaper and later editor of the Nyack College yearbook, *The Missionarian*. The others chose athletics. David was Most Valuable Player in his senior year of football, and Stephen was All-County tackle.

David said his dad was reluctant to give him permission to play football because Louis thought it would hurt his school grades. They reached an agreement. David could play football in the fall but would not do a winter sport. Then they would compare his grades in the fall and winter. David did play football—and his grades fell in the winter.

Instead of pursuing an athletic scholarship at Columbia University, David went to Nyack to prepare for missionary work. His favorite extracurricular activity was not football but dating an upperclassman named Sara. He liked music and she was an organ major. He liked to sing and she was in the same choir and chorale as he. They decided to make music together for the rest of their lives.

The boys' sports activities in high school meant that Esther again had to fill the role of double-duty Mom, representing her often-absent husband at the games. "She never complained," said Stephen, "and I never thought much about it. That's just the way it was. Mom never missed a band recital or sporting event I was involved in."

Esther did not heave reluctant sighs over this obligation because she loved sports as much as her boys and went the distance to support them. One rain-pelting day when Stephen was in only a practice football game, she and Mark sat undeterred beneath the bleachers and watched him play. "At the time," Mark mused, "I thought my mother had lost her mind, but it became an enduring, warm memory."

It was such support for her sons that prompted some of the players to call her the team mascot. Esther and her sons were such regular spectators at the high school games that other adults would save them seats if they were late.

Mark said he used to come home from school and find his mother had moved the ironing board in front of the television. She was watching a Yankee or Mets game while pressing their clothes. It may be apocryphal, but the story circulated that one Thanksgiving Day, Esther asked Louis not to pray too long over the turkey. She and the boys did not want to miss a football game.

On the few occasions Louis was able to attend a game, Esther had to explain what was happening. What did "first down" mean? What were all those gestures the referees used? Why the yellow flag? Because of his early heart condition, Louis had missed participating in sports as part of his growing-up years.

Esther, however, was not so engrossed in sports that she tuned out everything else. One day while watching a televised game, she felt a tremendous concern to pray for David, who was a missionary in Hong Kong. She immediately shut off the television and went to prayer until the burden lifted a half-hour later. She wrote to David and described the experience.

David explained what was happening at that very time she was praying for him. A surgeon was performing a biopsy on David with almost fatal consequences. "The doctor, visibly shaken, came to the waiting room afterward," he wrote. "He told my wife that while he was making the initial incision at the base of my neck, he almost cut into the jugular vein.

Usually the jugular is routed from the heart straight up the neck, but my vein made a jog and went up the other side of the neck. 'Had I cut into the vein, he might have bled to death before we could get it stopped,' the doctor said."

Off the playing field, the boys went different directions in their interests. Even as a boy, Stephen developed an interest in electronics. "Mom and Dad encouraged me to get my Amateur Radio Operator license at age fourteen," he said. "Their support helped me to pursue electronics engineering as a vocation."

After high school he enlisted in the Marine Corps and trained as an avionics technician. While he was serving in the Washington, DC, area, some of his buddies arranged a blind date for him. Stephen, however, was not blind, and when he met Mary Ann, it was a date for life.

Separating from the service after four years, he got a job as a research technician at the Johns Hopkins University Applied Physics Laboratory. "Working alongside engineers who were designing satellite instrumentation, it wasn't long before I realized I could design that stuff too," he said. Stephen eventually headed a company that provided engineering services to research institutes in the Baltimore area.

When Paul sensed God's leading to ministry in Taiwan and David to Hong Kong, however, their parents took a more cautious approach. While pleased, they were careful not to interfere in a matter they believed to be strictly between their boys and God.

Paul recalled, "When I was a senior at Nyack College, I applied for missionary service. From the beginning of that organizational affiliation, my father made sure there was not even a hint of nepotism in our institutional relationship. He excused himself from personally processing my application, did not participate in any of the interviews and absented himself from discussion and decision involving me at every level of the office."

While fulfilling her role as double-duty Mom, Esther still managed to have an active public ministry, especially the Women's Missionary Prayer Fellowship (WMPF). She believed what A.T. Pierson wrote: "Every step in the progress of missions is directly traceable to prayer." She was enlisted as the leader for WMPF (later called Alliance Women) at Simpson Memorial Church in Nyack and, shortly after, WMPF district president, a position she held for twelve years in two districts.

Widening Circles

Louis had Esther to manage the upbringing of their four sons while he faced challenges and conflicts that demanded his full attention and most of his time. He also had colleagues at "260" who stood with him and worked through many of the problems that arose.

From the beginning of his tenure as foreign secretary, he had the tireless support of his secretary, Jewel Hall. He was responsible for changing her plans to return to Thailand after a year of homeland assignment. He admitted to her years later, "When I watched you work during that first Bangkok conference, I determined that whoever became the new foreign secretary was going to have you for his secretary."

One of her most valuable skills was her understanding of the organization. "She knew the Alliance inside and out," Louis said. She made a special point of knowing in detail all the Board of Managers and General Council actions. Sometimes she marched into his office, holding a letter or memo, and declared, "You can't send this." She then referred him to the appropriate legislation, and that was that. "She was a sleuth if ever there was one," King conceded. "Between Esther and Jewel, the both of them kept me straight."

In the early years of his work as foreign secretary, he also could count on another assistant as dependable as Hall. H. Robert Cowles, former missionary to the Philippines who later became editor of the denominational magazine, proved a valuable and hard-working colleague.

In addition to the corporate officers—Nathan Bailey, president; William Smalley, secretary; and Bernard King, treasurer—the Foreign Department subcommittee initially included two area secretaries. Gentlemanly, efficient Robert Chrisman, former chairman of the Thai field, was King's chosen replacement for his vacated post for the Far East. His death due to illness in 1965 was a grievous loss to the foreign secretary. William Kerr, missionary to Thailand, replaced Chrisman. Two years later the large Far East area was reorganized and divided between Kerr and T. Grady Mangham, who had served as Mission chairman in Vietnam.

George Constance, area secretary for South America and Africa, had been chairman of the Colombian field when he, along with King, was appointed to the Foreign Department. He was a total contrast to his former peer and new boss. An affable and gregarious man who never met a stranger, he had problems staying strictly with policy. But King retained him as area secretary for South America and they worked together for eighteen years, until Constance's retirement.

Constance acknowledged, "Our relationship was at times a bit turbulent but always in a spirit of camaraderie with the object of reaching our goals for the glory of God."

When a young man appeared before the Foreign Department candidate committee, he was severely grilled by King. At one point, unsure of his answer, he asked the foreign secretary if the response was correct. King replied flatly, "We ask questions; we don't give answers." The interview completed, the candidate stumbled from the room, crestfallen at his poor performance and fearful of rejection by the committee. But Constance followed him out, gave him a hearty South American hug and said, "You did just fine. Welcome aboard!"

George Klein, former chairman of the Gabon field, was appointed area secretary for Africa in 1963. Gruff-spoken, always in a hurry and completely loyal to his boss and the Alliance, no one was ever in doubt where he stood on a issue. He brought something new to the department: an authentic representation for Africa based on years of experience.

King's world beat kept expanding. In 1958, West Africa was subdivided into three fields: Guinea, Ivory Coast and Mali-Upper Volta. China/Taiwan joined the family in 1962 and Jordan became a field two years later. By the end of his fourth three-year term in 1968, the Alliance work worldwide under his leadership had grown to twenty-six fields.

During that same period, the missionary staff increased from 822 to almost 900; organized churches more than doubled to about 2,500 and baptized members numbered 215,000.

Regional conferences, begun so successfully in Bangkok, played a key role in the expanding global boundaries of King's leadership. Especially after the second regional conference in Saigon, King saw the value of such meetings on a wider scale.

The South American Conference was held in Huanuco, Peru, in January of 1960. It was the first regional meeting outside Asia, bringing together seventeen Mission and Church leaders from the C&MA fields of Argentina, Chile, Colombia, Ecuador and Peru. In comparison to the Asian gatherings, it was small; Chile, with forty-seven organized churches, was the largest field.

Latin America at the time was still under the suffocating domination of the Roman Catholic Church, which was allied to the national governments. Most of the Alliance work was limited to the hinterland among villages and small-town populations. Almost nothing was being done in the cities to evangelize the middle- and upper-class groups who were the movers and shakers on the continent. Finding a convert in those socio-economic circles seemed as formidable as winning a Muslim to Christ.

But a self-inflicted problem also limited growth of the South American C&MA churches. King pinpointed the issue in a later report to the Asian Conference in Zamboanga, Philippines.

> Our work [in the five republics of South America] has not progressed as well as throughout all of the Orient. These countries are solidly Roman Catholic. Then too, the pastors felt like the Mission existed to pay their living. Furthermore, the missionaries on the field liked to have it that way because when they paid the salaries, they could tell them what to do. So the Foreign Department saw we had a difficult situation.
>
> We remembered, however, that the Bangkok Conference was so successful in achieving self-administration in national churches. We therefore thought it would be wise to have a meeting in South America like the Asian one. But there wasn't one national church in South America that was not receiving mission subsidy. All of them got it. We had no example among the churches of how to do it correctly.[1]

King solved this problem by inviting Florentino de Jesus, president of the C&MA Church in the Philippines, to be a resource person at the Huanuco meeting. He reported on how in his country the number of self-supporting churches grew from 13 in 1947 to 143 by the time he addressed the South American church leaders. He gave equally encouraging reports of other Asian churches. He told how, after the first Bangkok Conference, 251 churches had voluntarily gone off Mission subsidy, setting the stage for remarkable growth.

By the time de Jesus finished his report, the delegates forgot about pressing the Mission for more money. "Instead, they asked him question after question, day after day," King said. "I soon found out I should take a backseat. So at all times I sat at the rear ... because, being a national, de Jesus gave them better answers than I could as foreign secretary."

The South American pastors concluded that if the Asian churches could succeed in difficult times, so could they. The Colombian delegation went home and, despite continuing severe persecution of the Church, wrote to King that they no longer wanted American money. The Ecuadorian Church went completely off subsidy. Financial help to the Argentine Church dropped to $80 a month. The Peruvian Church adopted a five-year plan to eliminate all Mission subsidies.

"As iron sharpens iron"—nationals conferring with nationals—worked as well in South America as it did in Asia. King had learned the valuable lesson that, though leadership involves authority, there comes a time to step back and let people deal directly with God.

The first regional conference for Africa was held at Bouaké, Ivory Coast, in January 1964. By then, directives from New York had largely resolved the issue of foreign subsidy to the African churches. King credited Constance with getting all the African churches off Mission subsidy.

Another issue took center stage at Bouaké. King previously had reported that World Council of Churches representatives had been working behind the scenes with Alliance pastors in Congo, Gabon, Guinea and Ivory Coast to enlist their congregations as member churches. "It came as a surprise to the missionaries that the church brethren were being wooed by the ecumenists, and liked what they heard," King recalled. "It wasn't difficult to talk about an All-Africa Conference when the facts became known."

Seventeen missionaries and African delegates from four countries gathered at Bouaké. For resource persons, King invited Doan-van-Mieng, Vietnam, and Raghuel P. Chavan, India. As happened at the South American Conference in Chile, the two Asian leaders became the focus of attention while King and the missionaries took a backseat during the discussions. The two godly and skilled church leaders made a powerful impact on the delegates.

Area secretary Klein summed up perhaps the greatest achievement of the Africa meeting: "The feeling of aloneness dissolved into a feeling of oneness, with Christ being recognized as the unifying Lord."[2] The sense of belonging to a greater worldwide fellowship gave a much-needed boost to the often beleaguered and isolated African leaders.

It was the larger, more progressive gatherings in the Far East that led the way toward greater maturity. The third Asian convocation in Zamboanga, Philippines, 1961, became known as the missionary conference. The indigenous church policy was no longer an issue. The forty-three delegates from ten countries turned their attention to how to become sending churches. Guest pastors Albert Hashweh from Jordan and Ibrahim Oueis from Syria were amazed at the scope of missionary work already being done.

Sixty percent of the nearly 500 Filipino churches were giving offerings for missions. The Japanese Alliance supported a worker in Brazil. Indian missionaries worked in the Andaman Islands, and Vietnamese ministered in Laos. The Alliance churches in Hong Kong, especially the North Point Church led by Pastor Teng, were already sending missionaries abroad. Thailand and New Guinea (Papua) supported home missions programs. But these efforts were not considered enough.

Once it was settled that churches were either missionary or disobedient, the door opened to greater outreach. When asked who would like other national churches to send workers to their nations, the response was immediate. Z.A. Espa said, "We have been praying and longing for an Indonesian missionary to work among their countrymen in the southern Philippines."

M. Hon said, "There are 200,000 Cambodians in Vietnam. We hope to send a missionary to that area. In Cambodia we have many places that have not yet received the gospel. We would very much appreciate missionaries from other countries to help us."[3]

R.P. Chavan also invited workers from other areas to minister in India. Several church leaders later met in Manila to discuss coordination of their overseas efforts.

Their vision thus broadened, the delegates at Zamboanga expressed a desire for Alliance churches in all parts of the world to come together in conference. Momentum was building for a global fellowship.

The Fifth Asia Conference in 1969 took the suggestion a step closer to reality. For the first time in the eighty-two years of Alliance history, seventy-seven representatives from almost all overseas C&MA churches gathered in one place. Only four national churches were unable to send delegations.

Appropriately, this enlarged international gathering took place in Bangkok, scene of the precedent-setting first conference thirteen years earlier. That event brought together delegates from ten Asian fields representing 1,500 churches and 52,000 members. By 1969, the total jumped to 2,100 churches and 150,000 members. At the first Bangkok meeting, none of the national churches had their own missionaries. By 1969, nineteen missionaries were supported by six sending churches.

One feature had not changed during the intervening years: The air crackled with excitement and success. Reports treated very current and pivotal issues. Conferees were impressed by Vietnam's strategy of "divide to multiply" in its church-planting drive in the cities. But it was not the only way to go. The Templo Alianza in downtown Guayaquil, Ecuador, averaged one new church every two years for six years.

Missions was in everyone's thoughts. "It is an obligatory command to the Church. It must be obeyed," said one church leader. "The more Christians give [the gospel] outside their church, the more they have inside," testified a Vietnamese pastor. The Argentine representative reported that the church's missionary fund had more than the national church treasury.[4]

The fledgling missionary movement among the overseas churches did not happen by accident. From the very start, King believed strongly that a viable indigenous church was not the final step for missions. He impressed upon national leaders the principle that mission-founded churches reached maturity only when they became mission-sending agencies.

The Foreign Department developed a program that encouraged overseas churches to take the plunge. Workers sent out by the younger churches received aid to send their children to the same schools used by North American missionary parents. The Foreign Department helped with travel expenses to get them to their destinations. It also facilitated the workers' support through money exchange if the national currency of their sending church was not convertible on the world market.

This kind of cooperation prompted Ralph D. Winter, head of the US Center for World Mission, to recognize the C&MA as one of the few mission agencies encouraging missionary work by overseas churches, and doing it right.

Recognizing that fifty percent of the world's population in developing countries was under twenty years of age, the Fifth Asia Conference gave serious attention to Sunday school and youth work. After a good report by R.P. Chavan on ecumenism, a Vietnamese delegate commented, "We need to realize that when the bait is offered, there is a hook in the center."[5]

The conference ended with a broadly shared sense that this was just the beginning of something bigger than they had previously known, something on a worldwide scale. It was a fitting tribute to the man from New York who embraced the world as his field.

Collision in Gabon

What would have happened if an All-Africa Conference had been held in the late 1950s? If pastors of the Evangelical Church (C&MA) of South Gabon had been able to confer with Asian leaders experienced in dealing with the ecumenical movement? It may have averted a serious collision between Church and Mission in Gabon.

The conflict had been brewing before King became foreign secretary and toured Africa in 1957. He sensed a problem but perhaps even he did not realize how quickly it would erupt into an ugly crisis that brought the Mission to the brink of expulsion from Gabon.

Problems in the Central African nation began back in 1948 when it was still a French colony. The World Council of Churches launched a global strategy based on Christ's prayer to the Father: "that they may be one as we are one" (John 17:22). Ecumenical leaders and theologians interpreted that oneness as an organic unity, organizational as well as spiritual, integrating overseas missions and churches into national-level organizations with direct lines to the ecumenical headquarters in Geneva.

Looking at the plan from his perspective as foreign secretary, King said, "I figured the WCC wanted to begin by uniting all the Protestant missions and churches overseas. If it worked well there, eventually the US churches would get behind the effort as well and unite under the National Council of Churches."

This concept of unity resonated with the African Christians for two reasons. First, they were not involved in the historical development of Western churches justifying their existence and defining themselves by how different they were from each other. Lacking those denominational distinctions so important to the missionaries, Africans found the conglomeration of mission groups, often scores of them in a single country, very confusing.

Second, especially in French-speaking Africa where the Roman Catholic Church dominated, there was at least a surface unity of Catholic orders and congregations under one papal authority. Government officials, many of whom were also Catholic, appreciated the convenience of having a single leader to deal with, unlike the numerous and often competitive Protestant groups and their representatives.

There was a third but unrelated complication in African Church-Mission relations not found in Asia or Latin America. European colonial regimes by nature could not accept that African churches were capable of ruling themselves. The political implications were too obvious. Consequently, churches had to relate to the government under and through the Mission structures. The Congo church gained autonomy in 1932, but it was an internal arrangement with the Mission still being held accountable by the Belgian authorities for activities of the Africans.

Thus, Alliance missionaries in Gabon and elsewhere throughout Francophone Africa faced an enormous challenge in carrying out the Mission policy of establishing a strong indigenous church. Constance, area secretary for Africa as well as South America at the time, faced these obstacles as he moved to carry out the 1955 General Council mandate to implement the indigenous church policy worldwide.

When Constance arrived in Gabon in 1956 to initiate the autonomy process, there was almost no time to prepare church leaders in advance for the changes about to take place. Nevertheless, he presided at the meeting when the African church leaders elected a slate of officers and organized the autonomous national Church. No record of the meeting was preserved by either the Church or the Mission, but according to the field, "from that time on, the Church was self-governing."

An overview of the conflict between Mission and Church in Gabon reported that all sides contributed to the problem. It noted, "Prior to the arrival of the area secretary in 1956 there should have been communication with the field chairman and the executive committee announcing the Foreign Department's intention of having the secretary preside at the organizational meeting of the church during his visit."[6]

As a result, the Gabonese Church leaders were unprepared for the historic event; it seemed to go right over their heads. And no investigation of the legal aspects was undertaken. Even after the fact of autonomy, the report noted, the missionaries still did not cooperate with the

Church to make self-government workable, nor did they attempt to make it a legal reality. It would be years before a constitution and bylaws for the Church would be drafted, and the delay would further complicate an already difficult situation.

The Africans also contributed their share to the problem. The news from New York in 1957 about the end of subsidies for church workers "was received with little enthusiasm by the national brethren," reported the field chairman. Their attitude toward Mission finances and properties was equally unhappy. A later report commented,

> With increasing boldness in their sermons, national pastors exhorted the missionaries on loving the brethren and on unity, making it plain that unless missionaries shared cars and money, they were not fulfilling the commands of the Word.[7]

The Gabonese Church leaders believed their position was entirely justified on both political and ecclesiastical grounds. During the 1950s the French colonial administration was turning over authority and assets to the Gabonese people in anticipation of national independence. Furthermore, the Alliance area in southern Gabon was flanked on the north by the Paris Evangelical Mission and on the south by the Swedish mission across the border in Congo-Brazzaville.

Both missions were members of the World Council and embraced the concept of total fusion, placing all Mission personnel and assets under control of the African Church. Throughout the 1950s, the French and Swedish missionaries negotiated with their African counterparts on the basis of integration. The Gabonese Alliance leaders were kept informed about the discussions and they believed the Alliance should follow suit.

In 1961 the Church president, Jean M'Badinga, attended an impressive ceremony when the Paris Evangelical Mission capped years of negotiations by integrating with the national Church. Two weeks later he attended a similar celebration in Brazzaville, Congo, when the Swedish mission was absorbed into the Congolese Church on the same basis.

M'Badinga obtained copies of both constitutions and bylaws. These became the basis of the C&MA national Church's efforts to draft its own articles of organization. The missionaries had previously tried to draft a constitution for the Church to work on, but it was rejected by the Foreign Department as "too Western," and the Mission was instructed to let the Church draw up its own document.

The resulting Church-written constitution was in direct conflict with Alliance Mission policy. Its bylaws stipulated among other things that once the missionaries landed on African soil they would be under the authority of the national Church—where they would serve, what they would do, what houses they would occupy and what vehicles they could use.

All Mission funds were to be deposited in a Church account and administered by Church officials. The budget each year would be drawn up by the Church and submitted to the Mission for approval. Among the budget items were "expenses in carrying out pastoral duties, general expenses, and subsidies to local work."

King observed, "The bylaws were not intended by the Church for the Church, but by the Church for their control of the Mission." The stage was set for a three-way dispute between the Church, the Mission and the Foreign Department.

Months of confused communications and misunderstood directions crisscrossed the Atlantic Ocean between "260" and Gabon. Mission autonomy and Church fusion were hotly debated. Charges and counter-charges flew every which way. The future of Alliance work in Gabon was in serious doubt.

A Better Way

King surveyed the situation and said to himself, "There has to be a better way."

Winds of change were blowing in gale force across Black Africa. Churches as well as governments on the continent were certain to define independence on their own terms. Change was inevitable. Why not anticipate matters and work through them in advance? Wasn't that better than waiting until missionaries and nationals were at loggerheads with each other and future cooperation twisted in the wind?

A plan began to emerge in King's thinking. It would be innovative, a rare win-win situation, a direction never before attempted in the Alliance—and probably unprecedented in other evangelical missions, given the interest his plan attracted. It would certainly be totally contrary to contemporary thinking in ecumenical circles.

Concerning the Gabon crisis, he wondered, "How do we get our minds together, how do we solve this? Little by little, the concept of an agreement took shape. Of course, I saw it would be better to have the agreement before conflict ensued. Decisions then ought to be reviewed at five-year intervals so that if anything developed during that period it should be handled in a reasonable manner after a fair amount of time trying to work out the previous agreement."

The new way of doing missions was summed up in one phrase: partnership of equals. And since Gabon was just the first of similar situations in Africa and elsewhere, what transpired would set the pattern of future relationships between Alliance missions and overseas churches.

The rationale was really just a variation on King's basic theme about the indigenous church. The Church had to be free from Mission domination so that it could develop along authentic cultural lines and solid biblical principles. "The underlying basis is that the Church is the Body of Christ. The Mission is not," he often repeated. "Missionaries come and go at will, the chairman and committees change every few years, bringing new ideas and different ways of doing things. If the Mission is ruling over the work and giving all the answers, where does that leave the Church?"

The African scenario added to the indigenous church policy significance not as apparent in Asia and Latin America where nations were already sovereign states. As African colonies gained independence, King noted, "The Church's release from the Mission and assuming its national identity gave it stature with its governmental and non-Christian citizens. It was the right thing to do legally as well as spiritually."

King's vision of an affirming understanding between Church and Mission as partners had something else in its favor. Quite apart from scriptural, missiological and legal principles, it was workable.

In contrast, the ecumenical model of integrating the Mission with the overseas Church was operationally a fiasco. Through his contacts at the National Council of Churches on Riverside Drive, King was able to secure about sixty case studies of missions that merged with their national churches. His discussions with denominational leaders led to the same conclusion as the reports: "In every case where World Council-related missions chose integration as a solution to problems with the Church, it proved to be a disaster for the Mission."

David H. Moore, later the leader of the Alliance overseas effort, cited one example from the account by a Korean missionary in Thailand.[8]

The Presbyterian-founded Church of Christ in Thailand was by far the largest Protestant denomination. Other churches, resentful of paternalistic attitudes by their founding missions, demanded new relationships after World War II. Not the Church of Christ in Thailand. It simply invited Presbyterian missionaries to return and resume their work. Church-Mission relations were not an issue at the time.

The Presbyterian (USA) Board of Missions, however, considered integration to be the wave of the future and the best way to resolve tensions with the overseas churches. It took the initiative to impose fusion as the worldwide policy for its overseas fields. Ironically, the action had a reverse effect in Thailand.

Moore summarized the situation:

> The ceremony of integration occurred on August 16, 1957, almost 130 years after the first missionaries arrived. Thai church leaders seemed to accept it passively. . . . The document was signed by the leaders of both the mission and the church. One of those who had promoted the change said, "From now on there will no longer be missionary and national, giver or receiver, west or east. We are all one and equal in Christ. The foreign mission will be integrated with the national church as completely as salt dissolves in water."[9]

The arrangement quickly soured. One of the Thai church leaders observed acidly, "We still remember when they [the Mission] were having integration. . . . The integration ceremony was so gorgeous and gave much publicity. They distributed leaflets and documents which we framed on the wall for a while. For we did not know any real meaning and reality of the integration."

Other Thai leaders were more blunt in their hostility toward the policy. Moore quoted them: "Integration was a farce. The western missionaries cheated our Thai Christians. They forced us to accept this integration in order to control the Thai Church authority." One of their major criticisms was that foreign influence actually increased after integration because now the missionaries were inside the Church, whereas previously they were outside. More than ever, missionaries with their dollars dominated the Church, reducing its leaders to puppets.

Samuel I. Kim, a Presbyterian missionary in Thailand at the time, observed, "The consequences of the artificial and theoretical idealism of the integration architects, in fact, brought unprecedented problems between mission and national church."[10]

King did not need to consult the WCC case studies or look at Thailand to see that the policy of Church-Mission integration was a flop. It happened in Gabon even while he was working with the Alliance church to establish an ongoing cooperative relationship. He talked with the Paris Evangelical Mission treasurer who had been a leader in the integration plan but regretted his efforts. His colleagues could not tolerate the treatment given them by the African Church leaders. Their cars were taken from them. Their budgets, funds, even their living expenses were controlled by the Church. The Mission had fifty workers when it came under the Evangelical Church of North Gabon. But disillusioned, they left in droves. The treasurer, one of the two remaining French nationals, told King he was going in two weeks.

Meeting of Equals

Coupled with King's firm commitment to Christ as Lord of the Church was his respect for overseas church leaders. "I believed these were born-again men," he said. "My attitude in talking with them was not belligerent or adamant unless I had adequate reason from the Scriptures that what they wanted would not work. On their part, they had to be in agreement to do things correctly according to the Bible. Otherwise, they would be working contrary to Jesus, the Head of the Church."

Operating from this mindset, King positioned himself between Mission and church representatives in Gabon as an unbiased arbitrator. This came as a surprise to some missionaries who assumed their boss would automatically side with them. African church leaders thought the same. They all had to come to terms with the reality that the man from New York, sitting at the head of the table, would be scrupulously neutral, deliberately thorough and disturbingly impassive.

King's method of procedure in Gabon set the pattern for subsequent deliberations in other countries. In preparation for his arrival in 1963, African and missionary executive committees were asked to draw up their separate agendas. "I was there to pick up what both parties presented and talk together with them," King said. "My job was to solve the problem in a way that the New Testament pattern would be maintained for the Church and the Mission would be kept viable to do its work."

His insistence that the Church be free to be the Church and the Mission be allowed to be the Mission became known as the modified dichotomy policy, or simply, partnership. His adherence to this concept was total—even if it meant withdrawing the Mission from a country should agreement not be reached on this basic issue.

Even more important than the function of arbitrator, King believed his role to be pastoral. Harkening back to his days as a pastor, he refused to use the Bible to attack people or their problems. Rather, he allowed issues to arise through discussion and then he applied biblical principles.

"So much of the talk had to do with money at the beginning, control of Mission funds and the Church's perceived inability to pay anything themselves. So, as we got into this, I might turn to the Bible and give them more information. For instance, what Jesus had to say about pastors' support. I also used the section in Galatians, 'A man reaps what he sows' (Galatians 6:7). Strangely enough, most people think of that as an evangelistic text, but it has to do with giving to the Church. I would open that up to them, not driving it down their throats, but in a conversational way, talking it over."

All the issues in Gabon were not resolved during the 1963 meeting. It would take more high-level conferences before the separate and joint roles of the Church and the Mission were sorted out and the first agreement signed. But the parties stayed with it. The benefits eventually realized would be far beyond anyone's expectations.

Negotiations in Gabon provided King with experience to develop the Church-Mission agreement as a defining document for relationships in numerous other countries. Although details varied from field to field, the consultation followed a basic seven-step procedure.

1. *Explanation*: Chairman of the meeting, usually the foreign secretary or church president, explains the step-by-step process to be followed.
2. *Agenda*: Representatives of the Mission and the national church executive committees set the agenda from start to finish. A smaller group takes the lists submitted by the two groups and prioritizes the items for consideration. King noted that initially one topic always appeared on the church's list: What to do with missionaries who do not fit well with the working relationship.
3. *Discussion*: Each item is explored fully in plenary session. No decision is taken at this point and no name attached to remarks made. "Policy and procedure positions of the Foreign Department would

always be involved," King said, "so we had to explain where we could be flexible and where not. The church had to learn how far we could go."
4. *Draft Documents*: Church and Mission groups meet separately to draw up a draft of how they would like the agreement to read. These drafts go to the small agenda committee that combine the two drafts.
5. *Document Approval*: The joint committee's draft is read section by section before the full group. One section stipulates when the agreement takes effect and its duration, usually five years. Church, Mission and Foreign Department representatives meet separately to decide if they can agree on the draft document. "After three days or sometimes longer, we could come to a mutually acceptable document. Nothing was hurried," King explained.
6. *Document Signing*: Each conferee affixes his signature to the document in a formal and solemn setting. "We would put on our best suits and have a formal ceremony," King concluded. "The formality impressed on everyone the seriousness of the event."
7. *Communion Observance*: This service celebrates the unity of everyone in Christ, whether foreigner or national.

These formal agreements became the defining document of working relationships in most of the countries where Alliance missionaries served. Each consultation, however, differed from the others. In Vietnam and Hong Kong, the procedure went smoothly. In Congo-Kinshasa, by contrast, negotiations faltered because of dissensions within the churches. King and his colleagues first had to sort out which group truly represented the work.

In the Philippines, mature leaders of the Church cooperated fully in the consultation, but a young man named Jun Vincer, a pastor and recent graduate of law school, had other ideas. King recalled, "Like a lawyer, he came to the meetings to make demands, almost like a trial. Finally, I had to take him aside for a friendly discussion. I explained we were not a legal entity, but workers for the Lord, trying to come to an agreement for the glory of God. No doubt the older Church leaders also told him to cool it." Vincer went on to have a wide ministry, including leadership of the World Evangelical Fellowship.

Thailand proved surprisingly difficult at first and the consultation had to end without an agreement. The groups agreed to continue as they had been doing and come back after a few years to try again. Laos was another complicated situation. "The president of the Church bought the ecumenical position hook, line and sinker," said King. "He wanted to force the Mission into fusion with the Church. I had to take a very adamant stand contrary to my normal role in such discussions. It didn't become an issue of closing down the Mission, but it was within view that it could happen."

The Foreign Department gave high priority to Church-Mission agreements throughout King's tenure. He said, "As long as Church and Mission work together, I think they are essential. If we wish harmonious relations, if we want to know as foreigners where we get in and where we get off, an agreement of this nature is needed."

After David H. Moore became head of the department (now the Division of International Ministries), he participated in about twenty such agreements involving fourteen national churches. His view of the long-term value of the procedure, however, differed from King's: "The agreements were not viewed as a permanent tool. It was envisioned that sometime there would develop a close enough relationship so that issues could be openly dealt with in regular meetings between the church and mission teams."

That is what transpired. By the year 2001, the total of agreements in force dropped to approximately five. They had accomplished their primary purpose. The consultative procedure is no longer viewed as innovative and risky, but when King initiated the Church-Mission agreements they were considered both. Other missions followed the Alliance lead.

In fact, the concept triggered a momentous gathering of evangelical missions in 1971 known as the Green Lake Conference. The debate between fusion and partnership had become a full-blown issue for many groups. The C&MA's foreign secretary was the featured speaker in favor of the Church being the Church and the Mission being the Mission.

King's efforts to encourage cooperation between the North American Alliance and overseas churches sensitized him to a situation closer to home. Melvin Sylvester, first president of the Canadian C&MA, wrote, "It was in the late '60s, following his deputational role at a Canadian district conference, that he returned to Nyack and wrote a long letter to Nathan Bailey, telling of his impression of a growing sense of nationhood under prime minister John Diefenbaker. He predicted that the feeling would increasingly be reflected in our churches. He urged that a process be initiated to monitor, evaluate and offer guidelines that would lead to Canadian autonomy."

King's advice was rejected and he was forbidden by the president to discuss further the matter with the Canadians. He obeyed the order and never revealed the disagreement, even in retirement. "He was one of the lonely US voices affirming the Canadian C&MA in its move toward autonomy," commented Arnold C. Cook, a later president of the Canadian Church.

Congo Crisis

The widespread practice of negotiated agreements grew out of a very troubled period of disagreements in Gabon. It demonstrated a remarkable flexibility by King and his colleagues in the vortex of change to turn a negative situation into a positive one, all the while adhering to fundamental commitments. Pursuing the indigenous church policy and codifying it in a mutually acceptable document was obviously a workable policy.

But bringing a national church to the level of self-support, self-government and self-propagation did not immunize it from crises in relation to the founding mission.

The Church in Congo-Kinshasa was the oldest and one of the largest Alliance communities anywhere overseas. It was one of only two autonomous national churches for many years—Vietnam was the other—dating back to 1932. Its pastors were not on the dole; its leadership was completely African; its churches were constructed with local funds, and some of them were cathedral-sized, seating thousands. The hospital at Kinkonzi and its network of clinics were highly respected. Graduates of its Bible institute were reputed for their grasp of the Scriptures.

But this showcase church had not one but two Achilles' heels: a shortage of well-trained workers and a parochial school system that lagged behind the educational system used elsewhere in the Congo.

Complacency about the church was shattered when a cultic movement emerged in the 1950s. One missionary described it in rather stark terms as "an anti-missionary, anti-white, politico-religious movement combining paganism, Christianity, materialism and lust." Called Kimbanguism, after a Baptist catechist persecuted by the Belgian regime, the group rode the rapidly rising tide of nationalistic fervor and spread throughout the colony.

Nine thousand of the C&MA church's 40,000 adherents initially joined the movement. In areas where churches were poorly led, whole congregations deserted to the cult that promised freedom from white rule, seizure of the colonists' riches and salvation in the name of God the Father, Simon Kimbangu and the Holy Ghost. Even after Congo's independence in 1960, the movement continued to grow until it ranked third in size after the Roman Catholic and Protestant communities, claiming millions of followers.

As the Alliance Church attempted to recover from this external onslaught, it was hit even harder by a dissident movement within its own ranks. The schism began with a flawed educational strategy by the Mission for the Church's thousands of children. Resolving the issue and its consequences would require countless hours, a good deal of money and several trips by Foreign Department personnel. It subjected King's leadership to severe tests.

During the colonial regime, Congo had few public schools. In most places, children went to parochial schools or not at all. Since Belgium was ninety percent Roman Catholic, all colonial school subsidies for years went to establish a strong Roman Catholic school system. Protestant missions were obligated to pay out of their own pockets for the education of children in their churches. They protested loudly and long over the discriminatory colonial policy.

Finally, a socialist government came to power in Brussels and subsidies were made available in the early 1950s to Protestant schools in Congo. A grace period of five years was granted for non-Catholic schools to align their programs with the Belgian system and qualify for funds. Most of the missions complied.

The C&MA Mission in the Lower Congo refused the offer, choosing to continue its own separate way. A Belgian administrator warned, "The natives themselves would decide the issue by shunning non-subsidized schools where they would be required to pay tuition and buy their books and supplies."[11]

The warning went unheeded and problems began. By 1959 colonial authorities were receiving letters from people in the Lower Congo, asking for other missions to be brought into the Alliance area. The provincial commissioner warned the missionaries that unless they listened to their church people, he would act on the requests. Stung by the warning, the Mission started to get its schools in line with government standards, but the effort was too little, too late. Congo's troubled accession to independence in 1960 paralyzed the subsidy program.

A year later, when the country was in civil and economic chaos and the school system faced collapse, the Foreign Department agreed to pay all the teachers for 8 months, a total of $9,000 for 8,900 students in the mission schools. This was to give the Church time to get funding from the government for the schools that now would be in their hands. The bailout came with a deadline that gave urgency to the Church's efforts: by August 1961, all Mission subsidy would cease.

A dissident group called the Alliance of Congolese Protestants (APROCO) seized on the issue to foment trouble in the churches. Although it was mainly composed of non-Christians and former Church members, several men were related to the venerable but aging Church president, Thomas Paku. The group had more on its mind than just schools. It wanted to rid the area of missionaries, seize their properties and turn the Church into a power base that would launch it as a political party.

The showdown came in March of 1962 when Paku called all the pastors together and ordered them to sign a "Declaration of Affiliation" that contained matters clearly in violation of the church constitution. Despite threats by APROCO men surrounding the church building, some pastors refused and walked out. Led by Joel Kuvuna, the national church secretary, a new church organized. It adhered to scriptural doctrine and pledged continued cooperation with the missionaries. Of the nearly 30,000 church members, two-thirds sided with the Paku faction.

The conflict intensified later that year when finally the government agreed to subsidize 301 classes with a total of $250,000 annually. Two competing churches, each with its own slate of officers, used the legal name of the C&MA to lay claim to the school subsidy. Whoever got that money controlled the schools and children—and ultimately the parents and congregations. Threats and violence increased as the dissident group seized mission properties and pressed for full recognition as the legitimate church.

Responding to a request by the beleaguered Mission, the Board of Managers dispatched representatives with power to Congo in late 1963 to determine which church was the true Alliance one. President Bailey, area secretary Klein and King formed the delegation. They spent Monday, December 9, discussing the issues with the missionaries. Another full day was given separately to leaders of the two opposing groups.

The Paku-led faction tried unsuccessfully to bring APROCO men into the meeting but King insisted that only ordained pastors in good standing could participate. He conducted the sessions with courtroom solemnity and deliberation. Both groups were invited back the following Monday to hear the decision of the New York delegation. Since only the C&MA Mission had a charter recognized by the government, its action would be legally binding and final.

On the appointed day and time, the Kuvuna-led representatives filed into the conference room. The Central Government's district administrator also attended. The Paku group failed to appear. After a considerable delay and with the government official's suggestion, president Bailey announced the decision. The Kuvuna slate of officers and congregations were recognized as the church accurately reflecting Alliance teaching and practice.

He continued, "We do proclaim that Rev. Thomas Paku is no longer President of the Church of the C&MA of Congo. He and those associated with him have no authority in the affairs of the church. . . . From this date they must cease using the name of the Church of the C&MA of Congo."

It was a heartbreaking moment in the history of the longest existing overseas church of the Alliance. Paku, who for most of those years had given inspired leadership, and thousands of church people who had allied with him, were disaffiliated from the C&MA. There was no celebrating, no beating of drums, no derisive chanting such as the Africans were prone to do when one side prevailed in a dispute. Only a quiet sadness and sober awareness of what had just taken place.

If the New York officials had any doubt about their decision, it was quickly dispelled. That same day, as they started back toward Kinshasa, a truck filled with APROCO men blocked their way on an isolated section of the dirt road. They demanded that the Alliance officials disclose their decision. The tense standoff was abruptly ended when the district administrator drove up. With an air of authority backed by military clout, he ordered the truck removed so the delegation of foreigners could continue the trip.

The dissident faction continued the fight for another two and one-half years marred by violence, decrees from bribed government officials, conflicting court decisions and interference from WCC-backed religious leaders in Kinshasa. But eventually both sides had had enough. A mediator recognized that most of the church people wanted reconciliation. The reunited church was larger in size than before the split.

It helped that by this time biased local officials had been transferred elsewhere and the APROCO group was outlawed because of illegal political activities. At great cost, several principles were established. First: The new church administration was declared off-limits to nonmembers. Second: The church belongs to Jesus Christ and those who faithfully follow Him. And third: It must pursue a spiritual role, not a political one.

The Congo experience reinforced King's conviction that the Church's place in a nation is to produce godly people united in viable, indigenous churches that bear witness to Christ and demonstrate the power of His Word. Education and other social programs are the responsibility of government to its citizens—all of them. Later, when trends and efforts in other Alliance fields pointed toward parochial school involvement, he spoke with authority and finality against such moves, sparing those involved from incalculable grief.

Another Side

During that sorry church split in Congo when opposing sides were airing their dirty laundry in public, the work continued to grow and the gospel to spread. One story affirming this centered on a man named Justin N'Kokolo.

Justin was born into a Christian home, the son of a C&MA pastor. After he experienced for himself his father's faith, they became a familiar team on the circuit of church services and quarterly meetings. Justin began substituting in the pulpit when his father was away. It seemed certain he was headed for the ministry.

But the government had other ideas. In 1936 the village chief was ordered by the local administrator to supply two sturdy young men for the army. The canny chief knew better than to ask for volunteers. Instead, he picked two promising young men and sent them to the government post to do "road work." Justin was one of the two chosen.

Only after he had signed the papers did N'Kokolo, age twenty-three, realize he had just committed the next twenty years of his life to the army. An article published later noted,

> No one seemed more unfitted and unprepared for the brutal rigors of professional army life than Justin. He was gentle, retiring, and wanted to preach. Those qualities ordinarily are unknown to men paid to fight and to kill. It seemed but a matter of time before N'Kokolo's Christian integrity would choke in the dust of the parade ground.[12]

But boot camp did not dim his faith. Instead, he emerged from training as a soldier's soldier. He also developed a useful skill that gave him stature before his fellow soldiers—gunnery marksmanship. He was promoted in rank twice and decorated for bravery in a campaign against the Italians in Ethiopia during World War II.

After the war, Justin was sent to Belgium and appeared before King Baudouin as an outstanding example of the Congolese soldiers. But nothing swerved him from following Christ. Wherever he was stationed, Justin conducted Bible studies among the troops on base and preached in surrounding villages. When a group of converts was gathered, he led them in building a chapel. He even was allowed at times to use jailed prisoners to help with the construction.

His furloughs back to his father's house in the Lower Congo were legendary. Villagers marveled at this bemedaled, honored warrior who arose before dawn to sweep out his dad's church. When a relative seized some of his inherited land—sure cause for spilling blood—Justin responded by confronting his relative. "I could do you great harm," he said, "but because of Jesus, I can't." He dropped the matter.

N'Kokolo's twenty-year enlistment ended in 1956. By that time he was a sergeant-major and decorated eight times. But when he tried to separate from the service, his superiors balked. The Belgian commanding officer said that independence for the colony was drawing near and it would need experienced soldiers. Justin persisted in his determination to retire until he was summoned to the governor general's office. That did it. He withdrew his application.

In the halcyon days after Congo's independence in 1960, he was rapidly advanced to the rank of lieutenant colonel, second highest post in the army. He would have done much to help his bleeding country, but he did not have the chance.

In the gathering dusk of November 21, 1960, he approached the Guinean embassy to deliver an expulsion notice to the ambassador who was grossly interfering in the nation's affairs. Unarmed and unsuspecting, he was gunned down in an ambush on the embassy grounds.

Congo's President Joseph Kasavubu and many high-ranking officials paid tribute to the "nation's first national hero and martyr." More meaningful, a convoy of troop-filled trucks escorted the casket to his home village and father's church. Many of the soldiers volunteered for the trip because N'Kokolo had won them to the Lord.

The official army journal saluted him: "His faith was his governing principle. Not a dead faith, but one put in practice every day." The whole nation mourned his death and honored his Lord.

N'Kokolo's biography was published in Christian Officers Fellowship journals in Europe, North America and Africa and translated into several languages. Tragic though his death, Justin's life was a dramatic witness for Christ on the world stage during the dark days of schism and conflict in the Congo church.[13]

Indigenous Vindication

The workweek of May 1967 began routinely enough—until King received a phone call from the Canadian Office of Foreign Affairs. Had he heard that President Sekou Toure of Guinea, West Africa, had ordered all missionaries out of the country by month's end? What were his plans for evacuating missionaries of Canadian nationality? An hour later, the State Department was asking the same questions for American citizens employed by the C&MA.

The ultimatum should not have come as a complete surprise. Back in 1961, the Marxist-leaning leader of Guinea had said it was time for foreign missionaries to turn over leadership of their churches to the Africans. He called it "africanization." But in the ensuing years, he complained, missions had actually increased their numbers and their control over the work. He claimed this showed a paternalistic spirit that put down Africans as incapable of conducting their own religious affairs.

The 1967 edict was primarily directed against the Roman Catholic Church, its French archbishop and its 100-plus missionaries. Not only did the president resent them because of his Marxist-Leninist bias, he accused them of taking orders from Rome and blocking the progress of africanization in all sectors of the country. The C&MA, the only major Protestant mission, had about forty workers. It enjoyed normal, even friendly, relations with local officials, but the sweeping ultimatum included all foreigners. Muslim leaders saw to that.

"My immediate reaction was to negotiate with the government to see if there were a way around the decree," King recalled. "If not, then I needed to be on the scene to parcel out our missionaries and end our service in Guinea."

A phone call and a courier to Washington secured a visa in just a few days. King also got a briefing from State Department sources. They called him on May 10 to report that Sekou Toure had refused to see the American ambassador; it was time to evacuate the missionaries.

Two days later, near midnight, King landed in Conakry, the capital of Guinea. The missionaries who took him to the hotel were very apprehensive about the future. "Late as it was," King said, "before I unpacked my bags I asked for a complete briefing, especially about the basis of the president's decision."

Reviewing Sekou Toure's speech, they touched on his conviction that foreign missionaries were trying, through the churches, to control the country. King interrupted, "As soon as they got that far, I told them that I had found my wedge on how to talk with the president. I said we would meet in the morning and bade them good night."

King's plan was to remind the president that the Evangelical Church of Guinea had already gained its independence from the Mission in 1958 and four years later was completely self-supporting. The government had in fact officially recognized the church's status in 1964. Sekou Toure himself had been invited to the celebration of autonomy.

Furthermore, contrary to Toure's allegation, the Alliance Mission had *decreased* in size over the years. No missionary pastored a local church and no missionary was permitted to be part of the church's administration. Only two could attend the national Church's conference, and only by invitation and only as observers.

Since he needed the American embassy's help in gaining an interview with the Guinean president, King and a delegation talked with ambassador Robinson McIlvaine on May 13. The ambassador agreed the argument was a good one and worth trying. But he warned King that the

Papal Nuncio had flown in from Rome to request a change in the decree and was given short shrift.

When McIlvaine offered King an office in the embassy to prepare his case, King went a step further: "I haven't any experience of protocol involved in presenting a letter to such a high dignitary." The ambassador assigned his assistant to help formalize the appeal.

While they worked on the document, church president Paul Keita met with the Guinean secretary of state, a radical Marxist, but got nowhere. On May 14 the president repeated his decision to expel all foreign church workers.

The mission's appeal did not ask for a blanket revocation of the decree. It made a case for allowing some missionaries to remain and complete their specialized tasks: (1) To prepare men for churches without pastors; (2) To train an all-African faculty for the Bible institute; (3) To continue translation of the Bible into the major vernaculars; (4) To provide a pastor for the English-speaking international congregation in Conakry.

Preparing the appeal was only half the challenge. Time was running out. How could they get it past the various hurdles of bureaucracy and to the president who already had left the capital for a holiday? Providentially, the missionary taking the document to the government building on May 16 met the courier who was gathering mail from the various ministries for the president. The courier stuck the missionary's envelope in his pouch and delivered it directly to Sekou Toure's vacation retreat.

King worked out an evacuation plan with Ralph Shellrude, the Mission chairman, and left the following day. Word was quietly passed to the Mission from a government source, telling the missionaries to sit tight. Shellrude and Keita had an audience with the president on May 20. He indicated that his administration would give favorable consideration to the appeal.

At month's end, the French Catholic monsignor and all his personnel were "escorted" to exits of the country by civil and military representatives—some rudely put on trucks at night and driven to the border. All four of the other Protestant missions left, as did most Alliance missionaries. However, thirteen were allowed to continue their work in Telekoro (Bible institute and translation), Conakry (bookstore and international congregation) and Mamou (missionary children's school).

The Mission was still working in Guinea in 1984 when Sekou Toure died while undergoing heart surgery in Cleveland, Ohio. A bloodless coup the following year ended the Marxist regime and restrictions were gradually relaxed. Such was the new government's respect for the Alliance that only Protestant missions approved by the Mission were allowed to work in the country.

If the previous regime had intended to cripple the Church with the expulsion of foreign workers, it grossly miscalculated. The Church did indeed stagger from shock in the short term. Enrollment in the Bible institute dropped from ninety-two in 1967 to twenty-five six years later. But the number of students then started to climb, reflecting a recovery in the Church at large.

In the ten years following Sekou Toure's decree, the Church nearly doubled in size. During 1978 alone, 3,900 people turned to Christ. In 15 years the number of churches had tripled to 4,000 baptized members.[14]

The C&MA Church in Guinea proved anew—as in China, Cambodia, Vietnam and elsewhere—that establishing viable, authentic indigenous churches as the first priority of missions is the way to go.

Banmethuot Massacre

When 1968 dawned in Central Vietnam, relative quiet reigned in the provincial capital of Banmethuot, also site of an Alliance mission station. Four and one-half years had passed since Communist soldiers had abducted two Alliance missionaries and a Mennonite volunteer from the leprosarium. Continuing silence over their fate frequently reminded the mission staff that the enemy could strike again.

On January 30, the Lunar New Year, they did. Launching the *Tet* offensive, Viet Cong troops attacked almost every major city and important location in the long, narrow country. In a predawn raid on the Banmethuot station, the house occupied by Carolyn Griswold and her father, a short-term retired volunteer, disintegrated in a powerful blast. Leon Griswold died instantly. Carolyn lay trapped for hours in the wreckage before being rescued.

Other residences were also shelled, driving the missionaries to smaller shelters. Betty Olsen and Ruth Wilting, both nurses, tended to

Carolyn in a storage room. Olsen made a dash in her car to the clinic for medical supplies to treat her colleague and wounded tribal Raday Christians. The Viet Cong shot up her car and she was captured.

Edward and Ruth Thompson, followed by Marie Ziemer, had moved to a makeshift bunker. Robert Ziemer emerged to beg permission of the Viet Cong to take the wounded to a safer location. He was killed instantly with a shot in the head. Ruth Wilting rushed to his aid and was wounded. Soldiers tracked her back to the bunker, threw in a grenade and poured gunfire through the opening. The two Thompsons and Wilting died instantly. Marie Ziemer was lashed with grenade shrapnel.

Bleeding and dazed, she crawled from the shelter and perhaps was spared because of her white hair. They forced her to walk to another location where the Raday church leaders and several other Americans, including Olsen, were being held. The Viet Cong took Olsen, Hank Blood (a USAID worker) and several Radays when they retreated into the jungle. Only Blood, a tough ex-Marine, survived the trek and spent the remainder of the war in the infamous Hanoi Hilton prison.

Ziemer was released after two days and with the help of a Raday Christian walked to friendly lines. American military airlifted her to an army field hospital. She underwent emergency surgery and, almost miraculously, survived the whole ordeal. Griswold was rescued by Vietnamese rangers and put on the same flight but she died in the hospital.

All told, six Alliance workers and twelve Raday Christians died in the *Tet* offensive. It was the worst such massacre since the Boxer Rebellion in 1900, when thirty-six Swedish missionaries affiliated with the C&MA were murdered.

Banmethuot was the only mission center to suffer loss of life. A dramatic airlift by the US military rescued twenty-one missionaries at Dalat. Communist forces overran Hue and other places where workers were stationed but they all had escaped to safety.

King was winding up a four-week deputation trip to Africa when the tragedy occurred. He did not receive word until arriving in Paris on February 4. He immediately booked a flight to Bangkok where he hoped to get a plane to Saigon. But the unsettled situation forced him and T. Grady Mangham, area secretary, to remain in Bangkok. King's bout with malaria further delayed their arrival in Vietnam until February 9.

By that time, on advice by the State Department, more than forty C&MA women and children were evacuated to Bangkok. Another forty missionaries remained in Vietnam. Eventually the Vietnamese Mission returned to almost full strength and continued ministry with the *Hoi Thanh Tinh Lanh* church for another seven years.

Those years held many dangers, risks and tense times. Never answered was the missionaries' question why their colleagues at Banmethuot died or were taken, but they were spared. One of the missionaries, a single woman, expressed her attitude about it all. She had been interviewed by Hal Boyle, a nationally syndicated American columnist, before the Banmethuout massacre. He asked if she felt uneasy living in a war zone. Her reply: "I have no fear because I am in the center of God's will." Her name was Betty Olsen.

The Bottom Line

Turmoil roiled the decade of the 1960s in many areas where the Alliance worked. A tense Mission-Church situation in Gabon, a nasty church split in Congo, an anti-mission regime in Guinea, a horrible massacre of missionaries and local Christians in Vietnam. . . . But in those same locations the Church emerged stronger, taking its witness to a new level and new places.

Gabon, the field where the Mission was once on the verge of walking out or being kicked out, demonstrated the principle that it's always too early to quit.

During their field forum (conference) in 1997, missionaries decided it was time to launch an all-out effort together with the church to take the gospel to every one of the country's remaining twenty people groups that did not yet have the gospel. They pledged $25,000 to jump-start a village-by-village campaign to see "a church for every people and the gospel for every person" by 2000.

The combined Church-Mission team identified 55 villages with a population of 500 people or more who needed to hear about Christ. They named their initiative "Operation Villages for Jesus." Campus Crusade for Christ joined the effort by providing copies of the *Jesus* film and equipment to help get people's attention and whet their appetites for more.

Ralph Trainer, one of the workers taking part, described what happened next. "One day, two vehicles loaded with the trained Gabonese evangelists, a few personal belongings, a film projector, a generator and a map indicating neglected areas and target locations, left for fifteen months."[15]

During those fifteen months, the two teams saw more than 10,000 people pray to receive Christ. Thirty churches were started and forty established churches experienced revival. Trainer reported the "conversions of religious workers, witch doctors, village chiefs and government officials. Miraculous healings demonstrated the power of God."

He summed up "Operation Villages for Jesus" in triumphant terms: "There are no more unreached people groups in Gabon!"

Mission and Church leaders then raised their sights to see that every Gabonese individual was evangelized. To help achieve this goal, they initiated "Operation Barnabas," training follow-up teams to disciple the new converts.

From the 1960s, when the Africans and missionaries were at loggerheads, to 2000, when they worked in harmony to take the gospel to every unreached people group in Gabon, was a long journey, often rocky and painful for all involved. But the result was well worth the cost.

Notes

1. Louis L. King, "Report on the Third Asia Conference," *Report to the Foreign Department* (July 15-20, 1961), p. 6.
2. George C. Klein, "Historic Conference," *The Alliance Witness*, March 4, 1964, p. 12.
3. King, "Report on the Third Asia Conference," p. 12.
4. Louis L. King, "Report of the Fifth Asia Conference," *Report to the Foreign Department* (February 18-26, 1969), p. 25.
5. Ibid., p. 27.
6. "Extent," *Report to the Foreign Department* (December 1962), pp. 4-5.
7. "The Chairmanship," *Report to the Foreign Department* (January 24, 1963), p. 3.
8. Samuel I. Kim, *Unfinished Mission in Thailand: The Uncertain Impact on the Buddhist Heartland* (Seoul: East-West Center for Missions Research and Development, 1980), pp. 79-88.
9. David H. Moore, "Models of Church/Mission Relationships," unpublished study, p. 2.
10. Kim, p. 85.
11. Louis L. King, "Report of the Trip to Holland, France, West Africa, Gabon, and Congo," *Report to the Foreign Department* (March 21, 1959), p. 6.
12. Robert L. Niklaus, "Courageous Soldier and Gentle Christian," *The Alliance Witness*, May 17, 1961, p. 12.

The World His Field

13. Ironically, this author did little with this story until he was telling King about it—and was asked if he had written it up. Once written and published in the Alliance magazine, the article took on a life of its own.
14. Louis L. King, "Church Under a Socialist Regime" (case study, September 23, 1978), p. 14.
15. Ralph S. Trainer, "Villages for Jesus," *Alliance Life,* September 2000, p. 19.

NINE
Full Stride Worldwide

1969-1978
Time Markers

After the decidedly rebellious decade pf the 1960s, the 1970s were muddled and meandering. Overseas there were wars in Indochina and Israel and unchecked international terrorism; at home, an unprecedented crisis in the White House, self-doubting higher education and a death sentence on unborn, unwanted babies. Some called it the "un-decade," symbolized by a round and bland smiling face that could mean anything, or nothing.

Reacting to a new Communist offensive in April 1975, President Ford said flatly, "The Vietnam War is finished." Finished perhaps for the Americans, but not the tens of thousands fleeing Communism; 130,000 refugees came to the United States from Indochina as Cambodia and then South Vietnam crumbled in defeat.

The United States created the Environmental Protection Agency and mandated the use of unleaded gasoline. Conservationists celebrated the first Earth Day. For the first time in history, the majority of Americans lived in suburbs.

Despite wars and scandals, the United States looked good to Russian refugee Aleksandr Solzhenitsyn. The Dow-Jones average hit 1,000 for the first time in 1972, but cigarette stocks took a hit when the government mandated health warnings added to advertisements. The government also ordered non-discrimination in the workplace.

A NATO summit conference in Washington adopted a fifteen-nation mutual defense program. No one could have imagined the first time it would be called into action would be on September 11, 2001.

With polls indicating that thirty-four percent of Americans considered themselves born-again believers, 1975 was declared the "Year of the Evangelical." The ordination of a self-declared lesbian to the Episcopalian priesthood further widened the divide between liberals and conservatives. The presiding bishop hailed the event as "a sign of healthy change in attitudes toward homosexuals."

***

The threshold of the new decade held milestones for the Alliance. The annual report for 1970 cited the usual yet remarkable accomplishments of lay groups. The Women's Missionary Prayer Fellowship, more than 21,500 women in 1,355 local groups, collected over $390,000 for missionary outfits and projects and another $300,000 for the national project. The 266 chapters of Alliance Men were especially active in supporting "The Alliance Hour" programs broadcast over 60 stations. Both groups gave strong backing to "Alliance Key 73," a continent-wide evangelistic effort whose goal was saturation evangelism in every community with an Alliance church. "Operation Harvest," the final phase of "Alliance Key 73," reported a high of 23,791 conversions, but about half the churches did not participate. Another three-year campaign was launched.

In 1975 the Alliance suffered its most traumatic losses since the Boxer Rebellion of 1900. The collapse of Cambodia and Vietnam and dispersal of missionaries, and the subsequent flood of refugees, including many Christians, dealt a heavy blow to Alliance work in Asia.

However, the silver lining was the numerous Vietnamese and Cambodian churches formed by refugees coming to North America. That year Germany joined France and Holland in the scope of ministry in Europe. The Alliance Youth Corps had its biggest summer yet: sixty-four college students in sixteen countries.

When Nathan Bailey retired after seventeen years as C&MA president, he could report that all indicators, both foreign and domestic, were up. In North America since 1960, income was up 285 percent; number of churches, 35 percent; membership 65 percent; and baptisms 137 percent. More than any previous president, he involved the Alliance with cooperative evangelical organizations such as the World Relief Commission, of which he was president for nine years.

By the late 1960s and into the next decade, the Alliance reached full stride worldwide on an unprecedented scale. In some respects, it was a delayed result of the halcyon days of post-World War II, when the United States and Canada, unscarred by foreign invasion and riding high on the tide of military victory, relished a can-do attitude toward the world.

Years of marshaling resources and laying foundations were required before the C&MA in North America could join in the rewards of the postwar era. Former GIs, with an awakened vision of the world's unevangelized masses, first had to prepare for a new kind of conflict—spiritual warfare. And once overseas, they had to learn through time-consuming trial and error that veteran missionaries actually were doing some things right.

Conditions in overseas churches also required years of preparation for a broad advance. A new generation of church workers had to be trained. National churches had to divest themselves of suffocating Mission subsidies and find their place in new sovereign states or newly liberated countries. Paradigm shifts in strategies like McGavran's people movements and King's urban evangelism had to be fine-tuned through experience. Specialized agencies like Mission Aviation Fellowship, Wycliffe Bible Translators and missionary radio pioneers had to train personnel, raise funds and secure equipment before they could reach their potential in support ministries.

Missiologist Ralph Winter referred to the exciting postwar period of accelerating missions momentum as "the twenty-five unbelievable years." C&MA treasurer King concurred from his own perspective in funding overseas operations: "It was a great time to be treasurer," he said. "Budgets were met and surpassed. Giving to the General Fund increased percentage-wise every year."

The missionary rally that climaxed one of the General Councils indicated the spirit of the period. Louis King had given the challenge of missions and invited young people to surrender their lives to God's call. After waiting while a large group gathered at the front, he prepared to give the benediction. But a young man high in the balcony cried out, "Wait, Dr. King! I'm coming!" He hurried to the main floor and ran down to the front—part of a new generation that did not want to miss out on the blessing of serving God overseas.

By the 1970s foreign secretary King also reached full stride in his worldwide activities. He was aided by an enlarged and gifted Foreign Department staff that included an administrative assistant and four regional directors. Canadian-born and Congo-experienced Arni Shareski became his right-hand man; George Klein was director for Africa; David Volstad, for South America; T. Grady Mangham, Southeast Asia and the Middle East; and William Kerr, Pacific Islands and Hong Kong. The missionary staff numbered over 930 working in 34 countries. The Alliance overseas communities totaled nearly 7,000 churches and preaching points with 692,000 inclusive members.

King's commitment to indigenous church development, urban evangelism and other innovative strategies earned him widespread respect as a missionary leader in the evangelical community. He was president of the Evangelical Foreign Missions Association (now Evangelical Fellowship of Mission Agencies) and a board member for many years. He organized two historic missions conferences and along the way received two honorary doctorates in recognition of his efforts in promoting world missions.

Focused Style

How did he manage during those years of intense activities in different directions, often marked by crises and tragedies? Perhaps one word summarized his leadership style: discipline. It was the same quality that had carried him from a small-town church to a top-level role in world missions.

William Conley reminded King of a brief conversation at a field conference in Indonesia. "Another fellow and I were enjoying a chess game during a break in business sessions. When invited to take on one of us, you declined, saying that when you had nothing else to take your time you would rather sit and work out a theological problem in your mind! I didn't know what to make of that but we knew it was not an affectation on your part. Disciplined, I guess, would characterize your approach to your life and work."

R. Harold Mangham, later in several high-level posts of administration, recalled that when he was a young pastor, King gave him this advice: "The man who is successful is the one willing to take leisure time to improve his knowledge in his chosen field of endeavor."

King maintained that mindset throughout his ministry and set an example for others—and expected the same devotion to the job that he had. It did not make working for him an easy experience. During ten years as King's assistant, Shareski remembered there was little time for small talk in the office. His boss was all business.

Jewel Hall used words like *punctual* and *formal* to describe his relationship with her. She reciprocated by addressing him as "Dr. King," never by his first name. He was always very careful about appearances. If he intended to work in the empty office building on a weekend, he would tell her on Friday, leaving unsaid but understood that if she too planned to come in, she would have to bring another staff person with her.

Although he greatly depended on his secretary and appreciated her, King could be unconsciously abrupt and severe. Oddly, he explained that he was at his happiest when looking stern because that was when he was fully engrossed in his work. Nor was he reluctant to shovel papers off his desk to hers. Hall said, "He'd come out of his office at the end of the day and say, 'My work is done.' I'd agree, looking at him over the pile on my desk."

King's clean desk had another solution as well. What did not go to his secretary at the end of the day went into a deep file drawer of his desk. At times it was quite full. The papers would be retrieved for attention the following day.

Both Shareski and Hall agreed there was always an underlying compassion in their hard-driving boss. He was gentle and supportive of those who failed in an assignment or stumbled in moral failure, but insisted they give proof of recovery and change. Once confidence was restored, he, like the Apostle Paul with young Mark, did not refer to the matter again.

King did relax when he went to the national office lunchroom with his thin sandwich in a brown bag. He welcomed those who came to his table, listening with interest to their talk and adding comments from his own experience.

He didn't tell jokes because with so many good anecdotes from his travels, he didn't need to. Pastor Dana Lindsey recalled, "Your amusing stories from the mission field kept us in stitches, especially the one about the fainting bride whom you doused with a pail of water." However, he could enjoy a good joke by someone else, slapping his leg and letting loose a loud laugh, once with such gusto he knocked over a chair.

The same mixture of severity and warmth characterized his rapport with missionaries overseas. Arnold Cook, serving in Colombia during the 1960s and later as president of the Canadian C&MA, recalled King's firmness during one field executive committee meeting. The field director had purchased a piece of land without the Foreign Department's prior permission. "King did not mince his words. Looking directly at the director, he stated, 'This must never happen again!' "

The World His Field

Cook had his own heads-up from the foreign secretary. "I was church planting in a small city. He asked me about my role. When I told him I was serving as pastor of the small church, a missionary role he frowned upon, his response was direct: 'Arnold, it must turn out right!' In other words, it must be turned over to a national pastor at some point." When Cook had King as a guest in his home, he decided to have a "night off" with his children and watch some comedy films from the Canadian Embassy. He was apprehensive the foreign secretary would not approve of watching movies, but his fear was ungrounded. King joined in the laughter, enjoying the old flicks as much as anyone.

When retiring from full-time ministry, King received a letter from Peru that captured the change during his years of leadership. Richard and Elsie Abrams wrote to Louis and Esther,

> Dear Beloved Brethren:
>
> When we were young missionaries, the above greeting would have been untruthful. Louis L. King was anything but beloved! Respected, honored, obeyed with alacrity—all of these, yes. But loved—no! You were the distant and austere leader, the giver of commandments, always far more dedicated and disciplined than ever we could be.
>
> We remember an occasion in the early '70s when you and David Volstad [recently installed as area secretary] arrived in Lima to meet with the field executive committee. You had obviously dictated to David a series of measures to be communicated to us. We all filed into the conference room, took seats and exchanged the usual greetings. Then in the silent expectancy of the moment, with a slight nod toward Mr. Volstad, you said, "Read, David." Those two terse words became part of the folklore of the Peru field.
>
> But during the past decade, something happened. Gradually we have seen emerge a more mellow and human person, more tolerant and understanding, more ready to laugh and share with us. And somehow, those more human qualities have been more effective in communicating the Christlike character to us.

Marching on the Airwaves

Following World War II, radio technology caught the attention of some missionaries as a promising tool for communicating the gospel. Alliance workers helped organize some of the most powerful radio stations. HCJB, the "Voice of the Andes" in Quito, Ecuador, was cofounded by Reuben Larson, an Alliance missionary. ELWA was started in Monrovia, Africa, through the dogged and sacrificial efforts of William Watkins, son of Alliance missionaries to Guinea. TWR (Trans World Radio) grew out of the vision of Paul Freed, whose parents were former C&MA missionaries among the Arabs of the Middle East. Ralph Freed joined his son in the radio ministry.

TWR was to have a special relationship with the Alliance in Latin America for several decades. When King and Constance were touring the fields in the early 1960s, they repeatedly encountered requests by missionaries for money to start local gospel programming. The men from "260" were reluctant to parcel out small amounts to weak local stations scattered in different countries. Since the fields (except Brazil) used the same language to communicate the same message, why not focus funds on a powerful Spanish-language enterprise that could cover the continent?

In 1964 the two men visited a new radio station being built by TWR on Bonaire, an island in the Netherlands Antilles. The Freeds were in the process of installing powerful new transmitters that would accomplish the role King and Constance envisioned. And the Freeds were looking for program producers. They offered the Alliance the opportunity to be the first Spanish-language broadcaster on the new station. The proposal was for fifteen-minute programs four times daily at a reduced price too attractive to refuse.

Constance took the responsibility of getting the operation on the air—funds, programs, promotion, literature and staff. He didn't have to look far or long for a speaker who would be the radio voice of *Alianza en Marcha*.

Miguel Lecaro, pastor of the dynamic Templo Alianza in Guayaquil, Ecuador, was already a popular speaker on a local station. Volstad said, "People loved to hear Lecaro because he didn't preach at the listeners. He talked to them, as if one-on-one." The TWR staff agreed that he was the finest speaker of their Spanish-language department. Nyack College conferred an honorary doctorate on him in appreciation for his distinguished radio and pastoral achievements.

While Lecaro taped his messages in Guayaquil, a literature and correspondence office in Cali, Colombia, handled listener responses. Letters soon began coming in from Colombia, Venezuela, Dominican Republic, Puerto Rico and Cuba. By 1966 the Cali office was averaging 819 letters a month. Listeners responded from thirty-two countries. Correspondence rose in the mid-1970s to an average 2,000-plus letters a month. Broadcasts reached into Spain and could be heard as far north as Michigan and Connecticut.

The Roman Catholic Church unknowingly added to the success of *Alianza en Marcha*. Priests distributed small transistor radios pretuned to receive only Catholic broadcasts. But people soon discovered that with a bit of tampering they could pick up the Protestant programs from Bonaire.

An independent church in Colombia affiliated with the Alliance as a result of the broadcasts. Six Colombian congregations organized under the name of *Alianza en Marcha*. So did a church in Venezuela, and the response elsewhere in the country was so strong—over 3,000 listeners in a few years—that several national churches joined in supporting a missionary couple to follow up the inquirers.

Pedro Valdemar, a parochial schoolteacher in San Juan, Colombia, first heard the broadcasts in 1968. He responded to the gospel and gathered his family and friends to hear Lecaro's preaching. Eventually twenty of the group enrolled in correspondence courses offered by the Cali office. They met each evening in Valdemar's home and had a devotional service before the program. Soon the house was too small so the group moved to a rented hall and started Sunday services. This caught the attention of the local priest who had Valdemar fired from his teaching job.

The congregation contacted the radio office for help but the missionaries decided it was too far away—175 miles from the nearest Alliance church. They encouraged the group to unite with an evangelical mission in the area. The new converts persisted in sending reports about their growing numbers. Intrigued, Arnold Cook and Jake Hostetler went to San Juan to see what was happening. Hostetler's wife Margaret reported, "A delegation told the missionaries they would be Alliance whether or not they would ever meet the church leaders this side of heaven."[1]

While shortwave broadcasts from Bonaire reached listeners in rural areas, they were not widely popular in large cities where people preferred local stations, nor could the signal be clearly heard in the southern part of the continent. As missionary efforts shifted to cities, medium-wave broadcasts proved more effective and in keeping with Alliance urban strategy. In Lima, for example, one in every ten baptized converts said they first attended an Alliance church because of local radio.[2]

When the Alliance ceased airing shortwave programs from Bonaire after about thirty years, Lecaro, age seventy, was still speaking on local radio and still preaching two different sermons every Sunday in Templo Alianza, Guayaquil.

God Encounters

King was delighted to find workers in Latin America who shared his vision for reaching the major metropolises with the gospel. Lecaro's church used a strategy of assigning sizable numbers of members to start new works. Usually, within a year or so, new conversions and baptisms brought Lecaro's congregation back to full size.

Missionary Tom Kyle, a gifted evangelist in Brazil, committed himself to 100 days of continuous evangelistic services with the goal of establishing a new church by the conclusion of the series. "Give me a choir and a tent," he promised, "and I will give you a church." He started several churches using this strategy.

But the most successful plan, one that grew to continent-wide proportions, had a sputtering start. Kenn Opperman, missionary to Lima, Peru, proposed a plan with a vision that warmed King's heart, but its details left him cold.

"The program he concocted received a congenial welcome but it was so costly and so involved that I could not approve it," King noted. "My positive response was that something was being proposed about city work. I was of a strong opinion that the C&MA had to learn how to start churches that were large enough in size to gain the attention of people.

"Opperman had a good idea, but how he proposed to do it seemed to me not the way to go. He knew I didn't approve of his scheme, so he bypassed the field committee and Foreign Department and took it directly to General Council."

After Council turned down the proposal, King encouraged him to go back to the drawing board and draft a better plan of procedure. "It didn't take long for Kenn, his friends on the field and the LeTourneau family to come up with a new plan that would be suitable to my concept of how to do city work successfully in Lima."

The LeTourneau Foundation played a decisive role in funding the Lima vision into reality. The family owned a Texas-based corporation that pioneered in the design and manufacture of earth-moving equipment. One of the sons, Roy, was living in Lima to manage a road-building contract with the government. Seeing firsthand the spiritual needs of Peru's capital city, he helped the missionaries develop a strategy that not only won the Foreign Department's approval but also the LeTourneau Foundation's support.

King met with the board of directors when the 1971 General Council convened in Houston. "Out of the meeting," he reported, "grew a solid relationship that we could depend on, and the LeTourneaus would see that their investment resulted in almost certain success."

He described the Lima project in these words: "The aim was to enlarge two modest-size congregations so that each could have 1,000 people in regular attendance within fifteen months. Then these two congregations would 'hive off' and each start new congregations."

Even with the revised and scaled-down plan, King said, "This effort was very costly and intricate and could not have been attempted without a large loan and gift contributions from the LeTourneau Foundation for paying the cost of air travel and entertainment for about thirty evangelists from other countries, advertising through newspapers, bumper stickers, a church paper and television. There was also the expense of a radio program. Additionally, the Mission and the Church carried heavy financial loads."

From the start, King insisted the Lima endeavor be under the supervision of the Foreign Department, not the field. He knew that "because of the money involved and the project's size, it could become a problem on the field with so much attention given one church."

Other conditions helped shape the project and secure its success. Not only did the Mission have to relinquish its management of the project, it had to agree to the appointment of a missionary from another Latin American field to head the effort. King brought in Eugene Kelly from the Colombia field because he believed Kelly's personality and tireless energy would be a big asset. To its credit, the field committee accepted the decisions with grace.

One condition could have aroused negative reactions in the Peruvian Church. Evangelists from several countries and groups, not local preachers, would be invited for two to four weeks of ministry. Again, concerns for the kingdom overruled nationalistic sensitivities and the Peruvian leadership cooperated fully.

The Lima project could not wait for converts to materialize before providing adequate facilities to handle the response. The oversight committee, composed of four nationalities, surveyed potential sites and commissioned architectural plans before a single service was held. The LeTourneau Foundation provided most of the needed construction funds through a six-percent interest loan.

All these preparations would have been worthless had not the right churches been chosen to put the plan in action. The conditions were exacting. Each of the two churches had to agree to fifteen months of non-stop, intense outreach. Two weeks of evangelistic meetings every night were to be followed by two weeks with six evening Bible studies to disciple the new believers. Each church had to be willing to assume huge financial obligations and expand activities at a quickened pace. Members had to agree to join regular cell prayer groups and undergo training as counselors—in short, total mobilization.

The Lince congregation was the obvious candidate to launch the bold new plan. The small church had already shown initiatives in previous outreach efforts. It had conducted three campaigns and attendance had grown to 120 believers. Then a barren four years followed.

According to Miguel Angel Palomino, "a nucleus of believers began to realize that a stagnating church is not normal, but on the contrary, it should be constantly growing if it is alive and fulfilling the Great Commission. Thus, spontaneous prayer groups sprang up in homes and in the church itself. A spirit of great expectation developed within the congregation."

Palomino credited this surge in prayer activity, beginning in 1971, as the real beginning of the Lima project. "Most assuredly, the birth of [the program] can be dated from this period of transition and learning much before the campaigns began."[3]

One more element remained to be put in place before the Lince church could embark on the all-out effort: a pastor with strong pulpit and leadership abilities. Just as the Mission agreed to an outside coordinator and the national church accepted outside evangelists, the congregation graciously received a non-Peruvian pastor. Alfredo C. Smith, an articulate, educated and gifted leader, was called from Argentina to Lima in February of 1973.

He was delighted with his reception:

> As pastor of the church, I must give credit to the broad, affectionate and clearly felt support I received from the congregation. The atmosphere seemed similar to what must have pervaded the early church. Love, expectation, reverent fear and a will to work and to give sacrificially were clearly visible in the Lince congregation.[4]

Ripley-Style Response

The campaign began with an ambitious slogan that embraced the entire city of four million people: "Lima's Encounter with God" [LED in Spanish]. The first of the fifteen-month series of evangelistic meetings began in November of 1973. The astonishing results prompted one missionary to liken the program to one of Ripley's "believe-it-or-not" stories.

By the end of December 1974, the church reported that 2,050 people had received Christ, 205 were baptized and 700 regularly attended the church. Pastor Smith commented, "The operation must now adopt the name of 'Snowball.'"

To accommodate the rapidly growing congregation, a 1,000-seat sanctuary and education complex were ready on one of Lima's most important and heavily traveled avenues. The church's main entrance was fronted with glass doors so passersby could see what was happening inside—and give the lie to critics spreading ugly rumors about the church. "Accessibility, visibility and appearance became key factors and even influenced architecture in other Latin American cities," said coordinator Kelly.

Some people complained that the large and attractive building was too showy. But King insisted that the church's size and appearance were needed to make a statement that would catch the attention of Lima's residents. Indeed, the story circulated that if passengers asked taxi drivers where they could go for spiritual help, the cabbies took them to the Lince church.

With the church's outreach well underway, the planners turned to the second phase of LED, involving the Pueblo Libre church. Kelly expressed doubts about the choice of the smaller, less prepared congregation. "Many times I have asked myself why the Pueblo Libre church was included in the pilot project. Maybe it was to teach us how not to do it or how to come up with answers to a bad situation."

After more than a year of frustration and failures, some of the twenty-two church members agreed to cooperate with the new pastor, Francisco Perez, who was committed to the plan. The first campaign in January 1975 averaged between 350 and 400 attendees. Membership grew to 166 and regular attendance from 50 to 200. By the following year, membership more than doubled. The fired-up congregation dedicated its 2,000-seat sanctuary 2 years later.

The Lince congregation coped with its smaller 1,000-seat auditorium by commissioning groups of lay leaders and members to start new churches. In 1977 about fifty believers formed a cell group in the upper-middle class residential district of Miraflores; a year later another group from the mother church started a congregation in the El Augustino area of Lima; six more church plants followed, some in cooperation with Pueblo Libre members.

The LED churches kept pace with the growth through lay-training programs. The Lince congregation instituted an evening Bible academy to give new believers a firm grip on basic doctrines. In 1976 the Alliance Bible Institute was founded to prepare people for ministry. A group of forty-three students began classes two evenings a week. Five years later the first twelve students completed their studies and began pastoral work.

In 1993, twenty years after the first campaign, the Lima Encounter churches, now thirty instead of one, decided to celebrate the anniversary. They did so in characteristic fashion: All thirty congregations conducted evangelistic campaigns.

Much had changed during those two decades. The Lince church, now recognized internationally as a pacesetter in urban evangelism, still coped with its 1,000-seat sanctuary by conducting three services each Sunday for 4,000 attendees. The once-faltering Pueblo Libre congregation numbered 1,300 members. The daughter church in Miraflores filled its 1,000-seat facility each Sunday. The Alliance Bible Institute had expanded from 43 students to 290.

Richard Abrams, who succeeded Kelly as LED coordinator, estimated that in those 20 years more than 125,000 *Limenos* (residents of

Lima) had made some kind of commitment to Christ in the city's Alliance churches.[5]

The Lima effort encouraged the faltering nationwide Peru Encounter with God. Churches in other cities conducted their own campaigns with varying degrees of success and their efforts sometimes bore little resemblance to the original plan. But they could look to the Lima churches for advice and encouragement. The movement in 1991 went international, counting nearly 50 churches with 14,000 baptized members. Eight other denominations adopted similar urban strategies.

From the start, the Lima churches agreed to an open-ended commitment. Each of the congregations receiving financial help agreed first to pay back the loan and then continue paying into the fund for more church plants—until Christ returns.

Evangelical Ecumenism

About the same time the LED movement was picking up speed with King's encouragement, he was deeply involved in a project that would have wide-ranging significance. Harold Lindsell, then associate editor of *Christianity Today*, not one to indulge in hyperboles, said the 1966 Congress on the Church's World-Wide Mission held in Wheaton, Illinois, was an "epoch-making event" coming at a "junction point in Christian history."[6]

It was the largest ecumenical strategy conference on Protestant missions held in North America. In historical perspective, it was the most important such convocation since 1910 when the Edinburgh conference brought together a broad representation of denominational and independent agencies committed to world missions. The Wheaton event signaled the coming of age of the evangelical missionary movement that for the most part was less than 100 years old.

The historical junction referred to by Lindsell marked a crossroad when Roman Catholic and World Council of Churches paths intersected. The world of religion had been rocked by the apparent wide-ranging changes instituted by Vatican II. And after playing footsy with the Geneva-based ecumenical organization for decades, the International Missionary Council (IMC) formally joined the World Council. The merger took place in 1961 at its Third Assembly held in New Delhi.

What did these major events mean to evangelical missions and overseas national churches? What should be their response?

Many evangelicals and conservatives within the councilar denominations had participated in the International Missionary Council for decades. The 1961 merger forced them to face serious issues. The World Council position on such matters as universal salvation, inclusion of anti-evangelical Orthodox churches and the shift in focus from evangelism to social and economic changes conflicted with their biblical convictions. Those who withdrew from the IMC outnumbered those who remained.

This does not mean that evangelicals were united among themselves. The International Foreign Missions Association (IFMA), founded in 1917 by faith (nondenominational) missions, excluded all denominational and Pentecostal missionary organizations. For the 46 missionary societies and the 8,400 missionaries they represented, the IFMA offered spiritual fellowship and cooperation within narrow confines.

The C&MA did not join the organization. The reason may have been the Alliance policy of focusing on its mission and not becoming embroiled in theological controversies and feuding organizations. However, it did become a charter member of the Evangelical Foreign Missions Association (EFMA) founded in 1945 as the missions section of the National Association of Evangelicals. The EFMA organized as a voluntary group that welcomed denominational and nondenominational, evangelical and Pentecostal mission agencies. It specifically excluded non-evangelicals.

The organization drew together 59 groups with 6,452 missionaries working in 120 mission areas on all continents. The EFMA purposed to develop wider fellowship and greater spiritual unity among evangelical missions by encouraging consultation and cooperation among member groups.

Even so, the EFMA relationship with Pentecostal groups got off to a rocky start:

> Several conservative evangelical missions agencies refused to join the EFMA because of the existing membership of several Pentecostal organizations. In view of the developing resentment, the new association's unproved record of assistance, and the cost of contributions, Noel Perkin [Assemblies of God missions executive and a Nyack grad-

uate] reluctantly recommended withdrawal from the agency in late 1950. Three years later the department responded positively to the request of Dr. Clyde Taylor, executive director of EFMA, to rejoin the agency. Since then, the relationship of the Foreign Mission Department and the EFMA has been warm and cordial.[7]

Despite the many parallel beliefs and objectives of IFMA and EFMA, the two fellowships operated independently for decades—and at times with less than Christian fraternal ties. As late as 1960, when the IFMA organized a missions conference, EFMA members were not invited.

When the two groups finally got together, they issued a joint confession in the Wheaton Declaration:

> Christians having been regenerated by the Holy Spirit and who agree on the basic evangelical doctrines can experience a genuine biblical oneness, even if they belong to different denominations.... Evangelicals, however, have not fully manifested this biblical oneness because of carnal differences and personal grievances.[8]

Only six years after the all-IFMA conference, the world missions landscape had so drastically altered, thanks mainly to Vatican II and the WCC New Delhi Assembly, that walls between the two mission agencies began to crumble. The two groups gathered on the Wheaton College campus for an historic convocation that would define evangelical mission cooperation for the rest of the century and into the new millennium.

"It took a big vision and large faith to advocate another Congress with wider constituency so soon after 1960," remarked IFMA's Horace L. Fenton, general director of the Latin American Mission.

> It required much persuasion and debate to win commitment from Mission leaders to initiate Wheaton 1966. The very fact we gathered at all, on such a scale and under the sponsorship of these two groups, seemed a miracle in itself. For there had been among us strong differences in conviction that have kept us apart in spite of the basic theological unity we have claimed.[9]

The one man more responsible than any other for this "miracle" was Louis L. King. As originally planned, he was to be the EFMA cosponsor with IFMA's Ralph B. Odman, former director of the Regions Beyond Missionary Union. But Odman fell ill and died just before the Congress. Vernon Mortensen of The Evangelical Alliance Mission was chosen to replace him but too late to serve except in name only.

On King fell the dual responsibility of preparing for, and then chairing, the event. Though sobered by its significance and scope, he welcomed the role. It was consistent with Alliance involvement with broad-based, biblically ecumenical efforts dating back to Simpson's desire to have good relations with all true Christians. He had supported the Evangelical Alliance in England founded in 1846 and its North American counterpart established twenty-one years later.

King's own early experience as a pastor in the United States and then as a missionary in India forged a strong interest in inter-mission cooperation. During his years as foreign secretary he sought to widen his contacts with his peers in other organizations ranging from ecumenical to Pentecostal. He saw no problem in his friendship with Dr. Eugene Smith of the National Council of Churches. He also maintained a close and cordial relationship with Melvin L. Hodges, a missions leader of the Assemblies of God, whom he considered "a great missionary leader in his own right." Hodges presented one of the major study papers at the Wheaton Congress.

Despite the gulf between IFMA and EFMA for years, King and a few others sought in low-keyed efforts to bring them together. "Some of us in the EFMA and certain people within the IFMA were trying to get our two groups to be more cooperative and understanding of each other. We would have a small group to discuss this and that. This gradually developed into the idea we ought to have a world convocation to take up the prominent areas of problems and come to some agreed-upon solutions of understanding."

Preparations were time-consuming and had to begin a year in advance of the 1966 meeting. No instant communications such as the Internet or faxes were yet available to span the nations and oceans separating the speakers and organizers. It was mostly a snail-mail process and ultimately it all depended on King to keep the project on schedule. "It was an enormous load, to say the least," he admitted.

But he had the full cooperation of some outstanding men in both associations on the organizing committee. Men like Arthur F. Glasser (Overseas Missionary Fellowship), Kenneth S. Kantzer (Trinity Evangelical Divinity School) and Milton Baker (Conservative Baptist Foreign Missionary Society) were all busy men in their own work, but they freely gave of their time.

The World His Field

"You wouldn't know we represented two different organizations when we got together to work. There was a wonderful unanimity," King said. "There were always discussions, of course, but never in the sense of 'I'll separate if I don't have it my way.' None of that at all."

The planning committee agreed upon ten major mission issues that would be the backbone of the sessions: syncretism, neo-universalism, proselytism, neo-Romanism, church growth, foreign missions, unity, evaluating methods, social concern and a hostile world. A review group chaired by King was set up to "ride herd" on the writers of the position papers.

King flew to Chicago almost every month to review the drafts with colleagues like Merrill C. Tenney, dean of the Wheaton Graduate School, and G. Linwood Barney, dean of Nyack's Jaffray School of Missions. The authors had been given general guidelines but were not told what to write. King outlined the process for reviewing the papers: "Each of us already had received a copy and we debated the position taken by the writer. We didn't try to change his position, but we did suggest how to strengthen the paper. Some ideas had too much attention and perhaps some others not enough. Or the writer might be in error in some points.

"We didn't want a fluke on our hands, and these position writers knew what we were going to do. Sometimes the author had to rewrite his paper two or three times until we felt the balance was there and delegates would not be debating a paper with all kinds of erroneous concepts and flaws."

The Wheaton Declaration

All the preliminary pieces fell into place by the time the Congress on the Church's Worldwide Mission convened in Wheaton on April 9-16, 1966. It was an event of tremendous significance, drawing nearly 1,000 delegates from 150 mission boards in 71 nations. The American- and Canadian-based missionary agencies represented 13,000 workers, constituting two-thirds of all North American overseas workers.

Smith, head of the United States missions division of the WCC, was an observer at the conference. He termed it "a notable gathering, superbly organized, representing a larger number of missionaries than any previous missionary assembly in North America, seriously and creatively considering the evangelistic task of the Church in today's world."[10]

King opened the convocation with a keynote address that focused on his favorite topic: the supremacy and centrality of Jesus Christ in His Church. He based his thoughts on Ephesians 1:22-23: "And God placed all things under his feet and appointed him to be head over everything for the church, which is his body, the fullness of him who fills everything in every way."

The conclusion of his message left the delegates in no doubt as to the primary focus of the Congress: the Church, and the One who deserved their supreme loyalty.

> Christ's Person and Godhead, His offices and all His interest and His resources—all these in fullness have been given to the Church. Nothing, absolutely nothing, is withheld. All that He is as the Son of God; all that He is as Son of Man; all that He is as Mediator between God and Man; all of His service, His time, His care, His thought, and His very life—all these in fullness have been dedicated and given to the Church. With this sure knowledge, never let the words "weak" and "poor" be used again with reference to the Church![11]

One commentator observed, "The attention of the delegates was riveted on the speaker as he spoke with great authority and without reference to any manuscript. Some carried the message away as the sharpest memory of the Congress."[12]

Several Alliance men shared the speaker's podium during the week. Jack Shepherd, Jaffray School of Missions, gave the first major study paper, "Missions and Syncretism. "As the essential core of the Christian faith," he said, "we affirm this must include the utter lostness of man, 'there is none righteous, no not one,' and that the death, burial and bodily resurrection of Christ, God's Incarnate Son, has brought full expiation for sin and justification before God."

Philip Teng, Hong Kong, was one of the Bible expositors. Le-Hoang-Phu, Vietnam, presented the area briefing on Asia. Doan-van-Mieng, Vietnam, participated in the opening public rally.

After each major study paper was presented in plenary session, the delegates divided into groups to discuss its contents and report back to the main body. The draft committee led by King considered these comments when formulating the lengthy statement that became known as the Wheaton Declaration.

The intense process of preparing a joint declaration for such a large assembly of Christian leaders with cherished backgrounds and fervent convictions could have precipitated a verbal bloodbath. But the long months of careful preparation paid off. The meetings were serious but harmonious. Differences of opinion were expressed freely but without ultimatums. King said with a grin, "The sessions worked like a charm."

The 938 official delegates voted on each section of the 23-page Wheaton Declaration. Only one delegate registered dissent on two items, but withdrew his opposition at the end so that approval of the document was unanimous. "This is not to say that every delegate was in agreement with every particle of the Declaration," Lindsell observed, "but it did have the overwhelming support of most of them in every regard."[13]

After adopting the document, the delegates sang "A Mighty Fortress Is Our God" with an exuberance that seemed to rock Pierce Chapel. Thirty-five years later, King grew emotional with the memory: "It was one of the most moving experiences in my whole life. Even thinking about it still moves me."

King should have taken time off after the grueling week at Wheaton, but he didn't believe in vacations. Instead, putting the achievement behind him, he went immediately to Denver, where he was a main speaker at the National Association of Evangelicals.

But others did not dismiss so easily his pivotal role in the Wheaton Congress. Billy Graham asked him to be part of the organizing committee of the Berlin Congress of World Evangelism. King declined, saying, "I have to keep my head about me for the C&MA and can't take on any more."

In the following year, Wheaton College conferred on him the Doctor of Divinity degree. The citation read in part: "International and Interdenominational mission leader, author, ordained minister of the Gospel, and missionary, the Reverend Louis Ladner King currently serves as Foreign Secretary of The Christian and Missionary Alliance. As the distinguished chairman of the Wheaton Congress on the Church's Worldwide Mission, his executive ability directed the formulation of the now famous 'Wheaton Declaration.' " (Asbury Theological Seminary gave him a second honorary doctorate in 1980.)

Green Lake Conference

In his overview of the Wheaton Congress, Lindsell commented,

> What the delegates do now that the Congress is over will be more important than what they did when meeting together. Certainly the meeting was not a final act. It was only a curtain-raiser to other Congresses which must follow. It was a laudable start in the right direction.[14]

One of the first tangible results of closer coordination between the EFMA and IFMA was a joint publication. King was appointed to head an editorial group to organize such a periodical. The result was the *Evangelical Missions Quarterly*, now a widely respected missiological journal that represents the work of agencies and individuals in the two associations.

Another tangible result of the Wheaton gathering was not long in coming. The joint committee organized a meeting on the Baptist conference grounds at Green Lake, Wisconsin, near the end of September 1971. The 4-day conference drew 379 delegates from 102 evangelical missions, including 215 mission executives. Unlike the wide-ranging agenda at Wheaton, this conference would focus sharply on one issue.

King recalled, "One of the prominent problems at that time was Church-Mission relationships on the mission field. It was becoming acute and people involved in missions dealing with the problem needed to look at various patterns that might work for them. With the continuing friendly and cooperative attitude between EFMA and IFMA, we decided to go it a second time and the topic would be church relations."

Rapidly evolving political developments produced social changes, especially during the turbulent 1960s. Relationships between missions and the churches they had founded needed to be updated, but what should they be? On what enduring principles should new directions be based?

The obvious logical solution, according to WCC partisans, was integration of the Mission into the Church, "like salt dissolves in water." The C&MA foreign secretary, however, had faced this issue in the early 1960s and had distinctly different ideas. His innovative approach, especially in Church-Mission agreements, caught the attention of other Mission leaders searching for solutions.

While King agreed with the concept of a convocation, he disagreed with the committee's action in choosing him to be one of the two main speakers. Twice he refused the invitation but relented on the third try.

Part of his reluctance stemmed from a deep respect for the second resource person who would present a different and, in some respects, opposing view. He considered George W. Peters, professor of World Missions at Dallas Theological Seminary, a "remarkable man" and had no desire to engage him in what would be essentially a debate.

Peters had written several articles after the Wheaton Congress. Critiquing its declaration, he rightly recognized the principle of dichotomy running through the text. He did not think the concept "functionally most effective, filially most satisfying, scientifically most helpful," or that it expressed "the highest Biblical idealism."[15]

"In the end," King remembered, "the difference between the two of us was not as pronounced as some people thought it would be. George Peters was not advocating an outright fusion of Church and Mission as the ecumenical people had done in organizing their work so that the Mission ceased to exist. He envisioned a modified fusion."

King's own views on dichotomy would become modified, especially in view of his experience with the Congo (Zaire) Church. The situation with such a long-established Church almost mandated that certain missionaries would be appointed to work with the Church in areas like literature and education; others would be assigned specifically to evangelism and church planting.

But there was a marked difference between the Peters and King positions presented in two evening sessions of the Green Lake Conference. One was given by Peters, a seminary professor long on abstracts and short on specifics. The other was by King, a hard-nosed executive who dealt with practical realities.

"I was much more specific and had more evidence for my position of definite dichotomy as the C&MA was practicing it," the foreign secretary said. "I had over sixty documents from the ecumenical missions department of the World Council to prove that fusion was not the way to go. The course we were taking would preserve the Mission so it could do missions, preserve the national entity of the church and free the church from foreign dependence and all the hurt and resentment that went with such a strategy."

Fifteen years prior to the Green Lake meeting, King had confronted the relationship issue's thorny problem of foreign subsidy. In what he termed "a veritable miracle," in five years all overseas Alliance pastors were off subsidy and supported by their churches, leading the way to authentic autonomy.

It happened none too soon. The tumultuous decade of the '60s would test the mettle of the C&MA churches to the extreme in countries like Laos, Vietnam, Cambodia, Indonesia, Colombia, Gabon, Congo and Guinea. Cartmel observed,

> Without their self-identity established as distinct from the mission and their developed self-support policy, their problems would have been compounded. As he addressed the delegates at Green Lake, King could speak from experience. The indigenous church policy of the C&MA had not only been tested but the results positive.[16]

Peters also criticized the concept of separate identities for the overseas Mission and the Church because he could not fit it "into the body structure of the Church."[17]

King, although a passionate proponent of the indigenous church, did not view overseas churches through rose-colored lenses. He recognized that they might be vulnerable to "the inveterate tendency to self-centeredness" and that some in fact did display a "pathological anxiety" to control the founding Mission. Churches, he insisted, were never meant to be an end in themselves, absorbing funds from abroad for their own improvement and assigning missionaries to serve the church's unending needs. They came into existence to be the "means for enlarging and extending the spread of the gospel."[18]

Firm in conviction born of experience, King stood his ground: "The point is that mission administration separate from the church's control is valid and very often necessary for missionary endeavor."[19]

He summed up his position on dichotomy:

> As for me, I hold that the pattern of church-mission relationship ought not to have as its final criterion simply a compatible relationship. Rather, I look at the dichotomy pattern as I do that of fusion. I look to see if it allows both the older and the younger church to be New Testament kinds of churches. Does it meet the scriptural requirements regarding a church's function? Most essentially, does it foster or stifle a passion for evangelism and missions in both?

That, it seems to me, is the test of all tests. And dichotomy passes it quite well. The record of evangelism and missionary activity in both the older and younger churches that have operated under this system is well known to us and speaks for itself.[20]

No vote was taken as to who won the quasi debate, but for Donald McGavran, editor of the *Church Growth Bulletin* published by Fuller Theological Seminary, there was no question about the stronger presentation. Under the title "A Definitive Statement on Church-Mission Relationships," McGavran wrote that King's addresses described the situation most accurately and laid down biblical and practical guidelines for both Church and Mission.

He advised,

> This luminous statement should be translated into many languages and printed as news, as a pamphlet on church-mission relationships, as material for conventions of churches and assemblies of missions to study and discuss, and as advanced thinking on missions.[21]

1975: Pivotal Year

Leading up to his last term in the Foreign Department, King could look out on a world where everywhere the Alliance had been advancing and growing. To be sure, the coming years held promise of great things, but they would range across the whole spectrum between tragedy and triumph. It began with a collapse of nations in Asia to Communism. It ended with the triumphant formation of a global Alliance configuration.

Indochina, a French name that encompassed Laos, Cambodia and Vietnam, was in the final, futile throes of resisting Communist domination. Sensing total victory, the Russian- and Chinese-backed armies in all three countries launched an all-out assault in early January of 1975.

Cambodia was the first to fall. Alliance missionaries had begun the year with great expectations. From one small church in 1970, the capital city of Phnom Penh had twenty-seven places of worship five years later. Field director Eugene Hall reported, "In just the first six months of 1974, there were as many new worshipers as in the previous fifty years. The pace of growth continued in the first two months of 1975, when 210 people were baptized."[22]

Then the Khmer Rouge began its final push to overthrow the Lon Nol regime that was friendly to the United States and tolerant of Alliance missions. "Since January the Mekong River, the main supply line into the city, had to be closed," Hall reported. "With rebel forces gradually forming a line around the city, it was felt prudent for the missionary staff to leave."[23]

In February, C&MA president Bailey ordered them to withdraw temporarily to Bangkok. The next month when King was in Saigon for a similar crisis, he flew to Phnom Penh to urge the Cambodian Church leaders to leave the country. They all said, "No, we will stay with our people—we will die with them." A sense of foreboding yet calm acceptance hung over their last meal together. King returned to Saigon.

Chric Taing, general secretary of the Khmer Evangelical (C&MA) Church, mailed a final, handwritten note to King on April 7, 1975. "I have decided to end my life in Cambodia reaching out to millions of Khmer souls with the Gospel of Jesus Christ our Lord. When I left my family in Britain in October 1973, it was because the Lord spoke to me in Philippians 1:21, 'For me, to live is Christ and to die is gain.' Please pray for me that I may not forget it."

In a matter of days, the city fell and one of the most horrendous periods in human history began. The mass expulsion of 2 million people living in Phnom Penh ushered in the era of the Cambodian Holocaust. Few Christians survived. Most of the nation's estimated 5,000 believers and church workers were clubbed, shot or starved to death along with over a million other Cambodians.

Chric was spotted by Khmer Rouge soldiers as he distributed gospel tracts to people on the shore of the Mekong River in Phnom Penh. Without hesitation they shot him. Chric's witness was cut off, but the gospel could not be silenced nor the Church exterminated. It would outlive the Khmer Rouge holocaust and emerge stronger than ever while the Communist era was reduced to history.

In May of 1975 Laos slipped almost unnoticed under the control of the Pathet Lao forces. Evacuated to Thailand on May 16, Helen Sawyer wrote,

> We were not driven out of Laos by falling rockets and gunfire as our fellow missionaries had been in Cambodia. . . . It was threats and false accusations against us by protestors and strikers in the office of another Christian organization located near ours that made it seem wise for us to leave.[24]

Clement R. Dreger, the Mission leader, was allowed to return a week later to close down the work. Communist officials signed his exit visa—

and took his residence card. The message was clear: "You are free to go, but not to return." Contact with the Laotian and tribal churches was cut off. Reliable reports filtered across the Thai border that the victors took after the Christians with a vengeance.

The end of missionary work in Vietnam began with an assault on a familiar target of the North Vietnamese army and its Viet Cong allies: Banmethuot. In 1962 two Alliance missionaries and a Mennonite volunteer were seized and never heard from again. In 1968 the Communists returned during the *Tet* offensive, killed five missionaries and dragged an Alliance nurse, a Wycliffe translator and a USAID worker into the jungle. Only the civilian, a tough ex-Marine, survived the march to the infamous Hanoi Hilton.

The third and final attack on Banmethuot began Sunday night, March 9, 1975. The South Vietnamese defenses crumbled three days later and four more Alliance workers were captured: Canadian missionary Norman Johnson; Americans Richard and Lillian Phillips; and Betty Mitchell, whose husband had disappeared after the 1962 raid.

First held in a primitive stockade near Pleiku and then in Hanoi, the four would pass 234 days in captivity before being flown to Bangkok and freedom on October 30.

With the war reaching a critical stage in Vietnam, King and Mangham, regional director, flew to Saigon on March 19 to assess the situation and make on-the-spot decisions. They conferred with field chairman Jack Revelle and missionaries who had moved in from outlying areas, with Vietnamese church leaders and American embassy officials. At first the embassy people were not giving information "at the level I was accustomed to," noted King. A call to Washington quickly solved that problem.

The assessment was very grim. The Communists had overrun most of South Vietnam and in a pincer movement were encircling Saigon. Their superior numbers and firepower were smashing all resistance. A rumor circulated among the South Vietnamese forces that President Thieu had "cut a deal" with the Communists, further lowering their morale. The Pentagon, which had withdrawn American forces several years earlier, was ordered by Congress to send no more military aid.

Fifty-nine missionaries, crowded into the Alliance guesthouse in Saigon, awaited the decision of what to do next. Although they had lost everything and barely escaped the fate of their Banmethuot colleagues, King remarked on their excellent spirit: "At no time was there unrest, criticism or undue tension."

They sat together to draw up evacuation plans. Those who were due for retirement or furlough in six months were to leave immediately. Others who felt uneasy about working in the war environment were encouraged to talk with the field chairman. Women with small children were the next to go if conditions worsened. If complete withdrawal was necessary, the field chairman and a small core of men were authorized to arrange a legal transfer of all properties, assets and equipment to *Hoi Thanh Tin Lanh*. Even as the group worked out the details, it became quite obvious that all of the contingencies shortly would need to be implemented.

While in Saigon, King also met with the senior Viet Cong representative on the International Commission for Control and Security based near the airport. The commission was part of the Paris Agreement that led to withdrawal of American forces from Vietnam. He repeatedly pressed Lt. Col. Vo Tho Son for information about the missing Alliance missionaries. Apart from evasive, almost mocking responses, no new information or promises resulted from the meeting.

Concluding his visit to Saigon, King wrote with obvious heaviness of heart,

> Thus ended our twelve historic days in Vietnam, during which we dismantled our missionary enterprise that had experienced such blessing, dispersed fifty missionaries far and wide for the future spread of the gospel, and left behind three men in Saigon and four others—prisoners not of the Communists but of the Lord—who are the earnest of our return to that good land and people.[25]

The evacuation of missionaries, however, did not go exactly as planned. Tom Stebbins, a second-generation missionary to Vietnam, tried one last time to help Christians escape to freedom. On April 28 he returned to Saigon on an Air Force C-130 from the Philippines, "the only passenger flying in that direction," he said. He found Saigon in a total state of panic and confusion.

Stebbins went to the International Protestant Church, two blocks from the American embassy, where about 200 Vietnamese workers and believers were waiting to be evacuated. Working with several typists and with Doan-van-Mieng, Church president, he began processing the necessary papers authorizing the bearers to board the helicopters ferrying people from the embassy roof to ships waiting off the coast. He made several trips to the embassy with affidavits, each time more difficult than the previous.

The Church president did not fill out a form for himself, though he might have been given priority. When Stebbins urged him to add his name to the list and evacuate with the others, Mieng said the Church needed him and he had resolved to stay. They wept and embraced; then the missionary headed for the embassy with more affidavits for the last time.

An American official warned Stebbins that it was unlikely that any of the Christians would get on the few remaining flights. Stebbins stayed to help process Vietnamese already in the compound for evacuation. At midnight the embassy doctor advised him to take the next flight because time was running out. He telephoned the church to tell the waiting Christians he had done all he could. Around 1 a.m. he was airlifted off the embassy roof, the last Alliance missionary to leave Vietnam.[26]

All told, 137 missionaries to Indochina were furloughed, retired or reassigned to other countries. Unnumbered thousands of Christians in Cambodia, Laos and Vietnam were imprisoned, tortured and killed. Yet the work left by the missionaries not only survived but prospered. By the turn of the century, churches in Cambodia and Vietnam experienced remarkable increases. Only in Laos did state-sponsored persecution continue to hamper growth.

As often happens, unexpected blessings emerged when the Church suffered. CAMA Services, which began as a limited refugee effort in Vietnam, grew into the major relief and development work of the Alliance. Intercultural Ministries, which began as an effort to help Christian refugees from Indochina find new beginnings in North America, became a major factor in church growth in the United States and Canada. By the late 1990s, one in every four American congregations was an ethnic or minority church, many of them founded by Asian refugees.

New Base

While the war in Indochina was spiraling upward toward a tragic conclusion, two events were providing a new base for the C&MA's future.

One was a restructuring of the movement and the other was a move of operations from midtown Manhattan to Nyack.

The "society," as the Alliance was known historically, had been moving steadily toward the structure of a full-fledged denomination—although many old-timers choked on the word. But the reality was that, while founder A.B. Simpson recoiled from starting a new denomination, congregations bearing the name of the C&MA were forming all across North America. By 1973 the annual report noted that over the previous ten years an average of thirty-five people had been baptized every day and two new churches organized every week. The word "branches" was no longer used to identify Alliance congregations.

The 1974 General Council in Atlanta made it official: the reorganized Alliance would have a new identity. "After 87 years as a para-denominational organization dedicated to missionary activity," noted one Christian magazine, "The Christian and Missionary Alliance has formally recognized what many people have known for years: the Alliance is a denomination."[27]

King's only comment on this historic shift was, "The aim was to make a new structure so we could function as a proper denomination instead of a society. Since that was the overriding consideration within the constituency, I could not oppose the idea, and didn't."

In fact, he was mostly a bystander. "I had nothing to do with drafting the legislation," he said. "I agreed with the reorganization structure. It was a good one and I had no problem with it, probably because the Foreign Department was in no way restructured. It was only going to mean a new title."

Among the name changes, the four departments became divisions, and the department secretaries became vice presidents. King's new title was vice president for the Division of Overseas Ministries. Although the International Headquarters name hung on for a while, it was eventually replaced by the National Office in recognition of the fact that the C&MA in the United States was only one of many equally autonomous national organizations.

The office complex in New York City had served adequately for many years the needs of a growing movement. In an L-shaped configuration, the administrative offices faced Forty-Fourth Street; the "guest home," bookstore and Gospel Tabernacle were around the corner on Eighth Avenue. One of the connections was a walkway across the church roof.

By 1969, however, pressure was mounting to move the national office twenty-some miles up the Hudson River to Nyack.

One reason was the location in the city. Taxes were increasing and the neighborhood deteriorating. Prostitutes who had overrun the area often accosted people entering the buildings. The property was finally sold to a Roman Catholic social-service organization providing an escape and safe haven for teenage runaways who had come under the control of pimps.

The commute time by car to midtown Manhattan from the Nyack area, where many office workers lived, was growing longer. William Smalley estimated that in his years as corporate secretary, driving time to and from the city equaled three years of work in the office.

Another reason for the move was the need for more office space than "260" could handle as the Alliance grew in complexity and size. "I would have done a dumb thing," Bernard King acknowledged. "I would have remodeled every inch of space to provide more room. It would have been a cheap solution that didn't work for long. I wanted to do it so we would have more funds for our work overseas."

But the treasurer's proposals got nowhere. The office was Nyack-bound. So he organized a separate realty corporation and began putting aside money to pay cash for land in Nyack and also help the Gospel Tabernacle when it eventually moved to East Sixty-Eighth Street and became the First Alliance Church.

He also needed to find a mortgage loan to cover the estimated $2.5 million needed for construction. A senior vice president of the Chemical Bank, where the Alliance did most of its financial transactions, expressed interest. He invited the Alliance treasurer to lunch with top bank executives. "I learned subsequently," Bernard said, "that there were two main groups in the bank organization: one made up of Catholics and the other, Masons. I ended up with the religious group, probably a good thing as it turned out."

As the eight men sat down to lunch, his sponsor said, "Well, sir, give us a world view of what the Alliance does." Starting to speak, Bernard noticed that the president of the Chemical Bank mortgage division began to eat his lunch.

He interrupted his report, "Could we wait a minute to return grace? We are thankful for all God's goodness and I think it proper to recognize His provision for all our needs."

The chairman stammered in embarrassment, "Why, of course, you can pray," which the guest did.

The bank officer sitting next to him acknowledged, "I was within a month of taking priestly orders and now I am remembering some things I learned as a prospective priest." Another executive across the table said, "I am a graduate of Holy Cross [College]. I should have known better than not to have the Lord's blessing on our meeting."

"That broke the ice," Bernard said.

The group discussed his request for $2.5 million. The going rate was between nine and ten percent, which the mortgage division executive supported. Bernard's sponsor suggested, "Why not give it to him for eight percent? You can still make money at two points over prime." And that's what happened.

"I believe God used my prayer to trigger a favorable response to my application," the treasurer said. "Their connection to the church was not entirely dead."

The C&MA offices at 260 West Forty-Fourth Street relocated to Upper Nyack in the fall of 1974. Dedication of the building took place on May 24 of the following year. The treasurer considered the new facility one of his crowning achievements. The low-profile, two-story structure with its long, clean lines of tinted glass between white stucco layers of wall was as pleasing to the eye as it was functional. Each of the building's four sections was occupied basically by one of the four major operations: overseas work, stateside ministries, finance operations and general services. Executive administration gave oversight to all the divisions.

New Coalition

Like bookends, the 1975 General Council in Cleveland and the dedication of the new office building in Nyack bracketed an event that enormously dwarfed both: organization of The Alliance World Fellowship. The founding conference took place May 20-23 with nearly 100 participants from Alliance churches in 34 nations. Representatives from some nations, such as Vietnam, were unable to attend.

The event was a long time in coming. Back in 1952, when General Council reaffirmed commitment to an indigenous church policy, the hope was expressed that one day an international group would exist. In its April 1971 session, the Board of Managers went on record "to investigate the possibility of establishing a worldwide fellowship of Alliance churches."[28]

The Board approved a suggested "Act of Union" that was presented to the Sixth Asia Conference the following year. The document, drafted with the foreign secretary's supervision, sketched in broad strokes what the union could embrace: a nonlegislative means of consultation and cooperation in encouraging, examining and advancing the gospel; and promoting teaching of the Fourfold Gospel.[29]

The idea surfaced not only in North America. In the succession of eleven regional convocations, beginning with the First Asia Conference in Bangkok, 1955, interest was expressed with swelling insistence. The Asia meeting in Zamboanga, 1963, formalized the request for such a grouping.

The question about formation of such a world body was not "if," but "when," and proposed by whom. President Bailey took the initiative in the Board of Managers meeting in December of 1974. The result was a letter to each overseas church, inviting it to send up to four delegates and five observers to an organizational meeting after Council the following year. The Board offered to pay the expenses of two delegates.

Although overseas at the time, King welcomed the Board action and accepted responsibility to set up such a meeting. "I consulted with the Baptist World Fellowship and the Presbyterians to see how they formulated their organizations," he said. "I asked what they were set up to do, how they functioned and what authority they might have over member churches. After putting together the data, I began to see a way through, drawing up a rough draft of what needed to be done."

The world body would be built on the concept so successful in the regional conferences: "As iron sharpens iron,/ so one man sharpens another" (Proverbs 27:17). King believed the reward of honest and focused interaction would be greater success in establishing churches worldwide.

Bailey added another reason for the step: to strengthen churches to withstand ecumenical pressures. He wrote,

> The autonomy of the overseas churches has left them open to the overtures of continent-wide and world associations such as the East Asia Christian Council and the World Council of Churches. These organizations often accompany their subversive appeals with assurances of financial and sometimes personal gain in the form of sala-

ries and scholarships. In some cases these overtures have been very persuasive.[30]

The meetings took place immediately after the Cleveland General Council and before dedication of the new office building. Sessions were held in Simpson Memorial Church in downtown Nyack. As in previous regional gatherings, King deliberately limited the number of Americans and Canadians who could attend. One dynamic of such meetings was the ability of overseas church leaders to interact without undue influence by Westerners.

With many of the national workers familiar with each other and the groundwork already laid, the conference got off to a fast start and went well. English was the working medium with simultaneous translations in four other languages. The format differed little from other such meetings, focusing on major issues and providing spiritual renewal.

The agenda, however, did include a new item, namely, formal organization of the fellowship. Adriaan Stringer, conference moderator and former Dutch missionary to Congo, chaired with exceptional skill the thirteen-member committee that drafted the constitution. Conferees unanimously approved their work and then broke into applause.

The seven-page document affirmed the organization of a global community of national churches called The Alliance World Fellowship (AWF). It called for a conference every four years, established a seven-member executive committee to oversee the AWF between the quadrennial meetings and provided a financial plan for funding the organization by all member churches.

The constitution specifically defined the organization as a non-legislative fellowship, neither authoritative nor a physical unity. "An organic union is not now realistic," commented Bailey after the meeting. Given the obstacles he listed, that may have been his diplomatic way of saying it would never happen.

Looking ahead, King was more blunt in his concern for AWF's future: "I have a slight fear that [members] will assume more authority than a fellowship of that nature should have. Especially when it comes to missions, they may try to fall back on a failed policy of pooling resources to pay for workers to go from one country to another. It has happened in other denominations, and I'm always cautious about this kind of thing. The idea is latent in the attitude of some nationals. I know from past experiences and from my knowledge of what has happened with other world denominations and the push of nationals to be missionary on other people's funding."

He took specific aim at talk about internationalizing missions, an idea that "ticks me off for fair," he commented. "The responsibility for doing missions ought to be national and not international. Support should be as close to the grassroots as possible. Otherwise, you won't have responsibility and accountability."

The big plus of AWF, King believed, "is gaining world consciousness. They get a real feel for the needs of the world and progress of the gospel, and learn how to address these issues. It is a big encouragement to them as they consult with one another, hear stories of progress and solve problems in the process. All these things come to the fore when there are meetings like this."

Stretch Marks

While the collapse of Indochina had some unforeseen blessings, namely expanded operations for CAMA Services and numerous refugee-based churches in North America, it caused an unintended consequence related to finances.

CAMA Services did not pose a problem. King had established early in his administration that it should be a self-funded operation. While in favor of refugee aid and relief to disaster victims, he maintained that the money should come from specialized organizations with resources and expertise to handle such needs.

Furthermore, Alliance missionaries should take part only in programs that involved national churches and in cooperation with them should result in establishing local churches. It was a hard-line policy, but there was only so much money to go around. It was a case of determining priorities and then allocating available funds. The missions portion of the Great Commission Fund, he insisted, should be used to establish indigenous churches.

Resolution of the refugee crisis precipitated by the collapse of Indochina to Communism, however, was a stickier issue in financial terms. Several thousand Asian newcomers were Christians from Alliance churches who wanted to start life anew in North America. T. Grady Mangham, formerly regional director for Southeast Asia, became director of the World Relief Commission refugee program.

He hoped that C&MA people in North America "would at least sponsor Christians from the Alliance churches in Indochina." They did so and much more.

The Alliance resettlement effort was code-named "Operation Heartbeat." Louis T. Dechert, a retired military officer, ably administered the program. Churches responded generously to the appeal for emergency funds. But unresolved was the problem of long-term support.

As efforts shifted to establishing refugee-based churches, the Division of North American Ministries needed more money to supervise the work. How would Specialized Ministries, later named Intercultural Ministries, be funded? Would it be done by repeated special offerings or by regular support from the General Fund?

The matter came to a head in three separate reports during the 1975 General Council in Cleveland. The Council Committee on Finances reported "much concern about the multiplicity of special appeals." The Committee on General Services raised the same issue. The Committee on North American Ministries noted the division's demand for more financial resources and a projected appeal for Specialized Ministries. It cited "the current dilemma of insufficient money supplies" and called for a study commission "to recommend ways of providing adequate funds for North American ministries . . . without impairing the overseas ministries and without relying on special and crisis appeals."[31]

One study on funding spoke of "the mire of multiple appeals." On the national level, in addition to the missionary pledge offering, seven other appeals sought help for activities like World Literature Sunday, year-end budget needs and emergency situations such as the evacuation of missionaries from Indochina.

In addition, local churches were bombarded with an equal number of appeals from retirement centers, colleges, district projects and budgets and campground needs. The report noted "a growing grassroots protest against the special appeals."[32]

The Council committee reports brought to the surface tensions rising within the national administration over allocations from the General Fund. Homeland operations were taking a larger and larger slice of income from the General Fund. But the fund was promoted in missions conferences and generally thought by Alliance givers to be for missionary work. Since there was no defined minimum designated for overseas work, the percentage of income for that purpose was declining each year—a vexation for King.

Jewel Hall recalled one year when her boss's frustration boiled over. "I tried for twenty-two years to get him mad about things that made me mad, but I could not accomplish it. But one day he came into the office— I don't know how to describe it—he was putting his feet down more firmly than usual. I stuck my head around the corner and asked him what happened.

"He said, 'They have only given me a $510 increase in the Foreign Department annual budget!' When that recommendation got to the Board, though, they changed it."

King explained, "Little by little there was an erosion of money for the overseas work. For example, the Education Department already was allocated three percent of the budget for Alliance colleges; it asked for another two percent for higher education and got it. The Home Department wanted money for extension work, then asked for more to start ethnic churches with the help of C&MA refugees from overseas. Since all this had to come from the General Fund, more money was staying home and less going overseas."

Acting on the three committee reports concerned about funding, the 1975 General Council instructed the Board of Managers to address the matter and report back the following year. The Board, in turn, asked the president to form a "Task Force on Alliance Purpose and Planning" to study the problem and propose solutions. Bailey appointed seven non-administration men to join the seven denominational officers. He selected Don Bubna, pastor and Board member, to chair the meetings.

Knowing how difficult his task would be, Bubna asked the president to help him draw up a purpose statement for the group. It was "to produce a one-year and five-year plan for the Society, based upon our objectives and to include a philosophy of funding. The plan is to be more than percentages and numbers. It will include concepts and areas of emphasis."

The first meeting of the task force, renamed the Special Committee on the Philosophy of Funding, had a difficult start, a harbinger of things to come. It was held at the national office on April 5, the day before the next session of the Board of Managers. Several officers were on the road, and those present divided their time between the committee and their preparation for the Board meetings. At no time was the full group together, and those who attended could not agree on the three-step agenda the chairman proposed. He met comments like "This is a waste of time" and "I don't know why we have to meet."

To James A. Davey, secretary of the special committee, that first meeting was "a watershed experience. I had held the austere men from headquarters in awe. But I soon learned they were very human."

The chairman gave a verbal report to the Board about the unproductive first meeting. The Board responded by affirming the committee members chosen by the president and specifying that "they were to be full participating members." In other words, be there and get to work.

The next two-day meetings in June and November were held at a retreat center in Stony Point, not far from Nyack. Having the committee at full strength only served to accentuate the division between most of the denominational officers and the non-administrative members, with Louis King dissenting and Bernard King largely neutral. When it became clear that agreeing on objectives of the Alliance and a philosophy on giving was too ambitious a goal, the group turned to the one-year and five-year plans of the divisional vice presidents. This immediately brought the issue of percentages and numbers to the surface.

The committee report to the Board noted,

> While there is unanimity regarding the fact that our primary purpose is world evangelization, some feel that a more equitable balance of funds should be made in terms of North America and Overseas.
>
> Some feel, that on at least a temporary basis, less money should go overseas and more money should be used to develop stronger and newer works at home so that eventually more can be done overseas. Others feel that history is against ever returning a percentage of the budget to overseas once it has been allocated to home. Little progress was made in resolving this.[33]

According to Melvin Sylvester, committee vice chairman, the president and the vice president for North American Ministries advocated fifty-five percent of the budget for overseas work if a bottom-line figure had to be fixed. But they "preferred that the administration should continue to have the right to be flexible as the needs were presented in a given year."

Sylvester remembered that all the non-administrative members of the committee favored a sixty-four percent minimum for missions proposed by Louis King, adding, "It was very difficult for any of the vice presidents to oppose the president who had made his position clear." Because his views conflicted with the president's, King offered to resign, but Bailey refused to consider it. Bubna wrote to King later, "I watched you walk carefully, remaining loyal to the president while knowing you differed with some of his plans."

King stated his position in plain terms: "It would be fooling the people to use the income of the General Fund without due regard to the foreign work. If it was publicly stated that so very much went to the home and so small to the foreign, it would probably kill the C&MA's emphasis and the purpose for which we exist."

He warned in a working paper submitted to the committee:

> If too big a slice of the money pledged at the annual Missionary Convention is used for other than missionary purposes ... the contributors who consider that they have given a "missionary dollar" will question the financial integrity and credibility of the Society. We shall not know just when that invisible line is passed. There is always a time lapse. When, however, the question of integrity and credibility is raised, it will be too late to retrieve ourselves.[34]

The final committee report noted, "While all was conducted on a high level of interchange among men of good will, there were obvious and open differences." But some recalled that the debate was sharp and at times a little acrimonious. Sylvester commented, "Don Bubna did an excellent job in quite a tense and heated atmosphere." Bubna admitted later, "It was the most difficult committee I ever chaired."

Davey wrote in the minutes, "At this point there is question in the minds of some as to whether or not we can accomplish our mission to any meaningful degree." His own evaluation of the group: "a dysfunctional committee."

But a change happened during the June meetings at Stony Point. When the chairman tried a relational approach to getting the group together, he was rebuffed with comments like "This is fine for your staff in Oregon, but not here." So he changed his approach and got better results.

He recalled, "That evening I simply asked the men to share how they had come to commitment to Christ. Nathan volunteered and gave his testimony. It was very moving. He wept. It was a bit of a breakthrough."

Following the November meeting, the special committee presented its proposals to the December session of the Board of Managers. All three recommendations, with only one amendment, were adopted:

1. The general budget percentage for Overseas Ministries be set at a MINIMUM of 64 percent.
2. The Division of North American Ministries' general budget continue to include extension.
3. For a period of five years Specialized Ministries (including operational expenses) be funded by a "dual pledge" to be taken at the time of the annual Missionary Convention.[35]

The Report of the Secretary to the 1976 General Council in Norfolk had noted that a special committee had been appointed to study the whole matter of funding and would report to the September session of the Board.[36] No follow-up concerning the December's Board actions on funding was given to the 1977 General Council in Calgary or a later annual meeting. Proponents of a greater percentage of money for the home work apparently saw the handwriting on the wall. They decided not to pursue the matter at the Council level.

When asked about his evaluation of the committee's work, King said he was satisfied. Then he added, years later, why he still opposed the idea of more funding for home in order to have more eventually for overseas. "My experience in using money overseas for subsidizing pastors to open work was not a good one. And already it wasn't working smoothly in the United States.

"The ultimate result in decreasing allocations for missions to do other things is in effect just to rank overseas work with many things a denomination does. It is not *the* thing. It is one of many. If that happens, we would become just like the Methodists and Presbyterians or anyone else having a small missionary force, a dying interest in missions."

Strong Finish

When King moved on from his years as a missions administrator—beginning as an area secretary for two years and ending twenty-two years later as vice president for Overseas Ministries—he could look back on an era when Alliance interest in missions was far from dying. Between 1956 and 1978:

- Church groups totaling 3,982 on 22 fields grew to 12,292 in 36 countries.
- Baptized members more than tripled from 105,067 to 383,196.
- The staff of 822 missionaries working in 138 languages and dialects increased to 978 workers using 216 languages.
- National workers expanded from 2,702 to 7,891.
- Full-time Bible school students increased from 1,459 to 2,599.

One significant statistic for 1956 reported 1,547 self-supporting churches and groups. The 1978 summary had no such category because all 12,292 congregations were self-supporting. Another category in 1978 showed that inclusive members (baptized and non-baptized faithful believers) had soared to nearly 1,142,000.[37]

King would be the first to acknowledge that these statistics represented the sacrificial and courageous efforts of workers in the fields. But it is also true that without his innovative and disciplined leadership the numbers might have been far fewer.

If in fact success breeds success, would it follow King as he moved to a new level of leadership in 1978?

Notes

1. Mrs. Jake Hostetler, "*Alianza en Marcha* Church," *The Alliance Witness*, July 23, 1969, p. 16.
2. Louis L. King, "Report of the President," *Minutes of the General Council 1977 and Annual Report for 1976* (Nyack, NY: The Christian and Missionary Alliance, 1977), p. 7.
3. Miguel Angel Palomino, *Lima al Encuentro con Dios, A New Kind of Urban Missiology*, 1983, p. 8.
4. Ibid., p. 9.
5. Robert L. Niklaus, "This Encounter Keeps Going," *Alliance Life*, October 13, 1993, p. 15.
6. Harold Lindsell, *The Church's Worldwide Mission* (Waco, TX: Word Books, 1966), pp. 4, 10.
7. Gary B. McGee, *This Gospel Shall Be Preached: A History and Theology of Assemblies of God Foreign Missions to 1959* (Springfield, MO: Gospel Publishing House, 1986), p. 202.
8. Lindsell, p. 231.
9. Daryl Westwood Cartmel, "Partnership in Mission" (doctoral dissertation, School of World Mission, Fuller Theological Seminary, May 1980), p. 78.

10. Harold Lindsell, "Precedent-Setting in Missions Strategy," *Christianity Today*, April 29, 1966, p. 43.
11. Lindsell, *The Church's Worldwide Mission*, p. 26.
12. Cartmel, p. 81.
13. Lindsell, *The Church's Worldwide Mission*, p. 16.
14. Ibid., p. 17.
15. George W. Peters, "Mission-Church Relationships—I," *Bibliotheca Sacra*, July 1968, pp. 208, 211.
16. Cartmel, p. 105.
17. Peters, p. 212.
18. Louis L. King, "Mission-Church Relations Overseas—Part I: In Principle" (paper presented at Green Lake Conference, 1980), pp. 8, 10.
19. Ibid., p. 9.
20. Ibid., p. 19.
21. Donald McGavran, "A Definitive Statement on Church-Mission Relationships," *Church Growth Bulletin*, vol. 8, no. 2 (November 1971), p. 175.
22. Eugene Hall, "A Painful Break," *The Alliance Witness*, April 23, 1975, p. 18.
23. Ibid.
24. Mrs. Malcom M. Sawyer, "The Third Domino," *The Alliance Witness*, August 13, 1975, p. 9.
25. Louis L. King, "Report on Vietnam Crisis and Evacuation of Missionaries," *Report to the Board of Managers*, March 9-April 4, 1975, p. 296.
26. Thomas H. Stebbins, "Not Enough Time," *The Alliance Witness*, July 30, 1975, pp. 14-5.
27. "C&M Alliance Converts to Denominational Status," *Eternity*, August 1974, p. 8.
28. Nathan Bailey, "Annual Survey of the President," *Minutes of the General Council 1972 and Annual Report for 1971* (New York: The Christian and Missionary Alliance, 1972), p. 93.
29. Nathan Bailey, "Toward an Alliance World Fellowship," *The Alliance Witness*, February 26, 1975, p. 16.
30. Ibid.
31. "Reports of Council Committees," *Minutes of the General Council 1975 and Annual Report for 1974* (Nyack, NY: The Christian and Missionary Alliance, 1975), pp. 300-1, 303.
32. *Minutes of the Board of Managers* (New York: The Christian and Missionary Alliance, 1976), p. 511.
33. Ibid., p. 500.
34. Louis L. King, "Working Paper" presented to the Special Committee on the Philosophy of Funding, *Minutes of the Board of Managers* (New York: The Christian and Missionary Alliance, December 1976), p. 694.
35. Ibid., p. 531.
36. Robert W. Battles, "Report of the Secretary," *Minutes of the General Council 1976 and the Annual Report for 1975* (Nyack, NY: The Christian and Missionary Alliance, 1976), p. 249.

37. Louis L. King, "Report of the Foreign Department," *Minutes of the General Council 1958 and Annual Report for 1957* (New York: The Christian and Missionary Alliance, 1958), pp. 56, 90-1.
"Report of the President," *Minutes of the General Council 1980 and Annual Report for 1979* (Nyack, NY: The Christian and Missionary Alliance, 1980), pp. 8, 41.

TEN
"Stay on Course!"

1978-1987
Time Markers

As the '70s closed, Canada's future became clearer, both for the nation and its Alliance churches. Many businesses had begun to relocate from Quebec to English-speaking Ontario as a consequence of the province's 1977 law making French the official and principal language. At the end of 1979 the Canadian Supreme Court ruled the controversial bill unconstitutional. Voters in Quebec rejected their provincial leaders' independence initiatives the following year.

Autonomy for the Canadian C&MA in 1981 resulted from recognition on both sides of the border that the ministry would do better if the denomination were perceived as a fully Canadian operation. Subsequent growth in the churches confirmed this fact.

The new decade was dominated by areas of tension and violence. In 1980 Israeli jets destroyed a nuclear reactor sold to Iraq by France. It annexed the Golan Heights seized from Syria. Muslim radicals assassinated Egypt's Anwar Sadat after he made peace with Israel. Europe suffered an unprecedented rash of terrorist attacks and bombings in 1984 by Arab, French, Islamic and Palestinian groups.

A new and deadly enemy finally caught the world's attention in the 1980s: AIDS. Nowhere were the ravages of the disease more apparent than in Africa, a continent already in the throes of a terrible famine.

Entertainment media played a big part in American culture. An estimated 83 million people were glued to their TV screens for the *Dallas* series to find the answer to "Who shot JR?" The last episode of *M*A*S*H* drew 125 million viewers, the highest-rated show in television history to date.

The influence of entertainment may have helped an ex-movie star win the US presidency in 1980. But if the public expected fun time from "the Gipper," they were seriously mistaken. Ronald Reagan's vision of manifest destiny for the nation galvanized the "silent majority" and left liberals gasping for breath.

In religious terms, the 1980s became known as "The Great Divide," a decade of shifting majorities. Mainline denominations were in decline—Presbyterians and Episcopalians down more than twenty-five percent from 1965 to 1989, United Methodists down eighteen percent. Liberal churches' missionary forces shrank from over 4,000 to 1,200.

Evangelicals, however, were on the rise. A rousing "Washington for Jesus" rally attracted over 200,000 marchers. A Gallup poll reported that thirty-one percent of Americans referred to themselves as evangelicals or born-again Christians.

★ ★ ★

The 1980 C&MA General Council learned that the previous year produced a record net gain of sixty-six churches. Overseas the net total was 419 new churches with inclusive membership of more than 1 million. Korea joined the ranks of overseas fields. Reviewing these accomplishments, Council delegates approved a doubling campaign by the centennial year of 1987.

A string of 100-year celebrations began as the Alliance moved toward the centenary. Nyack College and *The Alliance Witness* observed theirs in 1982, Christian Publications, Inc., in 1983 and the Zaire Alliance community the following year.

The worldwide survey at the 1987 Centennial Council held in St. Paul showed all trends moving upward. Churches in the United States and Canada reached ninety-three percent of the doubling goal; inclusive membership achieved eighty-one percent.

The average church had 78 baptized and 144 inclusive members. Only 14 C&MA churches in North America had over 1,000 inclusive members. Two of the three largest were Specialized Ministries (later Intercultural Ministries) churches.

Overseas the doubling campaign noted a 100-percent increase in inclusive members, averaging 107,200 each year. Churches increased 90 percent to a total of 11,058. The goal of 1,200 missionaries was exceeded by 14. The total number of countries with Alliance churches rose to fifty-two.

The same upward pattern was evident in print production, radio broadcasts, medical treatment, translation work and leadership training, confirming the Alliance as a full-service missionary endeavor that encompassed the globe.

"Stay on Course!"

Why, when nearing age sixty-three and after forty years of almost nonstop ministry, would Louis King be open to an even larger, more demanding responsibility: president of the C&MA? Why would he allow himself to be nominated at the 1978 General Council when two other popular leaders with homeland-based work were also candidates?

His response, even years later, came in forceful, staccato bursts: "Stay on course! I was concerned the Alliance stay on course. As a missionary agency, finish the orders given us by the Lord. Organize, strategize, propagate with prayer and the Holy Spirit's blessing. Lock, stock and barrel!"

King believed the presidency could be the way to accomplish that goal. But despite this strong conviction, he refused to encourage his candidacy. "I always came to an election when my name was being considered as if I were not going to be chosen. So if it didn't happen, I was free from worry and apprehension of what might have been. I placed it in the Lord's hands. It was His business, not mine, and I would be content with the outcome."

His attitude going into the election at the Birmingham Council reflected his long-held principle that the call of the Church was the call of the Lord. "I believe that spiritual men and women who are my colleagues may know more about me than I do myself. They can seek the mind of the Lord and make their own judgments whether I am fit. We ought to rest in that instead of campaigning and conniving to get an office. I was so free from trying to be elected that I did not prepare a response if I were chosen."

King was elected on the second ballot as seventh president of the C&MA. He did not recollect any overwhelming feeling at the result, but Jewel Hall was watching him and said, "You should have seen the wide, wide grin on his face when the results were announced!"

Neither did he recall making an acceptance speech except to introduce his wife. Perhaps so, but his response was as crisp and concise as if he had written it out. The denominational magazine carried verbatim his remarks to the Council participants.

To his predecessor he said, "I want to speak a word of deep gratitude to Dr. Nathan Bailey. It has been a delight to work with him. We have traveled thousands upon thousands of miles together. We have sat together on many a platform and in many a waiting room. The graciousness that Dr. Bailey exhibited in all these instances has endeared him to me."

To his missionary colleagues he said, "For twenty-five years I have visited and worked with you. I have really been basking in the glory of your accomplishments."

In presenting Esther to the delegates he obviously struggled with his emotions: "She raised our four boys and did a magnificent job. Two of them went to the mission field and have served God there. Two of them are here at home and they love the Lord. . . . Some years I was only home two or three months out of the whole year because of the necessity of my work. Never once has my wife said it should be otherwise. Such has been her consecration, and I thank her."

He then addressed the 3,500 assembled representatives of Alliance churches across North America: "I covenant with you to be unbiased in the administration of the work of the Society. It is to be <u>both</u> at home <u>and</u> abroad—not one or the other, but both/and. I make this as a covenant before you that together we are going to work hard for the accomplishment of our task."[1]

Keeping in Touch

Some aspects of the incoming president's personal life and style of leadership would remain the same. "From the beginning," he said, "I had so given myself to the Lord and to the ministry that I was totally committed head to toe."

It meant first of all keeping in touch with himself despite the added pressures of work. This he did by maintaining as much as possible early-morning hours of personal study of the Scriptures and prayer before heading to the office. "It kept me abreast with the Word of God and it also kept me exceedingly keen on the will of God and what was right or wrong," he explained.

Another aspect of his life that would not change was his keeping in touch with troops in the field. It was commonly agreed that if King by chance met a colleague anywhere in the world he would recall immediately the person's name and current status. In this remarkable ability he was undoubtedly influenced by V. Raymond Edman. The first thing he mentioned in an article about his early mentor was an event at Wheaton College.

> In the fall of 1940 Billy Graham, a newly arrived student . . . was walking across campus when Dr. V. Raymond Edman, who had been recently installed as the college president, passed him and without stopping simply said, "Hi, Bill." Graham was amazed that Dr. Edman had any idea who he was. Encountering some students a little later, Billy remarked about this incident, and they laughingly said, "He knows everybody."[2]

King carried that habit into the presidency. Steve Bailey, a young worker with CAMA Services at the time, described his experience in 1982. "I remember well coming home from service in Nong Khai Refugee Camp and attending Council. Walking around the hotel with people who already had been serving the Lord for many years, I felt rather insignificant. One morning I was riding down the elevator and Dr. King also got on. [He] turned to me and shook my hand and said my name, where I had served, and that I had just returned home."

Ann Grinnell recalled in a letter at the time of King's retirement, "You surprised me in 1983 at the Board of Managers' banquet in Seattle when you spoke of my pre-Alliance employment. I marveled again later that year when we met at the missionary training seminar and you asked me about my interest to do computer programming upon return to Irian Jaya. The thrill of personal recognition filled me with gratitude."

Trudy Hawley had a similar experience. She wrote in a letter for King's retirement album, "Your concern to know each one of us missionaries by name has always impressed me. Even on my very first time in New York on my way to Congo in 1961, you knew me. I had run out for some last-minute purchase at the Woolworth store. You met me on the street and greeted me by name."

King's penchant for instant recall was not limited to adults. Oliver and Winnie Kaetzel, former missionaries to Laos, recalled, "Our children have commented about your remembering their names even years after we had left the field and our children were grown and gone from the house."

Nor was his attention limited to missionaries. Joseph S. Kong, then director for Cambodian Ministries, wrote, "You spoke one time to the Pacific Northwest Prayer Conference delegates about our work in Cambodia. You remembered all the Cambodian leaders by name with whom you met when you were in Phnom Penh."

One time, however, King's memory seemed to fail him. Ernie and Marilyn Klassen, missionaries to Peru, mentioned, "We met you in the hall [at the pre-Council missionary seminar in Calgary, 1977]. You could not place us and asked what field we were from. When we indicated that we were just candidates, you breathed a sigh of relief, indicating that for a moment you thought your memory was failing you!"

Some credit for his amazing recall of names and details must go to his laserlike concentration on whatever the matter at hand. But there was another, more personal aid to memory—a habit he and Esther started early in their work and continued into their retirement years. "As soon as breakfast is over," he said, "we read a minimum of three pages of Scripture. Then we pray through the *Prayer Manual*. We pray for families and single people and all their concerns. We pray for people who are in need—sickness and decisions that need to be made, or troubled situations."

This daily discipline helped Esther as well to keep in touch with workers during the years of her husband's presidency. Not that she didn't have her own work for the Lord. She was deeply involved in Women's Missionary Prayer Fellowships. One activity kept her connected to India. The Ramabai Mukti Mission, an orphanage for young girls, belonged to the Alliance but maintained its own system of support through groups in Europe and North America. For many years Esther served on the executive committee of the American council.

She had another ministry not widely known. "I might come back from overseas," King said, "and find one of the Nyack College students living in our home. Esther would explain, 'Well, he couldn't pay his bill and he would have to leave school, so I decided to help.' We had quite a number, mostly missionary kids. She took them in as one of our own boys at no charge until they could get back on their feet financially."

Tough at the Top

As King moved into the large corner office reserved for the president, many other things were different as well. Previously, in the Division of International Ministries, he had a capable administrative assistant in Arni Shareski, an excellent secretary in Jewel Hall and four regional directors—

all of them former missionaries who worked closely with him on a very focused agenda. He had managed a tight-run administration that followed closely the operations manual, referred to with irreverence by some colleagues as "the missionary's bible."

But as president he had no administrative assistant, though June Smith, who had been secretary to his predecessor, and later Pearl Swope performed well on a much higher level than mere clerk. In the Council-engineered reorganization of the National Office structure, the four vice presidents were to be, in effect, his assistants. Their role in the President's Cabinet was only to advise him on their widely diverse agendas, while decisions regarding the overall work were his responsibility and his alone.

"The presidency was different from administering the Overseas Division," he explained. "Directors were hand-picked and you saw eye-to-eye with them and had a direct line through to the fields. *Policies and Procedures* gave a full plan on how to work. Field directors were required to function according to the book.

"Other divisions at the time didn't have that kind of system and there were many intermediaries who could drag their feet if they didn't agree. Yet, as president, you only operated through the divisions; you didn't go over their heads. It was a much slower process with little hands-on leadership."

Fortunately, in putting together many overseas Church-Mission agreements, King had learned what Shareski called "his gentle art of negotiating. He was willing to yield on small items without losing sight of the big picture." King added, "I had to determine quietly the strategic points of discussion, yet be careful in my questioning not to castigate or accuse. People needed to see that I was fair in getting all the facts on the table and not simply dragging them to my conclusions."

Not that the President's Cabinet was hostile toward the new leader. The corporate officers, vice president Paul Alford and secretary Robert W. Battles, were fully supportive. So were the divisional vice presidents: Keith M. Bailey, North American Ministries; Merlin C. Feather, Finance and Treasurer; and Gordon M. Cathey, General Services.

King was able to hand-pick his successor to lead the Division of Overseas Ministries. David L. Rambo and his wife Ruth had served in the Philippines for five years before returning home in the mid-1960s. After he graduated from Fuller School of World Missions, they were ready to go back overseas. Instead, King asked Rambo to teach at Canadian Bible College.

Rambo objected strongly, his heart set on returning to the Philippines. The president invoked "the call of the Church is the call of the Lord." Rambo swallowed hard, went and taught. He later became a very popular president of the college. King recalled him to the States in 1978 to lead the overseas work.

Even with the full support of the C&MA officers, King found the presidency a tough assignment. He conferred often with Clyde Taylor, head of the Evangelical Fellowship of Mission Agencies, and Wade Coggins, his successor, as well as academics like Merrill C. Tenney of Wheaton College and Harold J. Ockenga, pastor of Park Street Church in Boston. Philip Hogan of the Assemblies of God was a friend and colleague. "I did not agree with his position on the tongues issue," King said, "but I was a guest in his home several times and if we were in meetings together we always managed to have a meal together."

Centennial Goals

An incoming C&MA president usually is expected to articulate the goals of his administration. King did not have to. The Birmingham Council took the initiative, approving sweeping goals to be met by the centennial celebration nine years hence.

The plan did not simply pop into the delegates' minds. A Council committee had taken aim at numbers suggesting the Alliance was losing momentum in growth: "While our President's 1977 survey provides many good reasons for gratitude and praise, a breakdown of the vital statistics on conversions, baptisms and membership gains, per church, presents continuing cause for the kind of concern expressed by this Committee last year.

"During 1977 our Society averaged, per church in North America, less than 12 conversions, just under 5 baptisms, and not quite 3 new members. Overseas the 'per church' averages were 4.7 conversions and 2.5 baptisms."

The report noted that the statistics represented a 16.4 percent decrease in inclusive members as well as fewer baptisms and professions of faith. It continued,

Adding to your Committee's concern in this regard is the fact that these current annual statistics reveal a decline, which has seen our conversion rate in North America drop to less than one per church per month, and not quite one per church every two months overseas.[3]

In response to this report, Council adopted ambitious goals for doubling the North American constituency with a comparable increase overseas—and do it all in nine years.

The Board of Managers later filled in the details, setting these goals to be met by March 3, 1987:

1. A net gain of 840 new churches in North America and 5,000 new churches overseas.
2. Inclusive membership in North America: 384,000; overseas: 1,904,000.
3. 1,200 missionaries and 3,200 official workers.[4]

That these challenging goals were put on the new president did not bother him in the least. "I was 100 percent in favor because it was right in line with what I had been working on for years overseas—perhaps not a doubling goal, but with a real effort to grow." It was an agenda, he said, that deserved his attention and that of the entire Alliance constituency "morning, noon and night, Sunday through Sunday, month after month, until we reached our Centennial and did it with the Lord's help."

One of the first churchwide efforts was "Project 10,000." Its goal was to train laypeople in regional evangelism seminars. The project actually attracted almost 13,000 participants.

The next denominational effort was "Target: Jerusalem." Organized and conducted by Francis W. Grubbs, the program helped churches study their surrounding communities and then plan their evangelistic outreach accordingly. Later, "Deeper Life Convocation" weekends emphasized the work of the Holy Spirit in witness and spiritual growth. "Tom Allen was up to his ears in the project," said King, "and it helped propel us forward."

One aspect of the doubling campaign gave special satisfaction to the president: the cooperation of Alliance Men and Women in a series of "Double in a Decade" banquets. The women's prayer groups gave their usual enthusiastic cooperation, while Alliance Men provided unusual logistical support. Alliance Men President Walt Meloon, with his corporate plane, then his successor, Raymond Kincade, with a chartered plane, enabled King to crisscross the continent in three-week tours.

He spoke at banquets in all the North American districts, motivating people to achieve the centennial growth goals. Seventeen such meetings were held in just one month. The tours in 1983 were so popular they were repeated the following year.[5]

"Those flying tours put the 'Double in a Decade' scheme before the people, and the whole thing was beautifully arranged by Alliance Men," King said. "You can't imagine the influence they had in helping with the forward movement we were enjoying then."

Doubling Progress

With all the special programs and unusual efforts, what was the progress toward the centennial goals? Here is a look at some of the progress that was made over the years.

1979 Campaign Update

Early on, the doubling effort produced encouraging results. In the first year, ninety-nine churches were started in the United States and Canada with a net increase of sixty-six new churches, the largest such total yet for one year. Inclusive membership gained 15,797, also surpassing the year's goal. Overseas statistics in 1978 (always a one-year lag due to difficulties in gathering information) included 137,447 new inclusive members. With more than one new church per day, the net gain was 419.

Finances also reflected broad and enthusiastic support of churches. The $218,500 over budget represented a 12.4 percent increase over the previous year. December income was almost $1.6 million, the largest monthly income yet recorded.

Rejoicing over these good reports at the 1980 General Council was tempered by the sudden death of former president Nathan Bailey the previous July. He and his wife Mary were en route home from The Alliance World Fellowship in Hong Kong, where he had been reelected as AWF president. Near Nottingham, England, their car collided with an oncoming truck. He was killed instantly.

Mary Bailey survived despite serious injuries, but after three years of painful yet courageous struggle she too died. King described her as "one of the Alliance's most valiant and truly remarkable members."[6]

The 1979 General Council in Lincoln reached a watershed event when delegates overwhelmingly authorized the Canadian C&MA to establish an autonomous Church body. It culminated a ten-year process and realized one of King's priorities when taking office. He commented repeatedly over the years to Melvin Sylvester, "This is in the best interest for our work."

During those years, pressures had been building north of the border. Some Canadian politicians were campaigning against links with the United States in industrial, agricultural and financial sectors. They branded these connections as akin to colonialism and cultural imperialism, stirring up anti-American sentiment.

Rambo, a member of the President's Cabinet, recalled that King considered Canadian autonomy a natural and desirable step—the same kind of recognition he granted overseas churches when foreign secretary. "It's time to stop the foot-dragging and get the job done," he told the cabinet members in one of their first meetings.

But some of the Council delegates were not so sure. They feared the Canadians could not be trusted on their own—forgetting that the Alliance movement was indebted to its Canadian roots and its Canadian founder. One delegate asked during the plenary debate, "If Canada becomes autonomous, what will happen if they fall into heresy?" To which King replied evenly, "Canadian autonomy means that the Canadians will be free to fall into heresy." Theology, however, was not an issue with most delegates.

Another delegate said the step was not a maturing of partnership between the two national churches. "It is a divorce," he heatedly declared. A Canadian observer was knitting as she followed the debate. She exclaimed, "What a nasty thing to say!" and accidentally jabbed herself with a needle.

Despite such objections, under the deliberate presiding of the president as moderator, the resolution easily passed. On January 1, 1981, The Christian and Missionary Alliance in Canada would become a fully autonomous Church body. The new relationship did not mean a total break between the American and Canadian constituencies. Since the doubling campaign began as a North American plan, statistics would continue to reflect in a single report advances on both sides of the border.

More importantly, missions would continue as a joint effort. The Division of Overseas Ministries, with Canadian representation in its administration, would oversee the work as a combined North American operation. Arnold Cook noted, "After autonomy Dr. King was very anxious that we continue to cooperate and learn from one another as two sister churches.

"During his time in office our overseas ministries were a seamless team of cooperation. He was very insistent that the Canadian voice in the division was a veto voice when it came to Canadian personnel. He also took the initiative to convene each December a joint meeting of the American and Canadian officers, alternating the venue between the two countries."

That missions relationship would undergo several revisions as Canadian lawmakers and some church leaders accentuated differences in Canadian identity compared to American culture. Legislation, for example, eventually would put an end to funds from Canadian churches sent to the US-based office for support of Canadian missionaries operating under the umbrella Division of Overseas Ministries.

1980 Campaign Update

North American Ministries again reported a record net gain of seventy-three churches in North America. Inclusive membership also surpassed its annual intermediate goal by approximately 10,000 new people. Overseas Ministries' progress, however, was "cause for some concern" even though 353 churches were started. In 1980 the total missionary force for the first time passed the 1,000 mark with 15 to spare.

In December 1980 King addressed a final official communication to all Canadian workers on the eve of their Church's autonomy. It indicated his depth of feeling and affection for them. He recounted a story Paul Rader told when leadership passed to him from the C&MA founder.

"Dr. Simpson was occupying a room at Headquarters across the hall from the Board meeting which he was unable to attend. At the close of the meeting I went into his room with Brother Senft and Brother Lewis.

"He put out his arm, and we knelt to pray. Oh, such a prayer! He started in thanksgiving for the early days and swept the past in waves of praise at each step, then to the present, then on to the future—the prophetic vision was marvelous.

"We all, with upturned, tear-stained faces, were praising God together with him as by faith we followed him to the mountain and viewed the Promised Land. He was so sure the Alliance was born in the heart of God. He lay there in a burst of praise, sure that God could carry it forward. So, reverently he lifted his hands as if passing the work over to God who had carried it all these days."

King concluded his final message as Alliance president for all of North America by simply stating, "This expresses my feelings about The Christian and Missionary Alliance in Canada as you begin a new era in your history."[7]

1981 Campaign Update

Moving closer to the midway point of the doubling campaign, churches in North America were still slightly ahead of the annual goal. Overseas churches reported on average almost two new churches every day, putting them well ahead of their target. But soaring inflation overseas heightened the cost of missionary work, and worsening economic conditions at home began to put strain on the doubling effort.

"Skeptics openly question whether we can afford to continue our rapid advance programs both at home and overseas," the president reported to General Council in Columbus, Ohio. "Our answer is that the world's economic conditions do not render sterile and empty our Lord's words, *Ye shall be witnesses unto me both in Jerusalem . . . and unto the uttermost part of the earth.* We cannot afford to stay stationary on any front."[8]

Indeed, after experiencing in 1981 the "biggest financial crisis experienced in our work since 1939," churches dug deeper in their pockets. Income by year's end showed $571,500 over budget.

1982 Campaign Update

Having intermediate or annually projected goals was a practical way to reach the long-range centennial objectives. But it did pose a problem. Raising the bar each year made it increasingly difficult to clear. Midway through the campaign to double, church growth in North America was barely making it over the hurdle.

The president pinpointed one of the difficulties:

> With no prospect of further large multiplication of churches formed mainly of refugees from Indo China, we now face the task of advance

through our usual means of church planting, namely, through district and fields, and by local churches mothering other congregations.[9]

Sustaining momentum by "usual means" would not be easy. The vice president for North American Ministries noted the following year that half the churches in the United States had either plateaued or gone into decline.[10]

Offerings were also slackening. *The Yearbook of American and Canadian Churches, 1982* tracked finances in many denominations. Per capita giving by full members of the US Alliance for all purposes was $693.31, ranking the Alliance in third place among American churches. But the same source indicated that per capita giving to missions by inclusive members was $73.67, dropping the C&MA to thirteenth place among all US denominations. King's observation: "Those who have recently come into our fellowship and are not yet full members have not yet partaken of the Alliance's genius for liberal giving."[11]

Meanwhile, overseas churches continued to gather strength, reaching nearly 1.5 million inclusive members in 9,500 churches. In 1981 (latest figures for the report), almost 190 new believers were added to the churches daily.

With the missionary work going so well, Rambo was very happy in his role as vice president for Overseas Ministries—until the president surprised him with another very difficult request. With Rambo's experience and academic credentials (four graduate degrees including an earned doctorate), King believed he was more needed at the time to lead the college and seminary at Nyack. Again Rambo resisted, and again King pulled from his pocket the "call of the church" principle. And again Rambo submitted to "the call of the Lord."

As a replacement for the overseas work, King had his eye on another educator and former missionary. King had seen David H. Moore in action under fire in Indonesia and commented, "His value was obvious to me." He referred to a crisis situation when differences between Church and Mission escalated to such a point that continued presence of the Mission in the country was threatened.

The Mission needed to take the first step in resolving the conflict and Moore was chosen to write a letter of apology to the Church. This he did effectively, and his part in the meetings helped bring the crisis to an end. He was teaching missions at the Alliance Theological Seminary when

King tapped him on the shoulder to become the new vice president for Overseas Ministries.

1987 Campaign Summary

The Centennial Council in St. Paul was a time of great rejoicing. No longer was attention fixed on the sometimes frustrating annual intermediate goals. The churches now looked at what actually had been accomplished, and the results were worth a hearty hallelujah. A sizable delegation from Canada joined in the celebration.

Four in every ten Alliance churches in North America in March 1987 were new since the campaign started in 1978. The drive netted a gain of 441 churches and nearly 89,000 new members and adherents. Specialized Ministries now embraced fourteen ethnic and minority groups. Win Arn, church-growth specialist, ranked the C&MA as the third-fastest growing Protestant denomination in the United States.[12]

Overseas churches claimed a worldwide community of nearly 2 million believers—about ten times larger than the North American constituency. They averaged 9 new churches per week over the 468 weeks of the campaign. Sharing in this remarkable record were 1,214 active missionaries.

The summary noted that in 55 years the Church in the Ivory Coast reached a membership of 133,842 inclusive members in over 1,100 churches, Vietnam to an estimated 350,000 believers in 75 years. The Indonesian Church, with 485,000 inclusive members, dwarfed the North American C&MA constituency.[13]

Although these figures were remarkable, the most dramatic push to open new churches in the United States was yet to come: "The Easter 100 Campaign."

Hope amid the Rubble

Meanwhile one of the overseas efforts during the doubling campaign was the "Good News for Great Cities" project. By this time, King's focus on urban church planting was a recognized priority in all overseas fields. This new plan targeted ten major cities worldwide, reaching from Colombia through Africa to Hong Kong. Special offerings helped cover expenses in starting new congregations in key urban centers.

Strangely, one of the most dramatic and successful church starts was not on the list. Beirut was perhaps the most strategic center for banking, commerce and culture in the Middle East. Then unrestrained sectarian strife for twenty years reduced the once-beautiful city to rubble. In that tragic conflict emerged a church that radiated hope and love throughout the capital of Lebanon and even beyond its borders.

It was known locally as "the church near the garbage dump." The Karentina district got its name from the French word for "quarantine." Adjacent to the church property was a holding area formerly used by the Port of Beirut to detain people seeking entry to Lebanon without proper papers or medical clearance.

Later it was given over to huge, reeking mounds of garbage, thanks to the city's indifference to unrestricted dumping. Even in the late 1990s the district was crisscrossed with narrow alleys, small factories that belched heavy black smoke and rusting hulks of abandoned equipment. But rising above the rubble and reputation of Karentina was a white cross easily seen from the main thoroughfare that skirts the district.

The founding and eventual prominence of the Karentina church are linked to one remarkable Lebanese: Sami Dagher. Trained in hotel management, moving up through the levels of management and earning citations, he had a promising career. Dagher was *maitre d'* of a restaurant in the elegant seaside Phoenicia Hotel when his future abruptly changed. Despite his successes, his marriage was falling apart. Through a mutual friend, he and his English wife Joy met an Alliance missionary couple, Harry and Miriam Taylor.

King was a guest in the hotel when the Taylors invited him to a weekly Bible study at the Daghers' residence. Asked to give whatever lesson God laid on his heart, King chose a passage in the Gospel of John and concluded with what Taylor termed "a very edifying challenge." King observed, "Sami began to perspire until it ran down his cheeks and chin as if someone had turned on a faucet." The sensitive counseling of Harry and Miriam Taylor later brought him to Christ and a transformation in his life.

One guest who frequented the restaurant for two weeks remarked to Dagher, "You are the only happy man in the whole crowd."[14] Among some of those regular clients were some of the world's richest people, but apparently their wealth did not make for a happy life. One of the more notable people Sami helped spiritually during his hotel days was a young American running from God. Dagher played a key part in redirecting him to the Lord.

The young man's name was Franklin Graham. Bob Pierce, founder of Samaritan's Purse, had been trying to help Graham through his spiritual struggles. He brought him along on a trip to Beirut. Franklin and his father, Billy Graham, would never forget Sami's timely witness. When young Graham took over as head of Samaritan's Purse, he would be a faithful supporter of the diverse ministries under Dagher's leadership.

Sensing God's call to ministry, Dagher resigned his position at the hotel despite the angry protests of the hotel management. The part-owner tried to dissuade his star employee from ruining a promising career in the hotel business. When that failed, he threatened to withhold the large compensation due Dagher, but relented and honored the commitment.

The supervisor also warned of dire consequences of such a hair-brained scheme—a pastor, indeed! He shouted that when Sami was starving and came to his house for help, he would not get even a crust of bread.

Both of Dagher's bosses were tragically wrong. The part-owner died when the hotel was totally demolished in the fighting between militia groups. And one day, Dagher's former supervisor showed up at his door for a visit. Actually, he was destitute and desperate for help but could not bring himself to admit he had nothing to feed his family—not even breadcrumbs. Sami sensed his need and loaded him down with food from his own kitchen.

After serving with the Taylors in the International Church of Beirut, Dagher felt led of God to start a church. In 1976 a new convert donated to the church two floors in an apartment building he owned in the Karentina district. Not only did the new congregation flourish, so did the area. The pastor gradually bought the apartment building and neighboring properties for church activities. One building owner was going to sell his holdings in Karentina, but when he saw what was happening, he moved there himself. "Sami has made the area so nice," he explained.

Threatened with death, shot at and kidnapped, Dagher experienced the promise of Psalm 91:7: "A thousand may fall at your side,/ ten thousand at your right hand,/ but it will not come near you." Although he sent his family to England for safety, he refused to leave Beirut. "We are immortal," he said, "until our work for Christ is completed."[15]

The congregation increased and so did its outreach to victims of violence crowding into the city. From 1984 to 1986 the congregation increased from 124 to 400 believers. With its own offerings and donations from abroad, the Karentina church provided food and shelter, clothing and utensils to needy people. It helped refugees start small businesses, repaired or rebuilt their houses and provided seed so they could return to their fields.

The story of Ramali, a mountain village, was just one instance of the church's work. A militia convoy of empty trucks led by tanks wound up the narrow road, intent on looting Ramali's houses and killing the inhabitants. But as some brave young men held off the gunmen, Alliance missionary Roger Elbel quickly organized a fleet of rickety buses to evacuate all 472 families to the coast. A ship chartered by Dagher took the 2,500 people to Beirut where Christians were waiting for them. The congregation provided essentials like mattresses, blankets and even some furniture.

Dagher said, "We noticed the sadness, the desperation, the lost look in their eyes. Once they had everything and now nothing. Everyone was angry and it was a heartbreaking experience."[16]

He took five families into his own apartment while they searched for housing in the city. The church found apartments for another twenty-five families and paid the rent two years in advance. As a result of the compassion they experienced, forty-five of the villagers put their faith in Christ.

The civil war forced Alliance missionaries living in West Beirut to become refugees as well. The Andrew Kerr and Darrell Phenicie families wanted to stay and tough it out with their fellow believers. But they were on the other side of the "green line," cut off from the church in East Beirut. Muslim militia who controlled the area were at best unpredictable. By 1984 the American government sent out word to its citizens in Beirut that it was pulling US troops from the country. When that happened, church leaders advised the missionaries to leave as well.

The two families still struggled over what to do. Their indecision ended when the embassy sent word that they should go immediately to the beach for evacuation. If they refused, the American government would not promise any further assistance. Overseas Ministries in Nyack concurred with the directive. A relieved Marilyn Kerr wrote, "At that time we could not have objectively made the decision ourselves."[17]

The Kerrs resettled in Jordan to have a much-needed ministry there. But for the Phenicies, who returned to Lebanon, the 1984 evacuation would be only the first of four such emergencies when they hastily packed suitcases and left everything else behind. The day after their hurried exit in 1984, the first American hostages were taken by Muslim militia.

Despite the savage fighting in Beirut, the Karentina church's outreach continued to grow. By the church's anniversary in 2001, four daughter churches would be established. Dagher started a Bible school in the 1980s to train young men to pastor churches that he envisioned would be established in neighboring Muslim countries. Some of the forty-three students came from Syria, where God was working in another remarkable way.

Through the leadership of Pastor Farid Khoury, a graduate of Alliance Theological Seminary, the Alliance church in Damascus not only became the largest evangelical church in the capital; over a ten-year period it also helped start six new churches in Syria. The strongest opposition came not from the regime of Hafez al-Assad but from the traditional Catholic and Orthodox communities from which most of the new converts came.[18]

Despite the secular nature of the government, any Muslim who dared to defect to the evangelicals paid dearly, possibly even with his life, at the hands of enraged family members. Those who escaped death were treated as second-class citizens deprived of rights and protection under the law.

Pastor Khoury was subjected to constant scrutiny by security agents. They attended his services, monitored his travels and kept close watch on who was in his congregation. He told of a visit by a high-ranking military officer whose son had become a Christian while studying in the States. The general, fearful for his reputation and job, urged the pastor to bar his son from coming to the church.

Khoury responded, "Would a Muslim cleric block the entrance to his mosque to anyone wanting to worship there? Neither can I forbid someone who wants to attend our services." Angered by the pastor's refusal,

The World His Field

the general had to leave and look for other ways to eliminate the disgrace caused by his son's conversion.

In Amman, Jordan, where the Kerrs settled, a miracle was occurring. A number of Alliance families wanted to start a church in West Amman. They located a building with an unfinished ground floor littered with debris and dirt. With help from the national Church, some funds from the United States and their own sacrificial giving, they furnished a sanctuary seating 200 people. The first service in the Sixth Circle Alliance Church, the first new church in Amman in thirty-five years, was held on New Year's Eve, 1985.

The largest C&MA church in Jordan was the Second Circle Church in Amman. It was pastored by Yousef Hashweh, national Church president and another ATS graduate. Under his ministry the Church not only grew, it became the sanctuary for several refugee congregations. Hashweh's preaching especially attracted business and professional Jordanians who committed their lives to Christ. The original meeting place blossomed into a beautiful church building designed and financed by the congregation. The Second Circle Church was a leading witness of the gospel in the Hashemite Kingdom. Its progressive congregation reached out to revitalize other churches in Jordan.

The church thrived despite a law forbidding any Muslim to change religion and the constant harassment of religious and government agents. A Sunday-night service typified the difficulty—and victory—of Christians in Jordan. When the pastor rose to conduct the Communion service, as if on cue, the loudspeaker in a nearby mosque began blasting the evening call to prayer, overwhelming the pastor's voice. The congregation began to sing, their voices rising strong and persistent until the chant from the loudspeaker ended. Then the service resumed as if nothing had happened.

The Jerusalem Alliance church moved against an even stronger current of hostility since both Jews and Muslims bitterly opposed all Christians, especially evangelicals. Nonetheless, the small, two-story building wedged between other equally historic structures in the Old City clearly displayed the C&MA logo for passersby to see.

Each Sunday a congregation of Arab Christians crowded into the immaculately white little chapel on the second floor. Worshipers spilled out onto the flat roof and other rooms on the first floor. Several believers would not speak to strangers or allow themselves to be photographed because of the risk of being exposed and persecuted. In some instances, even their Muslim families did not know they were Christians. Yet the vibrant little church held its ground in the heart of the spiritual capital of three world religions.

Conversely, after decades of witness to the Jewish population of Israel, the Alliance chose to forgo efforts to plant churches. Instead, they committed themselves to cooperate with messianic assemblies of born-again Jews. The decision to sublimate a denominational identity in order to promote an authentic Jewish witness in Israel won praise from messianic assembly leaders.

The baptized members of Alliance churches in the Middle East numbered less than a thousand. The total did not make a great contribution to the doubling effort in overseas churches, and their growth certainly did not match the potential of the "Good News for Great Cities" project of Overseas Ministries. But nowhere in the Alliance world community were there Christians who paid more dearly for their faith yet stood more resolutely. The Middle East believers represented the ultimate reality that church growth is not a numbers game but a faithful witness for Jesus Christ—even in the hardest of places.

Drawing the Line

King knew that if the Alliance were to stay on course as a missionary movement and denomination, maintaining sound doctrine must be a nonnegotiable priority. He took very seriously the Apostle Paul's instruction to Timothy: "Watch your life and doctrine closely. Persevere in them, because if you do, you will save both yourself and your hearers" (1 Timothy 4:16). That was one reason why he spent hours each day in serious study of the Word—both for himself and for the very soul of the Alliance.

He agreed with Harold Lindsell, then editor of *Christianity Today*, when he linked sound doctrine to missionary work:

> Embracing a doctrine of an errant Scripture will lead to disaster down the road. It will result in the loss of missionary outreach; it will quench missionary passion; it will lull congregations to sleep and undermine their belief in the full-orbed truth of the Bible; it will produce spiritual sloth and decay; and it will finally lead to apostasy.[19]

King developed his sensitive attitude toward sound biblical teaching as a teenager tutored by Pastor Topping in Grenloch. He never forgot the bitter conflict that split Princeton Seminary when it gave way to a liberal attack on the inspiration of Scripture.

Throughout his ministry, the authority of the Bible was impressed upon him by his mentors. In an article about Tozer's influence on him, King called him

> an intellectual beast of prey. ... Within him was a spiritual intuition that enabled him to scent the faintest error, name it for what it was and reject it in one decisive act. Through daily recourse to the Word of God, he had so thoroughly aligned himself with its teachings, commands, outlook and sentiments that this ability was ever present and active.[20]

King saw firsthand in his contacts with ecumenical leaders the debilitating drain of an eviscerated Bible. He recalled an incident that showed how the spiritually bankrupt National Council of Churches had lost its sense of biblical mission and become a mere political lobby. He recounted, "Twenty or more leaders of the missions department of the NCC met in the presiding Episcopalian bishop's residence in Greenwich, Connecticut. They wanted me to attend as an observer, so I had a grandstand seat to see how they operated.

"The big issue at the time [1950-1953] was Truman's decision to send the Seventh Fleet into the Taiwan Strait to protect the island from an invasion by the People's Republic of China. It was a major discussion all in favor of China as against Taiwan. Hour after hour, support was expressed for Communist China and opposition to the American policy of two Chinas. They insisted Taiwan was part of the mainland." The committee presumed to send a telegram to Eisenhower to state their position as that of all the NCC churches.

King received a letter in 1985 from a woman in Iowa. She asked about his contacts with ecumenical leaders. He replied, "For some time I have not had meetings with the leadership of the WCC and NCC. They have not changed for the better. I find it a waste of time to be dialoging with them."

Witnessing the dry rot of liberal theology that spread through the mainline denominations and sabotaged their missionary work, King was consistently diligent during his years as foreign secretary not to allow the same thing to happen in the Alliance. On one occasion, Professor

Tenney at the Wheaton School of Theology cautioned him about an Alliance missionary studying in the divinity program.

The student successfully passed all the courses but privately admitted he was a universalist, one who believed everyone would eventually be saved with or without faith in Christ. Tenney said he would have to grant the student a degree because he met all the academic requirements, but he regretted having him in the school. The missionary was quietly dropped from the Alliance roster. He joined a paramission group providing technical services to overseas missions.

The private manner of dealing with the missionary was consistent with King's views on how such matters should be handled. "Don't temporize, and don't dillydally. If you know it is wrong, deal with it as wrongdoing is supposed to be handled. Just make sure first you have all the facts accurate and not just hearsay. That goes for doctrine as well as for behavior."

Yet he realized in doctrinal matters the dispute could be explosive in public as well as destructive to the individual. "If it becomes a public issue," he said, "sides develop and friends are divided. It can become a controversy totally unchristian. I have always tried to keep the problem as tightly contained as possible. My concern is not to lose the person while dealing with the issue."

King's strict insistence on sound evangelical doctrine and his method of dealing with errant colleagues were put to a severe test in the 1960s. Wheaton College's Tenney warned him that an increasing number of professors in evangelical schools were giving lip service to the institutions' creeds but privately holding views of the Bible that conflicted with its teaching. He probably thought, "Not here in Nyack," but to his surprise and sorrow, King found he had to deal with that issue when it involved a close associate and friend.

Jack F. Shepherd had an impressive list of credits in his record. He and his wife Jean were Alliance missionaries in China until Communist pressure forced them out in 1949. They transferred to the Philippines with God's continued blessing on their work. He was later a very popular professor at St. Paul Bible College. He was asked, along with G. Linwood Barney, to start Jaffray School of Missions, an innovative approach that caught the attention of other schools and influenced their programs.

All was going well until King was confronted by a disturbing question. "I received a letter from six students," he recalled. "They asked why a professor was allowed to work at Jaffray when he taught false doctrine. I set up a meeting with Jack, along with another colleague. For one whole Saturday morning we discussed his theological views.

"I observed that he was hedging on some important issues so we met the following Saturday. At that time he agreed that he questioned whether the creative account in Genesis 1 to 11 was really history. He also suspected the biblical accounts of some leading figures in the Old Testament were not inspired."

Shepherd was starting down the slippery slope of Rudolph Bultmann's principle of demythologizing Scripture. Biblical accounts are not true history—not even the Gospels' account of the life of Christ. Although not yet at that extreme position, "Shepherd's stature was too influential to ignore," King said. "I asked for his immediate resignation in writing."

In his letter to the Nyack Board of Trustees, Shepherd did not raise the theological issue. Instead, he stated, "I believe my leaving could result . . . in the JSM program being strengthened and enriched academically . . . [and] in freeing me to do what I could probably do better than that which I am presently trying to do."

Relieved that the doctrinal matter was not raised at the college, King also allowed him to be released from the Foreign Department without the issue surfacing. He wrote to Shepherd, "My real aim is to 'buy time' in the earnest hope and expectation that a reassignment may become a reality. When the doctrinal matter is resolved, I have in mind something that should be of deep interest to you for a while."

Thus, deeply grieved by the defection of a friend and colleague, King left the door open for a return to ministry when, he hoped, Shepherd would once again believe in the full inspiration of the Bible. After leaving Jaffray, Shepherd served for a short time with the Latin American Mission. Then he returned in 1968 to the Alliance and pastored the Cranford (New Jersey) Alliance church.

Shepherd left no doubt about his renewed belief in the inspired, infallible Word of God. He wrote to a friend, "I have come to see the doctrine of inerrancy is crucial to a fully evangelical view of Scripture as the Alliance seeks to affirm it."

King wrote joyfully to Lindsell, "As you will remember . . . Jack had come to a position of not accepting the Alliance's statement on the inerrancy of Scripture. Well, I am writing to state he has now—through a long process of thought and study characteristic of him—returned to this position quite satisfactorily."

Shepherd was later elected education secretary of the C&MA and served as executive director of Alliance School of Theology and Missions, successor of the Jaffray school he helped found. Closing the circle, he and Jean returned to Asia, where he taught in the Alliance Biblical Seminary in Hong Kong.

King's policy of dealing decisively yet compassionately with a colleague wayward in doctrine was richly rewarded. However, drawing the line against theological error on at least one occasion brought him into sharp disagreement with other leaders in the Alliance.

Over the years he aligned himself with evangelical leaders concerned about declining belief in the Bible as the authoritative and infallible Word of God inspired in all its parts. These included Carl F.W. Henry, Gleason L. Archer and Wilber Moorehead Smith, among others. He also stayed in touch with Harold Lindsell who was writing *Battle for the Bible*, a defense of the inspiration of Scripture as the linchpin of evangelical theology. This was the book that precipitated the confrontation.

Lindsell defined inspiration

> as the inward work of the Holy Spirit in the hearts and minds of chosen men who then wrote the Scriptures so that God got written what He wanted. The Bible in all its parts constitutes the written Word of God to man. This word is free from all error in its original autograph. It is wholly trustworthy in matters of history and doctrine.

"The Bible," he continued,

> does not purport to be a textbook of history, science, or mathematics, yet when the writers of Scripture spoke of matters embraced by these disciplines, they did not indite error; they wrote what was true.[21]

The issue was much more than academic. In challenging the inspiration of Scripture, opponents of inspiration called into question the Bible's authority in the life of the believer. As neoorthodox scholar Karl Barth said, "What inspires me is inspired. What does not inspire me is not inspired."

Given this stand on inspiration, Lindsell took issue with liberals and neoevangelicals alike. One of the latter was Bernard Ramm, author of several theological books and for years a respected evangelical. But by the time he was approached to teach at Simpson Bible College, he had drifted from a clear-cut position on the inspiration of Scripture.

In doing research for his book, Lindsell learned that Ramm had signed a three-year contract with the college. He called King and alerted him to this development, adding that he was citing Ramm in his book and would identify him as teaching in an Alliance school.

"This was the first I had heard of this acquisition by Simpson College," King said. "I asked for some documentation to substantiate Lindsell's opposition to Ramm. Within a day or two, he sent me a massive amount of Xerox copies of quotes from Dr. Ramm's various books that provided indisputable evidence of his having definitely slipped from the 'faith once for all delivered to the saints.' "

In *Battle for the Bible*, Lindsell quoted Ramm's admiration and approval of H.M. Kuitert as "among the great theologians of our times." Yet Kuitert held the position that "to insist that everything happened precisely as it is read in the Bible is to read the Bible badly, or at least superficially . . . some things are reported that simply did not happen as they are told."[22]

The Genesis creation account, according to the Dutch theologian, is not real history and the story of Jonah is pure fiction. As for the Gospel accounts of the life of Christ, Kuitert believed that "the sheer fact that certain events are reported in the Bible does not guarantee that they happened. We do not insist that the resurrection of Jesus really happened just because the Bible says it."[23]

King said, "I immediately shared this information with Joseph Wenninger, secretary of education for the Alliance. He was aghast. We showed it to Nathan Bailey, and asked what to do."

Bailey and Wenninger flew to the West Coast to confer with the college administration. They were told that since the contract already had been signed, there could be a costly lawsuit if it were canceled. Bailey agreed with the college administration's assessment that Ramm should be allowed to teach until the contract expired and then it would not be renewed.

King stood his ground. Lindsell's book would expose the doctrinal errors of Ramm and identify him with Simpson Bible College. When the

Alliance constituency learned of this, he said, there would be real trouble. He rejected the suggestion that Lindsell be asked to drop references to Ramm's connection to the college in the book. "I prefer to let it be published. If Ramm is allowed to stay on, this would be the beginning of the school's going the way of Princeton Seminary."

Simpson College withdrew the contract and the issue was resolved. Ramm still was mentioned in Lindsell's book—without reference to the C&MA school—for drifting from the evangelical position on the inspiration of the Bible.

Showing the Way

Coming into the presidency, King realized that keeping the Alliance on course in the future would require more than only being reactive to situations that threatened to undermine the solid biblical foundation of the Alliance. The best deterrence to error, after all, is the strong, clear and positive presentation of truth. Over the nine years of his presidency, he wrote articles, preached sermons and delivered papers that showed the way to an enduring and vibrant future in worldwide evangelism.

Of particular concern to King was a doctrine that went to the very heart of evangelism and the missionary enterprise and was being questioned in some evangelical circles. He addressed the issue in a position paper entitled "The Lostness of Man—One Motivation for Evangelism."

He stated that the question is not whether a person who never heard the gospel will be lost, but that he or she is already lost. "Whether ignorant of, or ignoring, divine salvation in Christ, he has nothing to hope for beyond this world. Without God—whether ignorant of God or denying God or forsaken by God—he is truly immersed in darkness and misery. For being without God, he is without His help and mercy and protection."[24]

The position paper was published in pamphlet form and became the basis for a powerful sermon. Richard Bailey recalled his experience when he was a district superintendent: "I invited [King] to come to hold a conference on evangelism. He preached on the lostness of man. That message changed my life. I don't think I have ever been the same. It really revolutionized my ministry."

Richard Bailey was not alone. King's message on the fate of those without Christ became perhaps the most widely circulated and remembered of all his sermons. Right up to the time of his retirement, he received responses from men and women profoundly moved by the message. Even so, the question continued to resurface in the Alliance.

His conviction concerning the lostness of anyone who dies without Christ was reflected in a subsequent position statement in the *Manual of The Christian and Missionary Alliance*. It reads, in part: "We continue to adhere to what we believe to be the clear witness of Scripture that those who do not hear the gospel are lost as surely as those who hear the gospel and reject it."[25]

King believed strongly that if the Alliance were to stay on course it would require a constant review of basics that gave birth to the movement. An article on this principle appeared in the denominational magazine on the eve of his becoming president. "Remembrance: Key to Unswerving Purpose" indicated his hope for the future of the Alliance. He mentioned the warning by "one respected church historian [who] predicted that after ninety years of history the C&MA may rapidly change from an evangelistic, missionary, deeper-life movement to a solidified church that has lost its way."

King's response:

> In such a situation we need to look backward to examine our foundation, inward to discover our motives, and forward to settle our positive purpose. The powerful force of memory will be an aid to keep us true to our purpose for being, and certain concerning our destiny.[26]

After reviewing the history of the Alliance since its inception, he summarized his conclusion: "A careful study of the past discloses that the C&MA's very characteristic is that of a church which has within it the life and function of a mission. The Mission came first, and the Church grew out of the Mission.

"From the beginning the conviction has been maintained that along with deeper-life teaching, missions and evangelism are the primary purposes of Alliance churches and, therefore, a chief end for which each congregation exists."

He reviewed the positive evidences that this focus was being maintained, including the fact that "for every 114 members in Alliance churches of the United States and Canada there is an Alliance missionary serving overseas or a worker with Specialized Ministries."

He ended on a triumphant note:

> For ninety-one years, denominational home needs, isolationism, pessimism and the debates that are heard in some assemblies to "hold the line on missions" and to "do more at home" have never once been raised in our General Councils. What a record of consistent obedience to Christ's command to evangelize the world!
>
> Let the remembrance of this—out into the future—serve to keep us ever a "peculiar people."[27]

King returned to contemplation of the future in another article several years later. In his hopeful projection he relied on a truth so obvious it is often overlooked: the inner dynamic of Christ's life.

> I foresee that our work will never be in danger of ruin by popularity if the spirit and teaching of the Christ-life penetrate to every member of our congregations. God's truth and life received and experienced will forever spoil us for fashionable or worldly conformity and narrow sectarianism. Rather, they will exhibit themselves in our fulfilling His highest will and work.[28]

The president drew on his sense of Alliance history to underscore one of the chief means of staying on course. He wrote, "Along with the prominence given to foreign missions and the emphasis on biblical truths known as the Fourfold Gospel, giving probably ranks as the third great pillar of Alliance heritage."[29]

He referred to a quote by Henry Wilson, an Episcopalian clergyman and close associate of Simpson. Wilson called it "the gradual and solemn preparation for the offering." The two-week conventions at Old Orchard Beach in Maine and elsewhere were crammed with messages on the great themes of Scripture incarnated in Christ. Offerings generally were limited to the last day. In just two one-day offerings in 1896 at Old Orchard Beach and New York City, the outpouring amounted to $250,000.

King saw a contemporary relevance to the joyful and selfless outpouring in those early days to the giving by churches in the present.

> The principles on which the churches of yesteryear acted are as timeless as truth, for they are truth in action. Obedience to God's plan for world evangelism provides the mission. Patient, fulsome preaching and teaching of God's Word provide the motivation. Joyous giving to the point of hilarity provides the means.[30]

Toward the end of his presidency, King made an appeal to maintain at a high level two practices that were instituted by the Alliance and still crucial to the worldwide work: the local church missions conference and the faith pledge. He was aware that a growing number of churches, especially those led by pastors without a background in the movement, were resisting the one and ignoring the other.

He cited the missions conference as the centerpiece for sustaining the level of interest and commitment to world evangelism. He believed the New Testament model of missionaries personally reporting to their supporting church (see Acts 14:27) could not be substituted by something better.

He cautioned,

> Missionary interest in Congregational, Presbyterian and Methodist parishes was sustained so long as their men, women and youth ... conducted such Antioch-like missions conferences. Missionary interest, however, waned and died when these meetings were abandoned and members no longer had personal contact with overseas missionaries.
>
> It has always been the missionary himself who has kept the missionary movement growing. Unless local believers see missionaries and know their names and faces as well as their work and needs, before long missions becomes an anonymity to them.[31]

King reiterated one of his long-held beliefs that "homeland churches flourish when missionary interest flourishes." He referred to comments by R. Pierce Beaver of the University of Chicago:

> The overseas mission [after 1812] imparted the needed stimulus to stewardship; and provided the evangelistic impulse which brought vision, zeal, men and money for the apostolic task in the homeland.
>
> Home missions could not succeed until foreign missions gave example and inspiration. . . . It was the overseas mission which continued to cultivate stewardship and to carry forward all denominational causes and nondenominational enterprises.[32]

King further noted that the annual faith promise, like the conference, is rooted in the Bible. He referred to the Apostle Paul's instruction to the believers in Corinth that "each one" in the church with no exception should give, and further, that it should be given systematically, voluntarily and proportionately (see 1 Corinthians 16:1-2).

He recalled that Simpson, "originator of the faith promise method, suggested three steps in faithful giving: ability, sacrifice and faith. That is, determining what you can give for missions, then add some by sacrifice, then add some by faith in God's provisions."[33]

Laying the Tracks

Leaders of organizations and even of nations often attempt at the conclusion of their administrations to lay tracks for the future. They talk not only of possibilities but put their colleagues and constituencies on guard against potential dangers.

George Washington, for one, warned against being entangled in foreign alliances. "Ike" Eisenhower took aim at the military-industrial complex. King, in his last published article while in office, called attention to a concern much in his thoughts concerning the future.

In "Historical Drift" he warned of an affliction that almost inevitably overtakes organizations and movements. He also expressed the hope that it need not happen to the Alliance. "The process takes place," he explained,

> when a greatly gifted leader is raised up of God to call people to a new or renewed emphasis of truth and service. Others of similar heart and mind join with him to launch a new movement.
>
> As the movement ages and times change, however . . . a new generation of leaders takes charge. Possessing different motives, methods and goals, the leaders eventually alter the movement's character and direction.[34]

The C&MA was founded in such a historical context. Great denominations and agencies that had ushered in the remarkable Protestant era of missions had become largely moribund. Only a few hundred North Americans were serving abroad by 1880. The diminishing authority of God's Word and the resulting spiritual decline led one commentator to characterize religion at the time as "like having a toothache."

King saw many of the same problems apparent in his day.

> I refer to a heightened interest—even abnormal absorption—in restructuring missions to include almost everything the church does. In similar fashion, attempts to contextualize the gospel eventually result in what God condemns. Appeals are made to equate social concerns with evangelism, churches are urged to be involved in changing social, political, educational and economic structures.[35]

In another report King noted, "The lesson of church history is that the toning down of a church's original message and mission, and the elevation of new and different interests bring about a loss of the movement's thrust and Christ's favor."[36]

He took special aim at the idea of a "seamless Great Commission." Obliterating the distinction between work in the homeland and overseas—declaring even the terminology outdated—so that everything is seen to be the same and all needs given equal emphasis, he believed, only hastened the process of historical drift toward oblivion.

"As a denomination, we face the very real possibility of an imperceptible and gradual adding to ourselves all the self-serving practices and programs that the Alliance was purposely created to avoid."[37]

However, King hoped the Alliance could prove that historical drift was not an inevitable affliction. "We are not a Mission divorced from the normal activity of a church, but a church which has within it the life and function of a Mission." Demonstrating this was the fact that in the two previous years the C&MA fielded 241 missionaries—an all-time record. "Never in our 100 years of ministry have so many workers been sent abroad in so short a time," he noted.

How could historical drift be averted? King had a suggestion: "Memorialize every year by some new and greater venture of faith aimed at sharing the gospel with yet unreached peoples."[38]

He was already laying the tracks for one "new and greater venture of faith": renewed work in China, one of the oldest and largest Alliance fields before Communism forced a halt in 1949. The planned return to China actually began in December 1977, with a visit by King and William Kerr, regional director. It was the first time in twenty-eight years that C&MA leaders set foot on the mainland.[39]

Hosted by the China International Travel Service, the "tourists" followed a twelve-day schedule that visited only the sites and sights the government wanted seen. King and Kerr were sincerely impressed with the enormous progress in agriculture, industry, education and other aspects of life in the post-Mao era.

But they also observed the restrictions on personal liberties, especially freedom of religion. In all of China only two churches in Beijing were open. A rather large and imposing Protestant church was used once a week by six Chinese Christians and a dozen or so foreign diplomats. The Catholic church also was virtually abandoned. Unofficial house churches, where the real dynamic of faith flourished, were not on the itinerary.

The Alliance leaders did note, however, that recent changes would allow a few skilled foreigners such as teachers and engineers to live and work in China. The door was opening just a crack, but enough for Christian lay people to renew a witness for Christ among the 900 million Chinese.

While regional director, Kerr had drawn up the "China Policy" that would become the basis of how the Alliance should proceed in reentering China. In 1979 William and his wife Marion moved from New York to Hong Kong, where he opened the Office of China Affairs. In addition to helping Christian lay people find work in China and setting up mainland tours, Kerr was a keen China watcher who kept Alliance leaders well informed about developments in China.

He urged that evangelicals should try to build bridges to the churches of the Three-Self Patriotic (Protestant) Movement. According to Philip Teng, he said, almost all of them preach the gospel or else people would ignore them. The president agreed immediately.

"More than anyone else," King said, "Bill was responsible for the resumption of our links with China."

A delegation of the National Association of Evangelicals joined King and Kerr in an official visit to China in November of 1981. They conferred with Bishop K.H. Ting, chairman of the Three-Self Patriotic Movement. By this time, 200 churches had reopened and the cleric estimated there were more than 1 million Christians—most of whom worshiped in unofficial house churches.

Bishop Ting expressed concern for the pastoral care of the believers. The Nanjing Theological Seminary had resumed classes that year, but with just fifty-one students. Discussions led to a fraternal relationship between the Hong Kong-based Alliance Bible Seminary and schools training church workers on the mainland.[40]

Other aspects related to a return to China by the Alliance were done quietly. The Division of Overseas Ministries gathered documents on Mission properties in China. The information was sent to the US State Department so that if relations resumed between the two nations, reparations for seized properties could be part of the negotiations. Philip Teng was kept informed of these and other initiatives away from the public eye.

Kerr's efforts in assisting professionals from Alliance churches to find work on the mainland achieved growing success. By 1987 nineteen

Alliance laypeople engaged in "tent-making" activities, i.e., quietly witnessing for Christ while under contract for professional services. With King's encouragement the Division of Overseas Ministries formally organized this "new and greater venture of faith" that would eventually have worldwide impact.

The International Fellowship of Alliance Professionals (IFAP) sponsored its first couple to China in 1986. IFAP eventually sponsored dozens of skilled technicians and educators who spread out to nations where regular missionary work was banned by law. Some assignments of these dedicated laymen were so dangerous the link to the C&MA had to be confidential, their courageous exploits remaining a secret.

Easter 100 Churches

King's role as president began in 1978 with an unprecedented nine-year campaign to double the size of the Alliance in North America and abroad. His tenure culminated with a church-planting effort never before attempted by the Alliance and perhaps unique in American Church history.

On a single day, Easter Sunday of 1987, the denomination committed to opening 100 new churches. It was another "new and greater venture of faith" that would help the Alliance lean into the wind and blow off traces of historical drift.

Paul Radford, national director for church extension, spearheaded the campaign. He admitted that initially he was thinking of only twenty churches. But as he discussed the plan with some others in 1985, a pastor challenged him, "Anyone can start twenty churches. Let's ask God to stretch our faith and to aim for 100!" Richard Bailey, vice president for National Church Ministries, agreed: "That would be great!" The audacious campaign was born.[41]

The planners settled on basically a three-point strategy. First, a targeted area would be surveyed to determine certain community needs, and then a new church would be structured to respond to those needs. If people, for example, were concerned about their children, a registered nurse in uniform would supervise the nursery.

Second, a communitywide mailing would announce the opening of a church that would avoid objections commonly raised by unchurched people: boring sermons, unfamiliar music, long programs. The letter promised that the new church, its message and music, would be contemporary. Third, the worship style would be planned with non-Christians in mind. Among other things, the Scripture reader would announce the passage by page number in the pew Bible, not by book and chapter.

Pastors for these new churches received special training in how to conduct services made up mainly of unconverted people. Districts provided initial support for a period of time so pastors could devote their time to developing a self-supporting church.

Once again, Alliance men and women got involved enthusiastically. Radford said his phone was ringing off the hook with calls for information. Excitement spread through the whole denomination. "Starting 100 churches on one Easter Sunday absorbed our attention," King recalled. "It was a singleness of purpose rather than having many irons in the fire. It was designed to keep our focus and call on this one thing."

The single-focus effort paid off. "The planting of 101 new Alliance churches in a single day was the faith-stretching conclusion of our Centennial Advance," stated the final report with obvious joy. Average attendance was eighty-eight people; over 10,000 new people were introduced to the Alliance. More than 500 people received the Lord in the first 4 weeks of services.[42]

The smallest gathering was twenty-one people in Idaho; the largest was 302 attendees in Oregon. Radford called the campaign "an unfinished story." He mentioned a woman who kept for several weeks the letter announcing a new church in her area. Then when she and her daughter found themselves in deep trouble, they called the pastor. Both prayed for salvation in the pastor's office.[43] Along the tracks laid for the future on that Easter Sunday, new churches moved from blessing to blessing. Not all survived, but many flourished.

Mission Accomplished

The nine-year drive to double and the one-day surge in church planting culminated in the 1987 Centennial Council in St. Paul, Minnesota. The 5,700-plus delegates, hundreds of Canadian visitors and The Alliance World Fellowship leaders shared in the celebration. The Council theme "The King Is Coming!" fit right into their mood of jubilation.

The World His Field

The Alliance Witness editor Maurice R. Irvin compressed the event-bursting week into a few lines:

> The Council program each day was crammed full of special presentations that surveyed 100 years of progress at home and abroad. These employed speeches, interviews, audiovisual features, music and drama. A seemingly endless succession of banquets, breakfasts and luncheon meetings were held. More elaborate displays than had ever before been assembled were arranged in a huge exhibition hall (approximately 40,000 sq. ft.).[44]

Billy Graham preached in the opening service. His presence had special significance. Having started his ministry in the C&MA, he represented the hundreds, perhaps thousands, of evangelical leaders in other organizations and denominations upon whom the Alliance had had a positive and pivotal influence.

Presiding over the nonstop celebration, King entered into the spirit of the Centennial Council as much as possible. But the accumulated effect of forty-nine years and the impending reality of passing the torch of leadership to another affected him. Having had ear surgery just before Council didn't help either.

"The preparations for Council and being in the public so incessantly during that period, with hardly enough time to get adequate rest, did me in," he acknowledged. He was so weary at the conclusion of the week that he did something highly unusual—he asked an assistant to write the prayer he was to deliver at the dedication of the new president.

David L. Rambo, whom King had profoundly influenced over the years and who at the time was corporate vice president, was elected to follow King as the eighth president of the C&MA. One action taken by Council had symbolic import. It approved relocation of the National Office within a year from the Alliance-heritage-rich town of Nyack to a new site yet to be determined. It was time to move on.

King walked away from the Centennial Council with the sense that his God-given mission was accomplished. He said decades later, "I really felt that I had done as the Lord had directed me. I had no regrets at all for any part of my thirty-four years in the headquarters roles. To this day I don't have second thoughts, nor do I feel exultation for any particular thing that would puff me up and make me feel that I was important. I was quite willing for retirement and just to be a preacher again."

This author pressed him again, as he had done repeatedly during the weeks of interviews. If King had it to do over again would he have done anything differently? He replied firmly as always, "You keep asking me that and I must answer the same every time: no remorse, no questions. I gave my all for Jesus."

In his final president's report to Council, King lifted again the standard of what it meant for the Alliance to stay on course in the coming years. He quoted the stirring words of founder Simpson:

> Let the churches exist for this; let our ministers preach for this; let our seminaries and colleges be on fire with this one theme; let our laborers toil for this; let our consecrated women sacrifice for this; let our homes be furnished and our wardrobes be purchased with reference to this; and let a whole army of true hearts prove to the world around and the heavens above that they understand the meaning of the cross of Calvary, the cry of dying souls, and the glory of the coming Kingdom.[45]

Those words also aptly described the head-to-toe commitment of Louis L. King to his Lord Jesus Christ over a lifetime of service with The Christian and Missionary Alliance.

Notes

1. Robert L. Niklaus, "A Blend of Warmth and Work," *The Alliance Witness*, June 28, 1978, p. 7.
2. Louis L. King, "In the Presence of the King," *The Alliance Witness*, April 15, 1987, p. 22.
3. "Report of the Committee on President's Report and General Legislation," *Minutes of the General Council 1978 and Annual Report for 1977* (Nyack, NY: The Christian and Missionary Alliance, 1978), p. 249.
4. Louis L. King, "Report of the President," *Minutes of the General Council 1979 and Annual Report for 1978* (Nyack, NY: The Christian and Missionary Alliance, 1979), p. 4.
5. Staff report, "The President's Banquets," *The Alliance Witness*, January 4, 1984, p. 29.
6. Louis L. King, "Report of the President," *Minutes of the General Council 1983 and Annual Report for 1982* (Nyack, NY: The Christian and Missionary Alliance, 1983), p. 9.
7. Louis L. King, "Report of the President," *Minutes of the General Council 1981 and Annual Report for 1980* (Nyack, NY: The Christian and Missionary Alliance, 1981), p. 4.
8. Louis L. King, "Conclusion," *Minutes of the General Council 1982 and Annual Report for 1981* (Nyack, NY: The Christian and Missionary Alliance, 1982), p. 43.

9. Louis L. King, *Minutes of the General Council 1983 and Annual Report for 1982*, p. 3.
10. Louis L. King, "Report of the President," *Minutes of the General Council 1984 and Annual Report for 1983* (Nyack, NY: The Christian and Missionary Alliance, 1984), p. 43.
11. Louis L. King, *Minutes of the General Council 1983 and Annual Report for 1982*, pp. 5-6.
12. Staff report, "Growing Church," *The Alliance Witness*, May 7, 1986, p. 27.
13. Louis L. King, "Celebrating a Century of Blessing," *Minutes of the General Council 1987 and Annual Report for 1986* (Nyack, NY: The Christian and Missionary Alliance, 1987), p. 5.
14. Harry Taylor, "Only Happy Man in the Crowd," *The Alliance Witness*, January 30, 1987, p. 11.
15. Ibid., p. 12.
16. Andrew Kerr, "Suddenly Made Refugees," *The Alliance Witness*, September 11, 1985, p. 18.
17. Marilyn Kerr, "Evacuation from Beirut," *The Alliance Witness*, April 25, 1984, p. 18.
18. Andrew Kerr, int. with Pastor Farid Khoury, "A Growing Witness in Syria," *The Alliance Witness*, April 9, 1986, p. 20.
19. Harold Lindsell, *Battle for the Bible* (Grand Rapids, MI: Zondervan, 1976), p. 25.
20. Louis L. King, "First and Foremost a Preacher," *The Alliance Witness*, July 30, 1986, p. 22.
21. Lindsell, pp. 30-1.
22. Ibid., p. 136.
23. Ibid., p. 137.
24. Louis L. King, "The Lostness of Man—One Motivation for Evangelism" (position paper delivered at the pre-Council Missionary Conference, St. Paul, MN, May 14-16, 1973), p. 5.
25. *Manual of The Christian and Missionary Alliance, 1999 Edition* (Colorado Springs, CO: The Christian and Missionary Alliance, 1999), p. G5.
26. Louis L. King, "Remembrance: Key to Unswerving Purpose," *The Alliance Witness*, July 26, 1978, p. 4.
27. Ibid., p. 5.
28. Louis L. King, "What of the Future?" *The Alliance Witness*, June 23, 1982, p. 47.
29. Louis L. King, "A Rich Heritage of Giving," *The Alliance Witness*, October 23, 1985, p. 4.
30. Ibid., p. 5.
31. Louis L. King, "Now More than Ever," *Alliance Life*, April 1, 1987, p. 7.
32. Ibid., p. 7.
33. Ibid., p. 14.
34. Louis L. King, "Historical Drift," *Alliance Life*, May 13, 1987, p. 26.
35. Ibid.
36. Louis L. King, "Report of the President," *Minutes of the General Council 1985 and Annual Report for 1984* (Nyack, NY: The Christian and Missionary Alliance, 1985), p. 12.

37. King, "Historical Drift," p. 27.
38. Ibid.
39. Louis L. King and William W. Kerr, "We Visited China," *The Alliance Witness*, January 11, 1978, p. 18.
40. Staff report, "Evangelical Church Leaders Visit China," *The Alliance Witness*, February 17, 1982, pp. 7-8.
41. Paul Radford, "Get Ready for 100 New Churches," *The Alliance Witness*, November 19, 1986, pp. 24-5.
42. David L. Rambo, "Year One of Century Two," *Minutes of the General Council 1988 and Annual Report for 1987* (Nyack, NY: The Christian and Missionary Alliance, 1988), pp. 32-3.
43. Paul Radford, "Easter 100—An Unfinished Story," *Alliance Life*, June 24, 1987, p. 25.
44. Maurice R. Irvin, "A Day of New Things," *Alliance Life*, July 22, 1987, p. 14.
45. Louis L. King, *Minutes of the General Council 1987 and Annual Report for 1986*, p. 13.

EPILOGUE
"The Church; and the Church; and the Church"

1987-present

With the prospects of leaving office and retiring now at hand, King made two decisions. He put up for sale the house that had been the King family home for nearly thirty years. Then he and Esther selected an apartment on the beautiful grounds of Shell Point Village in Florida, fixing a date to move in September.

The house was no problem. He had a buyer before he left office at the end of July. But the closing formalities on the property did not move as quickly. They never do in New York. Progress slowed even more when lawyers for both parties went on vacation in August. King found the delay hard to take. "After my years in leadership, I wasn't used to no answers, no activity, no nothing," he admitted. "My wife said she had never seen me more frustrated and more worried."

Finally, on the Friday before Labor Day in September 1987, King's lawyer called. Everything was set. Could they close on Tuesday and be out of the house by Wednesday? The move to Florida took place as quickly as the closing in New York was slow.

David Moreland, an administrator at Shell Point Village, observed, "When people come here, we usually see them go through three stages: go-go, slow-go, no-go." The Kings were no exception.

At first, Louis maintained a heavy preaching schedule. In one 5-month period he had 95 speaking engagements, flying frequently and driving 7,500 miles. Invitations came from Mexico to Canada, coast to coast, from churches, conventions and summer camps. Commenting on his frequent visits to Canada over the years, Arnold Cook said, "He was the best known American leader in our Canadian churches."

He also maintained his personal discipline of early-morning study and prayer. He did not pine for the former days, but he admitted it was an adjustment. "It was like being completely cut off. Once out of office, you are out of information," he said. "Except for the Overseas Division, this is what happened. But when I was in office, I saw the same thing happen to those who preceded me, so I just accepted it."

Esther kept busy with her own priorities, especially getting involved in The Shell Point Village Church on the island. She took her usual place in the tenor section of the choir, participated in the women's meetings, played in the bell choir and kept her sense of humor.

After one performance of the bell choir, a visiting friend said to her, "I always said you were a bell-ringer."

Esther's prompt reply with a smile: "No. I'm just another ding-a-ling."

King's "go-go" schedule continued until 1993 when Parkinson's disease forced a halt. Esther also developed health problems. Still, they adjusted well to "slow-go" life in the Village. People who always had seen King in his conservative business suits and starched white shirts, exuding a no-nonsense demeanor, did a doubletake when they saw the Kings in casual summer wear tooling around the grounds in their electric golf cart.

In a few more years, "no-go" took over. The corner apartment in a high-rise condominium gave way to a two-room suite in The Pavilion, the Village's hospital. Then it was one room on the first floor near the nurses' station because of the increased need of assistance. Their health grew weaker but not their sturdy reliance on the Lord and their heart for His work.

King was asked what he considered the greatest accomplishments during his decades of ministry. Was it successful pastorates and positions of national leadership? Church-Mission agreements and urban-evangelism strategy? The Wheaton Congress and Green Lake Conference? Indigenous church measures and the *Policies and Procedures* manual? CAMA Services and the International Fellowship of Alliance Professionals? Regional conferences and The Alliance World Fellowship? Encouraging people movements and missionary activity by the younger churches? Prioritizing the training of overseas church leaders and making scholarships available? Defending the "faith once delivered" and launching the Jaffray School of Missions, the first Alliance graduate school? The centennial doubling campaign and "Easter 100 Churches" project?

Epilogue: The Church; and the Church; and the Church

In one way or another, all the above contributed to his crowning achievement. Of that he wrote in 1980,

> The indigenous church concept and our eventual faithful adherence to it is our crowning glory. Our early adoption of it has made us a unique phenomenon in missionary history. It should therefore be rehearsed in perpetuity, just as the Jews ever commemorate their deliverance from bondage in Egypt. For us and for the national churches it has been like a mighty deliverance from bondage.[1]

When Douglas MacArthur, graduate of West Point Military Academy, gave his farewell speech to the corps of cadets, he concluded eloquently, "Today marks my final roll call with you. But I want you to know that when I cross the river my last conscious thoughts will be of the Corps; and the Corps; and the Corps."

Louis L. King might well say as he contemplates crossing the river, "My last thoughts will be of the Church; and the Church; and the Church."

Best of all, awaiting him on the far shore is the Sovereign Lord of the Church, wonderfully familiar, with a welcoming smile and the longed-for accolade, "Well done, good and faithful servant."

Note

1. Louis L. King, "The Risks and Rewards of Self-Government," *The Alliance Witness*, October 1, 1980, p. 20.

BIBLIOGRAPHY

Articles

"A.I. Garrison, A Bond Servant of Jesus Christ," *The Alliance Weekly* (May 19, 1954).

Bailey, Nathan. "Toward an Alliance World Fellowship," *The Alliance Witness* (February 26, 1975).

"C&M Alliance Converts to Denominational Status," *Eternity* (August 1974).

Carlson, Paul E. "A Spiritual Answer to a Practical Question," *The Alliance Weekly* (January 20, 1954).

Carner, Lauren R. "India in Transition," *The Alliance Weekly* (October 12, 1946).

Chavan, Raghuel P. "Indian Churches Catch a New Vision," *The Alliance Weekly* (July 18, 1956).

"Evangelical Church Leaders Visit China," *The Alliance Witness* (February 17, 1982).

"The Fields in 1977," *Appendix VI, Minutes of the General Council 1978 and Annual Report for 1977* (May 16-21, 1978).

"Growing Church," *The Alliance Witness* (May 7, 1986).

Hall, Eugene. "A Painful Break," *The Alliance Witness* (April 23, 1975).

Herendeen, Dale S. "Buildings Built for Faith," *The Alliance Witness* (September 6, 1961).

Hostetler, Mrs. Jake. "*Alianza en Marcha* Church," *The Alliance Witness* (July 23, 1969).

Irvin, Maurice R. "A Day of New Things," *Alliance Life* (July 22, 1987).

"The Jaffray School of Missions," *The Alliance Witness* (May 18, 1960).

Kerr, Andrew. "Suddenly Made Refugees," *The Alliance Witness* (September 11, 1985).

_____, int. with Pastor Farid Khoury. "A Growing Witness in Syria," *The Alliance Witness* (April 9, 1986).

Kerr, Marilyn. "Evacuation from Beirut," *The Alliance Witness* (April 25, 1984).

King, Bernard S. "Financial Crisis in Indo-China," *The Alliance Weekly* (July 14, 1954).

King, Louis L. "Be Not Discouraged," *The Alliance Witness* (May 14, 1980).

_____. "Caring for the Church," *The Alliance Witness* (June 22, 1983).

_____. "Dr. Alfred Cookman Snead, Man of God and Missionary Statesman," *The Alliance Witness* (April 5, 1961).

_____. "First and Foremost a Preacher," *The Alliance Witness* (July 30, 1986).

_____. "The Gospel Outruns the Missionary," *The Alliance Witness* (February 24, 1960).

_____. "Historical Drift," *Alliance Life* (May 13, 1987).

_____. "In the Presence of the King," *The Alliance Witness* (April 15, 1987).

_____. "Now More than Ever," *Alliance Life* (April 1, 1987).

_____. "On the Homejo Trail," *The Alliance Weekly* (March 14, 1956).

_____. "Remembrance: Key to Unswerving Purpose," *The Alliance Witness* (July 26, 1978).

_____. "A Rich Heritage of Giving," *The Alliance Witness* (October 23, 1985).

---. "The Risks and Rewards of Self-Government," *The Alliance Witness* (October 1, 1980).
---. "Second Asia Conference," *The Alliance Weekly* (May 7, 1958).
---. "What of the Future?" *The Alliance Witness* (June 23, 1982).
--- and William W. Kerr. "We Visited China," *The Alliance Witness* (January 11, 1978).
Klein, George C. "Historic Conference," *The Alliance Witness* (March 4, 1964).
Kuhns, Janet. "God's Man in God's Place," *Alliance Life* (December 2001).
Larson, Gordon. "God Moved Upon the People of a Hundred Valleys," *The Alliance Witness* (March 25, 1959).
Lindsell, Harold. "Precedent-Setting in Missions Strategy," *Christianity Today* (April 29, 1966).
Maxey, Michael "Buzz." "Chief Amene," *Indonesian Insights* (April-May 2001).
McGavran, Donald. "A Definitive Statement on Church-Mission Relationships," *Church Growth Bulletin,* vol. 8, no. 2 (November 1971).
"Mission to an Urban World," *Church Growth Bulletin* (September 1975).
"News Flash," *The Alliance Witness* (September 18, 1963).
Niklaus, Robert L. "A Blend of Warmth and Work," *The Alliance Witness* (June 28, 1978).
---. "Courageous Soldier and Gentle Christian," *The Alliance Witness* (May 17, 1961).
---. "This Encounter Keeps Going," *Alliance Life* (October 13, 1993).
"North Point Alliance Church," *Foreign Field Flashes* (October 1966).
"Notice," *The Alliance Weekly* (June 1, 1955).
Peters, George W. "Mission-Church Relationships—I," *Bibliotheca Sacra* (July 1968).
Post, Mrs. Walter M. "Masses Move Toward Christ in New Guinea," *The Alliance Witness* (March 11, 1959).
"The President's Banquets," *The Alliance Witness* (January 4, 1984).
Radford, Paul. "Easter 100—An Unfinished Story," *Alliance Life* (June 24, 1987).
---. "Get Ready for 100 New Churches," *The Alliance Witness* (November 19, 1986).
Sawyer, Mrs. Malcolm M. "The Third Domino," *The Alliance Witness* (August 13, 1975).
Snead, Alfred C. "Advance Among the Tribes of Viet Nam," *The Alliance Weekly* (January 19, 1955).
Stebbins, Thomas H. "Not Enough Time," *The Alliance Witness* (July 30, 1975).
Taylor, Harry. "Only Happy Man in the Crowd," *The Alliance Witness* (January 30, 1987).
Trainer, Ralph S. "Villages for Jesus," *Alliance Life* (September 2000).

Annual Reports

Bailey, Nathan. "Annual Survey of the President," *Minutes of the General Council 1972 and Annual Report for 1971.* New York: The Christian and Missionary Alliance (May 17-22, 1972).

———. "Annual Survey of the President," *Minutes of the General Council 1976 and Annual Report for 1975.* The Christian and Missionary Alliance (May 11-16, 1976).

Battles, Robert W. "Report of the Secretary," *Minutes of the General Council 1972 and Annual Report for 1971.* The Christian and Missionary Alliance (May 17-22, 1972).

———. "Report of the Secretary," *Minutes of the General Council 1976 and Annual Report for 1975.* Nyack, NY: The Christian and Missionary Alliance (May 11-16, 1976).

Johnson, Gilbert H. "Report of the Education Department," *Minutes of the General Council 1961 and Annual Report for 1960.* New York: The Christian and Missionary Alliance (May 17-21, 1961).

King, Louis L. "Celebrating a Century of Blessing," *Minutes of the General Council 1987 and Annual Report for 1986.* Nyack, NY: The Christian and Missionary Alliance (May 18-24, 1987).

———. "Christ the Head of the Church," *Report of the Asia Conference.* Foreign Department. New York: The Christian and Missionary Alliance, 1956.

———. "Report of the Foreign Department," *Minutes of the General Council 1957 and Annual Report for 1956.* New York: The Christian and Missionary Alliance (May 15-21, 1957).

———. "Report of the Foreign Department," *Minutes of the General Council 1958 and Annual Report for 1957.* New York: The Christian and Missionary Alliance (May 14-19, 1958).

———. "Report of the Foreign Department," *Minutes of the General Council 1959 and Annual Report for 1958.* New York: The Christian and Missionary Alliance (May 13-18, 1959).

———. "Report of the Foreign Department," *Minutes of the General Council 1960 and Annual Report for 1959.* New York: The Christian and Missionary Alliance (May 11-16, 1960).

———. "Report of the President," *Minutes of the General Council 1977 and Annual Report for 1976.* New York: The Christian and Missionary Alliance (May 10-17, 1977).

———. "Report of the President," *Minutes of the General Council 1979 and Annual Report for 1978.* New York: The Christian and Missionary Alliance (May 15-20, 1979).

———. "Report of the President," *Minutes of the General Council 1980 and Annual Report for 1979.* New York: The Christian and Missionary Alliance (May 13-18, 1980).

———. "Report of the President," *Minutes of the General Council 1981 and Annual Report for 1980.* Nyack, NY: The Christian and Missionary Alliance (May 12-17, 1981).

———. "Conclusion," *Minutes of the General Council 1982 and Annual Report for 1981.* Nyack, NY: The Christian and Missionary Alliance (May 11-16, 1982).

———. "Report of the President," *Minutes of the General Council 1983 and Annual Report for 1982.* Nyack, NY: The Christian and Missionary Alliance (June 21-26, 1983).

_____. "Report of the President," *Minutes of the General Council 1984 and Annual Report for 1983*. Nyack, NY: The Christian and Missionary Alliance (June 22-27, 1984).

_____. "Report of the President," *Minutes of the General Council 1985 and Annual Report for 1984*. Nyack, NY: The Christian and Missionary Alliance (May 20-25, 1985).

Rambo, David L. "Year One of Century Two," *Minutes of the General Council 1988 and Annual Report for 1987*. Nyack, NY: The Christian and Missionary Alliance (May 31-June 5, 1988).

"Report of the Committee on Foreign Department Report," *Minutes of the General Council 1955 and Annual Report for 1954*. New York: The Christian and Missionary Alliance (May 11-17, 1955).

"Report of the Committee on President's Report and General Legislation," *Minutes of the General Council 1978 and Annual Report for 1977*. Nyack, NY: The Christian and Missionary Alliance (May 16-21, 1978).

"Reports of Council Committees," *Minutes of the General Council 1975 and Annual Report for 1974*. Nyack, NY: The Christian and Missionary Alliance (May 14-19, 1975).

Shuman, Harry M. "Annual Report of the President," *Minutes of the General Council 1953 and Annual Report for 1952*. New York: The Christian and Missionary Alliance (May 20-26, 1953).

_____. "Report of the President," *The C&MA: The Thirty-Sixth Annual Report* [for the year 1932]. New York: The Christian and Missionary Alliance (1933).

Snead, Alfred C., "Report of the Foreign Department," *Minutes of the General Council 1956 and Annual Report for 1955*. New York: The Christian and Missionary Alliance (May 16-21, 1956).

Minutes of the Board of Managers

"Covering Letter," *Minutes of the Board of Managers*. New York: Foreign Department Conference of The Christian and Missionary Alliance (October 7-14, 1926).

"Report #2: Preamble to the Report on Self-Support," *Minutes of the Board of Managers*. New York: The Christian and Missionary Alliance (1926).

Minutes of the Board of Managers. New York: The Christian and Missionary Alliance (1952).

Minutes of the Board of Managers. New York: The Christian and Missionary Alliance (1976).

Unpublished Sources

Barney, G. Linwood. "Jaffray School of Missions: A Vision Uncovered." Paper given at the thirtieth anniversary of the school's founding (1990).

Cartmel, Daryl Westwood. "Partnership in Mission." Doctoral dissertation, School of World Mission, Fuller Theological Seminary (1980).

"The Chairmanship." *Report to the Foreign Department* (January 24, 1963).

"Extent." *Report to the Foreign Department* (December 1962).
King, Louis L. "Church Under a Socialist Regime." Case study (September 23, 1978).
_____. "The Lostness of Man—One Motivation for Evangelism." Position paper delivered at the pre-Council Missionary Conference, St. Paul, MN (May 14-16, 1973).
_____. "Mission-Church Relations Overseas—Part I: In Principle." Paper presented at Green Lake Conference (1980).
_____. "Mission-Church Relations Overseas—Part II: In Practice." Paper presented at Green Lake Conference (1980).
_____. "The Practical Implications Arising from Dr. Charles E. Ryrie's Paper." (July 1963).
_____. "Remembrance: One Motive for Missions." Position paper for the Foreign Department (1974).
_____. "Report of the Fifth Asia Conference." *Report to the Foreign Department* (February 18-26, 1969).
_____. "Report on the South America Trip." *Report of the Foreign Department to the Board of Managers* (August 1957).
_____. "Report on the Third Asia Conference." *Report to the Foreign Department* (July 15-20, 1961).
_____. "Report of the Trip to Holland, France, West Africa, Gabon, and Congo." *Report to the Foreign Department* (March 24-26, 1959).
_____. "Report on Vietnam Crisis and Evacuation of Missionaries." *Report to the Board of Managers* (March 9-April 4, 1975).
_____. "South American Administrative Trip." *Report to the Foreign Department* (1967).
_____. "Urbanization and Missions." Foreign Department study paper (November 28, 1960).
_____. "Working Paper." Presented to the Special Committee on the Philosophy of Funding, *Minutes of the Board of Managers* (December 1976).
Moore, David H. "Models of Church/Mission Relationships."
Smalley, William F. *Alliance Missions in India: 1892-1972,* Vol. 1. Foreign Department of The Christian and Missionary Alliance (1973).

Books

Brinton, Howard H. *A Guide to True Peace: The Excellency of Inward and Spiritual Prayer*. New York and London: Harper and Brothers, in association with Pendle Hill, 1839 edition.
Bunyan, John. *Grace Abounding to the Chief of Sinners*. New York: Penguin, 1987.
Kim, Samuel I. *Unfinished Mission in Thailand: The Uncertain Impact on the Buddhist Heartland*. Seoul: East-West Center for Missions Research and Development, 1980.
Lindsell, Harold. *Battle for the Bible*. Grand Rapids, MI: Zondervan, 1976.
_____. *The Church's Worldwide Mission*. Waco, TX: Word Books, 1966.

Manchester, William. *The Last Lion: Winston Spencer Churchill, 1932-1940.* Boston: Little, Brown and Company, 1988.

Manual of The Christian and Missionary Alliance, 1999 Edition. Colorado Springs, CO: The Christian and Missionary Alliance, 1999.

McGee, Gary B. *This Gospel Shall Be Preached: A History and Theology of Assemblies of God Foreign Missions to 1959.* Springfield, MO: Gospel Publishing House, 1986.

Niklaus, Robert L. "The School that Vision Built," *Missionarian 1982.* Nyack, NY: Nyack College, 1982.

Niklaus, Robert L., John S. Sawin, Samuel J. Stoesz. *All for Jesus: God at Work in The Christian and Missionary Alliance Over One Hundred Years.* Camp Hill, PA: Christian Publications, Inc., 1986.

Palomino, Miguel Angel. *Lima Al Encuentro con Dios, A New Kind of Urban Missiology,* 1983.

Winter, Ralph D. *The 25 Unbelievable Years: 1945-1969.* Pasadena, CA: William Carey Library, 1970.

INDEX

Abrams, Richard and Elsie, 244, 251 (just Richard)
Africa, 5, 212, 218. *See also* Gabon, Africa, Church in
africanization, 231-2
Ahmedabad, India, 104, 117
Alford, Paul, 287
Alianza en Marcha, 245, 246
All for Jesus, 48
Alleine, Joseph, 71
Allen, Roland, 182
Allen, Tom, 289
Alliance. *See* Christian and Missionary Alliance, The (C&MA)
Alliance Bible Institute (Lima, Peru), 251
Alliance of Congolese Protestants (APROCO), 227, 228, 229
Alliance School of Theology and Missions, 194. *See also* Jaffray School of Missions (JSM)
Alliance Theological Seminary, 194. *See also* Jaffray School of Missions (JSM)
Alliance World Fellowship (AWF), 269, 271-2
American Leprosy Mission, 169
Amman, Jordan, 300
apostasy, trend toward, 171-5, 193-4, 301
Archbold Expedition, 152
Archer, Gleason L., 305
Argentina, 210
Arn, Win, 295
Asbury Theological Seminary, 258
Associated Medical Missions Office (AMMO), 169

Bailey, Keith M., 287
Bailey, Mary, 290
Bailey, Nathan, 209, 224, 228, 263, 270, 276, 283-4, 290, 306
Bailey, Richard, 307, 314
Bailey, Steve, 285
Bailey, Thomas P., 191
Baker, Milton, 46, 255

Bala, Benjamin, 115
Baliem Valley (Irian Jaya) crisis, 152-5
Bangkok Conference, 4-6, 9-12, 211, 213, 214
   discussion of self-governance, 18
   discussion of self-support, 14-7
   King's keynote address, 13-4
   pre- and post-, 148-152
   ripple effect of, 19-21, 151
Bangkok, Thailand, 2-3, 213. *See also* Thailand, Church in
Banmethuot (Vietnam) massacre, 196-8, 234-6, 264
Barney, Elsie, 193
Barney, G. Linwood, 190, 191, 193, 194, 256, 303
Barth, Karl, 305
Battle for the Bible, 305, 306. *See also* Lindsell, Harold
Battles, Robert W., 287
Beaver, R. Pierce, 310
Beirut, Lebanon, 296, 298, 299
Belgian Congo, Church in, 163
Belgium, 226
Bellig, Jacob, 49, 50, 51
Bellig, Kimber, 49, 50
Berachah Home, 46-7
Berlin Congress of World Evangelism, 258
Beyma, U.H. van, 176
Blanchard, Charles, 84
Blews, Ruth, 105
Blood, Hank, 235
Boon, Harold W., 191
Boxer Rebellion (1900), 235
Boyle, Hal, 236
Brabazon, James, 37, 40, 63, 114
Bridges of God, 124, 184. *See also* McGavran, Donald
Brown, R.R., 56, 83, 88, 116-7
Bubna, Don, 274, 276
Bultmann, Rudolph, 304
Bunyan, John, 78-9
Burley, Louella, 105
Byington, Helen, 137

Cable, John H., 53-4, 84, 85-6, 118
CAMA Services, 266, 272
Cambodia, 262-3, 266
Campus Crusade for Christ, 236
Canadian Christian and Missionary Alliance, 224-5, 291-3
Carlson, Paul, 141, 143, 183
Carner, Lauren R., 106
Cartmel, Daryl W., xi, 108, 109, 261
Cathey, Gordon M., 287
Chan, Ouch, 16
Chavan, Raghuel P., 10, 12, 17, 19, 120, 124, 151, 212, 213, 214
Chile, 164, 210-11
China, 169, 312-4
China Consultation, 169
Chrisman, Robert M., 5-6, 169-70, 209
Christian and Missionary Alliance, The (C&MA)
    budget for overseas work, 272-7
    centennial growth goals, 288-90
    as a denomination, 267
    Division of Overseas Ministries, 291-2, 314
    doubling campaign, 290-5
    faith pledge, 310
    financial operation, 146-8
    1955 General Council, 7-9, 148
    1956 General Council, 14, 158, 159
    1974 General Council, 267
    1975 General Council, 269
    1979 General Council, 291
    1981 General Council, 293
    1987 General (Centennial) Council, 295, 315-6
    local church missions conference, 310
    missionary allowances, 136
    as a movement, 57, 58, 136
    national office, 6
    policies and procedures for overseas fields, 136-8
    relocation to Nyack, New York, 267-8, 269
    screening process for new missionaries, 157

shortage of workers, 156-7
statistics about overseas work, 8, 242, 278, 288-9
See also Canadian Christian and Missionary Alliance
Church of the Brethren, 131
Church of Christ in Thailand, 220
Church-Mission agreements, 222-3, 224, 259, 287
Church-Mission dichotomy, King's position on, 260, 261-2
Church-Mission integration, 219-21, 259
Coggins, Wade, 288
Colombia, 164, 210, 246
Congo, church split in, 225-9
Congress on the Church's World-Wide Mission (1966). *See* Wheaton Congress
Conley, William, 242
Constance, George S., 132, 190, 209-10, 212, 216, 245
Cook, Arnold C., 225, 243-4, 246, 292, 321
Cooke, Leslie E., 176
Cowles, H. Robert, 209
Creer, David, 145-6
Crown College. *See* St. Paul Bible Institute
Cutts, William, 167, 168

Dagher, Joy, 296
Dagher, Sami, 296-8
Damal people group, 184-5, 186
Dani people group, 152-5, 187
Davey, James A., 104, 275
Davey, James E., 104
Davey, John H., 104
Dawan, Z., 10, 15, 16
de Jesus, Florentino, 12, 16, 18, 19, 211
Dechert, Louis T., 273
Deeper Life Convocation, 289
Delanco Camp, 26
Dennis, Ida, 25-6
Desai, R.B., 118-9
dichotomy. *See* Church-Mission dichotomy
Diefenbaker, John, 224

Dievendorf, Anne, 136
"Double in a Decade" banquets, 289-90
Drake, Clarence, 205
Dreger, Clement R., 263
Dulaca, J.A., 18
Dunbar, E.R., 45-6, 47, 49, 50, 61
Dunkers. *See* Church of the Brethren

East Asia Christian Council (EACC), 176-7, 270
Easter 100 campaign, 314-5
Ecuador, 163-4, 210
ecumenical movement, 175, 252-6. *See also* World Council of Churches (WCC)
Edman, V. Raymond, 52-3, 84, 284-5
Eicher, Bert and Artimese, 119
Elbel, Roger, 298
Ellenberger, John, 184
Emerson, Ralph Waldo, 21
Epp, Theodore, 90
Espa, Z.A., 213
Evangelical Church of Guinea, 232
Evangelical Church of Vietnam, 140, 142, 143, 175-9, 236, 265. *See also* Hoi Thanh Tin Lanh
Evangelical Fellowship of India (EFI), 122
Evangelical Foreign Missions Association (EFMA), 242, 253-4, 255, 259
Evangelical Missions Quarterly, 259

Feather, Merlin C., 287
Fenton, Horace L., 254
Fifth Asia Conference (1969), 213-5
Figg, Edna, 8, 132-3
finances, mission, 14-7
Fitch, Elmer, 46
Frame, John D., 169
Francis, Mabel, 136
Fraser, Kenneth C., 130
Freed, Paul, 245
Freed, Ralph, 245

Freleigh, Harold M., 53, 118
French West Africa, 163

Gabon, Africa, Church in, 163, 215-9, 221-2, 236-7
Gabrielson, John, 92
Gandhi, Mahatma, 85, 110
Garrison, A.I., 112
Garrison, Kyle D., 107, 108, 112, 118
Geddie, John, 40
Gerber, Dan, 197
Gibbons, Donald and Alice, 186
Glasser, Arthur F., 170, 255
"Good News for Great Cities" project, 295
Graham, Billy, 258, 285, 297, 316
Graham, Franklin, 297
Green Lake Conference, 224, 259-62
Grenloch, New Jersey, 25
Grenloch Presbyterian Church, 29-30, 35. *See also* Topping, William
Grinnell, Ann, 285
Griswold, Carolyn, 234-5
Griswold, Leon, 234
Grubbs, Francis W., 289
Guinea, West Africa, anti-mission regime in, 231-4
Gujarat, India, 101
Gujarati, 103-4
Gulbranson, E.F., 16

Haagen, Anna, 102
Hall, Eugene, 262
Hall, Jewel, 5, 11, 12, 139-40, 143, 167, 209, 242-3, 274, 283, 286
Hashweh, Albert, 213
Hashweh, Yousef, 300
Havelock Alliance Church (Lincoln, Nebraska), 88-92
Hawley, Trudy, 285
Henry, Carl F.W., 305
Henry, Paul, 46
Heredeen, Dale S., 178

Hess, Fannie L., 53, 118
Hines, Viola, 56, 59
Hmong people group, 193
Hodges, Melvin L., 255
Hogan, Philip, 288
Hoi Thanh Tin Lanh. *See* Evangelical Church of Vietnam
Holton, Genevieve, 134-5, 205
Hon, M., 213
Hong Kong, 184, 195, 196, 213
Hostetler, Jake and Margaret, 246
Howard, David, xi
Huyen, Ong-van-, 178

India,
    the Kings' missionary service in, 4, 100-25
        call to, 63, 80-2, 92-3
        delays to, 96-8
        disillusionment, 105-8
        language study, 103-5
        opposition to, 99-100
    political transition of, 105-6
    See also Ahmedabad, India; Gujarat, India; Maharashtra, India; Palanpur, India
indigenous church policy, 3-9, 20, 140, 149-52, 192, 214, 216, 219, 261, 323. *See also* self-support
Indochina, 138-42, 262, 266, 272
Indonesia, 149, 164, 191
Intercultural Ministries, 266
International Fellowship of Alliance Professionals (IFAP), 314
International Foreign Missions Association (IFMA), 253, 254, 255, 259
International Missionary Council (IMC), 252, 253
Irian Jaya, 184-7
Irvin, Maurice R., 316

Jackson, Fred, 50, 51
Jaffray, Robert A., 191
Jaffray School of Missions (JSM), 189-94, 303, 304

Jefferson, Thomas, 174
Jeffrey, D.I., 130
Jerusalem Alliance church, 300-1
Johns, Betty, 6
Johnson, Gilbert H., 191
Johnson, Norman, 264
Jordan, 300. *See also* Amman, Jordan

Kaetzel, Oliver and Winnie, 285
Kantzer, Kenneth S., 255
Karentina church (Beirut, Lebanon), 296, 298, 299
Kasavubu, Joseph, 231
Keita, Paul, 233
Kelly, Eugene, 248, 250
Kerr, Andrew, 298-9
Kerr, Marilyn, 299
Kerr, Marion, 313
Kerr, William, 6, 165, 169-70, 209, 242, 312, 313-4
Khmer Rouge, 262, 263
Khounthapanya, Saly, 10
Khoury, Farid, 299
Kim, Samuel I., 220
Kimbanguism, 225-6
Kincade, Raymond, 289
King, Bernard S., 9, 10, 143-8, 157-8, 190, 209, 268-9
King, Cordelia, 27, 28
King, David Jonathan, 84, 102-3, 117, 206, 207
King, Esther, 72-5, 115-6, 117, 129, 203-8, 284, 286, 321-2. *See also* India, the Kings' missionary service in; Martz, Esther Lillian
King, John Mark, 117, 129, 203, 204, 205, 207
King, Louis L.
  ability to recall names and details, 34, 285-6
  as area secretary for India and the Far East, 129-33
  balance in ministry, 76-8
  baptism, 33
  call to ministry, 36-9
  characteristics, 243

college education of, 43-52. *See also* Nyack College
disagreement with mission policy, 110-4
discipline, 71, 242
as foreign secretary, 159, 162-7, 168-71, 209
health problems, 34, 120-1, 322
home and family, 26-9
insistence on sound doctrine, 301-3
miraculous healing, 47-8
observance of the Lord's Day, 29, 86-7
as president of the C&MA, 283, 286-8
relocation to New York City, 133-5
role models, 52-5
semi-vows, 69-70
similarities to Albert B. Simpson, 40
spiritual conversion, 25-6, 31
as vice president for the Division of Overseas Ministries, 267
See also Havelock Alliance Church (Lincoln, Nebraska); India, the Kings' missionary service in; North Tonawanda (New York) Alliance Church; Westmont (Illinois) Alliance Church
King, Mildred, 26
King, Paul Lloyd, 74, 102, 103, 116, 117, 205, 206, 208
King, Raymond, 27, 28
King, Stephen Raymond, 98, 101-2, 117, 204, 205, 206, 207, 208
Klassen, Ernie and Marilyn, 286
Klein, George, 210, 212, 228, 241
Konemann, William and Harmina, 155-6
Kong, Joseph S., 285
Kuitert, H.M., 306
Kuvuna, Joel, 227
Kyle, Tom, 247

Landour, India, 102
Laos, 148, 223, 263, 266. *See also* Indochina
Larson, Gordon, 185-6
Larson, Reuben, 245
Latin America, 211
Lebanon. *See* Beirut, Lebanon

Lecaro, Miguel, 245, 246, 247
leprosy, 6
LeTourneau Foundation, 248, 249
Lewis, C.S., 37
Lima, Peru, 247-50
Lima's Encounter with God (LED), 250-2
Lindsell, Harold, 252, 301, 305, 306, 307
Lindsey, Dana, 243
Livingstone, David, 119
Loh, Philip, 183
Lon Nol regime, 262

ma-bop relationship, 108-10
MacArthur, Douglas, 323
Machen, J. Gresham, 32
Madcliff, Herbert, 39
Maharashtra, India, 101
Malone College, 172
Manchester, William, xi
Mangham, R. Harold, 242
Mangham, T. Grady, 197, 209, 235, 241, 272
Mar Thoma Church (South India), 119
Martin, Helen (Sherwood), 59
Martz, Clifford, 82-3
Martz, Esther Lillian, 56-62, 71-2. *See also* King, Esther
Martz, Myrle, 56-8
Martz, William, 56
Maxey, Michael "Buzz" and Myrna, 187-9
M'Badinga, Jean, 217
McGavran, Donald, vii, 124, 184, 186, 262
McIlvaine, Robinson, 232-3
McKay, Angus, 124
Meloon, Walt, 289
mentoring, 33-4
Mickelson, Einar, 153
Mieng, Doan-van-, 179, 212, 257, 265, 266
Miess, William, 51

Miller, Tracy, 77-8
Missionary Training Institute. *See* Nyack College
Mitchell, Archie, 197
Mitchell, Betty, 197, 264
Moore, David H., 219, 220, 224, 294
Moreland, David, 321
Moreland, William, 72
Morgan, G. Campbell, 55
Morris, Paul L., 11, 12, 103, 104, 115, 123
Mortensen, Vernon, 254
Moseley, Thomas, 45, 144

Nanfelt, Peter and Jerry, 165
National Association of Evangelicals (NAE), 171-2, 174, 253, 258, 313
National Council of Churches (NCC), 168, 173, 219, 302
Nehru, Pandit, 106
Nelson, H.E., 151
Netherlands, 163
Newbern, William, 4, 5, 11-2
Nhatrang Bible Institute, 178-9
N'Kokolo, Justin, 229-31
No, Y, 16
North Point Church (Hong Kong), 195-6, 213
North Tonawanda (New York) Alliance Church, 67, 68-9
Nyack College, 36, 43-5, 52, 55, 192, 245

Ockenga, Harold J., 288
Odman, Ralph B., 254
Olsen, Betty, 234-5, 236
Olsen, J.D., 141
Operation Heartbeat, 273
Opperman, Kenn, 247
Oueis, Ibrahim, 213

Paku, Thomas, 227, 228
Palanpur, India, 114-7
Palomino, Miguel Angel, 249

Paris Agreement, 265
Paris Evangelical Mission, 217
paternalism, 150, 151
people movements toward God, 184-7
Perez, Francisco, 251
Perkin, Noel, 253
Peru, 163, 164, 210. *See also* Lima, Peru
Peters, George W., 260, 261
Phenicie, Darrell, 298-9
Philippines, 149, 223
Phillips, Richard and Lillian, 264
Phnom Penh, Cambodia. *See* Cambodia
Phoopharot, Chom, 14
Phu, Le-Hoang-, 257
Pick, Franz, 147
Pierce, Bob, 297
Pierson, A.T., 208
Policies and Procedures manual, 137-8
Post, Harry, 85
Post, Viola and Walter, 184
postwar period of accelerating missions, 240-2
Princeton Seminary, 190, 302, 307
"Project 10,000," 289
Pueblo Libre church (Lima, Peru), 250-1

Rader, Paul, 292
Radford, Paul, 314, 315
radio stations, 244-7
Ramabai Mukti Mission, 286
Rambo, David L., 287-8, 291, 294, 316
Rambo, Ruth, 287
Ramm, Bernard, 306-7
Rash, Clifton, 83
Raysingh, Hiralal, 15, 16
Revelle, Jack, 183, 264
Roman Catholic Church, 211, 216, 226, 231, 246, 252
Roseberry, Robert, 4-5

Rosemont Alliance Church. *See* Havelock Alliance Church (Lincoln, Nebraska)
Ryrie, Charles E., 170, 172

Saigon, Vietnam, 181, 183-4, 264, 265
Sao, Ha, 141
Sather, Eileen, 166
Sawyer, Helen, 263
Scripture, inspiration of, 173-4, 301, 302, 304, 305, 306, 307
Second Asia Conference (1958), 179-80, 181
Second Circle Church (Amman, Jordan), 300
Selchow, E.G., 47
self-expression, 18-9
self-support, 7, 14-7, 20, 211-2. *See also* indigenous church policy
Senior, George, 25, 26
Shareski, Arni, 241, 242, 243, 286, 287
Shellrude, Ralph, 233
Shepherd, Jack, 191, 193, 194, 257, 303-5
Shepherd, Jean, 303
Sherwood, Helen. *See* Martin, Helen (Sherwood)
Shuman, Harry M., 7, 52
Simpson, Albert B., 43, 46-7, 69, 267, 292, 310, 317
   similarities to King, 40
   See also Berachah Home
Simpson Bible College, 306, 307
Singh, Bakht, 100
Smalley, William F., 110, 130, 137, 157, 190, 209, 268
Smith, Alfredo C., 250
Smith, Curwin, 183
Smith, Eugene, 171, 255
Smith, Gordon H., 142-3
Smith, June, 287
Smith, Raymond, 82
Smith, Wilber Moorehead, 305
Snead, A.C., 7, 9, 14, 62, 81, 97, 98, 112, 130, 158
Son, Vo Tho, 265
South America, 211
South American Conference (1960), 210-2

St. Paul Bible Institute, 91, 97, 144
Stebbins, Tom, 265-6
Stevens, William C., 189
Stowe, David, 193-4
Stringer, Adriaan, 271
Sunday, Billy, 30-1
Swope, Pearl, 287
Sylvester, Melvin, 224, 275-6, 291
Syria, 164

Taing, Chric, 263
"Target: Jerusalem," 289
Taylor, Clyde W., 170, 175, 254, 288
Taylor, Harry and Miriam, 296
Templo Alianza (Guayaquil, Ecuador), 214, 245
Teng, Philip, 194-6, 213, 257, 313
Tenney, Merrill C., 256, 288
Tet offensive, 234, 235, 264
Thai, Le-van-, 10, 12, 14, 18, 176, 179, 183
Thailand, Church in, 5, 6, 149, 163, 220, 223. *See also* Bangkok, Thailand; Indochina
Thomas, Cecil, 88, 97-8
Thompson, A.E., 48
Thompson, Edward and Ruth, 235
Three-Self Patriotic (Protestant) Movement, 313
Ting, K.H., 313
Topping, William, 30, 35-6
   as mentor to King, 31-4
Toure, Sekou, 231, 232, 233, 234
Tozer, A.W., 57, 58-9, 71-2, 84-6, 97, 129, 302
   King's friendship with, 79-80
Trainer, Ralph, 236-7
Trans World Radio (TWR), 245
Troutman, Ken, 154, 167
Turnbull, John, 35, 112
Turnbull, Walter A., 35, 112
Turner, Harry, 142

Ulrich, Ed, 153, 154
universalism, 174
urban church planting, 181-4
urban evangelism. *See* urban church planting

Valdemar, Pedro, 246
Van Dyck, Howard, 93
Van Stone, Lloyd and Doris, 153 (Lloyd only), 154
Vietnam, 140-2, 148-9, 163, 175-9, 181, 197-8, 225, 264-5, 266. *See also* Banmethuot (Vietnam) massacre; Evangelical Church of Vietnam; Indochina; Saigon, Vietnam
Vietti, Ardell, 197, 198
Vincer, Jun, 223
Volstad, David, 241, 244, 245

Wati, Ben, 122
Watkins, William, 245
Weidman, Claire, 147
Wenninger, Joseph, 306
West Africa, 210, 231. *See also* Guinea, West Africa
Westmont (Illinois) Alliance Church, 83-4, 86-8
Wheaton College, 84, 254, 258
Wheaton Congress, 252, 254, 256-8, 259, 260
Wheaton Declaration, 254, 256-8, 260
Whyte, Alexander, 70
Wible, Steve and Juniata, 166
Wilson, Henry, 309
Wilting, Ruth, 234-5
Wing, Myra, 105
Winter, Ralph D., 190, 214, 241
Women's Missionary Prayer Fellowship (WMPF), 208, 286
Woodstock (inter-mission school), 102
World Conference on Faith and Order (1963), 170
World Council of Churches (WCC), 170, 171, 173, 174, 176, 177, 179, 194, 215, 252, 253, 270

Ziemer, Marie and Robert, 235
Zwemer, Samuel, 32

"The World His Field *is God-honoring, soul-stirring, faith-challenging and vision-broadening. Just as the man I have known for over forty years—a world-trotter for missions."*

—Rev. Philip Teng, LLD, retired

It is high time for a new generation to read about Alliance principles and strategies that overseas have made us so successful under God. And it helps to "tell the story behind the story" of a towering leader on loan by the Almighty to show us the way. Read this book, so well written, and be biblically proud of a great person and a wonderful page of Church history.

—David L. Rambo, president (1987-1996),
The Christian and Missionary Alliance/USA

This is a valuable and fascinating record of a missionary statesman, a choice servant of God, who had vision and strategy for an indigenous church. It is an essential read.

—Dr. Melvin Sylvester, chancellor,
Alliance University College, Calgary, Alberta, Canada